D1715055

THE WHOLE WORLD WAS WATCHING

COLD WAR
INTERNATIONAL HISTORY
PROJECT SERIES

Edited by James G. Hershberg

Published in collaboration with the Woodrow
Wilson International Center for Scholars

THE WHOLE WORLD WAS WATCHING

Sport in the Cold War

Edited by
Robert Edelman and
Christopher Young

STANFORD UNIVERSITY PRESS
Stanford, California

Stanford University Press
Stanford, California

Printed in the United States of America on acid-free, archival-quality paper

Library of Congress Cataloging-in-Publication Data
Names: Edelman, Robert, editor. | Young, Christopher, editor.
Title: The whole world was watching : sport in the Cold War / edited by Robert Edelman and Christopher Young.
Description: Stanford, California : Stanford University Press, 2019. | Series: Cold War International History Project | Includes bibliographical references and index.
Identifiers: LCCN 2019012949 (print) | LCCN 2019014693 (ebook) | ISBN 9781503611016 (ebook) | ISBN 9781503610187 | ISBN 9781503610187 (cloth : alk. paper) | ISBN 9781503611016 (ebook)
Subjects: LCSH: Sports—Political aspects—History—20th century. | Sports and state—History—20th century. | Cold War—Influence. | World politics—1945–1989.
Classification: LCC GV706.35 (ebook) | LCC GV706.35 .W48 2019 (print) | DDC 796—dc23
LC record available at https://lccn.loc.gov/2019012949

Cover design: Rob Ehle
Cover photo: Nadya Comeneci, via Wikimedia Commons
Text design: Kevin Barrett Kane
Typeset by Newgen in 10/14 Minion

CONTENTS

ACKNOWLEDGMENTS

It began with a phone conversation in 2012. George Roy, one of the greatest of all makers of documentaries on sporting themes, was calling. He was planning to pitch a series of shows on sports during the Cold War to one of the leading cable networks. Was there, he asked, a particular book he should read? A quick search revealed that there was no such book, no authoritative history of this subject. There were instead various pieces of varying quality. Why not, we thought, fill that enormous gap? The first logical place to announce our intentions was the Cold War International History Project based at the Woodrow Wilson Center for International Scholars. The center's Blair Ruble set up a meeting with the project's director, Christian Ostermann, who suggested that we organize a multiyear, multisited international research project. We later learned that he made such suggestions to everyone, but some way, somehow, we took him seriously. Soon the Cold War Project's founder, Jim Hershberg, filled with enthusiasm and encouragement, was in touch. A scoping meeting, sponsored by the Tiarks Fund in the Department of German and Dutch at the University of Cambridge, convinced us to apply to the National Endowment for the Humanities, and we were successful in securing its invaluable support for the project.

We have organized and run three conferences, at the German Historical Institute in Moscow, the Jordan Center for the Advanced Study of Russia at New York University, and Pembroke College in Cambridge, UK, each of those institutions generously cofinancing and co-organizing the meetings. Fifty papers have been presented; twenty-five commentators have dispensed wisdom on the papers. Podcasts with interviews of our participants, recorded and edited by Vince Hunt, can be found on the Wilson Center's website, at https://digitalarchive.wilsoncenter.org/theme/sport-in-the-cold-war. Laura Deal of the Cold War Project took the lead in producing this site. Our first meeting was in

Moscow, supported by the German Historical Institute, which overcame the tragedy of a massive fire that destroyed its headquarters in 2015 as it was helping plan our first workshop. Nikolaus Katzer, the director of the institute, and Maria Chasovskaysa, his assistant, moved proverbial mountain ranges to find us a home at the Higher School of Economics, which provided an outstanding venue. Yanni Kotsonis, Fiona Neale-May, Heather Janson, and Natasha Bluth, his colleagues at the Jordan Center, created excellent conditions for a wonderful second meeting in the heart of Greenwich Village.

The essays in this volume are drawn from these two gatherings, and there are many people to thank. Given the lack of a sizable literature on Cold War sports, we wanted to create the basis for much further research. It is not an exaggeration to suggest that, in the process, we were able to create an international community of scholars, old and young, female and male. It is rare to find more than a single historian of sport at any institution of higher learning, but our attendees found areas of mutual interest and enthusiasm, now spawning a number of other books and articles. Along with our essay writers, we thank those who attended and took part inside and outside the meeting rooms: Irina Bykhovskaya, Sylvain Dufraisse, Travis Vogan, Anke Hilbrenner, Alexander Ananyev, Fabien Archambault, Pascal Charitas, Tony Shaw, Denise Youngblood, Sergey Radchenko, Yuri Slezkine, Erica Fraser, Vladimir Geskin, and Vladimir Titorenko in Moscow. In New York, the following contributed: Kate Burlingham, Tim Naftali, Mary Nolan, Tom Hunt, Mauricio Borrero, Jane Grimes, Carol Sagesse, John Nauright, Joanna Meilis, Amy Bass, George Vecsey, David McDonald, Jeremy Schaap, Nick Rutter, Kevin Witherspoon, and especially Lindsay Krasnoff.

We thank Mike Cole, David Nasaw, David Goldblatt, Steve Fagin, Steve Elig, Don Houts, Hasan Kayali, Pamela Radcliff, Manuel Morales, Jamie Ivey, Danny Widener, Luis Alvarez, Maria Carreras, Curtis Tyree, Ed Derse, Wayne Wilson, Harry Scheiber, Frank Biess, Victoria Yablonsky, Robert Horwitz, Angela Young, Simon Franklin, and Richard Holt for advice and feedback. Louis and Nicholas Edelman provided tech support and companionship; Peter Young, humorous perspective. Bob's pets Gus and Ted, his dour Scotsman, have also stamped their paws on this effort. The librarians and staff at the LA84 Foundation, the University of California San Diego (UCSD), the British Library, and the University Library of Cambridge University (where the inimitable Andrea Crossman carved out time in the acting librarian's schedule for ongoing discussions) have been exemplary and pleasant professionals. The

Russian State Archive of Contemporary History, led by the remarkable Mikhail Prozumenshikov, and the National Archive of the United Kingdom turned out to be great places to work. The Office of Research Affairs at UCSD helped guide us in finding funding, Sharon Franks provided outstanding feedback on our draft applications, Dan Sack at the National Endowment of the Humanities was more than generous with his advice, and Susan Winchester at UCSD kept track of accounts once we were successful.

Finally, we express our thanks to those who have made this book possible: Jim Hershberg, the series editor, and Christian Ostermann of the Cold War History Project, supporting us at the end as they did at the beginning; Margo Irvin at Stanford University Press for giving the manuscript such a gentle landing; and the two anonymous reviewers whose comments were welcomed by every contributor and made us think individually and collectively about what our project really meant.

The collaborative effort that has gone into the making of this book and the whole enterprise behind it is dedicated to the memory of Abraham Henry Edelman, who took me (Bob) to the Parade Grounds, played catch, and saved me for sport, and to Helen Fernandes, marathon runner and Cambridge neurosurgeon, who between our Moscow and New York conferences saved Angela Young's life and restored her to full health.

THE WHOLE WORLD WAS WATCHING

INTRODUCTION

Explaining Cold War Sport

Robert Edelman and Christopher Young

Sport was undeniably a major cultural phenomenon of the Cold War period. A fundamentally urban pastime and passion, its stock rose inevitably as migration from the countryside increased in the wake of World War II, with city populations doubling worldwide by 1970.[1] It was a constant source of innovation as the new medium of television spread and developed, from its household arrival in the 1950s through the advent of color in the 1960s and the cable and satellite revolution that followed in the 1980s. It played a significant role in the growth of leisure and health-related activities, particularly in the West, from the 1960s onward.[2] But crucially, the Cold War also changed sport.

More states than ever craved symbolic capital through athletic endeavor. Vast sums of money were poured into gaining it through fair and foul means; and the whole world, as the title of our book suggests, was watching. What its citizens—spectators, stalwarts, occasional viewers—were thinking, believing, hoping, and dreaming is a matter of rich potential for our understanding of the time. In every sense then, sport was a major phenomenon not just of the Cold War period but more specifically of the cultural Cold War. Given that subtle but important change in emphasis, it is surprising that the subject has been largely neglected in the impressive new field of Cold War studies that has emerged since the end of the conflict.

The fall of Communism coincided with the historical profession's "cultural turn," which began in the early 1980s. Topics once deemed marginal now assumed greater importance. As David Caute noted in his seminal *The Dancer*

Defects, the Cold War "was simultaneously a traditional political-military confrontation . . . and . . . [a] cultural contest on a global scale and without historical precedent."[3] Writers, dancers, musicians, filmmakers, artists, and playwrights were mobilized by the great powers to win favor with their own people and with the rest of the world. The goal of "victory by other means" was influenced by Joseph Nye's concept of "soft power."[4] Accordingly, scholars took the study of the Cold War beyond the purview of traditional military, diplomatic, and political history and established a broad context that looked at the mass reception and political meaning of cultural production.

This cultural Cold War has been a highly fertile area of research.[5] Students of the media have excavated the political in US entertainment films and the entertaining in their politicized Soviet counterparts and revealed how television on each side of the Cold War divide both created and challenged stereotypes.[6] Others have examined the successes and failures of international exhibitions of consumer goods and discussed the two systems' very different approaches to home design.[7] Scholars have also explored the open and secret roles of government in the production and dissemination of cultural products and shown how the American government conveyed the impression that pro-capitalist and pro-American arts and letters were the result of independent thought, when they were often heavily financed by the Central Intelligence Agency (CIA).[8] Many others went beyond high culture to reveal the broad extent of the covert actions of US intelligence agencies in a much wider range of activities and media.[9] Exhibitions of abstract Western art had a subversive effect in Communist states,[10] and government-sponsored jazz tours by African Americans failed to change postcolonial states' perceptions of racism in the United States because of statements made by the musicians themselves.[11] There was a profound interconnectedness between international and domestic politics in the United States.[12] Government and society actors came together to form a state-private network through which Western governments were able to pursue their soft-power goals.[13]

Concomitantly, the growing body of scholarship on the postwar USSR has gone far beyond the view that cultural production in the Soviet Union could be reduced to a binary between an official, philistine, and false art and a true, morally pure, and fully artistic dissident art. Instead, ambiguity features in a broad range of studies.[14] Soviet popular and middlebrow cultures were always torn between the conflicting needs of didacticism and entertainment. The result was a constantly evolving menu the public was free to ignore without serious penalty. The pioneering Russian historian Elena Zubkova focused on the enormous majority of ordinary Soviets who were neither jailers nor jailed,[15] while a large cohort of Western researchers bear the influence of Alexei Yurchak's pathbreaking *Everything Was Forever Until It Was No More*, which embraced the many uncertainties and contingencies of late Communism.[16]

Such work does not treat culture as an autonomous realm but rather connects it to the political. While studies of diplomacy and politics covered the circumscribed interactions of competing elites, the cultural Cold War literature expanded the terrain to include the societies that did or did not support them. This has undermined clichés about the independence of the arts and focused attention on the battle for the sympathies of the world's citizens. As this book demonstrates, the site at which this battle was most powerfully articulated is sport.

The very liminality of sport makes it both the hardest form of soft power and the softest form of hard power. In the Cold War, sport had many hard, tangible, and corporeal qualities: It produced easily measured results from which governments and their citizens could draw rapid conclusions; different kinds of states produced different kinds of sporting systems, which in turn reflected and influenced the development of those same states in different ways. More instrumentally, sport was used almost universally to inspire the fitness needed for military readiness, serving on both sides of the ideological divide the overtly political purpose of convincing citizens to become fitter workers, better soldiers, and loyal servants of one kind of political system or another. At the same time, ministries of defense deployed the ideas of many thinkers to inspire citizens to join armed forces and vote for politicians who supported spending on weaponry. Sport also has many soft qualities within and beyond the matrix of state ideologies. Sport operates through local and commercial enterprise; global media; and individual, group, urban, regional, national, and transnational identities. It feeds off deep personal and collective loyalties and fascinations; and as unscripted, unpredictable drama, more than any other social, political, or cultural entity, it is also innately subject to the strength and frailty of human performance as well as to the role of chance.

Surprisingly, sport has attracted only minimal attention from scholars of the Cold War, whether they study international relations or elite and popular culture. Despite its unrivaled visibility to billions across the globe and its inherent intricacy as an object of historical analysis, sport is all but absent from the mainstream historiography of the Cold War. Caute's *Dancer Defects* has but two cameos (Dinamo Moscow's British tour of 1945 and the diplomatic brouhaha surrounding the arrest of the Soviet discus thrower Nina Ponomareva on charges of shoplifting on London's Oxford Street in 1956);[17] compendious overviews such as Mervyn P. Leffler and Odd Arne Westad's *Cambridge History of the Cold War* and Richard Immerman and Petra Goedde's *Oxford Handbook of the Cold War* barely touch on it;[18] the journal *Cold War History* passed it over in its recent twenty-five-year retrospective special issue; and edited collections habitually overlook it.[19] Family, gender, sexuality, politics, mobility, race, film, literature, television, and poetry all feature, but sport is missing. If it is mentioned at all in serious literature, it is done so glibly, all too often portrayed as an alternative locus of the US-Soviet rivalry, with the rest of the world left watching from the stands. Or it is reduced to snapshots of such climactic moments as the Western boycott of the 1980 Moscow Olympics and the Eastern Bloc's decision to stay home four years later from Los Angeles—two connected dots seen from on high. This is no longer adequate. As Giles Scott-Smith and Joes Segal observe, "The narrative of absolute Cold War antagonism is looking increasingly misleading and disingenuous, to be replaced by a more differentiated and intellectually compelling interpretation."[20]

In the Cold War, "virtually everything, from sport to ballet to comic books to space travel, assumed political significance."[21] Virtually everything in that span has also received the serious attention of Cold War scholars. It is now commonly accepted that the international system cannot be fully understood without the inclusion of culture.[22] And it is equally compelling that Cold War culture cannot be understood without the inclusion of sport. Sport expands the cultural and connects it with the diplomatic. It also hits the sweet spot between "high culture," as favored by the Soviet Union, and "popular culture," as pushed by the United States.[23] The limited scholarly coverage of sport is not simply a gap that needs to be filled. Rather, the shape and contours of that gap need to be properly understood.

One reason, perhaps, for the time lag of sport within the study of the cultural Cold War is that there is as yet no authoritative account or collection that connects it to the big questions of the field. But sports history has been growing steadily over the last forty years,[24] and within it the literature on which such works could be based has gradually been accumulating.[25] This includes excellent foundational studies by individuals working in specific geographic areas—predominantly the Soviet Union,[26] the United States,[27] and East and West Germany,[28] but also in China,[29] as well as other countries in Europe.[30] New scholarship is appearing all the time, including diplomatic history,[31] and the field is reaching critical mass. For this book, we have been able to assemble a group of young and more experienced scholars from all over the world, from both strands of mainstream Cold War history as well as sports history. Although sports in Asia, Latin America, and Africa are still vastly understudied, we have elicited contributions from leading authorities in these respective fields.

Working closely with a vast array of sources, our contributors have produced authentic breakthroughs in many areas. Vitally, their scholarship respects the peculiarity of sporting systems while bringing their study into dialogue with mainstream scholarship. They are alive to the important dynamic between the specific and the general, which is sometimes missing in writing on sport, as scholars have been overreliant on the low-hanging fruit of bureaucratic paper, such as that preserved in archives and libraries. As proposed by the Italian scholar Mario del Pero in his recent commentary on sport and US diplomatic relations, "The real contribution that the study of sport can offer to our understanding of . . . the Cold War depends primarily on our ability to examine and highlight forms of interaction and exchange in which multiple players were involved, retrieving (and fully considering) the agency of all the parties and the complex connections they catalyzed."[32] This relational dimension of power—its forms, mutations, and contradictions—is precisely what our contributors have captured. Delving into the "extraordinary corpus of cultural production of the twentieth century," they know, as Caute noted, that Cold War culture "can be properly explored and understood only from multiple viewpoints."[33] This multiperspective approach applies both to the content of individual essays and to the range of the book as a whole.

As editors, we have been greatly influenced by the imperative of recent years to treat the Cold War as a global and variegated, rather than a binary and monochrome, phenomenon.[34] Our contributors range far and wide, in geography and in focus. In selecting them, we were ideologically agnostic about the recent debates for and against a broad conception of the (cultural) Cold War. Here we merely argue, on pragmatic grounds, that historians of sport should continue to cast their net as wide as possible since so much in the field is yet to be gathered.[35] Grouped according to significant geographic areas, our contributions reexamine critical issues of familiar players—the United States, USSR, and German Democratic Republic (GDR)—and open out to new ones, such as Asia and the postcolonial world. We have made a conscious decision to set aside for now the Olympic Games: these have received considerable scrutiny and thus have somewhat skewed perceptions of the field.[36] Instead, we consider lesser-studied but no less important regional games as well as quotidian sports with massive transnational fan bases (soccer, hockey, baseball); examine the global and local dynamics of drug abuse; and interrogate the social and political impact of celebrity. Many contributions extend beyond a single theme.

As the following brief descriptions demonstrate, individually these chapters deliver new—and often counterintuitive—insights that illuminate the multifaceted significance of sport for nations, groups, and individuals in the Cold War. Together, as our conclusion sets out, they allow us to distill the fundamental aspects of sport and the cultural Cold War on which future work in the field can build.

The United States

In the first half of the twentieth century, international competition gave the United States a platform to demonstrate its power and attractiveness to the rest of the world, and American sporting dominance seemed natural and normal, at least to Americans. But this changed with the Cold War. As the superpower rivalry that congealed into nuclear confrontation and proxy wars raised the political stakes of what was supposed to be friendly competition, sporting defeat at Soviet hands had to be explained and contested. This was a task the US government could not leave to the volunteer officials of the many national and international sports federations, and early on, American state actors became involved in the world of sport, as a private-state network emerged that simultaneously waged psychological warfare and turned profits for media conglomerates.

Looming all over this activity was the matter of race. As the empires of US allies crumbled and scores of new nations emerged into a postcolonial world, race became America's great handicap in the struggle for the sympathies of the world's citizens. It came up constantly in sporting encounters that went beyond the boundaries and limits of American domestic politics. Our essays shed light on the measures taken by the US government to control the sports world, the ways US media industries displayed it, and the problems raised internationally when African American athletes came to contest discrimination.

The cultural Cold War was quickly joined in the late 1940s. Both sides financed front groups, and in the West, a broad array of cultural organizations emerged to portray the greater attractiveness of capitalism and liberal democracy. Writers, dancers, artists, filmmakers, musicians, academics, and scientists were said to have made their choice of sides independently, free of state interference. But in 1967, the world learned that much of this activity was secretly financed by the CIA. Toby C. Rider has sought to find out if something similar happened in the world of sport, and his excavation of government, private, and Olympic documents reveals overt propaganda and covert control. The most salient moment of this process came in 1956 after the Melbourne Olympics, which had witnessed a particularly brutal water polo match between the USSR and the favorite Hungary in the wake of the Soviet suppression of the Hungarian uprising. When the Games ended, thirty-eight Hungarian athletes and officials chose to defect, mainly to the United States. These events were organized by the American weekly *Sports Illustrated*, a part of the Time-Life publishing empire of the powerful and well-connected anti-Communist Henry Luce. Rider shows that this intervention in sporting cultural diplomacy, still denied by the magazine, was funded by the CIA.

African American performers were always a conspicuous part of US sporting events and, in particular, of delegations abroad. Their presence was intended to demonstrate that the violence and disorder associated with the civil rights struggles of the 1950s and 1960s were only part of the American story. Sporting ambassadors admitted problems but offered an account of anticipated improvement. Elliott J. Gorn's account of the troubles of heavyweight boxing champion Muhammad Ali with the US government and his subsequent campaign against the Vietnam War presents a more complex and realistic picture of race relations in the United States. Throughout the twentieth century, boxing was a culturally hegemonic sport, and its heavyweight champion was seen as the world's toughest man. The polite and deferent Joe Louis was the sort of "Negro" white people could live with after the sexually threatening pre–World War I figure of Jack Johnson. The brash Ali won Olympic gold in 1960 followed by the heavyweight crown in 1965, announced his membership in the Nation of Islam, and a few years later refused conscription to fight in Vietnam. He had he said no quarrel with the Vietcong. If Ali did not initially see himself as a Cold War figure (and is often overlooked as such in scholarship), the Cold War certainly found him. He was stripped of his title, which he regained through court order and ring prowess, and his story dramatizes the centrality of racial politics nationally and internationally in the era.

The Soviet Union

Americans believed US sport operated autonomously, independent of government and detached from politics, while Communist sport was a realm of totalitarian control. But this is a classic false binary, and today it is hard to find students of the USSR who accept the concept of totalitarianism that so dominated academic and popular postwar thinking. Scholars now understand the Soviet party-state did more than simply deploy fear and terror. While repression did not disappear, the Gulag was abandoned by the mid-1950s, to be replaced by hegemonic strategies that could gain the consent of a population capable of exhibiting agency, autonomy, transgression, and careful resistance. Soviet domination of the Olympics might have seemed an expression of strong state power, but we have now moved well beyond the cliché of the "Big Red Machine." The pioneering research in this section deals with enlightened officials, fan groups, national republics, and international competition. Each essay points to a new way of understanding how Soviet sport worked in historical practice.

From the start of Soviet power in 1917, leaders, athletes, and officials had been ambivalent about the two sporting forms inherited from capitalism—Olympian amateurism and entertainment-oriented professionalism. Both approaches raised problems that could be sidestepped when the USSR operated in a situation of diplomatic and sporting isolation. After the war, however, elite Soviet athletes faced profound changes when the USSR elected to play by capitalism's rules. They accepted membership in the United Nations and began joining the many international sports federations, culminating in Olympic membership in 1951. While virtually all these organizations followed amateur codes, it was no secret that Soviet performers were well paid. Olympic officials knew this, and the Western press reported it.

Maintaining the fig leaf of amateurism proved a shrewd choice, enabling Soviet Olympians to dominate what was just a segment of the West's sporting talents. But this strategy also caused frustration, since under capitalism the top athletes were drawn away to the more remunerative sports and Soviet amateurs could not always test themselves against the best competition. In time a particular void opened up in the popular sport of hockey, which was habitually dominated by the professional stars of the North American National Hockey League. After decades of trampling their fellow "amateurs," the Soviets longed to compete against Canada, which originated the sport. This desire was eventually fulfilled in 1972, with an eight-game "Summit Series" that has gone down in the annals of the sport and is vividly remembered by all who witnessed it.[37] The Soviets' shock win in the opening encounter, the sharp contrast in styles between the "brutish" Western professionals and the "cultured" Eastern "amateurs," and the Canadians' dramatic victory in the dying embers in Moscow created a canvas on which the Cold War imaginary was played out for, and partly renegotiated by, millions of television viewers worldwide.

Yet, as James Hershberg has uncovered, this seminal event might never have happened but for the high-level negotiations and agile diplomacy of the talented Soviet prime minister Alexei Kosygin. Traveling to Canada to expand Soviet influence at a time of US troubles in Vietnam, Kosygin himself came under physical attack from demonstrators in Ottawa. It was only the generosity of a Vancouver crowd's welcome at a later hockey game—an event he almost skipped—that turned the trip into a success and led to both nations negotiating directly over the ultimate test of the world's best. As the forensic detail of Hershberg's essay shows, chance and personal inclination played a key role in the unfolding of one of the landmark events in the cultural Cold War.

While the Summit Series was abetted by Kosygin, it had the warm support of the Communist Party general secretary Leonid Brezhnev. If Stalin had been completely indifferent to sport and Nikita Khrushchev downright hostile to it, this changed in 1964 when Brezhnev became party leader. In contrast to his predecessors, Brezhnev had long loved sport and supported national teams and regional clubs at the many stops he made on his rise to the top. While the Brezhnev period in general has been described as an era of stagnation, the man himself took a keen interest in athletes' well-being and fostered success in the most popular pastimes of football and hockey.

Most important, he shared the dream of many sports officials from the mid-1950s of hosting the Olympic Games in the USSR and was a dynamic force in finally bringing the Games to Moscow. He championed this cause through thick and thin—riling his erstwhile advocate Khrushchev with Olympic visions at times of economic crisis and, once in power, playing the long game both internally and externally in regard to the politics of international sport. At various times, the Soviets trod a thin line between choleric allies (the GDR) and awkward allegiances (Franco's Spain, Israel, and South Korea) to gain mastery of the protocols that governed international sport. This paid off in 1974, when they were able to win the bid for the 1980 Olympic Games. In Mikhail Prozumenshikov's account, the leadership of a single man over several decades made a real difference, so much so that it is entirely plausible that the Eastern Bloc would not have boycotted the Los Angeles Games had Brezhnev not died in 1982.

Despite the boycott, the 1980 Games brought pleasure to Muscovites and the republics alike. What worked for the event of a lifetime, however, was more complicated in everyday practice. The center constantly sought to control centrifugal manifestations of nationalism, and open defiance could lead to severe penalties. Over the previous thirty years, the Soviet Union had wrestled with football's role as an engine for international success and social cohesion in the multiethnic Socialist state. While the capital's major clubs nurtured strong institutional identities, their leading provincial rivals such as Dinamo Kiev and Dinamo Tbilisi each effectively stood as its respective republic's national team. Georgian football developed a distinctive trickster style that set it apart from that of the rest of the Soviet Union. Likened to its dynamic national dance, this southern football, with its characteristics of beauty, ingenuity, and agility, was perceived as an alternative to that in the rest of the USSR—an idea that blossomed through association with the Argentinian and Brazilian game. Football allowed Georgians to consider themselves modern and to enjoy an identity that transcended Soviet borders. At the same time, as Erik R. Scott shows in his chapter, Georgian football allowed the Soviets to promote the multiethnic state—either by including players on the national team or by sending their club sides abroad, where they proved particularly flamboyant ambassadors to the postcolonial world and undermined stereotypes of the dour, physical Soviet. This was not always without tension. For while Georgian flair could promote Pan-Soviet as well as national success, the government's sponsorship also led to the advancement of the republic in its own right. Most astonishingly, Dinamo Tbilisi originally flourished under the patronage of Lavrentii Beria, survived his execution in 1953, and established itself as a model for post-Stalinist masculinity. With the spread of television, its reputation for playing the beautiful game became recognized and appreciated across the Soviet Union, even if resentment grew with Tbilisi's increasing success and its fans' aggressive ebullience.

Thus, while the various institutional structures of the USSR aspired to control independent activity, football was a blunt instrument in the hands of authoritarian rulers. While Soviet Communism privileged conscious control, citizens never relinquished the spontaneity that could lead to unintended consequences. Working in central and regional archives and conducting numerous interviews, Manfred Zeller is able to depict the complex and variegated world in which the authority of dominant political groups in the USSR was simultaneously accepted and contested by ordinary citizens in their complex roles as supporters. In Moscow as well as the republics, sport provided liminal spaces in which meanings were produced, digested, and changed. The regime and its press organs had exercised some measure of control over supporters in the 1960s and 1970s. And the dominant discourse had depicted fans as rational Soviet consumers, along with their extrovert behavior and more exuberant supporters described as "feverish fans." On the whole, however, this never reached fever pitch. For most of those two decades, it was difficult to tell who was supporting whom within Moscow stadiums. Things changed, though, in the late 1970s, by which time sport had increasingly globalized, with television transmitting images of youth behaviors from the West. Young Soviet fans followed suit, donning (hand-knitted) scarves in their team's colors, formulating partisan chants, and moving together en masse. But what was normal in the West was unusual in the East. While these fans saw themselves as part of a transnational youth movement, their articulation of it simultaneously expressed deeply Soviet messages. Appropriating state symbols from club badges for subgroup identity was a direct challenge to Soviet public life. It was also a means by which Muscovites, in whose city the scene developed with particular zeal, could express superiority over regional rivals. As the Cold War neared its end, it is little wonder that clashes between fans and police became ever more violent.

The German Democratic Republic

Much of what emerges from the Soviet case holds true for the GDR: the influence of strong individuals in high office; tensions and complications between center and periphery; sport as an arena for identity formation and a vehicle for protest of varying degrees; and the peculiarities of a sporting system that required considerable management and negotiation of local interests to produce the exceptional results it did. GDR sport is synonymous with Olympic success and doping. With a population of just seventeen million, the GDR ranked in the top three at every Summer Olympics at which it competed independently from 1972, defeating the United States in 1976 and coming in a close second to its Soviet ally as the Cold War reached its conclusion. Much, though not all, of this success was due to an extensive doping program, which the openness and volume of German archives have revealed more fully than for any other nation. Yet, as the three essays in this section show, there is more to tell. The quirky world of football gives a clearer sense of East German society and the breakdown of consensus within it than did any of the Olympic triumphs; rivalries, abuse, and naked ambition created an even darker side to doping than previously imagined; and a rare examination of ice-skater Katarina Witt shows the complex production of image and reception for domestic and international audiences. Like the image of Witt that emerges here, that of the GDR sport system as a whole appears more nuanced and complicated than usually assumed.

The GDR was not known as a football nation and was always in the shadow of Poland, Czechoslovakia, the USSR, and West Germany. In international competition, it qualified for only one World Cup (1974) and produced just a single winner of a European club competition (FC Magdeburg, Cup Winners' Cup 1974). But as elsewhere in Eastern Europe, football sustained a well-supported league, which rooted fans in national networks but connected them to transnational discourses and influences as well. As the Cold War reached its conclusion, it also provided citizens with an exceptional space in which to articulate discontent. Alan McDougall's essay, which focuses on the Stasi-sponsored Berliner FC Dynamo (BFC), explores "football's role as a political lightning rod," which "channel[ed] antiregime sentiment into areas that were not always as safe or sealed off as they seemed to be."

If an outlet for public frustration was ever needed, the state could not have created a better solution than BFC. With the personal support of Erich Mielke and constant pressure on match officials, the club broke the dominance of Magdeburg and Dresden and, starting in 1978–1979, brought the East German league title to the capital for ten successive seasons. In what is an important story for the final decade of the GDR, this stranglehold did not go unchallenged. Journalists lobbied members of the Socialist United Party of the GDR (SED); fans booed the club's players when they appeared for the national team; and the volume of petitions, to which the government always paid attention, grew exponentially. Fans drew unflattering comparisons with foreign leagues and vented their anger in the stadium. Eventually, the East German Football Association was forced to take action, and it is no coincidence that BFC's winning streak ended before November 1989. As McDougall notes, the sustained protest did not bring down the Berlin Wall, but it was a significant expression of dissatisfaction in the country, one that extended beyond all others in publicity and reach. That fans could challenge the regime so successfully says much about the dying days of the GDR, and that they could do it so visibly tells us something about the power of sport as a means of political engagement.

While BFC's ignominy was plain to see, the country's drug program lived in a netherworld that the public often suspected but never quite dared to mention; by the time the regime entered its final decade, though, parents had begun dissuading their children from engaging with serious sport. One thing the program shared with football, however, was the strong vested interests and disruptive effects of industry- and military-based clubs. Doping began in earnest in the GDR after the Munich Olympics in 1972. A report from 1974 outlined the need to keep up with the competition from the leading sports nations of the West—a claim that recent research on the Federal Republic has partly vindicated—as well as from the USSR. As Mike Dennis shows, the reason for central action had as much to do with wresting control from powerful national societies as it did with trumping international rivals. Vorwärts and Dynamo (the army and police organizations) went to particular lengths to defeat each other, competing between them for the best athletes, trainers, and medical facilities. Curbing the selfish and destructive drive of the clubs became a priority for sports officials as they sought to consolidate their own role within the country's hierarchy.

Despite central initiatives, "wild doping" became endemic to the system. This included wanton disregard for officially prescribed norms and the development of experimental steroid substances. Levels of dosage, bitter rivalries, and the right to ultimate control were recurring motifs in a circular battle between clubs, doctors, sports functionaries, and political leaders. Dissenting voices aside, it is clear that risks to human life were secondary to the imperative of success. Young female athletes were particularly vulnerable (many were doped without their knowledge or through coercion), while others, such as body builders, threatened the system with overt illegal consumption. Behind the "GDR machine" stood a system in disarray, one that damaged athletes and that even the Stasi could not monitor and control completely.

Katarina Witt, who dominated the sport of figure skating in the 1980s, was a conspicuous exception to the dreary world of most GDR athletes. While they were many, she was singular; while they had the brawn, she had the looks. Dubbed "the most beautiful face of Socialism," she presented the regime with an opportunity to counter the message that only hardened, muscular sportswomen had any chance of success in the East. The government took particular interest in Witt, monitoring her press contacts and promoting her image in the West, a process in which she herself was willingly compliant. Regime and athlete exploited the alignment of sporting talent and feminine allure—an aspect that was pushed to the limits with daring costumes and sensual routines—for political purposes. Witt talked often and openly about the benefits of the Socialist system and in 1988 became a goodwill ambassador for the United Nations International Children's Emergency Fund (UNICEF).

But as Annette F. Timm argues, this process involved more than simply selling sex to the West. In fact, the whole Witt phenomenon turns precisely on the different ways sex was coded in the capitalist and Socialist worlds. Witt was always surprised at the uptight nature of sexual relations in the West: as an athlete, she claimed to have a more natural relationship to her own body; she felt completely at home in the nudist scene, a movement with a long German tradition that had emerged as a form of overt protest in the GDR but had quickly become part of mainstream culture; and argued that the absence of economic dependency liberated sexual mores in Socialism. Witt's own self-understanding was distinctly at odds with Western tropes, which depicted attractive Eastern women as honey traps in the employ of the state and, more generally, as sadomasochistic and deviant products of totalitarianism. This fantasy both scared and soothed citizens in the West—they could sleep safe at night knowing what their governments were protecting them from. But for Witt, eventually, the tension proved too much, and her image began to fray even before the fall of the wall.

Asia

The Cold War played out quite differently in Asia than in Europe: the super-powers were caught in a quadrangular relationship with China and Japan, and two hot wars (Korea and Vietnam) ensued. Decolonization unfolded, and inter-nal conflicts left many countries in the balance. In this complicated mix, sport might seem irrelevant. Yet, as Tsuyoshi Hasegawa has argued, the "domestic politics of each nation developed in close connection with the external Cold War, and the Cold War profoundly influenced the media, sports, and people's consciousness."[38] Just as the conflict was configured differently in the region, so too was sport. A Western import, transported by imperial administrators, the Young Men's Christian Association (YMCA), and adherents of Muscular Christianity, it had largely remained the preserve of elites and educated male urbanites until the end of World War II. But in the wake of the Chinese Civil War and in the midst of newly emerging nations, sport became a critical tool for governments to boost legitimacy, secure a place on the international stage, and stake a claim for modernity. The three essays in this section address these themes in relation to China, Taiwan, and Thailand. Taken together, they show how, more than in any other region, political circumstances and sport's status as a relative cultural newcomer combined to project the Cold War as a shared and imagined reality containing both the threat of destruction and the promise of a better future.[39]

Before and after 1949, the People's Republic of China (PRC) cast its lot with the world Communist movement and looked to the Soviet Union for support and guidance. War weary and laden with embargoes, Mao Zedong adopted a "lean to one side" policy and accepted the Soviets as international Socialist leaders. Thousands of Soviet specialists in many different areas took up residence to help with the construction of Communism and drive forward the struggle for Socialist modernity. Sport was no exception. Facilities were constructed, scouts sent out to scour the mainland for talent, and athletes dispatched for long periods of time to the USSR. Coaches and athletic delegations also arrived in China from other Communist states, some of them—such as the Soviet gymnastics squad, fresh from Olympic triumph, and the superlative Hungarian national football team—of the highest international standing. As Amanda Shuman explains for the first time, Mao's embrace of sport had multiple, interlocking motivations.

Sport's previously close association with the Nationalists, who had just been driven into Taiwanese exile, allowed the new regime to connect with people not necessarily disposed to it. It also promised a way to capitalize on its most precious asset, the masses, by transforming the proverbial (and actual) "sick man" of previous decades into the healthy citizen of the one to come. The alignment with the Soviet Union enabled China to build legitimacy from the bottom up. The Soviet model, despite well-established indigenous practices, was taken over comprehensively; Soviet stars adorned the pages of Chinese magazines; and the USSR's preeminence in the international sphere was championed. The adoption of Soviet methods and the foreign recognition that sport brought with it formed an important part of the regime's strategy to increase support for the new Chinese state. Aspiration was vital: the improvised facilities and untapped talents of today would change tomorrow and propel China forward as it had the USSR. But for the Cultural Revolution and the radical change of course in the 1960s and 1970s, the successes of the 1980s would doubtless have come earlier.

For most of that period, the PRC was in dispute with Chiang Kai-shek's Republic of China (ROC), which enjoyed American support and occupied an inaugural seat at the United Nations. As the Olympic Games continued to grow in stature, they offered immense symbolic capital to both sides. The International Olympic Committee (IOC) sought naïvely to bring political enemies together, but—as in the case of divided Germany—a litany of petty point scoring ensued. Teams arrived late after others had withdrawn, banners were brandished at opening ceremonies, and host nations were placed in awkward situations they would rather have avoided. Even after the PRC abandoned the field to the ROC in 1958, the struggle continued. Most dramatically, decathlete and darling of Taiwanese sport C. K. Yang crashed at the 1964 Tokyo Olympics, as treacherous teammates turned by PRC agents robbed him of gold by spiking his morning glass of orange juice. In Montreal in 1976, the ROC came unstuck when the Canadian government, which had recognized the legitimacy of the PRC six years earlier, insisted it compete as "Taiwan." The ROC's subsequent boycott denied it the final opportunity to be the sole representative of China, as the PRC returned to the fold in 1979 and the ROC's fate as "Chinese Taipei" was sealed by Olympic formula.

Such high-profile politics were part and parcel of sporting encounter in the Cold War and have attracted considerable attention from sports historians. But as Andrew D. Morris shows, they were only part of the story. In the case of Taiwan, sporting developments were much more complex than a mere "two-dimensional, cross-strait struggle." The status of team sports on the island, for instance, was particularly nuanced. Basketball, an American sport that had taken root early in China, appealed to mainlanders in exile who yearned to return home, while baseball was the sport of choice of the native Taiwanese. Despite its association with the recent Japanese occupiers and failed attempts by the Nationalists to sinicize it, baseball became increasingly important as it gained in international reputation. Annual displays of massed physical prowess also assumed inordinate significance for the Nationalist cause. Drawing on thousands of participants, these aimed to buttress the regime's authority and inculcate a sense of discipline and devotion in its citizens. As hopes of renewed military action were fading, the events reminded citizens of their role in a future world when the promised land would be regained.

Mass events were important across East and Southeast Asia. The first Asian Games took place at New Delhi in 1951, providing a sporting terrain for the struggle between capitalism and Communism. Yet this event was but one of several regional competitions that simultaneously supported and challenged the work of the Olympic Movement. In the wake of decolonization in the southeastern part of the continent, governments and market economies surrounding North Vietnam organized their own games to help counter the spread of Communism. Alongside the Southeast Asia Treaty Organization (SEATO) nations, this much smaller competition became a sporting pillar of the US doctrine of containment. But as Simon Creak shows, it is important to transcend divisions between the diplomatic and cultural history of the Cold War and to highlight the national, regional, and international factors that simultaneously shaped this period of Southeast Asian history.

The authoritarian, US-allied military junta of Thailand took the lead by hosting the first Southeast Asian Peninsular Games in Bangkok in 1959. US diplomats with sports backgrounds at the Bangkok embassy played fully overt roles in organizing the movement and preparing the host's athletes; and Burma, Malaysia, Singapore, and South Vietnam participated. While the games had an obvious regional importance, they were equally significant for Thailand. In a postcolonial era, it shored up its previous special status as a noncolonialized nation by defining itself in close relation to the United States and its fight against Communism. Concomitantly, the games served distinctly local purposes by displaying the paternalistic intent of the military and its growing cult of the monarchy. Twenty thousand attended an opening ceremony in a brand-new stadium that drew heavily on Olympic ritual and included an address by the Thai king. While it would be a stretch to call the Peninsular Games a mega-event, the competition proved an effective vehicle for generating domestic support for regimes in the participating nations. The Philippines, Indonesia, and Cambodia joined later, and having outlived their Cold War purpose, the games continue to prosper today.

The Postcolonial World

Europe was the earliest theater of the Cold War, but its spread to Asia with the outbreak of war in Korea completely changed the terrain on which the larger conflict was contested. By the mid-1950s, a certain modus vivendi had emerged in the Old World, and the decisive struggles of the Cold War shifted to the rest of the world, where empires crumbled and new nations emerged. Latin America and Africa joined Asia as part of a global Cold War that others have even called an international civil war. Each side vied for the loyalty, support, and emulation of these new governments, most of which sought to be non-aligned. Led initially by Josip Broz Tito in Yugoslavia but, more important, by Jawaharlal Nehru in India and Sukarno in Indonesia, this postcolonial world witnessed a series of brutal proxy wars in which tens of millions lost their lives. If the nuclear stalemate minimized loss of life in the Northern Hemisphere, the Global South experienced carnage. It cannot be ignored.

As in mainstream history, scholars of sport must turn their attention to the new nations that emerged from the dying empires of US allies. Much like the proxy wars, sport in the postcolonial world can also be understood as classic contested terrain. This was not simply a story of the United States and USSR using athletes to deploy soft power to gain the sympathies of the citizens of the Third World. Even in the midst of the surrogate wars, nonaligned nations succeeded in developing sporting practices that afforded them a considerable measure of agency in relations with the Capitalist and Communist Blocs. New intercontinental formations were organized, and new regional events were created. The three essays in this section embrace the complexity and multidirectionality of these Cold War cultural flows. Africa, Asia, and Latin America had different relationships with the various empires that sought to control and exploit them, and the various empires deployed different strategies in ruling them, ranging from the formal to the informal and the neocolonial.

The harshest, most exploitative, and tenacious of the European empires was arguably that of Portugal. Yet in sporting terms, the country is recalled for its beautiful football and in particular for Benfica, the European Cup–winning club side of the 1960s with its star player, Eusébio, from Mozambique. As Todd Cleveland argues, the success of the game had distinct Cold War origins and indeed complications. Football in Portugal enjoyed little success in the 1950s, until it was greatly buoyed by a stream of players from its African colonies. Their arrival was part of the right-wing dictatorship's strategy for resisting calls to decolonize. Under pressure from both superpowers to grant its colonies liberty, the regime embarked on a program of integration to assuage internal and external critics. Treating the colonies as provinces, it changed its labor laws to increase the flow of overseas players and began to fete the successes of its club and national sides as a triumph of multiethnic tolerance.

With their potential to serve as symbols for both the left-wing African independence movements and a Portuguese regime that needed them desperately to justify its empire, the players had to adopt an unflinching apoliticism to protect their professional development and meager but meaningful earning power. Throughout, they trod a thin line but managed to alienate neither side. This was far from straightforward in the febrile atmosphere of 1960s Portugal, particularly after the outbreak of war in three of the five colonies. Radicalization occurred in university towns where many players studied while they trained and where they were enlightened about the exploitation of the countries they had left behind. Despite significant flashpoints when insurgent supporters exploited key sporting events, the players themselves opted for calm. And in opening up a gap between the fervor of their fans and their own actions, they kept a lid on a situation that would soon find resolution during the 1970s.

Rob Ruck's account of baseball in the Caribbean shows how formal and informal empire could lead to complex sporting patterns across large regional spaces. The spread of the US "national pastime" was largely accomplished by businesses and industries, with Cuba, emerging from Spanish domination, playing a central role in the diffusion of the game to the rest of the Caribbean basin from Mexico to Venezuela. Ties between the two countries were tight: a number of light-skinned Cubans found their way to Major League Baseball in the United States, while American players of African descent who were restricted to the Negro League found winter employment on the island. After World War II, however, concerns raised by the Cold War impinged on the sport.

The Brooklyn Dodgers' signing Jackie Robinson in 1945 and the subsequent integration of the major leagues might have portrayed some progress, but it hardly made the lives of Afro-Cuban players any easier when they came north and were confronted by a range of discrimination. The terms of this sporting trade in athletic bodies remained very much on the side of the US clubs. This held until the Cuban Revolution in 1959 began a process of moving away from the old relationship. By 1961, Cubans were no longer permitted to take up contracts in the north, and the openly professional structure of the island's elite league was transformed to conform to Soviet practices of paid amateurism. As the flow of Cubans dried up, Major League Baseball deeply mined the talents of Puerto Rico, the Dominican Republic, and Venezuela, signing scores of teenagers and establishing academies that attracted thousands of young men who pursued the elusive dream of big-time contracts. The Dominicans came to dominate the post-1961 flow of Caribbean talent in a minimally controlled process that replicated the primitive accumulation of capital. As a result, a Cold War–inflected rivalry between Communist Cuba and the capitalist Dominicans never emerged. The collapse of the USSR again changed Cuba's relationship with professional baseball, precipitating a wave of defections that often proved difficult for the players who came to the United States and trying for those they left behind.

The US relationship with the nations of South America can properly be described as neocolonial. In the twentieth century, the Monroe Doctrine, which had defined the US policy of limiting Old World power in the region for almost a hundred years, was replaced by a looser Pan-Americanism that sought to foster

trade and influence. In this context, the Pan American Games might seem like
a perfect vehicle for the United States: the possibility of a Western Hemispheric
event was first raised during the 1930s, and Avery Brundage, then head of the
US Olympic Committee and later president of the IOC, played a central role.
But as Brenda Elsey points out, there are different lenses through which to
view these acts of cultural diplomacy. The games failed to dispel doubts about
US intentions, and far from a festival of "good neighborism," the quadrennial
events proved to be yet another site of contested Cold War terrain.

The first games took place in Buenos Aires in 1951, as South American countries were realizing the adverse effects of the Marshall Plan on their access to
European markets and Juan Perón was seeking to foster a South American
third way between US imperialism and Soviet Communism. While the games
gave the Peróns an obvious opportunity to push domestic and international
agendas—encouraging workers to participate in traditional elitist sports, cham-
pioning women's sports at a time when suffrage had been secured—they also
heightened tensions with neighbors sympathetic to political dissenters. Yet the
United States hardly covered itself in glory: The New York Times compared
Perón with Adolf Hitler; a largely second-string team failed to triumph; and
American officials and journalists complained about food, facilities, and judging. However, the hosts dominated in a potent display of Argentinian modernity.
Mexico, four years later, impressed even more with its technological expertise,
and while English-speaking athletes were segregated at their own request, South
American solidarity grew. By the time the games arrived in Chicago in 1959,
the disdain of the organizers, who wasted little effort in putting them on, and
the public, which expended even less in watching them, was plain to see. In
such settings, the games cemented south-south ties while eroding north-south
relationships.

Conclusion

When one goes beyond the few highly visible mega-events, it is clear that Cold
War sport was implicated with what Michel de Certeau called "the practice
of everyday life."[40] In this book we place the emphasis on the quotidian and
ongoing character of sport to find the nuance and ambiguity that are obscured
by the blinding quadrennial glare of the Olympics and the soccer World Cup.
These essays are a first step toward broadening historians' concerns and changing the ways sport is implicated in the larger events of the era. Our project

seeks to show that sport is both integral to the study of the cultural Cold War and works out its difference from other forms of culture. Drawing the threads together now, we conclude by asking what our contributors reveal about a series of fundamental issues. What are sport's specificities? How are sports different from other cultural forms? And what false assumptions about sport in the Cold War need to be overturned? In answering these questions, we identify six key areas.

Fans

In sport, fans can have an impact on the outcome of the spectacle in ways consumers of other cultural forms rarely, if ever, can. With the audience part of the show, sport was capable of powerfully and swiftly projecting meanings with serious political implications, whether Georgian nationalism (Scott), opposition to the Vietnam War (Gorn), or anti-Communism in Southeast Asia (Creak). Despite the many successes of the historical profession's cultural turn, students of popular culture continue to struggle with the matter of reception. Texts and documents are easier to retrieve and analyze than more amorphous popular responses. Yet that task is more central and, thankfully, easier in regard to sport. We know how many watched and what they watched; we can make educated guesses about why they watched and how they understood what they had witnessed; the politics of the neighborhood or courtyard, pub or café, church or factory can be studied as part of ordinary people's daily lives. In making these their emphases, our contributors show how sport can provide a way out of what is too often a methodological cul-de-sac. In doing this, they examine how sport has informed identity formation and with it the world of mass politics within which modern sport evolved. In the Cold War, sport was a place for individuals and groups to think about who they were and make political choices based on that understanding. It was also a place for fans to revel in the fact that sport could slip through the hands of authoritarian regimes. Unjust and unpredictable, sport—particularly a team sport such as soccer—often defied logical, scientific, and rational attempts to control outcomes.

Media

Without the media and the public's attention to them, the resonance of Cold War sport would have been severely diminished. Its early stages corresponded to the arrival of television, a medium that quickly rivaled all others. In the United States, for instance, half of all households owned a set by the early

1950s; the number of regular moviegoers more than halved by the decade's end; and listening figures of popular radio shows collapsed in a matter of years.[41] In the Soviet Union, a similar development ensued with about a decade's delay.[42] Television played an increasingly important role in sport, particularly in the era of détente. In the 1960s, the IOC warmed to the idea of selling media rights,[43] with live, rather than limited, delayed coverage beginning in Tokyo in 1964 and ensuring such globally shared experiences of events as the 1968 Black Power salute of John Carlos and Tommie Smith and the 1972 terrorist siege in Munich.

Television had various effects on sport: its commercial hunger created competition that contributed to peace as much as it compromised it;[44] international coverage produced live shared experiences that drew on the fascination of difference but pulled the world together (Hershberg); pictures from afar gave fans novel modes of behavior and new measures to judge domestic offerings (Zeller, McDougall); and the visuality of the medium overlaid drab reality with pictures of grace and beauty (Timm). It would be a lazy assumption to imagine that all these effects were new. Many were evident in the interwar period, simply in different media that television would eventually oust. After all, as Peter J. Kuznick and James Gilbert observed, television was "only one of a series of dramatic changes in communications marking almost every decade of the century."[45] Future work in the field should, therefore, follow the example of our authors and ask what is specifically new or distinctive about television's contribution to sport in the Cold War. And researchers should pay specific attention to cable and satellite providers—the *real* revolution in broadcasting—which began toward the end of the period and quickly threw the delicate balance of viewing habits near the Iron Curtain out of kilter (Timm).

The False Binary of State Versus Independence

Any notion of a clear contrast between state-sponsored and independent sport is a false binary. Prozumenshikov, Rider, Zeller, Dennis, and Timm all tackle this matter in different ways. Indeed, the very variety of their essays undermines the argument that there was a clear distinction between capitalist and Communist elite, high-performance sport. The literature on Cold War culture has revealed that both superpowers used the camouflage of independence to hide state involvement. Few were fooled by Soviet efforts to create front groups, but global publics throughout the world were led to believe that pro-capitalist, pro-American sentiments were the result of free choices by individuals up until the 1967 revelations of CIA involvement. This was as true in the field of sport as it was in other arenas of cultural competition. The evolution of state-private networks assured that capitalist states were not asleep at the wheel.

The Communist side of the coin reveals the converse. Within the edifice of state-sponsored and controlled sport there were numerous areas of autonomy in which athletes, officials, journalists, and ordinary citizens could resist and negotiate the demands of authorities who were not always sure of what they were doing. The essays by Timm, Scott, McDougall, Zeller, and Dennis track well with the growing literature on late Communism, in which the binary of evil officials and good dissidents has been rejected in favor of complexity, nuance, ambiguity, and multiple shades of gray. How could it be that the leaders of the Communist Youth League loved Pink Floyd and Deep Purple? Yet they did.

The Inadequacy of Bipolarity

To the extent there is a master narrative of Cold War sport, it has been constructed more by journalists and politicians than by scholars. It describes a bipolar struggle between the United States and the Soviet Union played out in the distorting arena of the Olympic Games to convince the citizens of the nonaligned, postcolonial worlds to adopt one or another globalization project. Yet neither bloc was monolithic. While the Olympic Games may have been the most obvious site for an athletic proxy war, the essays in this book demonstrate how much more broadly and deeply sport was implicated in domestic political struggles. The competition between capitalism and Communism took place not simply between nations but within them as well. The essays of Prozumenshikov, Scott, McDougall, Rider, Gorn, and Zeller, in different ways, emphasize the Cold War's complex impact on what can be called the local.

Moreover, the Global South did not sit by passively while Communists and capitalists peddled their ideological and geopolitical wares. As the essays by Morris, Shuman, Ruck, Creak, and Elsey demonstrate, the new nations of Latin America, Africa, and Asia were able, through careful negotiation and cooperation among themselves and with nations of the East and West, to deploy sport to carve out institutions and movements of their own. The Pan American Games, the Caribbean baseball diamond, the Games of the New Emerging Forces, and the Portuguese football field were all sites at which the so-called periphery engaged a self-identified center. It is all the more remarkable that the postcolonial world was able to achieve these successes while it was the site of a series of proxy wars that cost tens of millions of lives.

Race

Race was an ineluctable element of the Cold War, one that was created, ironically, by the collapse of the very European empires (formal and informal) that had spread the practices of modern sport throughout the world. Race, and the racism it inspired, was an inescapable part of empire: the populations of the colonies were almost universally people of color, and whites justified their rule by claims of superiority to people who were black, brown, yellow, and red. When colonies became independent nations, the United States, with its history of slavery and continuing racism, faced huge obstacles in gaining the sympathies of the citizens and governments of nonaligned states (Gorn). While it peopled its international teams with African Americans and other minorities to create an impression of racial progress, this was a weakness the USSR was able to exploit in Africa, Asia, and even Latin America.

Racism had consequences that went far beyond mere external representation. The integration of Major League Baseball in the United States had deep resonance throughout the multiracial societies of the Caribbean and Latin America, and what was called "Organized Baseball" in the United States sought to reinforce a neocolonial relationship with the game to the south, until it was severely challenged in 1959 with the Cuban Revolution (Ruck). Even black athletes from other nations could have their natural antipathies to Soviet sport severely turned when they encountered discrimination while in the United States (Elsey). And at the same time, as Rita Liberti and Maureen M. Smith have shown in their recent award-winning book on Wilma Rudolph, the triple Olympic gold-medal winner in Rome, the challenge posed by the Soviets created an opportunity for poor African American women from the south—even if they did return from Olympic glory to decades of racial strife at home.[46] Race is a vital element to understanding the period, and its myriad patterns in sport should be traced with care.

Gender

When modern sport emerged in Great Britain during the nineteenth century, the popular and not altogether inaccurate narrative goes, it was constructed as a male bastion. If masculinity in the premodern world had been measured in terms of military service, the rise of capitalism created new elites who created wealth and power while sitting behind desks. To demonstrate their physical strength and its attendant privilege, they were drawn to pastimes that allowed them to perform their manhood. These should not be viewed reductively as a single expression of masculine identity but rather as a range of different articulations. From the beginning, men performed and projected themselves differently according to the sport they chose. Football was not rugby; nor was it cricket, tennis, or boxing. Later in the century, millions of workingmen were drawn to sport and, like their middle- and upper-class compatriots, had a range of forms (if somewhat more restricted) at their disposal. Football, in particular, came to occupy a leading position, while boxing remained a popular pursuit, both for spectators and participants. As the essays by Scott, Zeller, Gorn, Ruck, and McDougall show, sport continued to be a place "men could be men" even in the Cold War or, more accurately, a place where men could be different sorts of men. If one thing emerges across these essays, it is the nuanced ways in which men in different social and political contexts chose to articulate identities through sporting endeavor and spectatorship.

By the early twentieth century, women had come to contest the argument that sport was fundamentally male, and during the Cold War, the matter of gender produced great anxiety in the West. Women's sport was not a large part of capitalism's late 1940s and 1950s, but it most definitely was under Communism. During World War II, women had been massively employed in a variety of forms of physical and mental labor previously performed by men, but they were soon forced to revert to the private spheres of hearth and home when the "boys" returned and expected their jobs back. Such was not the case in the nations of Eastern Europe, which had lost millions of young men—a demographic disaster that hardly put an end to patriarchy in the USSR but nonetheless created opportunities for women. Throughout the first decades of the Cold War, up until 1972 and the enactment of laws calling for gender equality in the United States, Communist women held sway over their capitalist counterparts. Their success was dismissed as the work of lesbians or men dressing up as women.

With notable exceptions—such as gymnasts Olga Korbut and Ludmilla Turishcheva—these were long-held stereotypes. It would take until the 1980s for different versions of women's sport to gain acceptance in the wake of second-wave feminism and the early Cold War images of womanly Western athletes and asexual Communist ones to be challenged (Shuman). Even then matters were complicated, as was the aggressively sexualized figure skater Katerina Witt, whose image meant different things to different Cold War audiences (Timm).

The challenge for future research will be to interrogate the production and reception of such images, explore their tenacity, and uncover the reality that lay beneath. It will also be to look beyond the headline figures to discover the ways in which women played key and all-too-often overlooked roles as popular diplomatic ambassadors, such as at the Pan American Games, where their presence in numbers altered the tone and outcomes of a pro-female Peronist soft diplomacy that challenged reigning conceptions of bipolarity (Elsey).

As these key findings bear out, wherever sporting encounters took place, their impact and import were far from set. The aims of a state could be immaterial to its subjects; diplomatic priorities, irrelevant to friends and foe; the concern of one sport, the preserve of it alone. Sport has a deceptive simplicity, but in truth it is highly liminal and inescapably nuanced. There is no single point on a spectrum where its power can or should be isolated. Sport's fundamental elasticity is what sets it apart from other forms of culture that have attracted the attention of Cold War historians to date. To that one could add, of course, its unique range and visibility.

We are conscious of Thomas Lindenberger's caution that "the ways to live the Cold War predicament varied greatly depending on the place. . . . There were periods and places in which the Cold War was 'lived' in an acute and existential manner, in contrast to others in which it was only present as something rather remote, in the background rather than the foreground."[47] This is a useful reminder that Cold War sport did not always play out as intensely as it appears in the pages of this book. Like many other aspects of the Cold War—from missiles to box-office hits—the ideological implications of sport could be both intensely present and oddly absent from general consciousness. That said, we believe that sport, as much as—arguably more than—any other form of culture can take us to the "subjectivities, values, beliefs, and mentalities" of Cold War citizens, societies, and governments, to the "intangibles" that illuminate how people experienced the Cold War.[48] The job for historians is to trace these themes across a wide range of topics, where possible and appropriate, in granular detail. For Cold War sport, this book represents the first concerted effort to do so.[49]

PART I

THE UNITED STATES

IN THE "TWILIGHT WARZONE"

Overt and Covert Dimensions of the
US Sports Offensive

Toby C. Rider

In the early years of the Cold War, Americans began to discuss the nature of Soviet sport with increasing regularity. For the most part, they reached a consensus of opinion. A range of US sports officials and athletes, along with politicians, journalists, and academics, charged that the "Reds" had ruthlessly turned sports into a tool of state politics and propaganda. With equal conviction, many of the same people stoutly defended the role of sport in American society by celebrating its freedom from government control. To some extent they were right. The United States did not possess a state-directed sports infrastructure, and it did not directly subsidize its athletes.

Yet during this period, the government did deploy sport for propaganda purposes, regardless of what the majority of Americans might have said or thought. Under the presidencies of Harry S. Truman and Dwight D. Eisenhower, for instance, the US government's information program began to organize and fund overseas sports tours to protect America's image abroad. This form of cultural diplomacy was, of course, an exercise in state propaganda, even if the officials who ran the exchanges denied this fact in public. While historians have examined this government initiative, they have overlooked the various other sport-related activities undertaken by US propaganda services in the early Cold War years.[1] Declassified documents released in the past few decades reveal that tours and exchanges were but a single aspect of a far broader US cultural effort in the field of sports. The scale of this effort was truly global and sometimes veiled by a cloak of clandestine secrecy. Throughout the late

1940s and 1950s the overt and covert branches of Washington's information apparatus used sports to advertise and promote American culture and attack the regimes of the Soviet Bloc. Even if the US public collectively disapproved of Communist states mixing politics with sports, their own government was engaging in much the same thing.

Why the United States embarked on this propaganda campaign reveals much about the peculiarities of the Cold War. To avoid the unthinkable consequences of nuclear confrontation, the United States and the Soviet Union fought to gain a preponderance of power in world affairs through the mobilization and exploitation of ideas and culture. At the outbreak of the Cold War, however, the United States was ill equipped for such a battle. While it had created a sprawling propaganda machine during World War II, this machine was largely dismantled after the defeat of the Third Reich. Yet in response to the desperate realities of the fractured postwar world, the waxing power of the Soviet Union across Europe, and the sheer effectiveness of Communist propaganda, the United States soon began to reassemble its information network. The "realization dawned," a government analyst observed, "that here was a weapon which could be used in this twilight warzone in which we found ourselves living."[2]

Toward the end of 1947, a year that witnessed the intensification of Cold War antagonisms, the United States began to sketch the contours of its postwar propaganda apparatus. As had been the case in World War II, the program would be split along overt and covert lines. In December, the National Security Council (NSC) asserted that the Soviet Union "is conducting an intensive propaganda campaign" and pressed for the "immediate strengthening of and coordination of all foreign information measures in the U.S. Government designed to influence attitudes in foreign countries." The NSC subsequently approved NSC 4, a policy document that stipulated that the State Department assume responsibility for the fractured overt "information measures" strewn around a variety of "departments and agencies." A secret annex, titled NSC 4-A, gave the Central Intelligence Agency (CIA) authority to conduct "covert psychological operations designed to counteract Soviet and Soviet-inspired activities which constitute a threat to world peace and security."[3]

Just months later, in January 1948, the overt track of the propaganda apparatus was given legislative backing when Congress passed the US Information and Educational Exchange Act, which finally secured a permanent status for the overseas information program. Over the next few years, the size and scope of the Truman administration's cultural effort grew exponentially, as Congress

granted the State Department more funds to counter the "lies" of Soviet propaganda with the "truth" about the United States. By 1952, the United States
could boast that it was communicating to a massive global audience through
the international distribution of books, magazines, newspapers, and movies;
through more than a hundred information centers in more than seventy countries; through broadcasts carried on the airwaves of the government's radio
network, the Voice of America; and through a range of reciprocal cultural
exchanges. The Eisenhower administration continued to build on this platform
and, in 1953, consolidated the sprawling worldwide program into the United
States Information Agency (USIA).[4]

In the late 1940s, the officers who staffed the overt propaganda program
started to recognize that sport had become part of the total Cold War contest.
Reports from American diplomats overseas recorded the increasing number
of Soviet athletes competing in various international events and embarking
on cultural exchanges. Soviet propaganda, State Department officials noted,
hailed the achievements of its athletes, celebrated their victories, and praised
their contribution to global peace and goodwill.[5] The Soviets alleged, on the
other hand, that US sport fed the capitalist system and furthered the pursuit
of America's ruthless militaristic and imperialistic agenda.[6] "Both at home
and abroad," recorded a USIA intelligence analysis, "the Soviets have been
promoting the idea that only under their system can sports attain perfection
and embrace the masses of the population."[7]

As a result of this campaign, US information experts determined that foreign audiences had developed a distorted view of American sports and its place
in American society. Addressing the distortion required deploying a similar
approach. US officials realized that sport was a cultural medium that could
be successfully "exploited" because it had such immense range. In numerous
planning papers, American propaganda experts discussed the universal appeal
of sports, particularly to the "man-on-the-street," the "worker," and the coveted
opinion of the world's youth.[8] They recognized that sports topics easily stirred
interest on a global scale and allowed the United States to communicate with
audiences abroad in a shared language and culture. Sport was a medium that
was distinctly political but could be packaged otherwise.

Stories about America's sporting landscape became a staple subject as the
Soviet "sports offensive" gathered momentum. By 1952, the year in which the
USSR competed in the Olympics for the first time, the US government's over-
seas information *Bulletin* contained a regular column titled "Sports World."

Within two years the USIA established a monthly "feature packet" on sports full of cartoons, glossy photographs, articles, and carefully selected reprints from American newspapers and magazines. These materials were sent to US embassies, information centers, and public affairs officers around the world for distribution overtly and covertly in local and national media outlets. Moreover, the programming of the Voice of America included live sports coverage and stories in dozens of languages to an estimated audience in the hundreds of millions.

Without question, US propaganda had a defensive tone that attempted to refute Communist accusations about the role of sport in America. But there was more to the narrative than this. As Laura Belmonte has noted, for American propagandists, "life under democratic capitalism meant far more than escaping communist oppression. It signified a world of spiritual, material, social, political, and cultural benefits of which communists could only dream."[9] The content of US materials, then, sought to present America as a land of sports far more vibrant, and far more diverse, than the physical culture experienced under Communism.

In numerous stories, films, and pictures, propaganda experts tried to demonstrate that sports in the United States unified and enriched the lives of the national citizenry. On any given day, people across the country were said to be willingly participating in a range of sporting activities. In a recurring theme, these materials paid homage to the private and voluntary aspects of US sports, praising their place in forging a morally and physically sound community. Civic engagement exemplified the limited role of government in the everyday lives of Americans. Propaganda strategists continually contrasted the state-dominated model that prevailed under Communism with the citizen-led teams, leagues, competitions, charities, and philanthropic events in the United States. In a series of stories, US propaganda took great care to explain that the United States Olympic Committee was "self-governing" by soliciting charitable donations from the American public. "No government subsidy has been offered," a 1952 *Bulletin* article read. "If it were, it would not be accepted."[10]

More generally, propaganda experts endeavored to depict US athletes as normal people in just the same way they tried to present Americans as a community of ordinary human beings.[11] While Communist propaganda charged that American athletes were "rough, dirty-fighting, gangster-like competitors," the USIA deluged overseas audiences with stories on the hardworking, diligent, humble, and well-mannered individuals who represented the Stars and Stripes.[12] While Communist propaganda proclaimed America to be a "cultural wasteland," the USIA released materials about male and female athletes who had various hobbies, interests, and cultural talents. Unlike the one-dimensional figures in the Communist media, they enjoyed oil painting, drawing, writing, singing, listening to music, or expressing their religious freedom.[13]

The information program also portrayed American society as a place of social equality. Anyone could progress through hard work and honest forti- tude; anyone could become a paragon of "People's Capitalism."[14] In particular, the success and popularity of African American athletes helped counter one of the most powerful and persistent themes of Communist propaganda: racial discrimination in the United States. Propagandists attempted to deflect at- tention from racial segregation by portraying a gradual process of integration and change.[15] The USIA's selective approach to presenting race and sport in American society was perhaps best displayed in the agency's film on the ten- nis star Althea Gibson. It was released in 1957, the same year world audiences watched the unraveling civil rights unrest that gripped Little Rock, Arkansas. The Gibson film "appropriated" the athlete's victories in the US Open and Wimbledon championships to "show American democracy in a positive light." Rather than admit that Gibson's race had obstructed her tennis career, the film focused on her work ethic and inferred that her achievements were a "normal" by-product of the American way of life.[16]

Gibson's film touched on another important theme in US propaganda: the need to answer Communist accusations that American women were not only "on the verge of prostitution" but also "slovenly, ugly, and silly."[17] Instead, mul- tiple USIA profiles of female athletes sought to portray a wholesome, feminine, domesticated, and productive vision of American women.[18] Female athletes "enjoyed" doing housework and cooking, liked to sew and knit, hoped to marry and raise a family, and aspired to attend college or find a job. Once again, the narrative of progress was decidedly judicious. In the post–World War II era, women were vastly underrepresented on the US Olympic team, provided with few opportunities to participate in track-and-field events, and scrutinized for their ability to fulfill Western standards of femininity.[19]

While sport was used to construct a positive image of day-to-day life in America, US propaganda further explained that American citizens were noble participants in the far larger community of international sport. A host of fea- tures described the mutual transfer of ideas that occurred when foreign athletes, coaches, and physical educators visited the United States. There was also praise for Americans who traveled abroad to share their expertise on skills, techniques, and training. These overseas excursions, many of which were organized by the State Department, provided just the sort of copy information experts craved. Pictures and articles of Americans on missions abroad were proof of a nation committed to fostering amity and goodwill.

For the USIA, American athletes on tours were effective because they understood and preached the core moral values of sport. Thus, the information program was particularly keen to demonstrate that the United States was an upstanding affiliate of the Olympic Movement.[20] Propaganda strategists acknowledged that the Games were a globally admired festival driven by a compelling, if largely mythical, mission to make the world a better place through "friendly" athletic competition. They recognized that by describing to overseas audiences that the American public upheld and revered Olympic principles, they would be insinuating that the United States was also committed to the same goals. In leading up to the Winter and Summer Games from 1952 to 1960, the information program filled its overseas output with a range of materials emphasizing the "true spirit" of the movement and pumped out items highlighting US adherence to Olympic principles.[21]

While the main thrust of the US propaganda offensive aimed to counter Soviet "lies" about America's athletic culture, it also sought to tell overseas audiences the "truth" about sport under Communist rule. Conveying this message became even more crucial throughout the 1950s as Soviet athletes began to improve their performances at the Olympic Games and other international competitions.[22]

The bulk of the information program's stories about sport under Communism were based on accounts from Eastern European refugees living in the West. Fueled by a desire to end Communist rule in their homeland, refugees told deeply negative tales about the goals of Communist sport and the restrictive aspects of life in Eastern Europe. In one scathing attack broadcast on the airwaves of the Voice of America, Jozsef Halmay, a Hungarian émigré, explained that Communist states were solely focused on developing athletes for the sake of propaganda. Halmay, an Olympic canoeist who defected in 1954, also charged that athletes were locked in their hotel rooms during international competitions and locked in buses when they traveled to events. "I knew I was being used as a tool," he said.[23] Still, many of the information program's stories about refugees were also scripted to include a happy ending. The USIA frequently highlighted that émigrés were now living safely and contentedly in the "free world."

The overt US propaganda program relied on a high level of cooperation with private actors. Overseas output was littered with interviews and quotes from athletes, coaches, and sports administrators, while many of the tours described and pictorialized were organized by the State Department in tandem with American sports authorities. Yet the wealth of material gleaned from conversations with Eastern European exiles also masked the activities of the government's covert propaganda branch. The USIA did not tell overseas audiences exactly how some of these refugee athletes had managed to escape from their homeland in the first place. High-ranking American psychological warfare experts underscored the value of exploiting the propaganda potential of exiled athletes and, in some cases, began to fund and support defections. To shroud state involvement in these defections, they were sometimes organized by front organizations or other private groups supplied with government funds.

This use of nonstate intermediaries by the overt and covert strands of the information program was by no means limited to the realm of sports. During the late 1940s, the US government reacted to the unconventional nature of the Cold War by embarking on an unprecedented peacetime effort to work with and through private businesses, groups, and organizations to support US foreign policy objectives. In most instances, the public did not require convincing to join this fight. They were ready and eager to enter the fray, but they required resources and guidance to make their case effectively. The government filled this breach. Although this "state-private network" had an overt dimension, US officials understood that the general public, both at home and abroad, was wary of official government involvement in propaganda. The main thrust of the network was therefore developed covertly to shield the hand of the state.[24]

The covert dimension of the state-private network emerged as a component of US psychological warfare initiated by NSC 4-A. With the ink barely dry on this document, the US government immediately began sabotaging the Italian Communist Party's chances of winning the 1948 national election and undermining Communist influence in French labor unions. Buoyed by the outcome of these efforts, strategists sought to expand the range of clandestine initiatives even further. At the forefront of this diversification was George F. Kennan, director of the State Department's Policy Planning Staff. In a May 1948 memo, "The Inauguration of Organized Political Warfare," he and his colleagues called for the US government to undermine Soviet control in Eastern Europe by supporting "specific projects in the field of covert operations." One such project would involve the government sponsoring "liberation committees" led by refugees from behind the Iron Curtain. These refugees, the memo noted, would "act as foci of national hope and revive a sense of purpose among political refugees from the Soviet World."[25]

Kennan's plans were soon put into action. In November 1948, NSC 10/2 recommended the creation of a new covert directorate—later named the Office of Policy Coordination—within the CIA and charged it to perform a range of clandestine operations. The NSC directive emphasized that the activities "conducted or sponsored" by the United States should be "planned and executed" so that the government could "plausibly disclaim any responsibility for them."[26] In 1949, the Office of Policy Coordination established the National Committee for a Free Europe (NCFE), a group inspired by Kennan's blueprint for liberation committees and therefore designed to provide a voice for Eastern European refugees who wished to levy an attack on Communism. In an advertisement published in the *New York Times*, the committee announced that it would support Soviet Bloc refugees to "continue their stand against communism, anticipating the day when the Iron Curtain will fall and Eastern Europe will be ripe for democratic remaking." To anyone in the public who might be interested, the committee simply claimed to be a private philanthropic group led by prominent American citizens. In reality, it received millions of CIA dollars to fund Soviet Bloc émigrés in an astounding breadth of activities.[27]

A portion of this money found its way to the Hungarian National Sports Federation (HNSF), a refugee sports group based in New York and led by a Hungarian exile, Count Anthony Szápáry. The mission of the federation mirrored the goals of its financial benefactor. Yet unlike the multitude of other organizations funded by the NCFE, the HNSF sought to "deal the greatest possible blows whenever and wherever possible to the communists in the field of sports."[28] Indeed, the NCFE and HNSF cooperated on a number of projects and covert operations throughout the 1950s. They tried and failed to enter a refugee team at the 1952 Summer Olympics, created and distributed anti-Communist literature, publicly denounced the Communist sports system in the Western media, organized fund-raising events for the US Olympic team, demanded international sports bodies eject Communist nations from sports competitions, and helped Eastern European athletes defect and resettle in the "free world."[29]

Arguably the most significant of their collaborative efforts occurred in the aftermath of the 1956 Melbourne Summer Olympics, when they helped thirty-four Hungarians and four Romanians—including athletes, coaches, writers, and sports administrators—defect to the United States. Few knew of this at the time, and the details have been slow to emerge ever since. For years, most believed the explanation provided by the magazine *Sports Illustrated*. In a famous article published on December 17, 1956, just weeks after the closing ceremonies of the Games, journalist André Laguerre described in detail how he and *Sports Illustrated* had orchestrated the event. The thirty-four Hungarians in the group, Laguerre noted in particular, had chosen to live in a land of "freedom and opportunity" rather than return to their homeland, which had just witnessed a revolution crushed by the Soviet military. In the self-congratulatory piece, Laguerre claimed the athletes were "subjected to no pressure or propaganda. They had no contact with any U.S. official. They sought out representatives of *Sports Illustrated*."[30] While the article clearly emphasized that this was a private initiative and with minimal government involvement, it was, in fact, an example of far deeper state and private cooperation.

Aside from the HNSF and NCFE, other parties made pivotal contributions, none more so than Charles Douglas Jackson, a fascinating figure in the history of US covert operations. Like numerous other publicists and advertisers the government hired to assist in propaganda operations, he was plucked out of the private sector. Jackson graduated from Princeton in 1924 and spent his early career ascending through the ranks of Time Incorporated. During World War II, he was heavily involved with US psychological warfare, and his gift for propaganda made his services a commodity of great value after 1945. He regularly advised the Truman and Eisenhower administrations on Cold War planning and was instrumental in the creation of the NCFE.[31] Szápáry and the HNSF benefited from Jackson's connections in the government. He aided the group on numerous occasions and never swayed from his belief that exiled athletes living and competing in America were potent weapons in psychological warfare.

Jackson's ties to *Time* are also significant. The owner of the company, Henry Luce, was a founding member of the NCFE and well connected in covert circles. He was a close friend of Allen Dulles, Eisenhower's director of Central Intelligence, and Jackson's presence at the company meant that the media mogul had a further direct contact into the government's psychological warfare machinery. *Time* magazine assisted in various government projects, provided cover for CIA staff, and often published articles that gave the Eisenhower administration favorable coverage.[32] Yet to what extent was *Sports Illustrated*, a subsidiary of *Time*, caught in the US government's covert web? The magazine may not have had reporters on the CIA's payroll, but there is evidence to suggest it was not an innocent and objective vessel. The events that transpired before, during, and after the Melbourne Olympic Games indicate that *Sports Illustrated* was part of Luce's personal war against Communism and that this war was not isolated by any means from the White House.

Nevertheless, it is with the HNSF, not *Sports Illustrated*, that the story of the Melbourne defection must begin. On the afternoon of November 11, 1956, Szápáry and his wife, Sylvia, entertained Whitney Tower (a relative of Sylvia) at their home in Pound Ridge, New York. Also present was Dr. George Telegdy, secretary of the HNSF. The start of the Melbourne Olympics was less than two weeks away, and Szápáry had just returned from Vienna, where he had been trying to organize relief for Hungarians in the wake of the revolution. He asked Tower, the associate editor of *Sports Illustrated*, if his employer could assist in the defection of Hungarian Olympic athletes, many of whom had decided not to return home after the Olympics.[33] Tower agreed to help. He produced an "urgent and confidential" memorandum on the idea that soon landed on Jackson's desk. Tower told Szápáry that "outside of top government officials there is probably no man who has more influence with Ike [Eisenhower] and the State Department than C. D. Jackson."[34] Within days, Tower wrote Szápáry that "things definitely look promising" and that "Jackson is at the moment probing deeper into the matter in Washington." He added in a handwritten note, "I cannot over-emphasize the importance of maintaining the closest possible secrecy on this subject."[35]

Meanwhile, there had been some doubt surrounding the Hungarian team's participation in the Olympics. The Hungarian Revolution erupted in late October and was routed by Soviet troops on November 4. The Melbourne Olympic Games were slated to begin on November 22. Because of the upheaval in Hungary, the Associated Press predicted the national team would simply be unable to get to Australia. The report turned out to be wrong. The Hungarian National Olympic Committee sent a cable to the Melbourne Organizing Committee to confirm that its athletes would arrive in Australia on November 10, one week later than originally planned. The understated message blamed "unforeseen circumstances."[36]

As fate would have it, the water polo competition at the Games provided the Hungarians an opportunity to exact revenge, in a sporting sense at least, against the Soviet Union. With a formidable history of success in the pool, the Hungarians marched through the early rounds of the tournament, handily beating each opponent. The luck of the draw, though, pitted them against the

Soviets in the semifinal. The match is now part of Olympic folklore. From the first whistle, this tense and highly symbolic encounter was filled with physical confrontations and controversy. Feeding off the reportedly partisan support from the crowd, the Hungarians built up, and never lost, a 4–0 lead. Near the end of the game came the most famous incident of all. A Soviet player, Valentin Prokopov, punched the Hungarian star, Ervin Zádor, opening a nasty cut on his face. Such "a vicious and violent blow" that it "stained the water red," the London *Daily Mirror* embellished. The expatriate Hungarians in the stands vented their strong disapproval, and the referee stopped the game there and then. The Soviets were booed as they left the pool. The Hungarians moved on to the final, where they narrowly defeated Yugoslavia by a score of 2–1.[37]

As soon as the Hungarian team reached Australia, rumors of possible defections began to swirl in the Western media. Behind the scenes, the plan for a mass exodus was already coming together. The NCFE dispatched Telegdy to Australia, where he was soon circulating around the Olympic city and speaking with Hungarian athletes. He frequently imparted this intelligence to on-site *Sports Illustrated* reporters, including Laguerre, and this information was relayed to the magazine's headquarters in New York via coded cable messages. As might be expected, the athletes in question wanted reassurances that they would be granted asylum in the United States and assistance to resettle. Beyond this, Telegdy and Laguerre were in a race against the clock. With the Olympics scheduled to end on December 8, undecided Hungarians had precious little time to make an extremely difficult decision. Aside from leaving behind their country and loved ones, athletes feared government reprisals against family members and carefully considered whether their relatively privileged life as an athlete under Communism was worth giving up. Regardless, the *Sports Illustrated* leadership repeatedly assured everyone concerned that asylum would not be an issue.[38]

Believing that their journey to the United States would be unimpeded, dozens of Hungarian competitors eluded Communist security agents and began to disappear into the city of Melbourne. Just days before the Olympics closed, the first two to leave, Zoltán Török (a rowing coach) and Róbert Zimonyi (a coxswain), "strolled" out of the Olympic Village and "sprang" into a car bound for Telegdy's house.[39] Other athletes made similar plans once their athletic exertions were over. *Sports Illustrated* reported that members of the Hungarian water polo team "had barely dried themselves and tucked their gold medals into their pockets before they were unobtrusively driven off."[40] Telegdy was even approached by László Nadori, the chief of staff of the Hungarian Sports Ministry, who no longer wanted to serve the Communist regime. According to Telegdy, early one morning at 3:00 a.m., Nadori walked around the Olympic Village as though "indisposed" before climbing into a waiting car with the long jumper, Olga Gyarmathy. Both were taken to a nearby hotel, close to Telegdy's house.[41]

With the Games finally over, Olympic authorities allowed the Hungarians to stay in the US quarters of the Olympic Village from December 10 onward. Everyone waited for confirmation from Jackson that the athletes could legally land in the United States. Jackson had been active over the previous weeks, as he attempted to navigate and bend America's visa laws. In the wake of the revolution, the Eisenhower administration had relaxed its immigration policy to allow thousands of Hungarians into the United States and even increased the intake by admitting aliens into the country on "parole." This option was offered on an "emergency" basis, whereby refugees could enter the country if it "served the public interest."[42] Even though the option of parole was created primarily to assist the dire situation for refugees crossing the border from Hungary into Austria, Jackson was able to persuade the State Department to allow the Hungarian athletes in Melbourne to utilize this particular loophole.[43]

On December 18, *Sports Illustrated* sent a cable to Telegdy with the good news. The US government had granted "immediate" asylum to the Hungarians. A special Pan American flight, arranged by Jackson, carried them to San Francisco, where they landed on Christmas Eve.[44]

Although it is sometimes hard to gauge the impact or legacy of covert operations, the Melbourne defection certainly shook the regime in Hungary. It sufficiently troubled the government, sporting establishment, journalists, and academics to a degree that few wrote about it for years to come.[45] It is also possible to argue that the other joint ventures of the HNSF and NCFE left a mark behind the Iron Curtain. Telegdy even insisted that the Hungarian regime was fully aware of his federation and that "a special section of the Hungarian Sports Ministry" worked exclusively to "counterbalance the activities of the HNSF."[46] Yet determining, or weighing, what this meant in the context of defeating the Soviet Union or ending Communism in Eastern Europe is impossible. It is perhaps better to consider the actions of the HNSF as just one of many in an ongoing process of secret propaganda and cultural infiltration pursued by the US government throughout the Cold War.[47]

Judging the effectiveness of the overt information program is just as difficult. Did propaganda materials really sway the sympathies of the world's citizens? While government documents do herald the value of sports in communicating with overseas audiences, they also bemoan the symbolic power of international competitions. Strategists acknowledged that many of the foremost events demanded that all participating individuals or teams represented a nation, thus creating a sort of proxy battle. An American defeat to the Soviet Union at the 1956 Summer Olympics, argued one psychological warfare expert, "would certainly have an immediate impact on the man on the street, the worker, the rural citizen who reads little, the maiden who admires brawn. The mentality of 'my champion is stronger than your champion' reigns in every cafe in the world, and final proof is in deeds, not in arguments."[48] Policy makers came to realize that no matter how much they promoted the merits of the US system and denigrated the flaws of the Soviet model, the always unpredictable outcome of a sporting event carried a message that was hard to control.

There were glaring contradictions between the theory and the practice of the US sports offensive. The truth was often a flexible agent in American propaganda. Information officers were sometimes outrageous in their claims, proving little better than their Soviet counterparts. The links established with the HNSF and NCFE also reveal rhetorical problems. How indeed could a nation that forcefully endeavored to promote its ideological foundations of freedom and democracy work so diligently to mobilize the private sphere? Should the American people have been left to make such pronouncements if and when they wished to? The fear, however, was that the Communists were winning the war of words and deeds. Faced with the necessity of coming to terms with the "twilight warzone," US policy experts deployed methods that most Americans associated with their Soviet adversaries. "The choice between innocence and power involves the most difficult of decisions," noted one CIA officer. "But when an adversary attacks with his weapons disguised as good works, to choose innocence is to choose defeat."[49]

$$\textbf{2}$$

"NO QUARREL WITH THEM VIETCONG"

Muhammad Ali's Cold War

Elliott J. Gorn

Boxing was an American television staple during the 1950s and into the early 1960s, with weekly national broadcasts. American cities large and small regularly staged multifight cards, often featuring local heroes. Rising up from this broad base of talent, from lighter weights up to the big men, the boxing pyramid peaked with the heavyweight champion, the pinnacle of toughness, athletic prowess, and manly violence.[1]

Nationalism always attached itself easily to the ring. The most exciting matches of the nineteenth century featured an Englishman against an Irishman or an American against an Englishman or an Irishman against an American. The symbolism of two men fighting for supremacy was hard to resist. By the eve of World War II, no one had to be reminded what was at stake when Joe Louis twice battled Hitler's favorite fighter, Max Schmeling. Louis, as well as other black boxers, knew that American fans and sportswriters generally expected them to be polite and patriotic, humble, and grateful for their opportunities, model Americans. Mostly they complied.[2]

Cassius Clay from Louisville, Kentucky, was a promising young amateur coming up in the late 1950s. Clay's family was not poor but working class, his father a sign painter with artistic ambitions. Young Cassius was a less-than-average student who devoted himself with great discipline to training for the ring. Clay rose through the amateur ranks, won Golden Gloves championships, then won light-heavyweight gold at age eighteen at the 1960 Rome Olympics. A reporter from the Soviet Union, aware of the rising racial tensions in America, asked Clay about winning a championship for America when blacks were barred from eating in many restaurants. "Tell your readers we got qualified people working on that problem, and I'm not worried about the outcome. To me, the USA is the best country in the world, including yours." Public relations officers from the United States Information Agency (USIA) could not have put it better: Acknowledge the problem; then point to progress. Wilma Rudolph, another black US gold medalist, said Clay wore his medal with pride all over the Olympic Village.[3]

Asked about his victory at an impromptu news conference when he returned home, Clay was ready with what became his signature, a poem: "To make America the greatest is my goal / So I beat the Russian and I beat the Pole." Clay went on to say, in rhyme of course, that the Italians asked him to make Rome his new home. He thanked them for their hospitality and ended his little verse, "But the U.S.A. is my country still / 'Cause they waiting to welcome me to Louisville." The poetry was unusual for an athlete, but the patriotic sentiment was exactly what was expected from the young boxer, especially in an election year bristling with tensions over foreign affairs, missile gaps, questions about weakness abroad, even intimations of treason. But nothing Clay said had anything specifically to do with the Cold War, capitalism and Communism, the United States and the Soviet Union, "freedom" and "totalitarianism." Clay's words were conventional nationalism, in no clear sense addressed to particular ideologies. Yet ten years later, he was an international symbol of resistance to colonialism and US foreign policy.[4]

Four years after Rome, Cassius Clay took the heavyweight title from Sonny Liston, an ex-con who had been a leg breaker for the mob. Odds were 7–1 against Clay the night he won the championship. Liston was not only favored to win; he was just plain favored by fans and the press. Liston had the virtue of keeping to himself, saying little, but Clay during the four years he was undefeated through the professional ranks was outrageously verbal. He continued to celebrate himself in poetry, even predicting the round in which he would knock out his opponents. Once he turned professional, he gave up all vestiges of humility and gratitude. He was a master of self-promotion, and he later revealed that he modeled himself on professional wrestlers. For an African American prizefighter, proclamations like "I am the Greatest" or "I am the King of the World" did not sit well. He clearly was a black man who did not know his place.[5]

Worse, the day after Clay defeated Liston, he confirmed the rumor that he had converted to the Nation of Islam and soon thereafter dispensed with his "slave name," Cassius Clay. He announced to the world that henceforth he would be known as Muhammad Ali. In this era of "racial progress," of Martin Luther King, the March on Washington, and soon the Civil Rights and Voting Rights Acts, the champion openly consorted with the radical black leaders Malcolm X and Elijah Muhammad and with their militant movement that argued against racial integration. "I believe in Allah," Ali told reporters. "I don't believe in forced integration." And then, "I know where I'm going and I know the truth, and I don't have to be what you want me to be. I'm free to be what I want."[6]

That did not sit well with a very conservative guild of sportswriters. Ali's boxing style alone had raised eyebrows. Real heavyweights, most journalists believed, should be devastating punchers like Liston or, a decade earlier, Rocky Marciano. Though Ali was a big man for his era, he used his preternatural quickness more than his power. One of Ali's opponents, George Chuvalo, recalled, "He was just so damn fast. . . . He threw his punches when he was in motion. That is, he'd be out of punching range, and as he moved into range, he'd already begun to throw the punch. So if you waited until he got into range to punch back, he beat you every time." But finally it wasn't about the ring but about Ali's joining the "Black Muslims," as the Nation of Islam was disparagingly called, renouncing Christianity, endorsing black separatism, and above all, refusing to play the grateful Negro, thankful for all that America had given him.[7]

The widely syndicated sports columnist Jimmy Cannon wrote in the New York *Journal American*:

> The fight racket, since its rotten beginnings, has been the red-light district of sports. But this is the first time it has been turned into an instrument of mass hate. . . . I pity Clay and abhor what he represents. In the years of hunger during the depression, the Communists used famous people the way the Black Muslims are exploiting Clay. This is a sect that deforms the beautiful purpose of religion.[8]

In other words, Clay was a dupe, exactly the sort of stooge the Communists loved; only now the puppeteer was not Nikita Khrushchev but Elijah Muhammad.

To goad Ali and deny the legitimacy of his faith, opponents, sportswriters, and many fans continued to call him Clay. When other fighters did that, like Floyd Patterson and Ernie Terrell, Ali humiliated them in the ring, carrying them round after round, cutting them up, yelling, "What's my name?" Even Ali's supporters were appalled at his cruelty, but such moments were more grist for his detractors' mill. Two years after his first attack on Ali and the Nation of Islam, Jimmy Cannon widened his assault and, in so doing, summarized much of the animus against Ali. Cannon's was an often-quoted screed that bordered on incoherent, but his word torrent captured the uncomprehending, festering anger of the World War II generation at what we have come to think of as "the sixties":

> Clay is part of the Beatle Movement. He fits in with the famous singers no one can hear and the punks riding motorcycles with iron crosses pinned to their leather jackets and Batman and the boys with their long dirty hair and the girls with the unwashed look and the college kids dancing naked at secret proms held in apartments and the revolt of students who get a check from dad every first of the month and the painters who copy the labels off soup cans and the surf bums who refuse to work and the whole pampered style-making cult of the bored young.[9]

Cannon in his rage was on to something. Ali came to embody much of the spirit of the 1960s, the iconoclasm, the rejection of authority, the worship of youth. He was even placed under surveillance by the Federal Bureau of Investigation. It was not as if Ali had not thought about social injustice in the years when he contemplated joining the Nation of Islam: "I'm the heavyweight champion, but right now there are some neighborhoods I can't move into. I know how to dodge booby-traps and dogs. I dodge them by staying in my own neighborhood." And then on the Nation of Islam itself: "People brand us a hate group. They say we want to take over the country. They say we're Communists. That is not true. Followers of Allah are the sweetest people in the world."[10]

When the real troubles came for Ali in the late 1960s, the issue of course was Vietnam. After his Olympic victory, he was eligible for the draft, which could have sent him into combat or, more likely, as boxers had done since Joe Louis, onto the entertainment circuit for overseas troops. Eighteen years old, Clay registered for the draft in 1960; in 1962 the military classified him 1-A, eligible for service; just before he won the championship in 1964, he was ordered to take military qualifying exams. Clay had finished high school, but he was a poor student. His military intelligence tests put him in the sixteenth percentile. Tested again a few months later by three psychologists, he still came in below their 30 percent threshold. The army reclassified him 1-Y, not eligible for service. Sportswriters and fans grumbled and asked why this consummate fighter could earn big paydays in the ring and then avoid service while other men bled and died in combat. As the war ramped up and ever-more soldiers were needed, the army lowered its intelligence standards, and early in 1966, Clay—now Muhammad Ali—was reclassified 1-A.[11]

Reporters deluged him with questions on the day of this announcement. Robert Lipsyte, who was with Ali at that moment, remembered him as a naïve young man, not particularly attuned to world politics, one who had thought that his worries about Vietnam were behind him. Now suddenly the army's announcement put his life and career in jeopardy again. Reporters kept calling, questions kept coming for hours, about the war, Lyndon Johnson, the Vietcong. Ali became more and more agitated. "Finally," Lipsyte remembered, "after the tenth call—'What do you think about the Vietcong?—Ali exploded. 'Man, I ain't got no quarrel with them Vietcong.' And bang. There it was. That was the headline. That was what the media wanted." The champ was front-page news; his opponent, the United States of America.[12]

Lipsyte, one of the most sympathetic reporters covering Muhammad Ali, and certainly the most thoughtful, felt that Ali's Vietcong remark was the sincere expression of a frightened and harassed young man, not the summation of some deeper political analysis, which came only with time. Lipsyte was right if we are thinking narrowly about Vietnam. Still, Ali never backtracked from the words he blurted out that afternoon:

> Keep asking me, no matter how long,
> On the war in Vietnam,
> I sing this song,
> I ain't got no quarrel with them Vietcong.[13]

Ali's political ideas came out of his lived experience. Looking back on his boyhood, he invoked a famous name from the Freedom Struggle's past: "Emmett Till and I were about the same age. A week after he was murdered in Sunflower County, Mississippi, I stood on the corner with a gang of boys, looking at pictures of him in the black newspapers and magazines. In one, he was laughing and happy. In the other, his head was swollen and bashed in, his eyes bulging out of their sockets and his mouth twisted and broken. His mother had done a bold thing. She refused to let him be buried until hundreds of thousands marched past his open casket in Chicago and looked down at his mutilated body." Till was murdered in 1955, but the story kept taking on meaning for Ali as he thought about it through the years: "Emmett Till was the same age as me, and even though they caught the men who did it, nothing happened to them. Things like that went on all the time. And in my own life, there were places I couldn't go, places I couldn't eat. I won a gold medal representing the United States at the Olympic Games, and when I came home to Louisville, I still got treated like a nigger." In disgust, Ali claimed years later, he threw his gold medal in the Ohio River.[14]

Clay was twelve years old when the Supreme Court handed down the *Brown v. Board of Education* decision, desegregating, at least on paper, Southern schools. A year later came Emmett Till's lynching and, a month later, the murderers' acquittal. Three months after that, the Montgomery Bus Boycott began. Cold War rhetoric had been intense through the 1950s, the witch hunts, the Hollywood Ten, Joseph McCarthy's accusations, the hearings of the House Un-American Activities Committee, the trials of Alger Hiss and the Rosenbergs, and so forth. While civil rights and the Cold War seem distinct, the two were closely linked.[15]

If you were coming of age as Cassius Clay was during the 1950s, and if you were black and living in a border state such as Kentucky and paying any attention at all, you likely would be more familiar with the Cold War through racial issues than foreign policy ones. A young man like Clay would have seen in the newspapers and heard on the radio that Communists, outside agitators, and "Reds" were stirring up the black folks. It was a commonplace of Southern journalism that uppity blacks and white radicals were determined to destroy "the Southern way of life." Senators like James Eastland of Mississippi spoke of the Communist influence over the Supreme Court in the *Brown* decision; organizations that tried to register blacks to vote were tarred with the red brush; efforts of the National Association for the Advancement of Colored People at desegregation were routinely dismissed as Communist inspired. Simply put, Red-baiting was an effective tool against the Freedom Struggle. The White Citizens Council's founding document, a little book called *Black Monday* by Mississippi circuit judge Tom Brady, took it as an article of faith that Communists were behind civil rights agitation. Anti-integration and anti-Communism were cut from the same cloth; Red hunting followed the Freedom Struggle like night follows day.[16]

But it worked in reverse too. Beginning in the 1950s, the USIA was at pains to dispel the image of America wracked by racial turmoil. Decolonization movements swept Africa and Asia during these years, and winning the hearts and minds of nations freeing themselves from European domination became crucial in the struggle between the United States and the Soviet Union. Propaganda wars were fought over which superpower was the real friend of darker-skinned peoples. Every racial atrocity at home—every lynching, every "segregation forever" speech, every enforcement of white supremacy—made it harder to sell America as the world's beacon of freedom. The Emmett Till case that Ali remembered so vividly was a perfect example. After Till's death and the exoneration of his killers, a series of mass rallies, organized by civil rights groups, labor unions, and churches, broke out across the country. Again and again, speakers stressed that racism played into the hands of America's enemies, that we could not pretend to leadership of the "free world" while oppressing our own people, that we had everything to lose to the Communists. The acquittal of Till's killers in Sumner, Mississippi, in September 1955 brought a flood of outraged news stories throughout the world, questioning America's commitment to freedom and equality. The USIA did its best to minimize the damage with stories about racial progress and human brotherhood, but it is clear that the Cold War was emphatically entwined with racial politics.[17]

As the Vietnam War ramped up and the Selective Service forced Ali to think about the draft, his frame of reference was race, and he came to understand events in Southeast Asia through that prism. American involvement, its proponents argued, would stop Communist aggression in the Pacific. To fight in Vietnam was to defend America against a metastatic threat. Opponents of the war believed that US troops unwittingly did the Communists' bidding by making us into defenders of imperialism and oppressors of colored peoples. At first, young Ali was mostly disinterested in all of this; foreign policy, falling dominoes, and diplomatic chess little colored his thinking. But as he trained to become heavyweight champion through the early 1960s, race and the Cold War grew ever more closely linked for African Americans. Civil rights opponents even depicted the long successful struggles for passage of the Civil Rights Act of 1964 and the Voting Rights Act of 1965 as Communist victories. Ali would have been unusual if he *did not* think about Vietnam through the prism of American racial politics.[18]

By 1966 he had also imbibed ideas from the Nation of Islam, Elijah Muhammad, and Malcolm X. These were outlaw names, not only for most white Americans but also for blacks. The popular media often characterized the religion as little more than a hate group. The Black Muslims, as the press often referred to them, were critically aware of American racial politics, but their strategy was withdrawal, separate religions, businesses, and neighborhoods—segregation, not integration. Racism at home and imperialism abroad dictated an autonomous black world, uncontaminated by the evils of white men. The Nation of Islam was explicit about war—Elijah Muhammad went to jail for resisting the draft during World War II, and he insisted that his followers remain loyal to Allah, not the racist federal government. That meant not participating in imperialist wars against dark-skinned people. Equally important, decolonization was the order of the day throughout the Third World, including Muslim countries, so solidarity with the Islamic world and staunch anti-imperialism became part of the Nation of Islam's creed.[19]

Critics asked, Who was this semiliterate boxer, seduced by a cult religion, to have an opinion? Even his defenders, such as Lipsyte or TV commentator Howard Cosell, felt that when all of this began with Ali's reclassification to 1-A in 1966, the champ was callow and uninformed. Back in Rome in 1960, he seemed mostly ignorant of the stakes in international sport, and now he was ignorant of how Cold War superpowers jockeyed for influence. Certainly, he would have been hard pressed to articulate the ins and outs of politics, diplomacy, and warfare as well as, say, Secretary of State Dean Rusk or Defense Secretary Robert McNamara. "I ain't got no quarrel with them Vietcong" was literally the truth, ignorance that was wisdom, ignorance mercifully free of the mad logic of Vietnam and the Cold War.[20]

What Ali came to believe instead, no doubt under the tutelage of the Nation of Islam, was that his fame was an opportunity, that at twenty-four years of age he was a role model for the abstemious life of a Muslim (something he never quite got the hang of). In a remarkably rapid transformation from the parochial kid from Louisville, Ali became a "race man," that old phrase denoting one devoted to the betterment of African Americans. "Boxing is nothing," he told Robert Lipsyte in 1966, "just satisfying some bloodthirsty people." Of course, Ali loved the narcotic of the ring, went far too many years before he gave it up, but he also had a larger vision now: "I'm no longer a Cassius Clay, a Negro from Kentucky, I belong to the world, the black world, I'll always have a home in Pakistan, in Algeria, in Ethiopia." A month later he told Lipsyte, "In a few hours I could fly to another country. In the East, in Africa, where the people love me. Millions all over the world want to see me. I'm not going to sell my manhood for a few dollars, and a smile. I'd rather be poor and free than rich and a slave." Real manhood meant not a champion's money and success but solidarity with his people, African Americans as well as people of color throughout the old colonial world.[21]

Over the next year, Ali entered the ring several times, now managed by Main Bout, which consisted mostly of his Nation of Islam brothers, one more cause for white opprobrium. Arranging matches became increasingly difficult in the United States; no sooner would boxing promoters express interest in a particular city than the mayor or even the governor intervened. Politicians such as Chicago's Richard J. Daley wanted nothing but distance from the Nation of Islam and Vietnam draft resisters. Still, Main Bout arranged half a dozen commercially successful closed-circuit fights, including two in England, one in Germany, and one in Canada. Fighting roughly every two months, Ali defeated all of his serious opponents.[22]

Finally, on April 28, 1967, he was ordered to report to an induction center in Houston, Texas. Through his attorneys, he insisted he was a Nation of Islam minister and a conscientious objector, which meant he opposed all wars, not just the one in Vietnam. He maintained that as a Muslim, his life belonged to Allah, not the US government. Clearly, he had given much thought to his situation, and he began to articulate his position with more depth. He addressed a meeting in Louisville:

> Why should they ask me to put on a uniform and go ten thousand miles from home and drop bombs and bullets on brown people in Vietnam while so-called Negro people in Louisville are treated like dogs and denied simple human rights? No I'm not going 10,000 miles from home to help murder and burn another poor nation simply to continue the domination of white slave masters of the darker people the world over. This is the day when such evils must come to an end.[23]

The Johnson administration said the war was to save South Vietnam and other Asian nations from succumbing to the Communists; like a line of dominoes, when one fell, the others must go down too. Ali never engaged the "domino theory"; he simply ignored it, no doubt found it unworthy of refutation. The war was, as he put it, about white men sending black men to kill yellow men. Ali went on,

> I have been warned that to take such a stand would put my prestige in jeopardy and could cause me to lose millions of dollars. . . . But I have said it once and I will say it again. The real enemy of my people is right here. I will not disgrace my religion, my people or myself by becoming a tool to enslave those who are fighting for their own justice, freedom and equality. . . . If I thought going to war was going to bring freedom and equality to twenty-two million of my people, they wouldn't have to draft me. I'd join tomorrow. But I either have to obey the laws of the land or the laws of Allah. I have nothing to lose by

standing up for my beliefs. So I'll go to jail. We've been in jail for four hundred years.[24]

The key line is "the real enemy of my people is right here." Communism, the Cold War, the Soviet threat, the Vietcong were all distractions from the main issue or, maybe more precisely, masks that once ripped away, revealed the real enemy.

Twenty-six young men had been summoned to Houston's induction center on April 28. Each was asked to take a step forward when his name was called. They all did, except Muhammad Ali. Afterward, he told reporters in a prepared written statement that rather than go to jail or the army, he would fight in court for justice. An hour later, the New York State Athletic Commission withdrew his license and his title. Other states followed suit, taking away his livelihood, all of this without a shadow of due process, before any legal action—any indictment, let alone conviction—was handed down; Ali could not fight anywhere in the United States. Finally, he was arraigned on May 8 and released on bond. Deeming him a flight risk, the federal government forced him to surrender his passport so he could not fight overseas either.[25]

In June 1967, a Houston jury convicted Ali of violating the draft laws. He remained out on bail while his attorneys appealed, but there was every reason to think that he would end up serving at least part of his five-year sentence in a federal prison. For four years, the prime of his athletic life, Ali was not allowed to enter the prize ring—to practice his livelihood—while the legal process ground on. Men with criminal records and mob connections like Sonny Liston never much troubled the ethical beliefs of state athletic commissions or sports journalists. But Ali's political stance and his association with the Nation of Islam, with black separatism, and with opponents of America's foreign policy landed him in sporting purgatory.[26]

He became a public speaker, made a living on college campuses, and gave more than two hundred talks. He highlighted the irony of going to Vietnam to liberate others: "I'm expected to go overseas to help free people in South Vietnam, and at the same time my people here are being brutalized and mistreated." He bemoaned that the government had stripped him of his license and title, making it impossible to earn a living: "You read about these things in the dictatorship countries." He said things that upset people, especially progressives who supported his stance on the war. Staying in line with the Nation of Islam teachings, he spoke out for a separate black homeland: "Why don't we get

out and build our own nation and quit begging for jobs? We want a country."
He denounced intermarriage: "No intelligent black man or black woman in
his or her right black mind wants white boys and white girls coming to their
homes to marry their black sons and daughters to produce little pale half-white
green-eyed blond headed Negroes. . . . You want your child to look like you."
Integration was not the answer: "It's like we don't hate a tiger; but we know that
a tiger's nature is not compatible with people's nature since tigers love to eat
people. So we don't want to live with tigers. It's the same with the white man.
The white race attacks black people. . . . So we don't want to live with the white
man; that's all." And he upheld principle over money: "I could make millions
if I led my people the wrong way, to something I know is wrong. . . . Damn the
money. Damn the heavyweight championship. I will die before I sell out my
people for the white man's money." Robert Lipsyte recalled that remarks like
these sometimes offended his admirers. "Liberals who adored him for opposing the war were appalled by his sexist attitude toward women and his antigay
sentiments. Blacks who applauded his battles against racism cringed every time
he mocked Joe Frazier as a gorilla." Yet as Lipsyte observed, Ali, half-baked
Nation of Islam theology and all, opened windows onto otherwise taboo subjects, saw the world afresh.[27]

Would Ali have gone to jail? Those who knew him said yes, he was prepared to do it. When he fought George Chuvalo in Toronto months before his
scheduled induction, the possibility of taking refuge in Canada came up; he
refused. Most people thought some compromise would be reached with the
armed services, the usual star tour, but Ali apparently was not interested in
that either. "I'm being tested by Allah," he said. "If I pass this test, I'll come out
stronger than ever. I've got no jails, no power, no government, but six hundred
million Muslims are giving me strength. Why can't I worship as I want to in
America? All I want is justice. Will I have to get that from History?" And it
wasn't just millions of Muslims worldwide or black nationalists in America.
With time, a range of African American activists, from Martin Luther King
and John Lewis to H. Rap Brown and Stokely Carmichael, stood with him. All
became convinced that Vietnam and the Freedom Struggle were of a piece,
especially given the federal government's war on dissent.[28]

Prominent African American athletes spoke out for him too. Jim Brown
was the star running back for the Cleveland Browns, one of the most famous
football players in America. He also had become a vocal advocate of black
rights and black business and a partner in Main Bout. Brown gathered a small

group of athletes together in his office just before the Houston trial. Some disagreed with Ali's stance against the draft, a few might have hoped to change his mind, but before the meeting ended, all agreed to stand with Ali and, by their presence, to persuade other African Americans to support the champ. "But Ali didn't need our help," recalled Lou Alcindor, a college basketball star who years later converted to Islam and changed his name to Kareem Abdul-Jabbar, "because as far as the black community was concerned, he already had everybody's heart. He gave so many people courage to test the system." Bill Russell, perhaps the greatest professional basketball player of the 1960s, was there too: "I envy Muhammad Ali," he said a few days after the meeting. "He faces a possible five years in jail and he has been stripped of his heavyweight championship, but I still envy him. He has something I have never been able to attain and something very few people I know possess. He has an absolute and sincere faith. I'm not worried about Muhammad Ali. He is better equipped than anyone I know to withstand the trials in store for him. What I'm worried about is the rest of us."[29]

History vindicated Muhammad Ali. Most Americans today consider his life heroic, so it takes some effort to remember just how reviled he was in the 1960s, how rare his defenders were. Ali's lawyers argued his case all the way to the US Supreme Court, which handed down a decision on June 28, 1971. By that late date, half a million American troops had been on the ground in Vietnam for more than two years. The war escalated and escalated between Ali's first protest and the second year of the Nixon administration; thousands of American casualties became tens of thousands, bombing and troop movements expanded into Laos and Cambodia, and hundreds of thousands of Asians died. Protests and violence on college campuses grew routine, not just at Berkeley and Columbia and Wisconsin, but even at places like Miami of Ohio and the University of Alabama. Opinion polls indicated that most Americans now thought the war a mistake.[30]

With all that as background, the Supreme Court unanimously reversed Ali's Houston conviction, effectively dismissing all charges against him. The grounds were extremely narrow, purely procedural, not at all the endorsement of freedom of religion and conscience Ali had stood for. Rather, the court focused on the Houston Draft Board's failure four years earlier to make clear precisely why it rejected Ali's claim to conscientious objector status. Several of the justices were willing to see Ali go to jail, his conviction stand, but even they now lacked enthusiasm for the war. The procedural compromise garnered an 8–0 vote by avoiding the largest issues, especially the legitimacy of the Nation of Islam's claim on conscientious objector status.

After his state boxing licenses were restored, Ali fought his way back to the championship in the 1970s with a series of epic battles, against Joe Frazier, George Foreman, Ken Norton, and others, leaving no doubt that he was one of the greatest athletes of the twentieth century, *the* greatest, as he had long insisted. But as his friend Jim Brown said, Ali was much more. Thinking back on the late 1960s, Brown remembered, "He was above sports; he was part of history. The man used his athletic ability as a platform to project himself right up there with world leaders, taking chances that absolutely no one else took, going after things that very few people have the courage to go after." Brown compared later black athletes and entertainers to Ali, criticizing their unwillingness to take controversial stands on hard social and political issues. "These guys today are babies," Brown concluded; "Ali was a man."[31]

Bob Arum, an attorney–turned–boxing promoter, helped arrange some of Ali's matches before the suspension. Arum believed that Ali's opposition to the war in Vietnam was wrong and said he was "appalled" by the champ's refusal to be inducted into the army. Arum supported the war, called himself a "patriot." Years later, having changed his opinion on Vietnam, he reflected on Ali's stance: "It turned out he was right. It's amazing, really. Here he was, not an educated guy and certainly not at all knowledgeable about politics. And to my everlasting surprise, he was right about so many things where he didn't appear to have the background to know what he was talking about." Civil rights leader Julian Bond put it a little differently. He noted how divided the movement had become when Ali took his stand back in 1967: older more conservative leaders wishing not to upset powerful political allies all the way up to the president, but others, like Martin Luther King and Bond himself, coming out against the war. Ali, Bond noted, had not been part of those civil rights circles. Ali made up his own mind. "He was simply a guy," Bond remembered, "not sophisticated, not well-learned, not an expert in foreign policy, but someone who knew right from wrong and was willing to risk his career for it. I look back on that time, and I feel very strongly that Ali is part of every American's heritage. Every American should view him with pride and love."[32]

Ali took his stand on Vietnam at one of the hottest moments in the Cold War, not despite his so-called ignorance but because of it—more precisely, his ignorance of Cold War logic. He stood outside that logic for most of his life and paid it little attention; then when he could no longer avoid it, he zeroed in on how unjustly and arbitrarily Cold War ideology and rhetoric were used as a stick to beat anyone who got out of line, especially anyone who got out of line regarding black rights. He was not well educated in a formal sense, but he was thoughtful about his experience as a black man in America. That gave him the opportunity to attain moral vision. He seized that opportunity, refusing to do what was easy or expedient. He explored his conscience and then followed it.

There would be a lot to criticize Muhammad Ali for in subsequent years. He talked about the sacredness of the Muslim family, yet faithfulness to his wives eluded him; a race man, he made vicious racist remarks against his opponents, especially Joe Frazier; he remained loyal to Elijah Muhammad and the Nation of Islam long after others questioned their half-baked theology, their cavalier attitude to Islamic orthodoxy, and their assassination of Malcolm X. After his boxing career ended, Ali shilled for large corporations and for sleazy politicians. He let himself be transformed from a pariah into an America hero by denaturing his own message, letting himself be made into a symbol of love, togetherness, and tolerance, the sharp political critique now drained away. All of this is true, but it does not detract from the wisdom and courage he displayed over civil rights and Vietnam.[33]

Let me end on a personal note. I was in high school back in the late 1960s, a good student from a modest family of Roosevelt Democrats. I liked Ali from the time he became champ but disagreed with his stand in 1967. It was not that I bought the whole Cold War package—far from it. Anti-Communism always seemed crazy, surreal to me, and I was well aware of its abuses of civil liberties in the 1950s. Still, I listened to the arguments from the Johnson administration and half-believed them. I did not like the war, but the Great Society had accomplished so much; the president's inner circle seemed so polished and self-assured. Mostly I was just intellectually and morally lazy, not paying attention. A college deferment awaited me, so I was not forced, like Ali, to confront the war.

Finally I was startled awake by events in 1968. Mixed in with all the rebellion and repression of those days was the growing realization that Ali had been right all along. He rejected the "wisdom" of the experts, renounced everything, prepared to go to jail. Yes, it started with self-interest, a young man angry that his life and career were being upended. But in that exigency, he chose to educate himself, and he began that process with the tools at hand, a set of memories and ideas that came not from the foreign policy establishment and educated elites but from his community and his experiences as a black man in America.

Tuning out what officials said about Vietnam and the Cold War allowed him to develop his own insights. He took his stand and made it a little easier for the rest of us to do so too. It took far longer than it should have, but it mattered to me that Ali was talking sense as the world created by the best and the brightest went mad. Thus the champ, whom the army said had an IQ of 78, schooled the scholarship boy.

PART II

THE SOVIET UNION

BREAKING THE ICE

Alexei Kosygin and the Secret Background
of the 1972 Hockey Summit Series

James Hershberg

When Alexei Nikolayevich Kosygin landed at Vancouver airport on Friday afternoon, October 22, 1971, after a hectic and tumultuous week of traveling across Canada, the sixty-seven-year-old Soviet premier was dead tired. The last thing he wanted to do was go to a hockey game. After protracted pretrip negotiations, his attendance that night at a match between the Montreal Canadiens and Vancouver Canucks of the National Hockey League had been arranged, but Kosygin begged off.[1] His hosts pleaded with him to reconsider, and he grudgingly agreed. He was the first Soviet leader to visit Canada—reciprocating Prime Minister Pierre Elliott Trudeau's trip to the USSR five months earlier and tweaking Canada's southern neighbor at a sensitive Cold War moment.[2]

This essay, however, focuses not on the political or diplomatic aspects of Kosygin's Canadian excursion but rather its significance for sports and the Cold War. It explores the role of ice hockey in the Soviet's visit and the summit's part in spurring one of the iconic moments in Cold War ice hockey—the September 1972 ice hockey Summit Series between the USSR and Team Canada.

When Trudeau visited the Soviet Union in May 1971, Canada's hockey relations with the Soviet Union and the international hockey bureaucracy were in a deep freeze. Shortly before his voyage, the Soviet national team had won its ninth straight "world championship" organized each spring by the International Ice Hockey Federation (IIHF). That year's competition took place in Switzerland, and for the second year running, Canada did not take part, having tired of fielding "third-rate" teams composed of nonprofessional skaters who were routinely defeated by the Soviets, who continued to be regarded formally as amateurs. In 1969, a compromise agreement had been reached to allow Canada to use up to nine non-NHL (National Hockey League) professionals in the upcoming tournament, but that accord had collapsed after International Olympic Committee (IOC) head Avery Brundage warned the IIHF that amateurs would lose their Olympic eligibility if they played against professionals. Furious, the Canadians canceled plans to host the 1970 tournament, disbanded its national squad, and withdrew altogether from international competition.[3]

A report on the tournament in Switzerland from Canada's ambassador in Berne, James A. Roberts, underlined both the political tensions suffusing international ice hockey and the unsatisfactory situation blocking a true showdown between the best Soviet and Canadian players. The "Red Machine" cruised through the competition, mostly by lopsided scores, other than a hotly contested loss and tie to Czechoslovakia and a surprisingly tight win over the Americans. They were lustily booed by Swiss fans, as well as some Czechoslovak refugees, venting their ire at Moscow's invasion of their country less than three years earlier.[4] Canada's absence was "deeply resented," noted Roberts, who found most games "dull and even lackadaisical." On the eligibility dispute, he strongly urged Ottawa to stick to its "realistic" position until the IIHF saw the light, since it was "ludicrous and hypocritical" to consider the Canadians as professionals but the Soviets, Swedes, and Czechoslovaks as amateurs. The frustrated diplomat urged "some fresh thinking and a deep reappraisal of the Canadian position" to devise a new negotiating stand that could get Canada back into competitions such as the IIHF championships and the Winter Olympics against top international teams who were "openly professional in everything but name."[5]

The routine was even starting to grate on the Soviets, who found their domination increasingly tedious and yearned to test their mettle against the vaunted NHL pros. "For goodness sake, let's get the Canadians back in the championship," complained national team captain Boris Maiorov. "This is dull. Very dull."[6]

There is little indication, however, that hockey arose, at least not in any serious way, during Trudeau's May 1971 talks with Soviet leaders, although his tour of far-flung destinations around the USSR produced general agreement to enhance bilateral relations. Trudeau met with his formal counterpart, Kosygin, as well as with the Communist Party of the Soviet Union (CPSU) first secretary Leonid I. Brezhnev and President Nikolai Podgorny, but "there was little of substance to discuss," observed a leading scholar of Canadian foreign policy. Perhaps the most notable headline came when Trudeau, known for his criticism of the Vietnam War and other US international behavior, referred to America's "overwhelming presence" in Canada.[7] Some US officials worried that Trudeau was drifting too far from his nation's traditional, strategically essential alliance with Washington.

Trudeau conversed once in the Kremlin with Brezhnev, who, sitting across a conference table "peering at me with his powerful eyes from under very heavy eyebrows," struck the Canadian as imperious, "gruff and loudspoken, but with an occasional twinkle in his eye."[8] Trudeau spent much more time with Kosygin and seemed to hit it off with him. The premier's "easy manner and rational mind" appealed to the Canadian. The prime minister was a stern Communist but also considered a relative pragmatist and technocrat compared to more ideological comrades. Trudeau "genuinely liked" Kosygin, whom he later described as "Khruschev [sic] without the rough edges, a fatherly man who was a forerunner of Mikhail Gorbachev."[9]

In midsummer, Trudeau invited Kosygin to make a reciprocal visit, and diplomats and observers were startled when the Kremlin immediately accepted the idea and agreed to schedule it *soon.* Analysts suspected that Kosygin's sudden eagerness to tour Canada came not from sentimental feeling toward Trudeau but rather a general desire to expand Soviet influence at a time of US difficulties in Vietnam, as well as a specific desire to counter the dramatic Sino-American opening revealed in mid-July when it was announced that Henry Kissinger had secretly visited China and Nixon would follow early the next year.[10]

Moscow may have hoped to mix Canada into the "summit diplomacy" it was simultaneously conducting with Washington in August. Even as they prodded Ottawa to schedule Kosygin's visit, the Soviets, after long playing hard to get, finally agreed to a Nixon-Brezhnev summit in Moscow. In their internal assessment of Moscow's aims for Kosygin's visit, Ottawa's analysts sensed a wish for greater security by improving formal relations with key countries and keeping up the momentum generated by Trudeau's trip in May.[11]

In the run-up to Kosygin's trip, hockey seeped into Soviet-Canadian exchanges in a new, and more positive, way. The long-standing coach of the USSR's national team, Anatoli Tarasov, who had led the country's program since the end of World War II and turned it into a global powerhouse, expressed more passionately than ever his desire to compete against the best Canadian players.

In a *Sovetskii Sport* article in early September, "Let a Puck Settle All Problems," Tarasov reflected his impatience with the impasse. The brilliant, fiery, ebullient Soviet hockey pioneer argued for a direct confrontation between the best squads the two nations could assemble. He acknowledged that the Canadian "professionals" might win, but there was a big difference between "can win" and "have won"—and only battles on ice, not paper, could demonstrate which national hockey tradition would prevail. He concluded with a blunt, forthright, rousing (yet eminently reasonable) challenge:

> If they want to play against the united team of the USSR—World Champions for nine years running—they are welcome; let them organize a team of professional hockey stars. We are ready to accept this challenge also, but with one condition—both sides should be on an equal basis: a club should play against a club, a united team against a united team; the same number of games both on foreign and native rinks; neutral referees of the highest qualification should umpire the games. . . . So now what is your answer, gentlemen from the N.H.L.? Agree—and then your spectators in Canada and the USA, as well as Soviet spectators and hockey enthusiasts in Europe and the whole world will be able to enjoy hockey games with the participation of sportsmen of two principally different schools. And though each side will strive for victory, world hockey will not lose; on the contrary it will enrich itself.[12]

In mid-October, only a few days before Kosygin arrived in Canada, the Canadian embassy in Moscow cabled a translation of Tarasov's "very important article" and concluded that his challenge to the NHL was not mere rhetoric but the real thing: "In our view Tarasov is making no idle challenge. The Soviet Union intends to assure itself of the ultimate Olympic laurels at Sapporo next year and then it will be ready to risk the loss of amateur status of its best players, in order to dispute what Canada considers the real world Championship."[13]

Although the embassy did not explicitly link Tarasov's article to Kosygin's impending visit, the mounting evidence from Soviet hockey authorities influenced Canadian officials who were preparing Trudeau's briefing book. Taking a more optimistic tone than earlier, they provided an "extensively revised" background paper on Canadian-Soviet hockey relations. Perhaps not yet aware of Tarasov's article, the paper assessed the top Soviet hockey figure as "most interested in playing a Canadian professional team" yet unwilling to do anything that might endanger winning a gold medal at Sapporo. Once the Soviets achieved that goal, however, they might be ready to face Canadian professionals. Noting that recent talks between Canadian and Soviet hockey officials "indicated that the two countries may not be too far from agreement," it urged that the hockey authorities iron out the final details.[14]

For the hosts, the unprecedented visit afforded an opportunity not merely to conduct official discussions but also to showcase the country's culture and traditions. Devising Kosygin's detailed itinerary in Canada required weeks of intensive discussions in Moscow. Many matters were settled quickly—stops in Montreal, Ottawa, Toronto, Vancouver, and Edmonton; talks with Trudeau and parliamentarians; and visits to various economic, scenic, and cultural sites. Whether or not Kosygin would attend an NHL game, however, became a sticking point.

It seemed a no-brainer. On September 13, an aide in Trudeau's office urged that to convey Canada's uniqueness to Kosygin, the Soviet premier's itinerary should include economic, artistic, and athletic events that reflect Canadian strengths. In the sporting category, the aide suggested an NHL or Canadian Football League contest, with one of Trudeau's ministers accompanying the Soviet leader to assure a friendly reception.[15] From Moscow a week later, Canadian ambassador Robert A. D. Ford cabled Ottawa that a *Pravda* reporter who would accompany Kosygin thought the notion of his watching a hockey game was "wonderful" and that Soviet officials he had sounded out had reacted positively.[16] Back in Canada, officials decided on a match in Vancouver on Friday evening, October 22, against the legendary Montreal Canadiens. But when Ambassador Ford discussed Kosygin's proposed itinerary with Soviet deputy foreign minister S. P. Kozyrev, the hockey game suddenly seemed problematic. Kozyrev had several questions: Would the occasion be "official, semi-official or . . . unofficial"? Ford assured him that Kosygin "would be put in the most important box and be treated with every respect." Would the Soviet flag would be flown, national anthem played, and so on? What local dignitaries would attend? The Soviets, he said, were also "preoccupied" by the security problem, with "many thousands of hockey fans present."[17]

In Ottawa, the ambassador's message caused consternation. "We are distressed by Kozyrev's reaction to hockey game which we consider important public relations part of program," external affairs officials cabled Ford. Regarding the issues raised by Kozyrev, Ford was told the premier and his immediate party would be seated in a "special reserved area" of Pacific Coliseum. The Mounties felt confident they could handle security, but ceremonies such as flag raising or playing the Soviet anthem should be avoided. "Given propensity of hockey fans for vocal disapproval of formalities and delays we consider it appropriate only PM Kosygin's attendance to be announced on PA system seconds before opening faceoff." Kosygin would visit the teams in their dressing rooms, perhaps after the first period. The ministry urged Ford to make every effort to nail down Kosygin's presence: "As hockey is important part of our relations with USSR, particularly in eyes of public, we would greatly regret decision not to attend game."[18]

Meanwhile, at the Kremlin, Ford met Kosygin, who expressed "pleasure" at the upcoming trip and general satisfaction at the proposed arrangements.[19] The premier did not clarify his hockey preferences to Ford, and the ambassador's talks that day with foreign ministry aides suggested the issue was still unresolved. "Although discussion on hockey game in Vancouver is in hands of Kosygin," he reported, "there was speculation if in fact time will permit any clear expression of views."[20]

The embassy's contacts with M. N. Lunkov of the foreign ministry's European branch yielded only more uncertainty. During a lengthy planning session at the foreign ministry headquarters on October 5, the Canadians emphasized that Kosygin "would find game interesting" but Lunkov insisted on inserting the words "if desired" after the hockey game listing on the trip's printed official program "with confirmation possible only after Kosygin's arrival in Canada." The Canadian diplomats inferred that the Soviet foreign ministry "would mugwump matter without word from Kosygin himself"—and the premier was away on a visit to Algeria and Morocco, not expected back for a week or so. "This is not very satisfactory," they admitted to Ottawa, "but is perhaps better than outright cancellation."[21]

On October 6, Canadian officials in Ottawa told reporters that Kosygin had approved the itinerary for his impending trip,[22] but in Moscow, the hockey stop was still up in the air. When Ford called on Lunkov the next day, the Soviet remained ambivalent, reiterating that "if desired" should appear after the hockey game in the official program. For the first time, Lunkov added word on the issue from Kosygin personally, quoting the premier as saying he would attend "if he was not too tired." Even so, Ford indicated that arrangements would go forward, including setting aside tickets, but that "Kosygin could have quiet dinner if he wished."[23]

Despite these exchanges, when Canadian officials handed the press Kosygin's detailed itinerary on October 17, the day he arrived in Ottawa to start his eight-day visit, it included for October 22 in Vancouver a listing for him to watch the

Canadiens-Canucks hockey game that evening, after first meeting the team captains.[24]

Much to the chagrin of Canadian officials, the moment that got the most press attention during Kosygin's trip came on his first afternoon in Ottawa. Walking with Trudeau from the parliament to the Château Laurier Hotel under the autumn sun, he was assaulted by a man shouting "Long live free Hungary!" The assailant jumped on Kosygin's back before the Canadian prime minister and police dragged him off; dramatic photos of the émigré's attack graced front pages not only in Canada but around the world. Kosygin was not physically hurt but clearly shaken by what the Moscow press denounced as an act of "hooliganism." The incident dramatized the protests that would persist throughout his visit, by Jews, Ukrainians, Estonians, Hungarians, and other aggrieved groups. He already had a foretaste on his first night, when a crowd of fifteen hundred gathered outside the Soviet embassy in Ottawa behind a police cordon. The largest rally came two days later when seventy-five hundred marched in the capital to demand that Moscow allow Soviet Jews to emigrate. The protesters irritated Kosygin, who referred to them at a news conference as "certain riffraff."[25]

On October 18–20 in Ottawa, Kosygin and Trudeau had two lengthy bilateral meetings with aides present and a private lunch conversation. It is not evident that hockey was discussed, certainly not at any length. They did, however, sign a general accord on exchanges that established a "mixed commission to meet every two years 'to promote scientific, technical, cultural, academic and sports exchanges.'"[26] The closest Kosygin is known to have come to discussing hockey in Ottawa occurred when a parliamentarian presented him with a pair of CCM skates and told him, as a seventy-year-old contemporary, that "you certainly are not too old to skate—not in Canada."[27]

From Ottawa, Kosygin went to Montreal—where he met the provincial premier amid a surge of Quebecois nationalism and encountered more anti-Soviet protests.[28] On Friday, he flew west aboard a Canadian Air Force 707, inspecting the St. Lawrence Seaway from aloft and soaring over the Canadian prairies. At Vancouver Airport, in a mild drizzle, about a hundred protesters awaited him, demanding freedom for Ukraine, Poland, and elsewhere and an end to nuclear testing.[29]

When Kosygin arrived at the stately Hotel Vancouver, the presence of 150 shouting demonstrators "upset him badly and he told me he would not be attending the hockey game for which we had made full preparation," recalled Arthur Laing, whom Trudeau designated his personal representative to accompany the Soviet premier. Kosygin insisted he did not fear for his own safety but did not want to risk demonstrations that might "spoil the game." In trying to change Kosygin's mind, Laing, a member of the House of Commons from Trudeau's Liberal Party, resorted to a remarkably class-conscious argument: "I explained that all tickets to our arena had been purchased on a seasonal basis at costs as high as $500.00 for a pair and this was not the kind of person to engage in demonstration."[30] Another Canadian present, former foreign minister Paul Martin, also sensed that Kosygin "was anxious to cut the hockey game" on security grounds.[31]

Perhaps reinforcing his reluctance, the Soviet was simply uncomfortable at the prospect of being surrounded by thousands of people. "Unlike his predecessor, the late Nikita Khrushchev, Kosygin is a withdrawn and soft-spoken man who appears to be ill at ease when faced with large crowds," observed the *Washington Post*'s Dusko Doder. "He is apparently unable to establish a rapport with crowds, although in talks with small groups he displays an air of frankness, courtesy and intelligence that impressed his hosts."[32]

"Serious consideration was given to calling off the entire venture" until a few minutes before Kosygin left for the game, according to a Vancouver reporter. The Soviet premier, he wrote, was "seriously bugged by the recurring demonstrations" throughout his trip, and "Canadian authorities responsible for his safety" had a tip that "something worse than a demonstration" was planned for the game. Yet the Kosygin party had opted to go ahead, "apparently after Canadian security forces ascertained that any disturbance would be minimal."[33] Assured by Laing that protests at the game were unlikely, Kosygin finally agreed to take his chances and go.[34]

When he reached the Pacific Coliseum, before the 8:00 p.m. face-off, Kosygin met the captains of both teams: Montreal's Henri Richard and Vancouver's Orland Kurtenbach, each of whom presented him with hockey sticks as gifts. Comparing lengths, the premier was photographed holding one of the sticks alongside the "Pocket Rocket"—in a drab overcoat, to be sure, but a smiling contrast to the customarily grim Soviet image. The shot appeared in many newspapers. In return, Kosygin gave each captain gold cufflinks and tie clasps with pictures of Soviet athletes as mementos. All players on both teams received mini hockey sticks autographed by Soviet hockey stars. Kosygin "argued with Richard over the relative merits of Russian and Canadian hockey."

"We have a good team in Russia—good players," Kosygin stated. "Yes," Richard replied (prophetically), "but I think we can beat you once we get used to the style."[35] Giving them the highest possible Communist compliment, Kosygin praised hockey players as "great workers"[36] and said he had "great respect for them." Richard, in turn, later said Kosygin "seemed like a gentleman . . . a good man."[37]

The good feelings continued when Kosygin was seated in time for the opening face-off, in a VIP box alongside Vancouver's general manager, Bud Poile. Canadian notables sat nearby, and others in Kosygin's delegation received tickets elsewhere in the arena, while press rated only "standing-room" passes. On the Pacific Coliseum's walls, flags bearing the hammer and sickle and maple leaf hung side by side.

Shortly before the puck was dropped, Kosygin's presence was announced over the PA system, and the capacity crowd of 15,570 gave the Soviet leader a standing ovation that lasted almost a minute (forty seconds, by one account). The ovation even resembled, a *New York Times* reporter wrote, "the kind of applause and cheering that hockey fans normally reserve for stars such as Bobby Hull or Bobby Orr. If there were boos, they were drowned out." Some reporters, after speaking to fans, attributed the warm, even rousing reception to both general hospitality and a desire to compensate for his unfriendly treatment by protesters that "generated more sympathy for the Soviet leader than anything he could have done himself."[38]

Contrary to his fears, at the hockey game protesters were nary to be seen or heard, and for the first time in his entire stay in Canada, reporters sensed, he actually seemed to be enjoying himself: "Here his heart seemed to belong to hockey. His usually dour expression gave ways to smiles when there were good plays."[39] Though slated to depart during the first period, he stayed until the start of the third, leaving only after the Canadiens had put away the game by jumping out to a big lead; wags couldn't resist noting that, in evident tribute to the Communist guest, "left-wingers" scored all the goals he saw. The game ended in a 6–0 Montreal rout, a shutout for Canadiens' star rookie goalie Ken Dryden, but the hometown crowd could take solace from hints that they could count the Soviet premier as "a potential Vancouver Canucks fan." Kosygin attempted "to keep up an appearance of impartiality," only "smiling faintly when the crowd roared in outrage or approval at penalty calls." However, he "showed most emotion" when the Canucks attacked. After Vancouver "narrowly" blew a chance to score, he even "slapped the table in front of him." Yet he remained placid when Montreal threatened and "hardly clapped" when Frank Mahovlich and Marc Tardiff deposited the puck in the net. Perhaps, journalists suspected, he was merely being diplomatic, sitting beside Poile, and was grateful for the hometown hospitality.[40]

Afterward, Poile relayed to reporters some of Kosygin's remarks during the game. Though he "appeared tired," the Soviet had "watched intently" and seemed knowledgeable about the sport. And he left happy, saying not only that he "enjoyed it very much" but that the sell-out crowd had given him "the warmest welcome I have received outside my own country."[41]

Most important, however, were his comments about finally getting the best Soviet and Canadian hockey stars to face each other. Kosygin "said it was a fine game and it was a shame we couldn't get together and play internationally," Poile reported. "He said, 'How can you be the world's champ if you don't play anybody else?'" That clearly echoed Tarasov's argument, though it is not known whether Kosygin had met with the coach or even read his article before going to Canada. Hewing to the traditional Moscow line, Kosygin had half-heartedly tried to explain (or defend) to Poile the distinction between Soviet amateurs and Canadian professionals but sheepishly admitted: "I don't think I made it very clear since I can hardly understand it myself."[42]

Kosygin, who knew he was in a position to do more than bemoan the situation, "promised that he would look into the possibilities of Canada meeting Russia at 'this great game, hockey,' internationally," the *Vancouver Sun* reported, quoting him as saying, "I'll look into it. It's a pity we can't play each other at some level, somehow."[43]

The next night, at a banquet in his honor, Kosygin gave a speech that explicitly alluded to the possibility of closer Soviet-Canadian hockey cooperation. His exchanges of views with Prime Minister Trudeau that had begun in the spring in Moscow and resumed over the past few days were "already yielding positive results. . . . Our general agreement on exchanges reflects a desire to cooperate in science, technology, culture, art, education, sport—including hockey."[44] Although neither hockey nor even sports cooperation was explicitly mentioned in the lengthy final joint Soviet-Canadian communiqué issued a few days later, the evening in Vancouver had clearly boosted prospects to surmount the remaining hurdles blocking bilateral top-level competition.

Kosygin's attendance at the hockey game, despite his apparent prior diffidence, had gone off perfectly, allowing him to score, the *New York Times* judged, "his first popular success in Canada."[45] Later—as former foreign minister Martin recalled in a private report—the Soviet repeatedly expressed gratitude for "insisting on his attendance, since the hockey game was the hit of the tour."[46] The rousing ovation "delighted" the Soviet, Laing reported.[47] Another Canadian dignitary who had reviewed Kosygin's entire trip noted that he had endured some "terribly stuffy and rather dull" official occasions, but the hockey game and boat ride in Vancouver were "particularly enjoyable . . . and gave much more flavor of Canada and Canadian life."[48]

While implicitly included in the general accord to promote bilateral exchanges, concrete progress in hockey relations was not listed, publicly or privately, among the accomplishments or consequences for Soviet-Canadian relations of Kosygin's visit.[49]

However, stopping in Cuba on his way home, at a reception hosted by Fidel Castro, Kosygin told Ottawa's ambassador in Havana that the hockey game had been a highlight of his just-completed visit and voiced the hope that Canada and the USSR "would soon play together again."[50] And it did not take long after Kosygin returned to Moscow for the hockey follow-up to commence. On November 18, B. E. Kovalski, first secretary of the Soviet embassy in Ottawa, contacted the Canadian Department of External Affairs to make a startling proposal: the Central Red Army hockey club would be visiting North America around the New Year (for a tournament in Colorado in late December) and would like to visit Canada to play three games against teams of the "North American Professional Hockey League" in January 1972. The overture seemed striking because it was made directly between the two governments, through diplomatic channels rather than hockey federations or sports ministries. Additionally, it cut out the IIHF and IOC—in Canadian eyes, the two stodgy organizations whose arcane and absurd distinctions between "amateur" and "professional" had caused the logjam in the first place.[51] Canadian foreign ministry officials, uncertain what had prompted the unusual approach, wondered, among other questions, "Is this a direct result of Premier Kosygin's visit and the discussion with the Prime Minister and with hockey officials in Vancouver of Canada-USSR hockey relations?"[52]

Tarasov's eagerness to play the best Canadians and Kosygin's positive hockey experience in Vancouver, it appears, had combined to overcome the traditional caution of the Soviet sports and hockey bureaucracies. Indeed, at least some of those bureaucrats were left out of the loop. On December 1, the Canadian embassy in Moscow reported that its usual interlocutor on the subject—Sergei Pavlov, the head of the State Committee for Physical Culture and Sport's international section—"had just learned of" the Soviet embassy's approach in Ottawa and presumed it had been promoted by Tarasov. The sports apparatchik criticized the proposal, fearing it might imperil a gold in Sapporo.[53]

Having received the secret Soviet proposal, the next day the Canadian foreign ministry quietly conferred with bigwigs from the national hockey organizations (the recently formed Hockey Canada and the Canadian Amateur Hockey Association [CAHA]) and the Department of National Health and Welfare to craft a response. Besides raising questions for the embassy in Moscow to probe, the group agreed that the January 1972 dates were "impractical and self-defeating." Instead, they decided, "we would agree only to icing our best against their best," including "the best players in the NHL." The group "decided to propose an alternative date in September 1972" for a competition of top national squads. "It was agreed that in light of previous discussions on hockey exchanges between Prime Minister Trudeau and Premier Kosygin during the latter's visit last October, the Prime Minister's Office should be advised on any new developments in this field."[54]

A few days later, the Canadian foreign ministry cabled its Moscow embassy to inform it of the Soviet approach in Ottawa—which "may simply be follow up of Kosygin's conversations on hockey during Vancouver visit"—and of Canada's ("as polite as possible") rejection of the proposal for games in January and "firm counter proposal for highest standard Canadian professional exhibition games with Soviet national team at beginning of 1972/73 season."[55] On November 26, after consulting with NHL authorities, the Canadian external affairs ministry stated in a formal response for the Soviet embassy in Ottawa that the proposal for three games between Soviet and Canadian teams in January 1972, while welcome, was "inadequate and premature." Instead, it proposed a series of "exhibition games" to "begin in Canada in September of 1972, and be continued in the USSR in December. Each country would enter a team of its choice."[56]

It took several months of contacts and some tinkering before an agreement could finally be reached. The delay allowed the Soviets to take care of business by capturing another Olympic gold medal in February 1972 in Sapporo. Negotiations resumed in earnest between Canadian and Soviet ice hockey officials in the spring, at the world championship tournament in Prague, and a formal agreement was signed on April 18 by USSR Ice Hockey Federation boss Andrei Starovoitov and CAHA head Joe Kryczka, providing for an eight-game series in September 1972 (with four games in each country) between "a selected unrestricted Canadian Hockey team" and a Soviet national team.[57] The impetus for this early 1972 agreement had come in late 1971, from the combination of Tarasov's article in September and Kosygin's trip to Canada in October, culminating in the Soviet diplomatic overture and Canadian response in late November.

While CPSU general secretary Leonid Brezhnev likely had a role in the discussions leading to the series and certainly at least signed off on the final determination to go ahead with the unprecedented hockey showdown, the evidence presented here suggests that Kosygin probably had a larger role than previously suspected and that his October 1971 trip to Canada yielded the decisive breakthrough.

After the series, Kosygin exchanged friendly public messages with Trudeau, hailing the positive contribution this "great event in the sporting life of our countries" had made to Soviet-Canadian relations. Privately, however, he felt a bit ambivalent.[58] After attending the first game in Moscow, the premier did not attend the second game on September 24 but watched it on television and was not happy about what he saw. Not only had the guests won, 3–2, to stay alive in the series, but their on-ice behavior seemed to conform to the worst Soviet stereotypes of thuggish Canadian hockey. Penalty minutes in the game totaled thirty-one for Team Canada and only four for the Soviets, a disparity the hosts found fully justified but Canadian supporters angrily blamed on the West German referee. Even Canadian fans were hard-pressed to defend the most egregious act: Bobby Clark's vicious (and "unprovoked") slash to the ankle of star forward Valery Kharlamov, fracturing it, an act the eminent hockey journalist Red Fisher later termed "a major turning point in the series" for Team Canada.[59]

The next day in the Kremlin Kosygin received Arthur Laing, who had helped convince him to attend the match in Vancouver a year before. The parliamentarian, now minister of veterans affairs, was the highest Canadian dignitary Ottawa had sent to Moscow for the games. He was accompanied by Ambassador Ford (who had expected the Canadians to "slaughter the Russians" but was now presumably chastened).[60] For the Soviets, Pavlov, the chair of the state committee on physical culture and sport, and the foreign ministry's Lunkov sat in. In general, the premier declared, the series enhanced bilateral Soviet-Canadian ties. It was "a great cultural event and brought our peoples closer together," he claimed, asking his guests to tell Trudeau that Soviet spectators had shouted "friendship" (*druzhba*) even when their team trailed in the game he had witnessed, and reasoning that the players had "good relations" even if "these might be forgotten in heat of battle." He had particularly friendly words for Trudeau personally, calling him the best-known and most popular Canadian leader ever in the Soviet Union and undiplomatically voicing support for him in upcoming parliamentary balloting: "We are convinced PM Trudeau will win election. If he needs any support," Kosygin joked, "we will send some people to vote for him." [61]

In regard to hockey, however, he was less jovial. Though Kosygin congratulated the Canadians on their victory the day before, Ford reported that the Soviet premier was "obviously concerned with roughness of play," which he found "upsetting." Echoing past hockey-ideological polemics, he said he "had expected professionals to show how to combine a game of strength with beauty but professionals were not what he had thought they were. He said he realized their lives depend on how they play 'unlike our players who are not professional.'"[62] Although Kosygin said his remarks were personal, Ford cabled Ottawa that they quickly "were fed out to the Soviet press and, although he was not quoted directly, clearly served official justification for line that CDN professional hockey was brutal, rough, ruthless and alien to the Soviet system."[63]

Nevertheless, despite some hard feelings, the frozen ice hockey landscape had definitely melted. Far from backing off, the Soviets continued to pursue competition with Canadian professionals for the remainder of the decade, alongside East-West détente. Two years later, in 1974, in another Summit Series, the USSR national team defeated all-stars (including Hull) from the upstart World Hockey Association. In the winter of 1975–1976, two Soviet clubs (CSKA Moscow and Kryla Sovetov Moscow, known as the Soviet Wings) played a "Super Series" against NHL teams. This competition is best remembered for CSKA's 3–3 tie with the Canadiens at the Montreal Forum on New Year's Eve, featuring Vladislav Tretiak's brilliant goaltending, and an ugly 4–1 army loss to the defending Stanley Cup champion Philadelphia Flyers, whose rough tactics prompted a Soviet protest "skate-off" that interrupted play; the contest, once again, perfectly fit the trope of barbaric capitalist hockey goons. Still, top-level ice hockey competition between Canadian professionals and Soviet teams became regular occurrences, even after détente collapsed. That elite hockey rivalry continued through five Canada Cup tournaments, each held before the NHL season began between 1976 and 1991. In 1986, the IOC finally threw in the towel and permitted all to compete at the Winter Olympics.

Transcending entrenched Cold War ideological tensions, bureaucratic politics and self-interest, and various personal and institutional idiosyncrasies, the sport of international ice hockey had finally been raised to its highest level ever. It is fair to say that the ice really began to thaw that one night in Vancouver.

ACTION IN THE ERA OF STAGNATION

Leonid Brezhnev and the Soviet Olympic Dream

Mikhail Prozumenshikov

During the seven decades of Soviet power, sport and politics were inseparably connected. Yet the Soviet people were persistently indoctrinated with the idea that these two things were absolutely incompatible. In practice, politics not only actively interfered in sporting matters; it even affected the results of competitions. This approach to sport was, of course, not the preserve of the leaders of the USSR; rather, it was found throughout the world. But if one were to speak about specific politicians, virtually none can be compared with Leonid Brezhnev in his attention to sport and in its use for political purposes.

Brezhnev, who led the USSR from 1964 to 1982, was born and raised in Ukraine, near the city of Dnepropetrovsk. He first studied as a surveyor, then worked in a steel plant, and even served for a year as a tank driver in the Red Army. But even before World War II he had begun a career in the Communist Party, becoming third secretary of the Dnepropetrovsk regional party committee. During that time, Brezhnev had already developed an interest in sport, especially football. The local team, Steel, did not achieve great success, but it did enjoy the active support of the local party leadership.

After the war, Brezhnev continued to climb the party hierarchy. In 1952, Joseph Stalin noticed this young, active functionary who was now based in Moldova. As the leader of the Moldovan Communist Party, Brezhnev arrived in Moscow at the Nineteenth Congress of the Communist Party of the Soviet Union (CPSU), but after the congress he did not return to Moldova but became secretary of the CPSU.[1] After Stalin's death in 1953, Brezhnev briefly dropped from the ranks of principal leaders of the country,[2] but he soon came to enjoy the support of Nikita Khrushchev. The two men had worked together in Ukraine, and when Khrushchev gained power, he remembered his protégé. From this moment, Brezhnev became one of the top political leaders of the Soviet state, and the active period of his political life corresponded to the years of the Cold War when big-time sport became an important instrument in that larger global confrontation.

Brezhnev's name is most often associated with the 1980 Olympic Games held in Moscow, which he managed with considerable difficulty to organize and run. The idea of holding the Olympic Games in a Communist country first occurred to Brezhnev as early as the 1950s. In February 1956, after the Twentieth Congress of the CPSU, where Khrushchev made his famous "secret speech" about the cult of Stalin, Brezhnev was returned to Moscow from his post in Kazakhstan and appointed secretary of the Central Committee of the CPSU. Two months later the Soviet leadership received a proposal from the USSR State Sports Committee to organize the Summer Olympic Games of 1964 in Moscow.[3] Perhaps the return of Brezhnev and the proposal of the Sports Committee were just a coincidence. Yet such projects were discussed in the USSR only after a preliminary reconnaissance at the highest echelons of power, and Brezhnev even then was known as a big supporter of sport. In the difficult postwar years, he had regularly found time to visit sports competitions. He supported the initiative of the Sports Committee and brought up the matter for discussion at a meeting of the Secretariat of the CPSU Central Committee.[4]

Brezhnev was not alone in his desire to use sport for the benefit of Socialist society. In the 1950s, sport began to play an increasingly important role in Soviet foreign policy. Before World War II, sports competitions in the USSR were considered a means of training future defenders of the Communist system, intended primarily for domestic use, but after Stalin's death the situation changed. The new leadership realized sports victories could successfully advertise the Soviet way of life and demonstrate the superiority of the Socialist system. In 1956, the USSR made a brilliant debut at the Winter Olympics in Italy by winning the team competition. Four years previously, the Soviet Union had performed no less successfully at its first Summer Olympics in Finland. In December 1956 the Soviet Olympic team repeated its stellar performance in Australia. This event took place even though the USSR had broken off diplomatic relations with Australia in 1954 because of a spy scandal, with some Soviet leaders opposing participation at Melbourne. They insisted on a number of restrictions, demanding that Soviet athletes should not live in the Olympic Village but stay aboard the ship *Georgia*, which was to be anchored in the port of Melbourne.[5] Brezhnev was among those who strongly fought against these manifestations of a Stalinist closed society, and it was decided that the Olympic Games in Melbourne should witness the complete triumph of Soviet athletes and that the whole world would see how beautifully Soviet people lived in the country of victorious Socialism.

Brezhnev and his allies then raised the idea in the Politburo of holding the 1964 Games in Moscow. On the financial side, the leadership made preliminary calculations; the estimated cost of 36 million rubles was to be offset by income from foreign delegations to the tune of almost 420 thousand dollars.[6] Yet it soon became clear that there were many obstacles to the implementation of these ambitious plans. Among the objective obstacles was the fact that Soviet infrastructure was not yet ready to host such a large-scale event. Moscow was desperately short of new sports arenas. Just built in 1956, the new national stadium at Luzhniki Park would not be sufficient in itself. There were not enough modern hotels, cafés and restaurants, or transport. The World Youth Festival in Moscow, which took place in 1957 and did not compare in scale with the Olympics, only highlighted all of these problems. The subjective factors were the product of the Cold War orthodox Stalinist thinking of many Soviet leaders. Despite the beginning of the "thaw" and some democratization of Soviet society, the uncontrolled access of foreign tourists and the Western press to Soviet citizens was still considered highly undesirable. Even worse, the country that hosted the Games would have to make a commitment to invite all member countries of the International Olympic Committee (IOC), whether or not they maintained diplomatic relations with the USSR. At the time, the Kremlin could not imagine the flags of such countries as Taiwan, South Korea, and Israel hanging in the Soviet capital. As a result, the idea of organizing the Olympic Games in 1964 in Moscow never got off the ground.

The figure leading the country, Nikita Khrushchev, represented another subjective obstacle to hosting the Olympics in the USSR. Despite his earlier support for Brezhnev, he was not interested in sports and considered them frivolous. Nonetheless, Khrushchev was forced to put up with sporting competitions being organized in the Soviet Union because they raised the prestige of the country. Khrushchev also suppressed the attempt to hold the Olympic Games in the USSR in 1968. Before discussing this question in the Central Committee, Khrushchev read the note of the Propaganda Department, which stated that the 1960 Olympics in Rome incurred losses of about 2.5 billion lire. The Soviet economy was suffering from very serious difficulties at the time, and the note, prepared by party specialists who knew Khrushchev's attitude to sport, achieved its negative goal. Khrushchev, who was skeptical about the idea of holding the Games, became angry. How, he asked, could you spend so much effort and money on the organization of sports competitions when the country was facing more important and complex tasks?

It may seem like a coincidence, but the fact remains. Khrushchev's negative reaction to the Olympics proposal coincided with his idea to remove Brezhnev from the post of chairman of the Supreme Soviet of the USSR, which he had occupied since 1960.[7] Although he was essentially a figurehead in the Soviet nomenklatura system, it afforded a good opportunity to visit different countries and establish contacts with various individuals and organizations, including international sports committees. Brezhnev, as the nominal head of the Soviet state, opened the 1962 session of the IOC that took place for the first time in Moscow. He organized the reception of heads of international sports federations and discussed with them the problems of the world sports movement. All of these ties would later prove very useful when Moscow submitted an official bid to host the Olympics, but in 1963 Khrushchev, who was generally supported by Brezhnev, believed that his protégé should work more for the benefit of the party and not engage in such "nonsense" as sport.[8] A year later, Brezhnev was removed from the post of chairman of the Supreme Soviet of the USSR.[9] This move may well have played a role in Brezhnev's decision to join the 1964 plot by members of the Presidium of the CPSU Central Committee that ended Khrushchev's time in power. They also resolved that in the future, one person should not occupy two posts simultaneously—that is, leader of the party and head of the government. Accordingly, Brezhnev was elected first secretary of the CPSU Central Committee, and Alexei Kosygin was elected chairman of the USSR Council of Ministers.

The politics of the Cold War had a tremendous influence not only on sports competitions themselves but also on the choice of Olympic host cities and the internal organization of the Soviet Olympic Movement. In addition to the actual sporting confrontation between the United States and the USSR, the Soviet leadership was well aware of an earlier statement by the new US attorney general, Robert Kennedy, that the prestige of a country is determined by both missiles and Olympic gold medals. The Games quickly became a place of political struggle. In one case, it seemed the Olympics of 1968 in Mexico City might not take place at all because early that year the IOC reversed its position and allowed South Africa, which had previously been excluded from most international sports federations, to take part. It seemed the Soviet Union and other Socialist states would join the African countries in boycotting the 1968 Games because the USSR had always acted as a "consistent fighter against the apartheid regime."[10] Yet Moscow was not interested in splitting the Olympic Movement in which the USSR had come to play a leading role. So the Kremlin placed quite a difficult task before its sports functionaries within the IOC. They were to take the line that the Olympic Games should still be held in Mexico City, that the USSR should take part in the Olympics, and at the same time that relations with African countries should not be spoiled. Not surprisingly, the Soviets could come up with no answer of their own, and the problem was resolved only when the IOC reversed its own decision and South Africa was again excluded from the Olympic Movement. The Soviet Union received particular appreciation from the leadership of Mexico. As noted in a Committee for State Security (KGB) secret paper prepared for the highest Soviet leaders, the Mexican president "said in the circle of his closest associates that he feels a great sense of gratitude to the Soviet Union for its strong support of Mexico on the issue of the XIX Olympic Games, and he is ready to show the Russians that Mexico can appreciate the friendly support."[11]

Following the logic of their policy, the Soviets turned a blind eye when the Mexican authorities brutally suppressed the massive student protest that took place on the eve of the Games, saying that it was an internal matter for the country. Moscow itself faced serious sporting and political problems during these Games. The Mexican climate forced the organizers to hold the Summer Games in the fall, meaning that the Olympics of 1968 began two months after Soviet troops had entered Czechoslovakia and crushed the Prague Spring. As a result, as at the Summer Games of 1956 and the Winter Games of 1980, which took place in the wake of the Hungarian uprising and the invasion of Afghanistan, respectively, Soviet athletes became hostages of Kremlin policy. They were exposed to criticism and accusations, and the Czechoslovakian athletes demonstratively refused to communicate with their so-called Soviet friends. In these circumstances, the Soviets fell back on the timeworn slogan of "sport out of politics" and constantly appealed to the representatives of the IOC, which supported the USSR in this matter. However, in contrast to their actions in the case of the African American athletes Tommie Smith and John Carlos, who famously expressed political protest in Mexico City and were banned from the

Games, the IOC decided not to disqualify the famous silver-medal winner, Czechoslovakian gymnast Vera Caslavska, for her behavior during the medal ceremony. Standing on the podium, Caslavska turned in the opposite direction when the Soviet anthem sounded. The new Czechoslovakian leadership that had come to power with the Soviet army subsequently corrected the IOC's "mistake" by banning Caslavska from foreign travel for several years.

In the second half of the 1960s the USSR Sports Committee tried once again to apply to host the Games in Moscow in 1972. It was expected that Brezhnev, now general secretary of the party, would support this issue, but at the time the leader had to strengthen his position in power and was not up to dealing with matters of sport. Once again, the application of the Sports Committee sank in the bureaucratic corridors of the Kremlin. Interestingly, the main domestic opponent of bringing the 1972 Olympics to Moscow was the future Soviet ambassador to Canada and one of the closest associates of Mikhail Gorbachev, Alexander Yakovlev. At the end of the 1960s, he was the deputy head of the Agitation and Propaganda Department of the Central Committee and acted as one of the more ideological fighters in the party.

Yakovlev, who in the 1960s was an ordinary party official, strongly opposed the Olympics in the USSR, not for economic or other reasons but solely on ideological principle. He was deeply aware that Brezhnev's desire to host the great sports festival completely contradicted the embargo on inviting athletes from the "forbidden" countries to Moscow. These included some with whom the USSR had no contact, and inviting them to Moscow would seriously damage the ideological principles advocated by the Soviet Union and that Yakovlev actively defended in those years. Moreover, Yakovlev was among those who were most active in the preparation of the well-known resolution of the Politburo of the CPSU Central Committee in 1968, in which Soviet scientific, cultural, and sports organizations were strictly forbidden to have any contact with a number of countries.

Despite the USSR's decision not to bid for the 1972 Olympics, the Cold War made the choice of who should host that event an unexpected headache for the Soviet leadership. The main contenders were Munich and Madrid. Munich caused a nervous reaction in the Socialist German Democratic Republic (GDR), which saw it as "a political provocation of the West," with the leaders of East Germany begging Brezhnev to use all his influence to prevent the Games going to Munich.[12] Yet the Soviets did not want to vote for Madrid, as they had not maintained diplomatic relations with the Franco regime since the Spanish Civil

War. Ultimately, the pressure from East Berlin was so great that the Soviet leadership decided to vote for Madrid. For the Soviet Union at that time such a decision could only be called sensational, and it is not surprising that the document revealing the CPSU Central Committee's resolution was hidden behind numerous secret classifications for many years. It is unknown what arguments were used, but even the leader of the clandestine Spanish Communist Party Dolores Ibarruri made clear that "the Communist Party of Spain had no objection to the Games in Madrid."[13]

At the last minute, however, when the Soviet delegation was already participating in the IOC session in Rome, it received fresh instructions from the Kremlin to vote for Munich. The archival documents suggest that this 180-degree turn was made by Brezhnev, who had his own plans in this regard. The USSR received considerable dividends from this decision. For Bonn it was extremely important to hold the Games in the new Germany, especially during the negotiations on the German problem in the early 1970s. West Germany's leaders remembered Soviet support for the candidacy of Munich and expressed their sincere gratitude to Brezhnev.[14] The Soviet team in Munich was greeted with unusual warmth and hospitality. Brezhnev's peace-loving policy contributed to the signing of a peace treaty with Germany. That atmosphere extended to the playing fields, with the Soviet secret service reporting to the Kremlin, "West German fans more often supported Soviet than American athletes."[15] In response to the wishes of the Soviet Union, the organizers concluded a secret agreement with the anti-Soviet radio station Radio Free Europe, located in West Germany. In return for accreditation to the Games the representatives of the station pledged "not to interview any of the participants from Eastern Europe."[16] The Soviet Union justified its decision to vote for Munich by saying that it was a part of a larger compromise agreement, which, with all its limitations, opened the path to formal international recognition for East Germany. East Berlin was well aware of all this but still expressed its displeasure and made various demands on Moscow. In particular, the ambassador of the GDR to the Soviet Union refused to let the traditional Olympic torch relay go through his nation.[17]

International sports competitions during the late 1960s and early 1970s demonstrated a new political line pursued by Brezhnev. Soviet policy became more flexible and less ideological. There was a military coup in Greece that brought a military junta to power in 1967. Moscow condemned the regime of the "black colonels" but did not cut either diplomatic or sporting ties with Greece.[18] Competitions with Greek teams continued, but if they took place in the USSR, they were not held in Moscow. These events were staged in the provinces, and almost nothing was reported in the Soviet press.[19] It is, however, true that the entire Soviet leadership did not share the general secretary's views on sports. When the World Cup in Athletics was held in Athens in 1969, a large number of international organizations (including Communists) made an appeal to boycott the competitions. Soviet leaders decided to discuss this issue at a Politburo meeting, where Brezhnev's point of view won, and a special decree approved by the Politburo repeated the 1968 slogan "sport out of politics." The Politburo noted that the Soviet athletes would go to the event in Greece because this is an "international rather than a national event," and the victory of Soviet athletes would cause a favorable international response and "provide moral support for democratic forces in Greece."[20]

These and similar actions of the Soviet leadership were ultimately aimed at removing the long-standing obstacle to bringing the Olympic Games to the USSR—the obligation to invite all members of the Olympic Movement regardless of their political relationship (or lack thereof) with the Soviet Union. At the same time, Brezhnev tried to convince the orthodox forces in the Central Committee and his international allies to sacrifice old principles. No steps along this path were easy. Israel was invited to the 1973 University Games in the Soviet Union, a decision that led to protests from many Arab countries. A year later, also for the first time, a team from Taiwan came to the Soviet Union to participate in the Biathlon World Cup. Information about this visit was kept to a minimum. The event was held in the Belarusian town of Raubichi, near Minsk, rather than Moscow. Yet it was a secret only for the majority of Soviet citizens. Outside the USSR, the topic of Taiwanese biathletes in the Soviet Union occupied the headlines of the sports pages for a long time. Mainland Chinese propaganda paid special attention to this matter with sharp anti-Soviet comments. At this time too, various teams from South Korea began to arrive in the Soviet Union for international competitions, which provoked protests from their northern Socialist neighbors. All of these athletes came to the USSR to participate in large international rather than dual competitions. Nevertheless, a precedent was created. These countries still had no diplomatic relations with the Soviet Union, and the invitations were clearly a rehearsal for a Moscow Olympics.

Brezhnev's time in power could also be called a golden age for Soviet athletes. As the general secretary of the CPSU Central Committee and leader of the largest Socialist state, Brezhnev dealt with a huge number of foreign and domestic political problems. Nevertheless, he did not neglect sports.[21] During his rule, Soviet athletes received maximum support from the state, new stadiums were built, and numerous national and international sports events were organized. Brezhnev himself appeared at many competitions, especially ice hockey. Despite the sensational defeat of the so-called Red Machine at the Winter Olympic Games of 1980 in Lake Placid (the "Miracle on Ice"), Brezhnev insisted that the Soviet players be awarded governmental medals.[22] The main task of elite Soviet sport, to advertise the Soviet way of life with the help of victories and medals, continued. Yet much also changed. Under Brezhnev, losing athletes did not suffer repressive consequences as in the past, when teams were disbanded and defeat in sports was regarded almost as state treason. Instead, different levers of influence were deployed, including administrative resources. After the Summer and Winter Olympic Games of 1968, when Soviet athletes were unsuccessful, occupying only second place, the Central Committee mobilized ministries, departments, and public organizations to work in the field of sport. All of these bodies were supposed to report on a monthly basis to the Soviet leadership on the preparations for the next Games, and thanks to these measures, the USSR was the top-ranked nation at both the Winter and Summer Olympics of 1972.

In late 1969, the Politburo finally decided to proceed with the official nomination of Moscow to host the Games of the XXI Olympiad in 1976. The letter addressed to IOC president Avery Brundage contained the key phrase that "all participants of the Games, representatives of international sports federations, the press, radio, television and all those involved in the organization of the Olympic Games, will be provided with free entry to the USSR."[23] However, despite the great work done over the next six months, the Soviet bid failed, as did a rival one from Los Angeles. Instead, at the IOC session in May 1970 in Amsterdam, Montreal was chosen as a compromise candidate. After that defeat, Brezhnev had to fight yet again for his Olympic dream, this time with his internal opponents. Some members of the Soviet leadership regarded the results of the voting in Amsterdam as a "capitalist conspiracy against the Soviet Union." Accordingly, the Soviet leader began to receive such radical proposals as the elimination of the IOC or the organization of the so-called Spartakiads of workers instead of the Olympic Games.[24] In the early 1970s, these proposals appeared absurd, but Brezhnev and his supporters had to work hard to dampen emotions and start a new pre-Olympic campaign, which this time led to winning the Moscow Games of 1980. In the conditions of the Soviet authoritarian system, this success became possible largely because there was a man at the head of the Soviet state who was personally interested in having the Olympic Games take place in his country.

At the end of 1975, when Moscow had already been named host of the 1980 Games, Brezhnev was working on a summary report for the upcoming Twenty-Fifth Congress of the CPSU. For this report, he and his assistants received broad and extensive information on the country's situation, which led many to conclude that the economy of the Soviet Union was on the verge of serious crisis. After reading these documents, Brezhnev took an unexpected action. While he had always dreamed about the Olympics in Moscow, he wrote a note to his closest colleague, Konstantin Chernenko, inviting him to consider rejecting the Games. "It was," he wrote, "not too late," noting that the main argument would be the "enormous cost" the Soviet state would have to bear. In conclusion he proposed discussing the issue at a meeting of the Politburo.[25] This note remains the only documentary evidence of Brezhnev's doubts about the correctness of his Moscow decision. These doubts were never again raised or discussed, and preparation for the Moscow Games picked up momentum rapidly.

Some scholars, however, refer to the memoirs of Anatoly Chernyaev, who was one of Brezhnev's assistants and who describes the heated discussion on this issue among Soviet leaders at the dacha in Zavidovo in early 1976.[26] With all due respect to memoirs, one should treat the entries made in them with a certain degree of caution because of their specifics, especially when it is impossible to verify exactly when they were created and whether any changes or additions were made to them subsequently. Still, there is a difference between the records, for example, made by Vladimir Malin, head of the general department of the Central Committee of the CPSU during the time of Khrushchev, and the notes by Chernyaev. The former were stored in the archive from the very moment they were created, it is easy to verify their authorship and the terms of their creation, and there is an official document recording their provenance. That cannot be said with certainty about Chernyaev's memoirs. Moreover, no other archival document mentions that this problem was discussed at one of the meetings of the Politburo of the CPSU Central Committee (as Brezhnev insisted).

It is important to emphasize that to the end of his life Brezhnev remained a principled opponent of political boycotts of sports competitions. On such rare occasions when boycotts did happen during his leadership—for example, the refusal of the USSR's football team to play a World Cup qualifying game in Chile two months after the military coup in 1973, a stance that ultimately disqualified the USSR from the 1974 finals in West Germany—he regretted the necessity of observing certain rules in sports and politics during the Cold War. One can only imagine how the history of the Olympic Games might have worked out if Brezhnev had not died in 1982. So far we have not found any document in which Brezhnev officially or unofficially talked about a possible boycott of the Olympic Games in Los Angeles. Despite the boycott organized by the Western countries during the Moscow Olympics, it appears Brezhnev was prepared to allow athletes from the Soviet Union and other Socialist countries to travel to the United States in 1984.

Of course, it would be wrong to make one person responsible for everything (even if he was at the summit of Soviet power for eighteen years). But the Soviet Union had its own specific power structures. As is well known, since the time of Stalin a political system developed in which the head of the party not only was the leader of the country but also determined its general policy by his actions, habits, and preferences. The leader's closest circle tried to please him, copying his habits or interests, and then things snowballed throughout the country. Sometimes it was useful; sometimes it was base stupidity. Khrushchev liked corn, for instance, so corn was grown immediately in all regions of the country, even in the north. However, Khrushchev tried to fight with the party bureaucrats and invented the Committee of People's Control for this purpose. Accordingly, the officials had to create branches of this committee throughout the country. Party functionaries were not fond of these committees, since they acted largely independently and could also control the activities of the party leadership. However, while Khrushchev was in power, they were forced to tolerate these organizations and to praise them at every opportunity. When Khrushchev was removed from office, party functionaries immediately liquidated these committees.

It was the same with Brezhnev. Wanting to please the leader of the country, party and state officials tried to play on his weaknesses and preferences. He was very proud of his active participation in World War II, for instance, so as soon as he came to power, the military theme began to prevail in the USSR: the annual celebration of Victory Day, increased care for war veterans, new awards, and so on. The general attitude to sport also changed, as everyone knew that Brezhnev was a fan (his diaries published in 2016 record the many times he attended sporting events and watched football and hockey matches on television, for example). Accordingly, in this situation Soviet officials also tried to show their love of sport. A great deal of money was allocated to the construction of new stadiums; athletes began to receive much larger salaries (by Soviet standards), new apartments, and cars; the most famous athletes were constantly awarded state orders and medals; and athletes could make requests that party bosses, worried for their careers, found hard to turn down. Therefore, in the Soviet Union, love (or vice versa, the indifferent attitude) of the party leader to sports was of great importance for the development of sport and the athletes themselves.

SOCCER ARTISTRY AND THE SECRET POLICE

Georgian Football in the Multiethnic Soviet Empire

Erik R. Scott

An official fan guide published for Dinamo Tbilisi in 1960 depicted the stars of Soviet Georgia's leading soccer team in stylized sketches that showed them singing while engaged in acrobatic leaps toward the ball. The guide's illustrators knowingly linked Georgian football to the explosive, colorful, and competitive style of male folk dancing that the small republic was famous for throughout the Soviet Union. On one page, Avtandil Ghoghoberidze, the team's striker, was depicted performing the *kartuli*—a Georgian wedding dance—with his hands while balancing on the ball. Throughout, the guide implied that the dazzling techniques of Georgian football and the ethnically distinctive movements of Georgian dance were facets of the same national repertoire of body culture.[1] The intimate association of football and dance worked both ways. Around the same time that the guide was published, the Georgian State Dance Ensemble introduced a piece whose playful choreography included passes of a ball made between the dancers.[2]

Football was the most popular sport in the USSR, and it reflected and sometimes reinforced social and national divisions in the multiethnic Socialist state. Although the game received government sponsorship, it presented Soviet citizens with a diverse array of competing imagined communities, each with its own symbols, heroes, myths, and grievances.[3] Separate communities formed around Moscow's strong club teams, the largest rivalry being between Dinamo Moscow, patronized by the secret police and state functionaries, and Spartak Moscow, supported by trade unions and large segments of Moscow's working class.[4] Successful clubs in the national republics that could take on the center's leading sides, the most prominent examples being Dinamo Kiev and Dinamo Tbilisi, in effect became national teams supported by large segments of the Ukrainian and Georgian populations.[5]

While club teams throughout the Soviet Union earned praise for skill and effectiveness when victorious, Georgian footballers were known to represent a distinctly ethnic style of play. The Moscow teams had different fan bases but were mainly cheered for winning or castigated for losing. Dinamo Kiev's style of play was closely linked to Russia; there were many Russians on the team, and their trainer for many years was from Moscow. Similarly, Dinamo Minsk, though less successful than Dinamo Kiev, was difficult to distinguish from a Russian club; many players who failed to make the Moscow teams went to play in Minsk. Ararat Yerevan and Neftianik Baku occasionally upset the Moscow-based teams and were sometimes characterized as displaying a "southern" temperament, but their success was attributed to skill and training, not to the way they played. Georgians seemed to offer a visibly ethnic alternative to the style of play present throughout the Soviet Union.

The techniques of Georgian football and the mythology surrounding them emerged from the encounter between a centralizing Soviet state and an assertive Georgian republic. The name of Georgia's most successful team suggested a certain tension: Dinamo was a Pan-Soviet organization run by the police and headquartered in Moscow; Tbilisi was the capital of the Georgian nation and the destination for a massive twentieth-century migration from the Georgian countryside.[6] In Tbilisi, local party leaders supported the establishment of folk troupes that gathered the dances of rural Georgia and choreographed them as recognizable sets of body movements. Meanwhile, the Georgian capital's leading soccer club assembled the republic's best players to produce a dominant team that could represent the Georgian nation.[7] Central authorities in Moscow oversaw these developments.[8] They invited Georgian dancers to the Kremlin to showcase the state's commitment to multiethnic diversity, and they called up Dinamo Tbilisi's top players to join the *sbornaia*, the all-Soviet team. Georgia's dancers and footballers embodied national particularity; policy makers in Moscow sought to ensure that Georgian difference served the needs of an imperial state.

While Georgian football was a hybrid product forged through interactions between periphery and center, it was perceived as a nationally defined alternative to the default way of playing found elsewhere in the USSR. Georgian fans and athletic promoters consciously appealed to its associations with the national style of dance, claiming that it displayed the same qualities of beauty, ingenuity, and agility. Georgian football was also defined by what it was not. Georgian and Russian commentators alike saw it as emotional instead of calculating, dominated by dribbling rather than physical defense, and defined by artistic improvisation instead of brute force. Yet it was still held that Georgian players could form a complementary part of the all-Soviet team.

The mythology surrounding Georgian football was burnished by its imagined connections with the "beautiful game" played by successful South American teams.[9] Interestingly, South American footballers were also held to move on the pitch in ways that evoked dance. The elaborate dribbling of Argentinian football recalled the tango, while the playfulness of Brazilian soccer was associated with the samba.[10] The international successes of Argentina and Brazil's teams were a source of pride for domestic audiences in the two countries; victories seemed to prove that criollo Argentinian culture and racially mixed Afro-Brazilian culture could succeed against the cultures of larger and more developed countries. Football transformed the cultural qualities associated with South America's alleged backwardness into assets in a modern and global sport. Local promoters and players often went out of their way to emphasize the ethnic distinctiveness of their team's style of play, and the gaze of international audiences offered confirmation of these differences.[11]

Soviet Georgia sought similar recognition through football, cultivating a mythology of national distinctiveness on the pitch that, at least for a time, served Georgian and Pan-Soviet purposes. Yet like Argentinians and Brazilians, Georgians also dreamed of a global sense of belonging through soccer that transcended Soviet borders. During the Cold War, Georgian footballers gained a prominent place on the world stage by taking part in the soccer diplomacy that was a crucial component of the Soviet Union's outreach to the postcolonial world. Just as the United States sought to demonstrate that it had surmounted its racial problems by sending hundreds of African American athletes on overseas goodwill tours, the Soviet Union used soccer to cast itself as a harmonious multiethnic alternative to the United States in postcolonial countries with a past of racially defined foreign domination.[12]

This essay examines Georgian soccer's twentieth-century evolution and considers how its mythologized embodiment of national difference was used to convey both Georgian nationality and Soviet multiethnicity in the context of the Cold War. It reveals that the Soviet promotion of Georgian soccer had some unintended consequences. On the pitch, Georgian nationality and Soviet multiethnicity took on new meanings that did not always conform to official ideology. Promoted abroad by the Soviet state, Georgian football's greatest successes were ultimately claimed as evidence of national triumph rather than Soviet achievement.

Like most national myths, the mythology of Georgian soccer emphasized its long-standing pedigree. In truth, Georgia could rightfully claim football as a direct import from Britain rather than a secondhand artifact handed down from Russia. Around the same time that English mill owners introduced soccer to Moscow in the late nineteenth century, English industrialists and workers brought soccer to Georgia via the Black Sea port of Poti.[13] Soccer took hold in Georgia before the Bolsheviks came to power, and observers pointed to a distinctly national style even before the official establishment of Dinamo Tbilisi in 1925. As early as the 1920s, Georgian soccer players were called the "Great Uruguayans" (*didi urugvaelebi*), a reference both to Uruguay's dominance in the soccer world and to a supposed southern style of play that valued artistry over athletic discipline and improvised attacks over coordinated effort.[14]

However, Dinamo Tbilisi, which came to stand for Georgian football in general, was forged in the Stalinist period and bore the imprint of Stalin's Georgian compatriot Lavrentii Beria. This was no coincidence. The All-Union Dinamo Sport Society had been linked to the state's security and secret police apparatus, the NKVD (People's Commissariat of Internal Affairs), since its founding at the initiative of Feliks Dzerzhinksii. As Georgia's leading *chekist* (Soviet secret police officer), Beria played an important role in promoting Dinamo Tbilisi's early development.[15] The Georgian team, which played its first competitive matches in 1936, considered Beria its "first honorary member."[16] Dinamo's stadium in Tbilisi was even named in his honor.

Sometimes, Beria weighed in forcefully to support his club. In 1939, the semifinal match between Spartak Moscow and Dinamo Tbilisi for the Soviet Cup, which Spartak Moscow handily won, was declared invalid and a rematch ordered. According to Spartak team president Nikolai Starostin, this decision was made at the "very highest, and no longer athletic," levels of power, quite possibly at the behest of Beria, who continued to serve as the president of the Dinamo sports club even after being promoted to head the NKVD in Moscow.[17] The patronage of Beria, who remained a passionate supporter of Dinamo Tbilisi despite his ascent to the center, was crucial in establishing a lasting institutional basis for soccer in Georgia; he oversaw the development of top-notch facilities and ensured his team a relatively privileged position in the world of Soviet football.

Under Stalin, however, representations of the team's national distinctiveness tended to adhere to semiofficial ethnic hierarchies. While the "temperamental game" of Georgian footballers was praised for its "highly individualized technical mastery" and "interesting tactical combinations" in a 1949 guide published in Moscow, this exciting, if impulsive, style of play was implicitly contrasted with the hallowed iconography of the Soviet goalkeeper, who stoically stood ready to defend against any attack.[18] In this context, it was significant that Dinamo Tbilisi's goalkeeper and coach were often Russian. The Georgian side was frequently described as an inconsistent "moody team" in the Soviet press.[19] The pairing of flamboyant Georgian artistry with steely Slavic discipline at the goal line and in the coach's box may have struck team organizers as a plausible solution to this perceived problem. Such an arrangement was also ideologically appropriate, fitting with Stalinist assertions of the primacy of the Russian people in leading the Soviet Union.

A distinct period in Dinamo Tbilisi's history came to a close with the death of Stalin and the subsequent imprisonment and execution of Beria by his political rivals in 1953. Despite the incarceration of the team's patron, Dinamo Tbilisi remained dominant on the pitch that year. On September 4, the team appeared to clinch at least a tie for the Soviet Top League title with a 2–1 victory over Torpedo Moscow. In a turn of events that recalled the role Beria likely played in annulling Spartak Moscow's victory in 1939, Dinamo Tbilisi's win was declared invalid. The Soviet press announced that a rematch had been ordered in part because of the "rough play" of two of Dinamo's players.[20] The speed at which the decision was reached, however, suggested that party leaders deemed it politically undesirable to have the Georgian team claim the title while its patron faced charges of treason.[21] Three days later, a despondent Dinamo Tbilisi lost its rematch with Torpedo Moscow and its share of the title. Georgian fans, regardless of their opinion of Beria, no doubt felt that the central authorities had robbed them of a championship.

Given the team's close associations with Stalinist authority, Dinamo Tbilisi's transformation in the wake of Stalin's death and Beria's execution was rather astonishing. Although it remained part of the police-sponsored Dinamo organization, the name of the team's stadium was changed, all references to Beria disappeared from fan guides, and the team in effect went from being a vehicle for Stalinist policies to an embodiment of post-Stalinist ideals of Georgian masculinity. With the disappearance of Georgians from top political posts in the Soviet Union after Stalin, Dinamo Tbilisi's players became the new heroes for an emergent generation of Georgians, and, in some ways, rooting for the team became a way of expressing nationalist frustrations with the center.

The experience of being a fan also changed in the post-Stalinist period. Fan literature proliferated, Georgian soccer became the subject of popular movies that mythologized its prerevolutionary origins and showcased the extreme devotion of its supporters, and televised matches drew larger audiences, with fans able to watch Dinamo Tbilisi on screens throughout the Soviet Union.[22] Emphasizing the team's unique artistry, the most famous announcer for Dinamo Tbilisi's matches was Kote Makharadze, a widely recognized dramatic actor from Georgia whose emphatic expressions, poetic turns of phrase, and heavily accented Russian linked a recognizably Georgian body culture to an audible sound track of readily appreciable difference. When Dinamo Tbilisi finally emerged as the champion of the Soviet Top League for the first time in 1964 (after coming in second in 1939, 1940, 1951, and 1953), the team also gained a new song for its repertoire. Recorded by Orera, a Georgian band that enjoyed Soviet-wide popularity, "Chveni orkros bichebi" (Our golden boys) spoke of "dreams fulfilled" and "goals fulfilled" but made no mention of the Soviet Union or Socialism.[23] Set to a guitar and employing traditional Georgian polyphonic harmonies, the song was at once modern and grounded in national culture.

Thanks to the efforts of Georgian promoters, whose claims of national uniqueness resonated with Georgian fans, Georgian soccer possessed a unique mythology that fit the skills of Dinamo Tbilisi's stars. While there were other competitive Georgian clubs that enjoyed passionate local support, such as Torpedo Kutaisi, only Dinamo Tbilisi had a consistent shot at the title and succeeded in winning the Soviet championship. The team stood for Georgian football beyond the borders of the Georgian republic, and its national distinctiveness came into sharper focus when contrasted against the Russian teams it routinely faced. Although the sport was originally a foreign import and had made advances thanks to Stalinist patronage, Dinamo Tbilisi's success on the soccer field was perceived as part of an innate Georgian artistry.

The Cold War saw the Soviet state mobilize Georgian soccer skills for international audiences, giving Georgian footballers prominence on the all-Soviet *sbornaia*, which made its Olympic debut in Helsinki in 1952. Two important, if potentially contradictory, criteria shaped the formation of the *sbornaia*: the team had to reflect the ideal of the USSR as a multiethnic union defined by a fraternal "friendship of the peoples," and it had to be successful. In the iconography of the "friendship of the peoples," Russians were typically given the leading role, and the other titular nationalities of the Soviet republics ascribed supporting roles, each with its own distinctive characteristics, which together were meant to constitute a harmonious whole.

The ideal *sbornaia*, therefore, might have featured Russians in key positions, with support from a representative selection of non-Russian players drawn from each of the Soviet Union's fifteen republics (while there are only eleven positions in soccer, one imagines that the smaller republics might have provided substitutes). In reality, the Soviet team that competed in the Olympics and the World Cup looked rather different. Stars from the Moscow-based clubs, along with players from the successful Dinamo Kiev and Dinamo Tbilisi teams, dominated the Soviet *sbornaia*, reflecting the uneven distribution of success in Soviet football. Even though Georgians made up only 2 percent of the overall Soviet population, they were consistently overrepresented. For the first Soviet Olympic football team, the second-largest contingent of players from a club team came from Dinamo Tbilisi, which provided six footballers.[24] When the Soviet Union made its World Cup debut in 1958, one-fifth of the players on the roster were Georgians from Dinamo Tbilisi, a trend that would continue through the rest of the Soviet period. The first time the Soviet team was captained by a player unaffiliated with a Moscow-based club was in 1972, when Dinamo Tbilisi's defender Murtaz Khurtsilava took the helm. The second time was in 1980, when the position was assumed by his teammate from Tbilisi, Aleksandre Chivadze.

Soviet authorities often saw the overrepresentation of footballers from the Moscow-based clubs, along with the dominance of players from Dinamo Kiev and Dinamo Tbilisi, as a problem. A report on the performance of the Soviet *sbornaia* in the 1970 World Cup written by its coach, Gavriil Kachalin, attracted concern with its admission that the "core" of the Soviet team was made up of players from just four Soviet clubs: Spartak Moscow, Dinamo Kiev, Dinamo Tbilisi, and the Moscow-based Tsentral'nyi sportivnyi klub armii (TsSKA).[25] Delegates to the Football Federation of the USSR from republics that rarely supplied players to the Soviet team frequently complained about their lack of representation.[26] Georgian representatives, in contrast, boasted of the success of their southern republic. At the 1970 meeting of the Soviet Football Federation, Tsomaia, the delegate from Georgia, suggested that other republics could learn from the Georgian model: "Maybe we can all carry things out the way we do in our republic. Many of our soccer players play for Soviet youth teams and for the all-Soviet team." Irritated by Tsomaia's boasting, Valentin Granatkin, the federation's chairman, interrupted by exclaiming, "Because you have no winter!"[27]

An even more pressing issue was the Soviet team's lack of success in international competitions. The Soviet team made it to the semifinals of the World Cup only once, in 1966, where it lost to West Germany, 2–1. While the Soviet press consistently praised the collective team spirit embodied by the *sbornaia*, and Soviet fans dreamed of finding a harmonious mixture of the disciplined and athletic style attributed to Slavic players and the dexterity and inventiveness associated with Georgians, the team never really coalesced. Some of its problems were those faced by any national team: it was difficult to coordinate national- and club-level schedules, and club-level organizations had more stability and structure. In the Soviet context, however, officials grew concerned that the national team's shortcomings undermined the state's ideological message of multiethnic harmony. One alternative pursued by Soviet authorities was to promote the USSR's more cohesive club teams abroad. Club teams gained some impressive international achievements, with Dinamo Kiev defeating the top teams of Europe to take both the Cup Winners' Cup and the Super Cup in 1975. Dinamo Kiev's successes led to a plan to make the Ukrainian club the basis for the Soviet national team.[28] Dinamo Kiev, however, turned out to be a less-than-ideal representation of the Soviet Union. The club's identity was difficult to separate from that of its coach, Valerii Lobanovskii, who was known for a hyperrational approach to soccer. This reputation may not have been entirely deserved, but it was a popular stereotype associated with the coach and, by extension, his team.[29] Internationally, Lobanovskii seemed to confirm undesirable Cold War–era depictions of the USSR; foreign journalists described him as an emotionless person and derided his players as "Sputniks" and "Russian robots."[30] It was also nearly impossible for Dinamo Kiev's players to simultaneously serve the needs of the national and club teams. Shouldering the burden of extra matches and practices, they were overworked and exhausted. The approach ended in 1978, when the Soviet team, formed on the basis of Dinamo Kiev, failed for the first time in history to qualify for the World Cup.[31]

While Dinamo Tbilisi never dominated Soviet football to the same degree as Dinamo Kiev, Georgian difference on the football pitch arguably better served Soviet ideological needs in the Cold War. Unlike their Ukrainian counterparts, Dinamo Tbilisi's stars were portrayed as colorful and individualistic. As non-

Russian and non-Slavic representatives of the Soviet Union, Dinamo Tbilisi's players were called on to serve as cultural ambassadors to the postcolonial world and dispatched to Latin American countries thought to have an affinity for a similarly southern style of play. Often, they lived up to these expectations. In exhibition matches, they were greeted with cheers in Brazil and Argentina.[32] In 1961, Avtandil Ghoghoberidze was sent to Cuba along with other representatives of Dinamo Tbilisi to meet with Fidel Castro, and photographs show the visiting Georgians posing with Castro after dressing him in a traditional Georgian hat.[33] An even more famous photograph, taken immediately after a 1965 friendly match between the Soviet *sbornaia* and the Brazilian national team, showed the four Georgian stars of the Soviet team, Anzor Kavazashvili, Mikheil Meskhi, Slava Metreveli, and Giorgi Sichinava, posing arm in arm with a shirtless Pelé, football's greatest celebrity. The photograph, disseminated widely in the Soviet press, revealed the admiration the Georgians clearly had for the Brazilian football legend but also linked the Soviet team's Georgian contingent with the idea of a southern style of soccer that could allegedly be found throughout the world.

In principle, members of Dinamo Tbilisi were meant to evoke Georgian distinctiveness while conveying the cohesiveness of a multiethnic Soviet Union. Sometimes, personal, national, and Pan-Soviet interests coincided: by most accounts, Georgian footballers were initially eager to serve state needs, especially since international travel opened up a world inaccessible to ordinary Soviet citizens. Breathlessly recounting his first visit to Paris in 1954, Ghoghoberidze recalled, "In those years, and even after, an air of magic hung around the words 'international match.'"[34]

Decades later, the team's domestic and international successes had bred a greater sense of confidence among Dinamo Tbilisi players and supporters. The team won its second Soviet Top League title in 1979 and bookended this achievement by taking the Soviet Cup in 1976 and 1979. Bringing its distinctive style of play into the international arena, the team sought to claim its place among the top European clubs, which, as Soviet officials and footballers recognized, set the standards by which others were measured around the world. Accordingly, Dinamo Tbilisi's 3–0 victory over Liverpool in a 1979 European Cup match played before ninety thousand ecstatic supporters in Tbilisi was heralded as a signal achievement. Afterward, Georgian journalists proudly quoted Liverpool manager Bob Paisley's statement that Dinamo Tbilisi had "pleasantly surprised him" with their level of play.[35]

Dinamo Tbilisi would go on to score the biggest victory in the club's history, defeating Carl Zeiss Jena to win the 1981 Cup Winners' Cup. Admittedly, it was less prestigious than the European Cup and played against a fellow Socialist club from East Germany rather than a storied Western European competitor. Nevertheless, it was a major coup, both for the Soviet Union, which had a poor record in international football competitions, and for the small nation of Georgia. Soviet authorities and supporters in Georgia both sought to take credit for the victory. Leonid Brezhnev wrote, "It was not in vain that we all rooted for them [Dinamo Tbilisi]" and claimed the victory as one for the entire Soviet Union. Georgians, however, saw the team's success as a national triumph. Letters and telegrams congratulating the team poured in from Georgians living throughout the Soviet Union, including a woman residing in the Komi Autonomous Soviet Socialist Republic (ASSR) who proclaimed, "Henceforth European football will be spoken with a Georgian accent."[36]

The 1981 Cup Winners' Cup victory seemed to offer an opportunity for Dinamo Tbilisi to transcend the hierarchies of Soviet multiethnicity by superseding their reputation as a "moody team." When the club had gained its first Soviet Top League title in 1964, the success of Dinamo Tbilisi's "golden boys" had been linked to their Russian coach, Gavriil Kachalin. In the judgment of Nikolai Starostin, it was Kachalin who had "skillfully guided this sharp, but not always well-balanced ensemble to victory" by "reinforcing the team's psychological strength."[37] However, Dinamo Tbilisi's 1981 team was successfully managed by a homegrown Georgian coach, Nodar Akhalkatsi. After Dinamo Tbilisi's Cup Winner's Cup victory, journalists from *Pravda* wrote about the team's temperamental reputation in the past tense: "Earlier Tbilisi Dinamo was often called a moody team, one that could defeat a strong opponent in brilliant style and then, not preparing for their next match, lose to an even worse team."[38] Now, according to Russian soccer celebrity Valentin Ivanov, the team's "long-standing skill in improvisation" had finally been "united" with effective organization.[39]

Returning to Georgia, Dinamo Tbilisi's players were carried off the plane in the arms of supporters and cheered as national heroes as they paraded with their trophy in front of tens of thousands of fans packed into their home stadium. A jubilant song recorded by the Soviet Georgian band Iveria, which blended rock and polyphonic Georgian harmonizing, memorialized the team's victory. The song's Georgian-language lyrics left little doubt about the national nature of the team's achievement. Its narrator praised the "boys" of Dinamo Tbilisi, whose victory had "glorified Georgia"; their success was "like radiant light shining on the mountains and valleys" of the Caucasus nation.[40] This sentiment was echoed by Davit Kipiani, one of the stars of the 1981 squad, who described international matches as a forum for proving the strength and vitality of Georgian national character. Speaking to a fellow Georgian journalist, Kipiani explained, "It's worth remembering that football is not just composed of feints, dribbling, and passes. Football is also a contest of different character and personality types. And character types, in their essence, are national."[41]

Dinamo Tbilisi's success exposed tensions arising from the centralized Soviet state's reliance on Georgian soccer to achieve its ideological goals. For some Soviet observers outside Georgia, the achievements of Dinamo Tbilisi and the behavior of its fans represented a growing challenge to Russian dominance and Pan-Soviet solidarity. While Georgian players continued to be valued for their contributions to the Soviet team, the victories of Dinamo Tbilisi against opponents from larger Soviet republics was sometimes cause for popular resentment.

Dinamo Tbilisi's Georgian supporters gained a reputation for pushing and sometimes exceeding the boundaries of acceptable behavior in the multiethnic Socialist state. At a 1971 meeting of the Soviet Football Federation, the Georgian representative spoke out against what he saw as a crude depiction of Dinamo Tbilisi supporters as "overly expansive and emotional" in the newspaper *Sovetskii Sport*.[42] Meanwhile, Georgian sports officials sought to have a greater say in which players were called up to play for the *sbornaia*, likely because they wanted to protect the interests of Dinamo Tbilisi. At the same Football Federation meeting the Georgian delegate framed the issue as one of national sovereignty. The delegate explained that the Football Federation had the right to "recommend" players, but to "make demands of the sports committee of a sovereign republic with its own constitution is simply unfair and offensive."[43]

Dinamo Tbilisi's politically connected patrons in Georgia also asserted local control through the informal use of republic-level institutions. When the team's top prospect for goalkeeper, Anzor Kavazashvili, sought to leave the club to play in Russia, he was prevented from purchasing a plane ticket and had to depart Georgia in disguise, traveling on a ticket made out in a friend's name. Tracking him down in Leningrad, representatives from the Georgian KGB came to the apartment where he was staying.[44] Although Georgian authorities relented once Kavazashvili officially began playing in Russia, they used back channels

to induce him to return. While playing for Spartak Moscow, Kavazashvili received a call from Givi Chokheli, a footballer from Dinamo Tbilisi who had
played with him on the Soviet team. Chokheli, who had been asked by the
Georgian sports minister to make a personal appeal to Kavazashvili, asked
the goalkeeper, "Don't you want your parents to live well in their old age?"[45]
Kavazashvili was nearly tempted to return to his homeland and his family but
ultimately refused when he learned he would not be guaranteed the starting
spot at goal for Dinamo Tbilisi.

A nagging concern for Dinamo Tbilisi's supporters was that the team was
gaining international recognition as a Soviet rather than a Georgian club. The
Georgian national repertoire, which linked an ethnically distinctive style of
football to familiar Georgian dances, could be readily recognized by Soviet
spectators. However, attempts to use Georgian football to convey the multiethnic diversity of the Soviet state abroad depended on the intelligibility of
this repertoire on the international stage. Some foreign observers understood
Georgian football as it was intended; a French journalist, for example, described
the 1964 Dinamo Tbilisi squad as "the best Eastern representatives of South
American football traditions."[46] Yet the terms of Georgian national difference
on the pitch were not always recognized by international observers, and some
Georgian supporters grew worried that Soviet sponsorship led foreigners to see
the team as Russian. They were particularly irked when publications like the
West Ham United newsletter alternately described the victorious 1981 Dinamo
Tbilisi team as "the Russians" and "the Soviets," as if the terms were equivalent.[47]
Beyond the Soviet Union, it was common to conflate Russia and the USSR, but
because Soviet citizens were categorized by nationality and perceived national
distinctions to be significant, Georgian supporters blamed the lack of foreign
recognition on the inability of their team—and, by extension, their country—to
truly stand alone on the world stage.

In 1990, Dinamo Tbilisi withdrew from the Football Federation of the USSR,
and the club was renamed Iberia Tbilisi, a reference to the ancient kingdom of
eastern Georgia.[48] Georgian football's efforts to pursue international success
independent of Moscow were linked to the push for national sovereignty. A
Georgian journalist writing in the republic's main newspaper in November
1990 described the Soviet Football Federation as an "imperial structure" that
prevented Georgia from "entering the international arena." Once again linking soccer to dance, the author noted that Georgians had been forced to suffer

foreign press accounts that spoke of their republic's famous dance ensemble as a group of "Russian performers."[49] Even though the central security organs of the Soviet state had supported and promoted the development of Dinamo Tbilisi, Georgian football became a forum for advancing nationalist separation.

The failure to field a truly successful all-Soviet team reflected the tensions of the multiethnic Soviet empire, which had grown more apparent in the post-Stalinist period. Putting together a cohesive *sbornaia* became more difficult as national republics sought to push their own agendas through formal and informal means and central sporting authorities had to coordinate among teams backed by different government ministries. The authorities' reliance on republic-level teams to represent the Soviet Union abroad generated some expected grievances, since Moscow advanced the prospects of these teams with funding and infrastructural investments but controlled the terms of their international participation and claimed their monetary gains.

Emboldened by the international prominence they had gained playing for the Soviet Union, Georgian footballers sought more independence and better salaries. Fueled by these ambitions, Georgia established one of the Soviet Union's first professional soccer clubs, Mretebi Tbilisi, in 1988.[50] However, the harsh realities of post-Soviet Georgia made dreams of a South American–style football paradise seem increasingly distant, a development that was wryly observed in the 1991 film *I Am Pelé's Godfather!* (*Me, peles natlia!*). In the movie, a middle-aged Georgian man magically travels between a run-down Tbilisi and a sumptuous Brazil full of football legends, scantily clad women, and carnival celebrations. He returns with stories of how he befriended Pelé's father and taught his son, the Brazilian soccer legend, how to play; however, in Tbilisi his wife is unimpressed, his creditors hound him, and he remains stuck in a low-level job inspecting Georgia's crumbling electrical infrastructure. In reality, most Georgians with significant football talent left the country; the trends of globalization that accompanied the end of the Cold War made transferring to a more prominent foreign team easier and far more lucrative. After living through the Georgian Civil War from 1991 to 1993 and witnessing the collapse of the nation's economy, Mretebi Tbilisi's former top prospect, Giorgi Kinkladze, ultimately joined Manchester City for a fee of approximately two million pounds.[51]

While the link between the two was always tenuous, in the post–Cold War era it became increasingly difficult to see soccer as representative of national character. Storied franchises were bought up by foreign investors and the game's stars purchased by the highest bidder, turning the English Premier League into a global operation in which less than a third of the players were English.[52] Europe's national teams also grew more diverse, drawing on immigrants and minorities from former colonies; these squads were praised by many for embodying multiculturalism but criticized by others for failing to live up to expectations of national homogeneity.[53] By the early twenty-first century, even the concept of a distinctly Brazilian style of play embodied by Brazil's national team was more of a myth linked to a successful global brand than a reflection of the team's actual techniques on the pitch.[54] While Georgians sought to redeploy football as a national institution following the Soviet Union's collapse, the rules of the game had changed.

6

RUSSIAN FEVER PITCH

Global Fandom, Youth Culture, and the Public Sphere in the Late Soviet Union

Manfred Zeller

The first crowd of soccer spectators that Iurii Mikhailov (b. 1967) ever encountered was clad in green and white.[1] He was about ten years old and living with his parents in Budapest. The fans were wearing scarves in their team colors and waved flags on the metro ride to and from the stadium. Young Iurii had never seen anything like it. In an interview in 2008, this Spartak Moscow fan described the event as a "revelation." Retrospectively, the encounter was no doubt an important moment in Mikhailov's biography. It was presumably not until much later that he figured out that they were fans of Budapest's Ferencváros club. Still, when he returned to Moscow in 1979, he was undoubtedly astonished to find that many of his friends were now also wearing similar scarves. His young companions were not wearing the green-and-white colors of Ferencváros, however, but the red-and-white colors of Spartak Moscow. Often referred to as the "people's team," Spartak was the most popular team in Moscow and throughout much of the Soviet Union.[2] Followers of Spartak Moscow were the first fans in the Soviet Union to adorn themselves in their team's colors, wave club flags, sing fan songs in the stadiums, and travel en masse to away games. Groups of the so-called fan movement (*fanatskoe dvizhenie*) quickly developed around other local clubs and by the mid-1980s had spread throughout the Soviet Union, with the notable exception of the Central Asian and Caucasian republics.[3] Spartak's *fanaty* (fans) had led the way to the creation of this new subculture that reinforced the special status of Spartak and its fans in the Soviet Union. Their fan culture, however, was quite similar to the practices of other new fan groups. Through scarves, chants, and away games, but also through fighting, they sought to create a sense of cultural superiority. By the 1980s, Soviet security forces were confronted with violent clashes with opposing fans on a regular basis.

This essay traces the history of fan culture and its globalization from a Soviet perspective and points to the impact of globalized sports at a local level.[4] It describes the development of fan culture within the Soviet Union as an example of the broader impact of images of Western fan culture on fan cultures around the world since the 1960s. It focuses on the local consumption of Soviet media images of global fan culture and the resulting transformation.[5] How were Western fan images and practices adapted and shaped within Soviet culture?

New mass media created new fan cultures on the local level by creating connections between previously unrelated contexts. More specifically, the expansion of the Soviet media occurred in parallel with the various steps of contestation and détente in the context of the Cold War. In the mid-1970s, Moscow teenagers were inspired by televised images of cheering Western fans who publicly marked themselves with visual signs of allegiance and enthusiasm. Unlike earlier Soviet soccer fans, who had expressed their enthusiasm by means of less visible practices such as whistling during matches or writing letters to the authorities,[6] fans now began to openly celebrate their affiliations, along with their aesthetic independence and involvement in a global youth culture. In doing so, their aspirations and practices ran counter to the propagandized goals of the omnipresent Socialist state.[7] This was the result, however, of a two-decade cultural penetration of the Soviet sports media with images of Western fandom.

I understand globalization as the diffusion of practices, norms, and technologies around the world.[8] In the second half of the twentieth century similar forms of fan behavior and aesthetics developed in the field of spectator sports in many regions around the world. As new forms of media connected audiences across the globe and (at least in the West) travel grew more commonplace,[9] spectators began to imitate the practices of more distant fan cultures. However, the fact that fan practices in various regions *seem* similar at first sight does not infer that they *mean* the same things to different protagonists. After all, the imitation of cultural practices unfolds within the varying contexts of local media, societies, and milieus.[10] Shaped by these conditions, they evolve concurrently and in interaction with their sources, but their development is neither simultaneous nor similar. Histories of transnational fandom will have to deal with "more specificity and less generality," to quote Ramón Spaaij's appeal in regard to approaches adopted within the social sciences to transnational hooliganism.[11]

In the Soviet Union the transformative impact of modern mass media (in particular television) was one of the major preconditions for the development of an informal fan movement.[12] From the late 1950s, a consumer society emerged within the Soviet Union as the Nikita Khrushchev administration and the Soviet elite sought to stabilize their rule by improving the general population's standard of living. The Soviet media were used to "educate" the population on the benefits and practices of "rational consumer culture."[13] Analogous to this process, sports media began to produce "visual and textual representations" of fan culture and replicate the imagery of "ideal consumers" that accompanied media coverage of other consumer goods.[14] These images were intended to introduce the idea of "rational consumerism" into spectator sports: from then on, images of decent, "cultured," and "objective" fans would serve as informal guidelines for many soccer fans and indicated how far one could go in expressing popular subjectivity in a state of collective norms.[15] At the same time the media also produced models that fans would later draw on; in the long run the coverage of fan practices in the West unintentionally established alternatives to the figurative norms of "decent" Soviet public behavior.

Young Spartak Moscow fans and, a couple of years later, fans of TsSKA (Tsentral'nyi sportivnyi klub armii), Dinamo Moscow, Dinamo Kiev, and other teams, began to imitate these models by traveling to away games and wearing their teams' colors inside and outside stadiums, developing a "new sense of the global" in the process.[16] Within the context of late Soviet reality, their "Western" style of expressing their commitment was unique. As with Soviet consumption of Western popular music, this adaptation of Western cultural practices entailed a "process of selective borrowing and appropriation, translation and incorporation into the indigenous cultural context."[17] Although the images of Western fans that inspired their Soviet counterparts were equally products of the Soviet sports media, these practices ran counter to the established norms of cultural sophistication and uniformity that defined Soviet public life.

This set of cultural practices can also be interpreted as the masculine-encoded "emancipatory impulses" of a generation of young citizens who sought temporarily to exclude themselves from the norms of Soviet public life.[18] Fans expressed these sentiments primarily through acts of visual embodiment in the public sphere, including graffiti, the use of fan paraphernalia, and collective travel to away games. These "liberating" practices exposed sociocultural rifts within Soviet society, and the authorities soon felt that it was necessary to combat the growing movement. Scenes of Spartak fans battling fans bearing the emblems of Dinamo and TsSKA (teams closely linked to the security and military forces) could not easily be tolerated.

While these young soccer fans outwardly positioned themselves on the margins of Soviet society, as pupils, students, and employees the overwhelming majority of them chose to tolerate the limitations placed on them in late-Soviet society.[19] My main sources of information are contemporary media reports, interviews with former fans, and a variety of Russian and Ukrainian archives. The use of media reports and archival sources as comparative points of reference serves to counteract the effects of the retrospective distortions that are an inherent aspect of oral accounts. However, no other source comes closer to the actual historical actors, their values, myths, and beliefs than an interview. Even though personal memories are invariably distorted to some extent by the passage of time, it is possible to detect specific images that accurately convey values and aesthetics typical of the time frame in question. Retrospective by nature, a carefully compiled oral history can reveal which images and events really mattered to the interviewees.[20]

A number of developments within Soviet media in the 1950s and 1960s set the preconditions for a new fan culture in Moscow. Two key factors were the extended geographic scope of TV broadcasts and the wide availability of TV sets, which transformed isolated urban leisure practices into a media-driven consumer culture that permeated the entire USSR. This immediately altered the nature of Soviet spectator culture and set the stage for the conspicuous adoption of Western practices by fan groups.

During the Stalinist era fan practices were restricted to the stadium. Outside the stadiums nonvisual forms of participation were rare and generally limited to radio broadcasts.[21] Likewise, the Soviet sports press seldom produced images of spectators. "Active" sportsmen rather than "passive" spectators were considered to be more meaningful propaganda models for the fostering of Socialist ideology.[22] The focus of Soviet media in the late Stalinist era was directed toward the "hooligans" and heroes of the Socialist order rather than fans. An article from 1946, for instance, makes mention of "hooligans in the stadium,"[23] while a report from 1952 mentions "a young Stakhanovite" who sat "next to a composer who is known to all the people."[24] In their references to the terraces the press conjured up an image of crowds of Soviet spectators who spent their well-deserved leisure time following the games from the stands with an air of detachment and impartiality.

In contrast, in the late 1950s and early 1960s Soviet authorities began to regularly supply fans with visual representations of the "ideal" soccer fan through the sports press. As was the case in the construction of other contemporary consumer discourses in the Soviet Union, the media offered an image of fans as "rational consumers" by describing them as "cultured" and praising their "objective" behavior.[25] While the "rational consumer" was generally a feminine construction,[26] the image of the ideal soccer consumer was predominantly male.

The sports journal *Futbol*, a weekly founded in 1960, distinguished between two diametrically opposed classes of soccer fans. According to the press the overwhelming majority of fans were "feverish" (*bolel'shchik*) fans—a term with particularly positive connotations. With its associations with suffering the term connotes a level of subjective emotional involvement that was unknown in earlier descriptions.[27] The ideal feverish fan expressed his affiliations inside the stadium, but these expressions of devotion never transgressed the norms of Soviet "refinement."

The negative element in this dichotomy was the hooligan. In 1960, a report was published on a court trial against *khuligany* (hooligans) in connection with an incident at the Luzhniki stadium. The prosecutor accused the defendants of bringing feverish fans into disrepute. The defendants, the prosecutor claimed, had nothing in common but their love of vodka.[28] In the press the distinction between "cultured and uncultured masculinity," which formed a "significant part of the rhetoric of Soviet sports,"[29] was applied increasingly in descriptions of fans, thus contextualizing the negative part of the dichotomy within the broader phenomenon of public hooliganism in the Soviet Union.[30] Images featuring more recent Western fan customs also began to be published at this time. In March 1964, for instance, a photograph was published depicting fans cheering for Inter Milan at the European Cup quarter final against Partizan Belgrade. The caption read: "The flags were waving in the stands of San-Siro. They were not moved by the wind, but by the arms of hot blooded Internazionale fans."[31]

While Soviet media reasserted the previously established identification of negative forms of spectator behavior with hooliganism, it also made two significant gestures toward soccer fans. By introducing the image of the feverish Soviet fan, the media acknowledged the principal legitimacy of fan subjectivity. Furthermore, Soviet media also sought to fulfill customer demand for information on recent developments in Western soccer and fan culture.

As is the case in other consumer discourses, the images of fans published in the media implied "multiple usages, symbolic meanings, and conflicting perceptions."[32] Soviet citizens were able to multiply their agendas and strategies through the "performative reproduction" of the ideal Soviet *bolel'shchik*.[33]

Interview narratives and archival sources such as fan mail show that soccer fans envisioned and shaped their identities according to these models of cultured Soviet fandom (as opposed to images of Western fans), precisely because this enabled them to express a variety of meanings within the Soviet value system.

This is true not only of members of the Soviet technical intelligentsia involved in the fan culture. Workers also acted in a similar fashion by signing petitions calling for their local team's promotion.[34] Television viewers lodged official complaints about what they felt were biased decisions or overly aggressive tactics.[35] They thus claimed for themselves the image of the cultured and objective fan while attributing the negative element in this dichotomy—"uncultured behavior"—to their opponents. Fans even wrote to referee associations to protest about a particular individual's performance.[36]

Although the strategies pursued by these feverish fans can be reconstructed from archival sources, it is important to note that these innovations did not have a significant impact within the larger public sphere. The more conspicuous signs of these changes within 1960s Soviet fan culture include the occasional use of simple banners and primitive terrace chants.[37] Later practices including the widespread use of paraphernalia, fan blocks, and massed chanting were still unknown at the time, and it was not always apparent during play which team the majority of fans actually supported. On the surface, the fan culture of this period does not appear particularly diverse, and little mention is made in interviews of the fan practices of the 1960s *bolel'shchiki*. When interviewees (in particular, members of the informal fan movement) do refer to these practices, they invariably describe them as "passive."

In fact, the strategies of the feverish fans were far from passive, but they lacked *visibility* and *permanence*.[38] Most soccer fans chose to draw on the subtle codes of feverish fan culture rather than openly reference Western fan cultures; hence the dearth of signs, symbols, and statements that might have indicated that these fans viewed their actions within the context of an imagined global community of soccer fans linked by a set of universal cultural practices.

On a global level the late 1970s and early 1980s were a period of political turmoil as tensions rose time and again between the Soviet and Western Blocs. Events such as the Soviet invasion of Afghanistan, the NATO Double-Track Decision, and the reciprocal boycotts of the Moscow and Los Angeles Olympic Games in 1980 and 1984, respectively, underlined the epochal significance of this period of international relations.[39] However, in the shadow of the troubled international relations that dominated newspaper coverage of the time, the international standardization of modern sports had already led to the dissemination of a variety of cultural practices, precipitating the formation of a fan culture that, like many other popular youth cultures of the period, manifested many of the most common features of cultural globalization.

Unlike earlier fans, the protagonists of this new movement worshipped their teams in ways that were highly visible and contradicted the very foundations of late-Soviet public life. The creation of a specifically Soviet spectator/consumer culture was a prerequisite to the formation of this new movement, as it supplied the protagonists with models of Western fan behavior. Never before had the Soviet authorities had access to a medium "for reaching so many people with its messages, and never had a medium appeared so potentially out of sync with the messages it was to deliver."[40] It is important to note that although this new fan culture relied heavily on images produced by the media, its protagonists dismissed earlier fans for their highly "Soviet" passivity and "refinement."

Developing as it did under the conditions of late-Soviet rule, the organized fan culture that emerged in Moscow, Kiev, and other cities adopted public displays of affiliation that diverged from those common in the West. In a society characterized by state-controlled collectivity, wearing a hand-knitted fan scarf potentially challenged the conventions of public uniformity. As a colorful statement of youthful independence it implied that its wearer was a member of a global youth culture of Western origin; the scarf contradicted the gloomy uniformity of daily life in the Soviet Union and challenged the educational aims of the Socialist propaganda state.[41]

For more than a decade images of cheering Western fans clad in their team colors had circulated throughout the Soviet Union. Most important, the Soviet Union joined the European Cup competitions in 1965, and the away games of the Soviet sides were shown on TV in the Soviet Union on a regular basis.[42] This, as Robert Edelman points out, "had a significant cultural impact on the nation's teams, their supporters, and television viewers."[43] For instance, Soviet fans gained firsthand experience of their German counterparts when they traveled to Kiev to support Bayern Munich. Television coverage of the event contrasted the colorful Bayern fans with the civil Soviet audience.[44] In 1972 Soviet audiences watched as Scottish fans invaded the pitch after the final match of the European Cup between Dinamo Moscow and Glasgow Rangers. It was this game in particular that inspired Spartak fans to go to games in their team's colors and to sit in a block together at the stadium, where they would actively support their team with terrace chants.[45]

Spartak Moscow's relegation from the first division in 1976 is also widely considered to be a seminal moment in the history of informal fan movements in the late Soviet Union. On its return to the first division Spartak won the championship in 1979, thus accelerating the evolution of its fan culture.[46] Inspired by a constant flood of images from the West, younger fans began to act in a more Western and less Soviet manner at a time when economic crises were making it increasingly difficult for the authorities to fulfill the population's expectations.[47]

Not surprisingly, the practices of these fans were at first very similar to those of their Western counterparts. As fan paraphernalia was as yet nonexistent, most fan scarves were hand-knitted. Fans often adopted melodies from popular songs and changed the lyrics to suit their purposes—a practice that highlights the link between pop and fan culture.[48] One of these fan chants was a modified version of the popular hit "The World Is Not Easy" (*Mir ne prost*) by the group Samotsvety.[49] According to the unofficial song brochure *Fanatskii Fol'klor*, the chant was written in 1978.[50] The song was the chosen anthem of the Spartak fans, who sang it at literally every game.[51] While the melody is pleasant, the lyrics are clearly intended to antagonize other teams from Moscow and Europe: "All other clubs must pay their tribute—Dinamo, the Horse Stable, Milan, and Haiduk!"[52] Meanwhile, the emergence of blocks of fans supporting their teams en masse in soccer stadiums marked yet another cultural transfer.

Interview narratives support the notion that this new form of soccer fan culture was unchallenged by the authorities in the first years of its existence.[53] The first press report on informally organized Spartak Moscow fans, published in 1977, was reasonably neutral in its tenor. It identifies the fans as a group of "boys," who are "mostly workers, but also include pupils and students." Unlike that of their feverish counterparts, their response to the game was not restricted to whistling or applauding good play; instead, their displays of support varied and "matched the pace of the game." The article also mentions that it had recently become "en vogue" in Moscow to wear a red-and-white scarf and that the movement had even spawned its own poets. Overall, the article presents these new fans as young, decent, and cultured individuals from the heart of Soviet society.[54] The authors of the article refrained from criticizing the first visible signs of audience fragmentation (old versus young); instead, they chose to describe the practices as if they were a form of poetical, "cultured" fan behavior. Clearly, the authors sought to integrate the emerging movement into the cultured consumer practices of Soviet masculinity,[55] just as the press had previously attempted to integrate feverish fans. The fact that this was, in all like-lihood, a conscious strategy is further highlighted by the omission in the article of any reference to the obviously Western origins of these new fan practices.

This integrative approach soon proved to be ineffective following the formation of fan groups affiliated with Dinamo Moscow, TsSKA Moscow, and Dinamo Kiev in the early 1980s. Unlike earlier fan groups, which generally refrained from public displays of their club affiliations, these various groups were aware of each other in the stadiums and on the streets and used fan paraphernalia to visibly mark their allegiance. Although the new fan culture stood in a long tradition—not of dissent but of popular subjectivity—it was the first time that soccer fans had sought to represent their group affiliations *visually* in the stadiums, on the streets, and at away games.

This innovation proved to be crucial; unlike in pluralistic Western societies, in the Soviet Union there always was the possibility that expressions of subjectivity that breached the boundaries of Soviet uniformity within the public sphere could become problematic per se. This was certainly the case when fans of Spartak Moscow, the so-called people's team and the archrival of the state-run police and army teams Dinamo and TsSKA,[56] began to openly appropriate state symbols, such as the emblems of the Spartak and Dinamo sports clubs, in their struggle to dominate the city of Moscow.[57]

The struggle was more than a symbolic battle for the stadiums. In interviews fans described the increasingly violent conflict, which escalated throughout the 1980s and culminated in large clashes between various groups.[58] But the violence was at its worst when fans traveled to away games to support their teams. As Dinamo Kiev fan Aleksandr Ponyrev put it, the fans felt as though they were setting off on a "pirate ship" when they traveled to away games.[59] These accounts emphasize the strong impulse to enact emotional experiences within the public sphere—an impulse that fans inherited from their Western role models and enacted in their travels throughout the vast Soviet territory.[60]

This tendency to favor increasingly visible cultural practices significantly shaped the self-image of fanatical fans, as is clearly illustrated in contemporary interviews. Spartak fan Amir Khuslutdinov (b. 1965) described his companions as "shiny" (*iarkii*) and "free" (*svobodnii*) people. Khuslutdinov, a savvy and knowledgeable expert on fan history and an important *avtoritet* (authority) within the movement, is known as "the professor" in fan circles.[61] Iurii Mikhailov was also keen to emphasize his attention to detail and even went as

far as to contact me on my cell phone after the interview to correct a miscel-
laneous detail.[62] In the memories of former fans, *visibility* figures as a central
element of manhood in the 1980s.

It is very difficult to reconstruct precisely how such fan practices were perceived by the majority of the population at the time. The total number of "fanatical" fans in Moscow in the early 1980s is estimated at around thirty thousand.[63]
While this figure is impressive, it should be noted that the vast majority of fans
were not involved in the fanatical movement. Moreover, few fanatical groups
existed outside Moscow, and those that did were much smaller.[64] The wider
public presumably associated fanatical youth culture not so much with Western
fan practices but with the annoying arrogance of adolescents from the capital.[65]
A research perspective that focuses too strongly on the situation in Moscow
cannot provide an accurate impression of fan culture in the Soviet Union.

Most of the fans that I interviewed who did not belong to the fanatical scene
expressed a dislike of fanatical youth culture. Their aversion had grown over the
years, and it is difficult to pin down the origins of their disapproval. However, it
should be noted that many ordinary Soviet soccer fans and citizens of the early
1980s presumably had little direct knowledge of informal youth culture and
its practices. On October 20, 1982, for instance, about ten thousand spectators
had made their way to the stadium to watch the Union of European Football
Associations (UEFA) Cup group qualifier between Spartak Moscow and FC
Haarlem from the Netherlands. By the end of the game, a catastrophe occurred
in one of the stairways, as the militia tried to get hold of young fans who had
thrown snowballs during the game, resulting in at least sixty-six casualties.[66]
In the aftermath, rumors circulated that "something really bad" had occurred
at the stadium. It was also alleged that punks (*panky*) were responsible for the
disaster.[67] Soccer fanatics did indeed have a lot in common with other youth
subcultures such as the "Soviet flower children." In many of these subcultures,
teenagers formed loosely knit gangs bound together by friendships, informal
gatherings, and spontaneous actions.[68]

Fanatical fans themselves contributed to the movement's blurred public
image in the early 1980s. Most of them refrained from openly challenging the
Soviet order by creating *permanent* signs of their group affiliations. As Iurii
Mikhailov explained, "[While] this was a protest against the Komsomol [the
Soviet youth organization], everybody stayed in the Komsomol."[69] Fanatical fans
did not have a coherent political strategy; while testing the boundaries of Soviet
society, they were careful to keep one foot inside the Soviet order. Organized

fans imagined themselves as members of a global youth culture, yet only one of my interviewees actually turned his back on official youth organizations.

Testing the boundaries of Soviet authority in this manner already demanded a considerable degree of juvenile courage or naïveté. The fans' imitations of Western practices contradicted the way in which public processes functioned within the Soviet Union. Indeed, at the time of the Luzhniki Stadium disaster Soviet authorities had already begun to combat the growing movement. Interviewees point out that police tried to ban the most important and visible sign of group affiliation from Soviet stadiums: the (generally) hand-knitted fan scarves. As rivalry between various fan groups intensified, fans choosing to wear their team colors often found themselves involved in violent altercations both with other groups of fans and with the authorities. Iurii Mikhailov, who was also trapped in the stampede at Luzhniki Stadium, claimed that the catastrophe was triggered by altercations between attending fans and police forces.[70]

In the aftermath of the catastrophe, the Moscow Executive Committee ruled that the interior organs had frequently failed to react with the appropriate degree of force to "antisocial acts" at sports events in the past. The comprehensive catalogue of measures ordered by the committee was clearly designed to subdue the movement. These included organized trips to sporting events at which fans were instructed on how to behave inside the stadium. Meanwhile, the interior security organs were instructed "to prevent any disturbance of public order and to resolutely thwart any violation."[71]

This two-pronged strategy of prohibition and integration was bound to fail for at least two reasons. First, the fan practices were part of a way of life that differed from that prescribed by Soviet institutions such as the Komsomol—it was simply impossible for fans to identify their aesthetic practices with the officially sanctioned idea of the cultured fan. Adventurous tales of fans stealing flags from official sports organizations and cutting up Pioneer ties to make new scarves are indicative of the lifestyle in the fan movement (*fanatskoe dvizhenie*).[72]

Second, the organized fans that I interviewed did not consider themselves uneducated or uncultured. Although they realized that their behavior at away games was not proper in the Soviet sense of polite citizenship, their narratives combined courage and a potentially violent masculinity with a sense of *cultural superiority*. Young fans perceived themselves as the Soviet vanguard of a movement that spanned the entire globe. It was they who had established an authentic stadium culture in all its beauty within an environment that did not care for such aesthetics at all.

The state's heavy-handed approach and the new policing tactics transformed the nature of these localized fan practices;[73] they also strengthened the prejudices held by fans from Kiev against Moscow and the Russian Soviet order. Kiev fan Aleksandr Ponyrev's account of his journey to an away match in Moscow sounds more like a wartime mission through enemy territory. The fans faced communication difficulties and were forced to use secret meeting points at metro stations. Hiding their fan scarves, they gathered in secret to prevent their "neutralization" by the militia before arriving at their destination near the stadium, where fighting soon broke out.[74] Police strategies for dealing with fans were modified several times in the 1980s. The periodical threats issued by the authorities shaped the fans' behavior and even the composition of the movement's active core.[75] Only the most courageous and dedicated organized fans of the 1980s continued to participate in the movement's activities throughout the increasingly violent 1990s.

Cultural transfers have an enormous impact on societies in a globalized world. In the 1960s and 1970s, Soviet media produced idealized visions of decent, rational Soviet *bolel'shchiki*, while also covering developments in Western fan culture. Many soccer fans slyly adopted the model of the feverish fan to express their particular affiliations in a more ambiguous fashion. From the late 1970s onward a minority of young Muscovites began to imitate the highly visible fan practices of the Western model. Soviet teams were tied to Soviet sports organizations, but fans wrenched these symbols of the Socialist state from their official context to publicly demonstrate their joy. This confronted the Soviet public with the sociocultural fragmentation that was otherwise expressed between the lines.

The history of Soviet fan culture challenges earlier Cold War stereotypes about cultural interdependence between East and West. A careful analysis of late Soviet fan movements reveals that despite being influenced by Western fandom, the countercultural potential of their actions led to specifically Soviet meanings of fandom. The *fanatskoe dvizhenie* combined violent behavior with a sense of cultural superiority. As students, workers, or Komsomol members, they remained integrated members of Soviet society, without having ever known anything else, but as football fans too they imagined themselves in a specific Soviet way. To belong to an almost global fan movement meant to trump fans from other Soviet republics that had not yet introduced such practices. The big movements in Moscow especially elevated themselves above others—thereby reproducing earlier hierarchies of the multinational Soviet Union.

PART III

GERMAN DEMOCRATIC REPUBLIC

EULOGY TO THEFT

Berliner FC Dynamo, East German Football,
and the End of Communism

Alan McDougall

On March 22, 1986, Lokomotive Leipzig welcomed defending champions Berliner FC Dynamo (BFC) for a match vital to the destiny of that season's East German football championship. The hosts took an early lead and then withstood heavy second-half pressure and a red card for defender Matthias Liebers. As the match entered injury time, Lok still led. The referee, though, did not blow the final whistle. In the ninety-fifth minute, a cross was sent into the Lok penalty area—and a BFC player fell to the ground, following a clash with a Lok defender. To the crowd's fury, the referee pointed to the penalty spot. BFC equalized with the last kick of the game. The team from East Berlin eventually beat Lok to the league title, their eighth in succession, by just two points.[1]

BFC's 1–1 draw with Lokomotive Leipzig in March 1986 caused public uproar. It was no isolated incident but the latest in a long line of dubious decisions that benefited the team sponsored by the East German secret police, the Stasi. Many elements in the supposedly muzzled media spoke openly about refereeing ineptitude or worse. Fans from across the country flooded the offices of the Communist Party (SED; Sozialistische Einheitspartei Deutschlands) and the Football Association (DFV; Deutscher Fußball-Verband der DDR) with anti-BFC petitions. BFC supporters, meanwhile, reveled in their club's notoriety, embracing the villain's role in the same way as supporters of Italy's most successful club, Juventus, whose long history of referee-influenced success was once celebrated in a pamphlet titled *Eulogy to Theft*.[2]

Two of the petitions were sent by Heiko H., a student and photographer who was at the Lok-BFC game. In the second, written in May 1986 after his first went unanswered, he remarked, "For me it's all reduced to the question of whether you are hopelessly unqualified to do your job responsibly or whether you are rather misusing your position for deliberate cheating." H. referenced BFC's ongoing failings in European competition, where refereeing help was not readily available, and the attractiveness of the West German Bundesliga (Federal League) to GDR citizens. "I too," he concluded, "see how football can look at Bayern Munich."[3] The Communist authorities were not deaf to such angry voices. The referee in question, Bernd Stumpf, was suspended from top-level football. Two members of the DFV's referee commission with ties to BFC were sacked. The SED even sent conciliatory replies to some of the petitioners who complained about the Lok-BFC game—though not to Heiko H.[4]

The fallout from this controversial match reveals a great deal about football's singular place in "the world's most authoritarian and monitored sports system,"[5] a system that by the mid-1980s had established the small and otherwise largely unheralded German Democratic Republic (GDR) as an Olympic superpower. It highlights football's role as a political lightning rod, channeling antiregime sentiment into areas that were not always as safe or sealed off as they seemed to be. BFC's success, and the high price at which it was bought, tells us more about Cold War sport in East Germany, and indeed about the fatal weaknesses of the East German state, than the quadrennial gold rushes in Montreal, Moscow, or Seoul.

This essay examines popular responses to BFC's contested dominance of the final decade of GDR football. Situating this story within two broader frameworks—the complex web of domestic club rivalries (most notably between BFC and Dynamo Dresden) and the transnational world of Cold War sport—it uncovers a sporting scandal that prefaced the breakdown of Communism. No other form of dissent in the 1980s, certainly not in the GDR's small peace and environmental groups, was as widespread, public, and united as the anti-BFC campaign. Protests about one unpopular football club did not bring down the Berlin Wall, but they were emblematic of a deep sense of disenchantment with Socialism. BFC's abrupt decline at the end of the 1980s paralleled that of the East German state. It also found echoes beyond the GDR's tightly policed borders. BFC may have been sui generis, but its rise and fall showcased a Cold War story that transcended East-West binaries, revealing the extent and limits of sport as a vehicle of cultural exchange and the ways in which GDR football, for all of its isolation, was part of the post-1945 European history of sport, a site of "strong national histories" and "trans-national patterns and connections."[6]

BFC Versus the Rest? An Introduction to GDR Football

"The GDR Oberliga [First Division]," wrote Christoph Dieckmann in 1999, "was the most conservative league in the world."[7] Founded, like the GDR itself, in 1949, East Germany's top competition could hardly avoid the charge of insularity. Fans and officials recognized that GDR football tended to "stew in its own juices,"[8] promoting defensive mind-sets on and off the pitch. Players and coaches were drawn from a small, domestic pool. Even when Czechoslovakia, Hungary, and the Soviet Union allowed older athletes to transfer to clubs in the West during the perestroika era, the GDR held its ground.[9] It was only in 1990, after the collapse of SED rule, that the embargo was lifted. As the first foreign players then came to the Oberliga from Poland, Hungary, and even the United States, East German players headed west in far greater numbers. By the time the Oberliga opened itself to the world, it was beyond salvation.

Yet Dieckmann's characterization of the Oberliga, like the Cold War stereotype of the smoothly oiled East German "medal machine," does not tell the full story. The GDR, despite its reputation, was never a "closed society."[10] The same was true of East German football. The GDR was a founding member of the Union of European Football Associations (UEFA) in 1954. The national team participated in the qualifying rounds for UEFA's inaugural European Championships in 1960, and club sides entered UEFA's three club competitions when they were founded in the mid-1950s. Two of the national team's earliest coaches, János Gyarmati (1955–1957) and Károly Soós (1961–1967), were Hungarians. DFV coaches, meanwhile, pressed for closer contacts with their peers in France and England. They lauded the skills of Real Madrid's Alfredo Di Stéfano and the ultramodern training facilities of North London's Arsenal.[11]

The transnational elements in East German football were thus more pronounced than at first seemed to be the case. Equally, the authorities had less control over the Oberliga than they did over other parts of the GDR's elite sports program. Far from guaranteeing uniformity and an acceptance of central directives, the production-based structure of GDR football—established around such sports organizations as Chemie (chemical industry), Dynamo (police and state security), Lokomotive (railways), and Vorwärts (army)—created a multilayered system of competing interests, in which the turf wars of party bosses fed into older rivalries. The result, at least until the 1970s, was an Oberliga that was often unpredictable.[12] It was in this distinctive landscape that BFC's controversial rise to the top took place.

True to form, even BFC's origins were divisive. As part of a major restructuring of GDR football during the 1954–1955 season, eight of the fourteen Oberliga clubs were converted into state-favored sports clubs (SCs). One of them was SC Dynamo Berlin. In November 1954, with the season already under way, the nucleus of the team of Dynamo Dresden, defending Oberliga champions, was transplanted with little discussion or publicity to the GDR capital to bolster football's flagging fortunes there.[13] The party-mandated relocation sent the surviving shell of a team in Dresden into a decline from which it took fifteen years to recover and unwittingly kick-started the bitter rivalry between Dynamo's Berlin and Dresden clubs that defined GDR football in the 1970s and 1980s. The "painful" move to Berlin was not forgotten by older Dynamo Dresden supporters.[14] Yet Dynamo Berlin, known after further reforms in the mid-1960s as Berliner FC Dynamo, was no overnight success, despite the patronage of Stasi boss Erich Mielke. The only trophy to arrive before 1978 was the East German Cup in 1959.

Underachievement kept BFC's unpopularity in check. But as a representative of the secret police and the GDR capital, the club always engendered more suspicion than affection. A match against Dynamo Schwerin in 1968 ended in a riot, amid suspicions of bent refereeing that created in Schwerin, a small town in the GDR's northeast, a unanimous anti-BFC front—encompassing fans, players, media, and even the local Stasi office.[15] Following a derby defeat to BFC in 1977, two supporters of Union Berlin wrote to the DFV in outraged tones that would be familiar in the coming decade. One described referee Adolf Prokop's performance as "beyond the pale. . . . Sure, referees are only human . . . but this was something else." The other argued that such an officiating performance "endangers fair play, . . . not only on the pitch, but in the stands."[16]

BFC always had a bad reputation, but there was no correlation between its apparent status as the regime's favored team and its results until the late 1970s. Why, if the Stasi were so powerful, did Mielke wait so long to flex his muscles? If match officials always favored BFC, why did it bear fruit only after 1978? The archives have never yielded a document that mandated Stasi bribery of referees and linesmen. As one BFC fan put it, "There was no state decree that BFC had to win."[17]

A confluence of factors likely brought BFC to prominence. There was the decline of such rivals as FC Magdeburg, winners of the 1974 European Cup Winners' Cup, as well as the growing stranglehold of the Stasi on elite sport and the more general "psychological slavery" of officials toward top teams (a phenomenon hardly confined to the GDR).[18] BFC's excellent youth program was important, as was Mielke's annoyance at the success and popularity of Dynamo Dresden. No GDR club was the exact equivalent to Spartak Moscow, the people's team of the Soviet Union, but Dynamo Dresden—despite its ties to the GDR's police state—had the strongest case. Oberliga champions five times between 1971 and 1978, Dynamo Dresden was the GDR's best-supported side. In this period, the club drew an average attendance of 26,930 to the Rudolf Harbig Stadium, more than double the Oberliga average of 12,024.[19] The Dresden area was a black hole for Western media reception, known as the "valley of the clueless," a factor that restricted local access to, and interest in, West German football.[20] Dynamo, like Spartak Moscow, enjoyed a nationwide following, as fan mail from the 1970s and petitions from the 1980s both attest, though not everyone was sympathetic. As one Lokomotive Leipzig supporter later put it, "For me, Dynamo is pretty much Dynamo."[21] The Dresden club found support in all sectors of society, from children (including many girls) to pensioners, and from Vietnamese "guest workers" to prize-winning authors.[22] Dynamo Dresden's appealing "modern and attacking style of play,"[23] first displayed to a large international audience during the 7–6 aggregate loss to Bayern Munich in the European Cup in 1973, contributed to its popularity. Interesting parallels can be drawn here with another popular, technically adept police team from the Soviet Union, the Georgian side Dinamo Tbilisi, winners of the 1981 European Cup Winners' Cup.[24]

After a fractious encounter between BFC and Dynamo Dresden in 1978, Erich Mielke apparently walked into the Dresden dressing room and told the players, "You must understand, the capital city needs a champion."[25] The 1978–1979 season marked the first of ten consecutive seasons in which BFC won the league, an extended period of dominance that bored many of BFC's supporters and angered supporters of everyone else. After the 1–1 draw between BFC and Lokomotive Leipzig in March 1986, one petitioner—bemoaning the "farce" that GDR football had become—claimed that BFC's hegemony was unparalleled: "This has never happened in Albania or Malta, to say nothing of England, the Soviet Union, Czechoslovakia, Hungary, or Italy."[26] The claim was not entirely accurate. In the period when BFC swept all before them, Liverpool won the English league title eight times (1978–1990); and Sparta Prague, the Czechoslovakian championship on seven occasions (1984–1991). The GDR was certainly not the only place in Europe where one club's dominance encouraged public apathy, smaller crowds, and a lack of skilled play.[27]

Unhappy GDR football fans may not have recognized comparative cases, but they were certainly aware of another international element in the story: BFC's failure to replicate domestic preeminence in European competition. The club's record in UEFA's premier club tournament, the European Cup, was modest. BFC never got beyond the quarter finals and suffered several embarrassing early-round defeats during the 1980s. Domestic cakewalk and European failure went hand in hand. Media, fans, and players alike were conscious of this discrepancy. The final part of an anti-BFC poem distributed by FC Karl Marx Stadt supporters in 1988 spoke for many in asserting, "When the ref is just a neutral / Then BFC is merely second level / In the European Cup there are difficult times: / BFC weighed and deemed too light!"[28]

BFC's struggles looked worse because weaker GDR clubs fared better in Europe. Carl Zeiss Jena and Lokomotive Leipzig, for example, reached the final of the European Cup Winners' Cup in 1981 and 1987, respectively. Other Eastern Bloc clubs with powerful institutional support went one better. In 1986, the Romanian army team Steaua Bucharest defeated Barcelona to become the only team from behind the Iron Curtain to win the European Cup. Eleven years earlier, Dinamo Kiev, under the pioneering coaching of Valerii Lobanovskii, won the European Cup Winners' Cup and the UEFA Super Cup (defeating Bayern Munich) amid a run of six Soviet league titles in ten years. While Kiev enjoyed greater international success than BFC, its methods—stockpiling the best young players through Ministry of Interior contacts and employing the infamous "away" model, whereby Lobanovskii's teams only ever played for draws on the road—were equally unpopular. Yet the Soviet national team, like its GDR counterpart, failed to benefit from one-club dominance. As well, there were widespread rumors that Dinamo Kiev, like BFC, fixed matches by buying off referees.[29]

Crooked Champions: Anti-BFC Protests

The mid-1980s marked the peak of anti-BFC feeling. The club, as one fan proudly recalled, was "hated by everyone."[30] The groundswell of public opinion manifested itself in numerous ways. There was frank media discussion of the

BFC problem. Journalists privately lobbied the SED to take measures to change the public perception that BFC handpicked its referees and sportswriters.[31] Some of the sportswriters, one Stasi informant claimed in June 1985, preferred to feign illness than to report on BFC home games.[32]

BFC's machinations were given added spice by the increased spectator violence of the decade, an ugly phenomenon that transcended the Iron Curtain, stretching from England to the Soviet Union and taking in both halves of divided Germany.[33] In the 1985–1986 season, clashes with visiting supporters in and around BFC's ground in the Prenzlauer Berg district were routine. The Stasi reported, for example, "brutal" fighting and "serious disturbances" between BFC and Lok and Hansa Rostock fans at subway stations and at Alexanderplatz in the city center.[34] Violence was just the tip of the iceberg. At grounds across the republic, especially in the Saxon cities of Dresden and Leipzig, BFC players were booed while playing for the national team. Anti-BFC banners, such as "We welcome the GDR champions and their referee," were on frequent display.[35] Anti-BFC terrace chants were ubiquitous: "Every second person a spy"; "down with the cops' team"; and "Zyklon B for BFC."[36] In the Soviet Union, similar chants were directed against another unpopular police team, Dinamo Moscow.[37] In both cases, the relative freedom and anonymity of the stadium provided a space in which structures tied to state power could be criticized.

The anti-BFC debate was also advanced in a more private forum: the petition (*Eingabe*). Amid a paucity of democratic options, letters to state bodies offered one of the few means of complaining about life under Socialism. Football-related petitions of the 1980s covered subjects ranging from the national team's struggles to crumbling recreational facilities, but one topic outweighed all others. After Dynamo Dresden defeated BFC 3–2 in the 1985 cup final, the DFV received seven hundred letters of complaint about the referee's blatant if ultimately futile attempts to help the side from East Berlin.[38] The match against Lokomotive Leipzig the following March inspired a similar deluge. Though petitions arrived from all parts of the GDR and were written by people from various backgrounds (including workers, students, ex-referees, and party comrades), the voices raised most frequently and loudly in complaint came from Dresden.

Anti-BFC petitions combined blunt criticism with the ability to "speak socialist,"[39] a mode of address typical of communications to the authorities on all complaint-worthy subjects, from housing shortages to inedible oranges. A petition from the factory worker Günter D. in 1982 contained strong criticism of Communist institutions. The DFV and the media, he argued, enabled BFC's crooked dominance and ignored the hooligan behavior of BFC supporters. Additionally, there was ritualized rhetoric about the lack of "political-ideological education" among players and coaches. Three years later, the academic Alfred I., like Günter D. a Dresden resident, asked Erich Honecker for advice about how to placate young people at his college about "mistake-ridden, provocative refereeing performance(s)" in games involving BFC while hiding any personal interest in the issue behind the desire to see "clean sport" in the GDR.[40]

In 1986, an anonymous petition sent "in the name of thousands of chemical industry workers" from Halle lamented the enforced transfer to BFC of star striker Frank Pastor from local side Hallescher FC Chemie. The smaller club, it claimed, now played before "empty terraces": "people are watching only Western football; youths are putting on awful Western [football] shirts."[41] Such references to the lure of capitalist football highlight another important feature of the petitions: their awareness, and even exploitation, of football's international power. There were many ways in which the GDR belied its status as a closed society, from medical conferences and the Leipzig international trade fairs to popular music and cinema. Despite the apparent insularity of the Oberliga, football was central to this story of cultural exchange.[42]

Petitions repeatedly brought up BFC's struggles in the European Cup. An anonymous letter from 1985, for example, concluded that "we all know that [BFC] are a very good team and don't need the help of the men in black, the football association, etc. Quite the opposite—it only does BFC harm. The club is becoming ever more unpopular in the GDR and there's payback every time on the international stage. . . . Here you can't bring along 'your' referees and you have no possible influence at all."[43] Less frequently, but no less significantly, petitioners recycled the "rumor" that referees favored BFC to gain selection for matches abroad.[44] There was even talk of taking the problem beyond East German jurisdiction. One petitioner, rebuffed in his attempts to get BFC's 3–2 win at Rot-Weiß Erfurt in October 1985 overturned, threatened to write to UEFA and the Fédération Internationale de Football Association (FIFA) if nothing changed.[45]

In these dialogues with the state, football in the West served as a yardstick and a cautionary tale. After the 1985 cup final, the petitioner Alfred M. expressed relief that Dynamo Dresden beat BFC, despite the referee's efforts to the contrary. He suggested that the result forestalled a repeat of the Heysel disaster that had taken place ten days earlier, in which Liverpool fans charged and killed thirty-nine Juventus supporters at the European Cup final in Brussels. Alfred

M. then criticized BFC's players and officials for not publicly congratulating their opponents, contrasting this lack of sportsmanship with a recent game in England, at the end of which players from Liverpool and Manchester United left the field arm in arm.[46] Not unlike the Communist authorities—forever torn between opening up football to best practices from the West and sealing off the game from its inimical "capitalist" features such as hooliganism or professionalism—supporters used the international game as a flexible means of expressing dissatisfaction with domestic football.

"Small Revolution"? Responses to the BFC Controversy

After the 1985 GDR cup final, a mechanic from Bischofswerda wrote that the refereeing bias toward BFC had been so blatant that "even the party leadership must have seen it."[47] He was right. The state's responses to the BFC crisis undermined the image of the GDR sports system as a smoothly oiled machine in which unity and hierarchy were sacrosanct. BFC officials fiercely defended their corner, bewailing an orchestrated media campaign against the GDR champions, but powerful voices in the SED and the DFV now attempted to rein in BFC.

Complaints about institutional bias toward BFC were as old as the club itself, yet not until the mid-1980s was anything done about it. What caused this "small revolution"?[48] First, there was media coverage of BFC. Certain newspapers and journalists were reluctant to keep quiet about bad refereeing performances in BFC games. Additionally, many of the most egregious errors were seen by millions of television viewers. The second reason related to institutional changes in the DFV, most notably the appointment of Karl Zimmermann as general secretary in 1983. A Leipzig native, hostile to BFC's strong influence at the DFV's head office in East Berlin, Zimmermann wanted GDR football to clean up its image—and was supported in his endeavors by Politburo member Egon Krenz.[49] Third, there was, of all things, public opinion. The volume of anti-BFC protests had become so loud by the mid-1980s that it demanded an official response.

Under increased scrutiny, the DFV commissioned an extensive report on refereeing performances during the 1984–1985 season. The findings were clear. BFC accrued just sixteen yellow cards all season, but there were thirty-one for Lokomotive Leipzig and forty-five for Dynamo Dresden. Nine matches were identified as probable sites of crooked officiating. The report spoke of "targeted pressure" on referees and the press from BFC officials.[50] Video analysis of the 1985 cup final was equally damning. It showed that seventeen of the referee's sixty decisions were wrong, a very high ratio for an experienced, FIFA-accredited official. Fourteen of the seventeen errors benefited BFC.[51] Privately at least, the DFV came to the same conclusions as the ordinary spectator. There was clear favoritism toward BFC, and it was damaging GDR football.

As public anger and private evidence mounted, the authorities began a charm offensive. Petitioners received individual responses, sometimes delivered in person, from high-ranking party officials, including the head of the SED's department of sport, Rudi Hellmann. This was not a new approach. When Günter D. complained about the refereeing of a Dynamo Dresden–BFC match in 1982, he was welcomed to SED headquarters in Dresden and invited (along with interested colleagues) to watch a Dynamo training session.[52] Such efforts were stepped up in the mid-1980s. In reply, for example, to the outspoken Hans-Jürgen H., whose six-page missive from 1986 asserted his "damned right to watch honest sport," Hellmann conceded that "your basic position is completely justified."[53] Hellmann's response to another petition, sent by Alfred I. in 1985, was longer than the original communication and outlined detailed measures to quiet public unrest about BFC and the declining standard of GDR football.[54] This Socialist version of customer care emphasized the consequences for inept officiating. The referees who took charge, respectively, of the 1985 cup final and the March 1986 match between Lok and BFC (Manfred Roßner and Bernd Stumpf) were banned, as were the officials responsible for BFC's dubious 3–2 win at Rot-Weiß Erfurt five months earlier. The DFV's referee commission was overhauled too, as Heinz Einbeck and Gerhard Kunze (both BFC members) were sacked, with the former replaced at its head by the man who refereed the 1970 World Cup final, Rudi Glöckner.[55]

These were, it might be argued, cosmetic changes, far less extensive than those made in Bulgarian football after spectator and player violence at the 1985 cup final between Central Sports Club of the Army (CSKA) Sofia and Levski Sofia led to the disbanding of both teams.[56] BFC, after all, made it ten in a row, winning the league title again in the 1986–1987 and 1987–1988 seasons. The scapegoating of referees did not address the underlying causes of the scandal. This required an open reckoning with the secret police, whose network of informers included leading referees (such as Prokop and Stumpf), coaches, and players (including eighteen of the seventy-two first-teamers at Dynamo Dresden between 1978 and 1989).[57] Nobody in football could countenance this—nobody, that is, except the fans. Their role in challenging BFC's hegemony was extremely important. Public pressure forced the state to take action. Even if that action was limited, the inversion of the power dynamic (and the real shift in policy) points to football's role in articulating alternative voices and identities in a one-party dictatorship. It also illustrates an estrangement from SED rule that found much broader popular expression in the dramatic events of 1989.

Amid the back and forth between anti-BFC petitioners and the state, it was rare to encounter anyone who, like Ralf R., criticized media silence about bad refereeing against BFC.[58] Another interesting aspect of the story emerges here. Like Juventus fans in Italy, who tended to laugh off opposition chants of "you only know how to rob" (*sapete solo rubare*),[59] supporters of "FC Stasi" took a perverse delight in the club's unpopularity. A siege mentality emerged by the mid-1980s and found various outlets, from the development of a violent hooligan following to mockery of the more popular Union Berlin's lack of success and phony working-class identity. One BFC fan later claimed that accusations against the team "hardly bothered us."[60] Attendance figures, however, told a different story. BFC's string of triumphs drew supporters away from the stadium rather than into it. Between the first and last of BFC's ten straight titles (in the 1978–1979 and 1987–1988 seasons, respectively), the average home gate fell by more than 40 percent, from 14,923 to 8,792 spectators.[61] Such numbers suggest that BFC's dominance of GDR football, like the SED's dominance of East German society, rested on increasingly shaky foundations.

BFC and the End of the GDR

On November 8, 1989, BFC drew 0–0 at home to Stahl Eisenhüttenstadt. The result was in keeping with a recent decline in the club's fortunes. The run of ten straight league titles had ended in 1988, as Dynamo Dresden returned to the summit of GDR football. With a strong squad and young talent seemingly available on tap, nothing then suggested that BFC's decline would be terminal. Everything changed, though, the next day. On November 9, flustered Communist officials—faced with mass protests, an uncertain party leadership, and the momentum of events elsewhere—opened the Berlin Wall. By nightfall thousands of GDR citizens were joyously entering West Berlin. Egon Krenz, now interim leader, scrambled for position, using an unconvincing metaphor to remind Moscow of its responsibilities: "You know, in a game of football, when a free kick is awarded, a wall is formed in front of the goal. Free kicks are the results of fouls by the other team. Let us make sure together of fair play."[62] But Moscow was no longer listening.

BFC's collapse is a useful microcosm of the collapse of the GDR. A seemingly unassailable institution, outwardly successful despite widespread domestic grumbling, but always struggling for international credibility, was suddenly rendered powerless. Awaiting trial in 1992, a bemused Mielke asked, "How did it come about that we simply gave up our GDR, just like that?"[63] The events of 1989 revealed that the mighty resources at the disposal of the secret police, and its football team, were ultimately props on an empty stage, as shifting Soviet priorities and popular unrest destroyed the GDR and its lauded sports system. BFC's transformation from feared and despised GDR institution to football backwater appeared to happen almost overnight. Yet it was the protests earlier in the 1980s that first pulled the rug from beneath BFC's feet, creating a climate in which unaccountable authority was challenged and made accountable.

By the end of the 1989–1990 season, BFC—stripped of secret police support—had been renamed FC Berlin. Its star players led the cut-price exodus to the Bundesliga. Financial negligence effectively left the club bankrupt. In the final Oberliga season (1990–1991), the club finished eleventh, thereby failing to make the ranks of postunification professional football. Average home attendance was just 781, many of whom ("the lunatic majority" in Simon Kuper's words) were hooligans.[64] There was further to fall too, before the club reclaimed its original name in 1999 and began a modest revival. During the 2015–2016 season, BFC was to be found in the regional fourth tier of German football. Home matches at the Jahn Stadium in Prenzlauer Berg took place in front of crowds as small as 750. Less than thirty years earlier, the same club contested sold-out European Cup ties at the same venue against the likes of Liverpool, Roma, and Hamburg. For BFC and other leading East German clubs, international cultural exchange was paradoxically richer and more extensive during the years of Cold War division than it was in united Germany.

Fan power alone did not bring the GDR's serial champions to this reduced position, but the impact of the grievances of the 1980s in eroding BFC's seemingly impregnable position was significant. Using the limited powers of protest at their disposal, ordinary supporters drew attention to a blind spot in the GDR's sports system and in the process revealed that the Olympic gold medals were smoke and mirrors, masking sporting and political structures that were in decay. Caution must be exercised in regarding football under East German Communism as a means of hidden resistance. The sport's vast appeal, in the

GDR and elsewhere, lies in its unusual visibility, regularity, and unpredict-ability as a leisure pursuit—a flexible site of play and the consumption of play that allows people to escape from, as well as to engage with, politics. Yet, in appropriating the narratives and spaces of state-supported football culture for their own pleasurable ends, fans engaged in subversive acts that had political consequences. The anti-BFC protests of the 1980s offer compelling proof that Cold War sport, and Cold War football in particular, was anything but a "bread and circuses" distraction.

SPORTS, POLITICS, AND "WILD DOPING" IN THE EAST GERMAN SPORTING "MIRACLE"

Mike Dennis

Despite a small demographic pool of about seventeen million, the East German "David" scaled the heights of the Cold War sports ladder to rank alongside the "Goliaths" of international sport, the United States and the USSR, and to show a clean pair of heels to its West German "class enemy." How the East Germans managed to reach and then stay at the summit for almost two decades can be attributed to the intensity of inter-German rivalries at the epicenter of Europe's Cold War, the relentless sociopolitical instrumentalization of sport by the ruling Socialist Unity Party (SED), and an integrated scientific-technological support system, including a comprehensive state-inspired doping program. Given its political sensitivity and its crucial role as a means to combat the German Democratic Republic's (GDR's) legitimacy deficit, the doping program was classified as a state secret, and several thousand athletes, both minors and seniors, were put under close surveillance by the Ministry of State Security (Stasi). Despite the delivery of a "sports miracle" and the establishment of an elaborate doping "master plan" by the mid-1970s, the elite sports edifice was beset by intrinsic operational malfunctions and divergent group interests and rivalries.

The contestation underlying GDR sport is exemplified by "wild" doping in the clandestine pharmacological enhancement cabinets of the tightly knit institutional sports networks. This form of doping, narrowly defined, is characterized mainly by the exceeding of and disregard for officially prescribed norms on the level, frequency, and type of dosages administered to athletes. It should, however, be stressed that wild doping was not extraneous to but an integral element of the hothouse of East German high-performance sport. Beyond centralized top-flight sport unauthorized doping was widespread in semiautonomous sports such as bodybuilding and powerlifting. Wild doping in this sphere was regarded by officialdom as a threat to the state doping program because it increased the risk of exposure to the detriment of the GDR's public stance as an advocate of "clean" sport. The notion of wild doping also encompasses the development and widespread application of experimental steroid substances, notably STS 646 (mestanolone), which did not receive formal clearance from the appropriate medical bodies and posed potentially serious health risks to athletes. Such substances were even distributed to minors whose universal right to care should have placed them beyond this kind of abuse or what, in retrospect, Dr. Rainer Hartwich, a senior figure at the Jenapharm pharmaceutical concern, called a *Riesenschweinerei* (absolute scandal).[1]

Although evidence has emerged of extensive state-directed doping in Czechoslovakia, the Soviet Union, and some other Communist states during the Cold War, the GDR remains by far the most thoroughly researched and well-documented case. The Stasi archival materials constitute a rich treasure trove of primary sources ranging from state and party policy documents to records of controllers' meetings with informers. In investigating the various forms of wild doping, this chapter draws heavily on the files of Dr. Manfred Höppner, Dr. Lothar Kipke, and other informers intimately connected, whether as sports physicians, officials, or trainers, to their Stasi controllers. Other invaluable sources include the files of the SED, the Ministry of Health and other government bodies, and pharmaceutical companies. The trials of former GDR officials, doctors, and trainers, especially those held in Berlin from 1998 to 2000, have produced important legal documents and substantial primary material, which, together with Ines Geipel's diary of the trials as well as interviews with athletes, form a much-needed counter to the self-exculpatory recollections by Manfred Ewald and other members of the GDR doping hierarchy.[2]

Doping in East Germany was framed by international developments. International sports bodies in a series of disjointed administrative, scientific, and technical measures banned key substances for contravening sports ethics. The International Olympic Committee (IOC), the leading international sports organization, prohibited amphetamines in 1967, anabolic steroids in 1974, and testosterone in 1983. Three main periods can be identified in the evolution of doping in the GDR:[3] the 1960s, when amphetamines made up the main performance-enhancement substance with anabolic-androgenic steroids coming to the fore as the decade closed; from the 1970s into the early 1980s, when steroids, notably the anabolic-androgenic Oral-Turinabol (4-chlorodehydromethyltestosterone), were predominant; and a period of flux from about the mid-1980s, when the palette was more diverse as scientists were mobilized to develop other drugs and techniques, for example, human growth hormone and peptide hormones, in an increasingly desperate effort to protect the GDR's status as a sporting superpower. The doping of minors followed a slightly different trajectory from that of seniors. According to René Wiese,[4] a doping program started in earnest after the Munich Olympics, especially among young females and in early-maturity sports. The subsequent sharp rise in numbers took place in such an uncontrolled manner and a frenzy of experimentation that, at the beginning of the 1980s, planners incorporated youngsters into the centrally administered doping system while also extending doping to top performers in almost all sports in the Children's and Youth Sports Schools.

While the extent of wild doping and an individual athlete's level of drug consumption are difficult to assess with precision, the periodization of wild doping tends to follow the stimulant-steroid chronological pattern: the amphetamine phase coincided with widespread semiautonomous doping by organizations such as the powerful Dynamo and Vorwärts Army Sports Associations.[5] To bring order to this situation, a doping master plan was ratified by the Central High-Performance Sports Commission in October 1974 and implemented in the succeeding months. The centralization of doping was part of an ambitious overhaul of top-flight sport initiated by the Deutscher Turn- und Sportbund (DTSB; German Gymnastics and Sports Federation, the central mass organization for sport and home of the top civilian sports clubs) president Manfred Ewald in the late 1960s in accordance with SED sports policy goals and is frequently viewed as crucial to the development of an efficient medal factory. While the changes undoubtedly curtailed many autonomous activities and enabled the GDR to avoid embarrassing positive tests at international sports events, there is nevertheless considerable evidence to show that wild doping was by no means eradicated and that, in the third and final phase, from about the mid-1980s, unregulated doping became endemic when the elite sports system became entangled in what proved to be the terminal decline of the East German Communist system.

The House That Manfred Built: State Plan Theme 14.25

The clandestine state-directed doping program inaugurated in 1974–1975 was part of a major restructuring process that set criteria for a high-performance sports model toward which other countries, whether capitalist or Socialist, would move. With the GDR coming in from the diplomatic cold in the late 1960s and early 1970s, a process in which sport had been invaluable as a form of soft power in countering the Federal Republic of Germany's (FRG's) Hallstein Doctrine, success in the sporting arms race remained crucial to bolstering the state's international reputation and reducing its internal legitimacy deficit. To ensure global sporting success and to defeat the class enemy on its own territory at the 1972 Munich Olympics, top-flight sport in the GDR underwent a grand reconstruction between 1967 and 1975. This included the reconstitution of the High-Performance Sports Commission as the main decision-making body and the clinical division of elite sport into two tiers. Funding was ruthlessly diverted into the upper tier, comprising sports with the greatest medal-earning potential, such as swimming and track-and-field athletics. However, mass sport was severely disadvantaged despite regime propaganda on an alleged symbiosis of mass and elite sport. With the exploitation of youngsters so crucial, the three-tier pyramid for the identification and development of talent was refined and further systematized by the introduction of the complex Uniform Inspection and Selection System (Einheitliche Sichtung und Auswahl) in 1973. The goal was to ensure a supply of highly talented athletes for the twenty-five leading sports clubs via the Training Centers at the base of the pyramid and the Children's and Youth Sports Schools on the middle level. In the late 1980s, as many as sixty-five thousand to seventy-thousand youngsters were incorporated into this structure.

With the backing of SED leaders such as Erich Honecker, Central Committee secretary for security, political organs, and sport,[6] the driving force behind the elite sports model was the ambitious and autocratic Manfred Ewald. Appreciating the importance of the increase in anabolic-androgenic steroid use internationally and of the threat posed by tighter in-competition tests,[7] Ewald was anxious to develop a state doping program that would deliver on performance targets, combat club "egoism," and stop the unsystematic and excess dosages taken by athletes. By reining in organizations, in particular Dynamo and Vorwärts, with their own scientific expertise and systems, Ewald envisaged that the systematization of doping would act as a lever in his and the DTSB's ongoing struggle with their rivals for control over elite sport.[8] During the 1960s, the often bitter rivalry between clubs and associations had been a major factor in a veritable plague of wild doping as club officials, athletes, sports physicians, and coaches pursued a competitive advantage and the internal and external benefits from success in such a prestigious and well-funded sphere of society. Ewald had, however, to tread carefully in his dealings with the Dynamo Sports Association (SVD; Sportvereinigung Dynamo) because its chairman, Erich Mielke, was minister of state security and since 1971 a member of the SED Politburo. The SVD, the umbrella sports organization of the Stasi, the Ministry of the Interior, and the Customs Administration, had a large active membership and numerous elite sports clubs such as SC Dynamo Berlin.

A key top-secret planning document initiating the state doping program in 1974 refers to the widespread application of pharmaceutical means in the United States, France, the FRG, Great Britain, the USSR, and other European Socialist countries and concludes, not without an element of self-justification, that the GDR had little if any option but to continue and improve on its own use of "supportive means" (unterstützende Mittel).[9] This term frequently appears in official documents as a euphemism for anabolic-androgenic steroids and other doping substances. The reference to the GDR's fraternal allies is a reminder that sportive nationalism fueled not only clashes between ideological foes on either side of the Iron Curtain but also an acute rivalry between the GDR and its Soviet mentor. By 1974–1975, the state doping program had taken concrete form under the cover name of State Plan Theme (SPT) 14.25 of the Ministry of Technology, and an intricate web of SED and state institutions had been spun. Research and development were conducted by specialist groups in university departments, institutes of the Academy of Sciences, the Dynamo and the Vorwärts Sports Associations, and state-owned enterprises such as the Jenapharm pharmaceutical concern. The Research Institute for Physical Culture and Sport (FKS) in Leipzig, part of the State Secretariat for Physical Culture and Sport's empire and much coveted by Ewald, was the country's leading research center for performance-enhancing substances.

Extant data from research projects into anabolic-androgenic steroids and other substances and techniques as they came on stream, such as erythropoietin (EPO), human growth hormone, neuropeptides, and blood doping, are highly revealing in regard to their performance benefits and side effects.[10] Time and again, researchers emphasized that to achieve maximum results, performance enhancers had to be integrated into training programs with due regard for levels and timing of dosages as well as age and gender. Given the complexity of the research program, a special Research Group on Supportive Means (Forschungsgruppe unterstützende Mittel) under Manfred Höppner was set up to coordinate projects. It met regularly with a second important group established in 1975, the Working Group on Supportive Means (Arbeitsgruppe unterstützende Mittel), also under the direction of Höppner. The two groups were pivotal to the operation of the integrated state doping program, or what Brigitte Berendonk has aptly called the "Manhattan Project."[11]

The Working Group on Supportive Means oversaw the elaborate chain of substance distribution within the context of four-year plans formulated by the experienced triumvirate of Ewald, Höppner, and the FKS deputy head Alfons Lehnert. The trio's endorsement was also required for the annual plans regulating the application of substances to club athletes.[12] The guidelines on the administration of dosages were worked out in advance by the FKS and Höppner's Working Group on Supportive Means. Each sports federation's annual doping plan was agreed on in discussions between its trainers and doctors. With regard to the sports clubs directly under the wing of the DTSB—Dynamo and Vorwärts were sufficiently powerful to retain their own pharmacies and channels—the chain of drug distribution usually ran from Höppner's High-Performance Sport Department 2 at the Sports Medicine Service (SMD) in East Berlin via the fifteen SMD regional sports medical advisory offices and then on to the two hundred or so doctors of a specific section or discipline in the elite sports clubs. The next stage was for the doctor to hand over the substances to a club trainer according to the dosage prescribed in an athlete's individual training plan. Athletes were not to be informed about what they were receiving; the blue Oral-Turinabol tablets, for example, were mixed with safe supplements, often in drinks such as tea, and the mixtures described as vitamins.

The magnitude of the operation can be gauged by selected statistics: an estimated two thousand athletes, both seniors and juniors, were doped each year from about 1972 onward, and perhaps as many as ten thousand down to the collapse of the GDR; fifteen hundred to two thousand coaches, administrators, secretarial staff, top officials of the sports federations, sports scientists, doctors, and medical personnel in the SMD were directly engaged in the program;

perhaps as many as two million doses of anabolic-androgenic steroids were used annually as part of officially authorized guidelines; and about twenty thousand urine samples were tested each year by the Central Doping Control Laboratory in Kreischa.

The lab in Kreischa was crucial to the success of the doping program. Founded in 1977 as an organ of the SMD Central Institute, it was an IOC-accredited laboratory involved in international doping controls. Its head was Dr. Claus Clausnitzer, a Stasi informer, Inoffizieller Mitarbeiter für den besonderen Einsatz (IME) "Meschke," and a member of the five-man IOC Subcommission on Doping and Biochemistry. Clausnitzer and his colleagues at Kreischa were part of an extensive, top-secret operation to ensure that no GDR athlete tested positive while competing abroad, as had happened to the star shot putter Ilona Slupianek at the 1977 European Athletics Cup. Although the vast majority of the tests proved negative, when a positive test was confirmed or thought likely, the athlete was withdrawn from competition. Positive testing might indicate mistakes in the dosage levels or timing of their administration but also the likelihood of unregulated doping. Manfred Höppner addressed this issue in 1986 when testing had revealed widespread wild doping. The trainer of javelin throwers at the SC Einheit Dresden had administered three and six times above the agreed dosages. Höppner was also highly critical of the many trainers who administered anabolic-androgenic steroids recklessly and sometimes in "uncontrolled dosages" in the belief that the requisite training could be neglected.[13]

Inevitably, given the social and political significance of elite sport, the Stasi cast a long shadow over the doping program. The monitoring of the sport behemoth was carried out primarily by Main Department XX's special section for sport, whose full-time staff was responsible for steering more than three thousand unofficial informers (IM; Inoffizielle Mitarbeiter) in elite sport in any given year during the 1970s and 1980s. Among the major institutions monitored by the Stasi were the FKS, the Kreischa laboratory, the Children's and Youth Sports Schools, and the top sports clubs. Probably the most important informer in sport and the ministry's biggest eyes and ears was the ubiquitous IMV/IMB (Inoffizieller Mitarbeiter mit vertraulichen Beziehungen zu im Vorgang bearbeiteten Personen/Inoffizieller Mitarbeiter der Abwehr mit Feindverbindung bzw. zur unmittelbaren Bearbeitung im Verdacht der Feindtätigkeit stehender Personen) "Technik," the cover name for Manfred Höppner, who as a long-serving member of the International Amateur Athletic Federation Medical Committee kept watch on the development of new tests for drugs that might threaten the GDR doping program. Among his many offices were head of the SMD High-Performance Sport Department 2, deputy director of the SMD (1967–1990), medical officer to the GDR Athletics Federation (1964–1977), and leader of the two working groups set up as part of SPT 14.25 for the coordination of research and drug distribution. Consequently, his multivolume Stasi file contains invaluable information on a wide range of topics, for example, the chain of drug distribution and the numbers and some of the names of athletes and trainers involved in the doping program. As an architect and guardian of the doping guidelines, his reports to his controller are essential sources for uncovering evidence of wild doping and the attendant health risks.

An Epidemic of Wild Doping

By the mid-1970s, a highly regulated state-sponsored doping program was in place that, together with the reforms of the late 1960s, was a major factor in the GDR's sporting preeminence. Ewald and Höppner's monolith was, however, by no means as sound a construct as they intended, as can be seen in the persistence of the many internal tensions and rivalries that had been endemic before the organizational restructuring. While rivalries abounded both between and within organizations over the fruits of success and status, a collective interest in the maintenance of the GDR state ensured that disagreements did not spill over into a rejection of the Socialist system per se but rather over its operation. The long-standing and fierce rivalry between the two largest sports associations, Dynamo and Vorwärts—and, of course, for sporting glory with clubs under the DTSB wing—manifested itself in competition for talented athletes, trainers, and medical expertise. Victories in national and international contests would, it was envisaged, help boost the prestige and influence of the associations. Dynamo itself was plagued by internal conflicts, many of them rooted in club egoism and regional and local sensibilities to interference in their domain by central SVD officials and clubs based in the capital. In 1965, for example, the football supporters and officials of SG Dynamo Schwerin and local SED politicians protested bitterly and successfully against the aspiration of SC Dynamo Berlin—Mielke's favorite club—to exercise its right to draw on talented players from the provincial team.[14]

Football was one of several sports where the intensity of competition led to unregulated doping on a widespread scale. Although doping was officially sanctioned for the national football team, it was banned in the domestic league, partly for security reasons.[15] Doping among East German football clubs can be attributed to the prestige accruing from success in a sport with an extensive popular base and strong roots in the community. Even local and regional SED bodies, as in Dresden, were more than willing to countenance pharmaceutical means to outstrip rival clubs and regions. It is ironic that the SVD's own leading clubs, Dynamo Berlin and Dynamo Dresden, resorted to the illicit practices that the Stasi was entrusted to combat as part of its mission to safeguard GDR sport.

Höppner's observation to his Stasi controller in 1984 that all top football clubs engaged in unauthorized doping has been confirmed by research detailing the use of amphetamines, psycho-stimulants, and anabolic steroids since the mid-1960s. When measures were initiated by Ewald in 1985 to bring wild doping under control throughout the top division (Oberliga), two Union Berlin players tested positive for the anabolic steroid Depot-Turinabol despite advanced warning to Union and other clubs. The checks revealed not only that wild doping occurred at top clubs such as Dynamo Dresden, Dynamo Berlin, Magdeburg, Carl Zeiss Jena, and Lokomotive Leipzig but that it was also common on lower levels of the footballing ladder. The Jena club, generously supported by the local Carl Zeiss optics conglomerate, took advantage of its networks to establish illicit doping schemes in the 1970s and 1980s. The club's national team representatives returned to Jena with information on drugs such as amphetamines; moreover, the club had access to the Oral-Turinabol tablets that were produced by the local Jenapharm pharmaceutical enterprise and also distributed to elite members of SC Motor Jena and other sports clubs.[16]

While football is perhaps the most visible arena in which conflicts regularly played out, rivalry also spread across track-and-field athletics and many other sports. In regard to track and field, the 1986 dissertation of Hartmut Riedel, the medical officer of the Athletics Federation, provides invaluable insight into serious excess in several athletics disciplines. Although he advised that the annual level of Oral-Turinabol should not exceed 1,500 milligrams (mg) for males and 1,000 mg for women, two of his own long jumpers, Uwe Lange and Frank Pasheck, recorded dosages of 2,453 mg in 1982–1983 and 2,145 mg in 1980, respectively.[17] The problem was even more disturbing in the heavy-throwing disciplines and the shot. Throwers topped the list of all androgenized female track-and-field athletes in the 1980s, registering staggeringly high annual dosages: for example, the shot putter Ines Müller Reichenbach, 3,680 mg; and the discus thrower Irina Meszynski, 3,190 mg.[18]

Swimming was another sport in which the GDR excelled, most spectacularly when the women's swimming team, mainly consisting of juniors, won fifteen of sixteen golds at the 1976 Montreal Olympic Games. The Swimming Federation's physician Dr. Rolf Kipke was a particularly aggressive doper, criticized by Höppner for the brutality of his injections without due care for his charges, who were deceived into believing they were receiving vitamins.[19] Kipke, himself one of the Stasi's most informative sources (IM "Rolf"), was a member of the FKS Research Group on Additional Performance Reserves and also sat on the International Swimming Federation's Medical Commission. As training could not, in his view, secure the vital performance edge, it had to be combined with anabolic-androgenic steroids despite a "certain risk." Body changes among girls were not necessarily permanent, and while voice changes could not be removed completely, they could, or so he reasoned, at least be ameliorated.[20] Other physicians and trainers were also egregious dopers of minors, such as the SC Dynamo and national swimming trainer Rolf Gläser and the SC Dynamo physician Dr. Dieter Binus, who both administered dosages in excess of prescribed levels.[21] The side effects exhibited by youngsters as a result of injections with testosterone persuaded another leading SVD sports physician, Dr. Bernd Pansold, that they might originate in a disregard for official guidelines by clubs, such as those in Karl-Marx-Stadt and Dresden. He attributed most of the blame to the club sports sections, especially trainers who put enormous pressure on their athletes to use supportive means, a practice that some sports physicians likened to a criminal offense.[22]

Höppner was most alarmed by negative reactions to the Montreal Olympics, both at home and abroad, regarding the deep voices and profusion of body hair of East German swimmers and other competitors, the result of being administered anabolic-androgenic steroids. He shared Pansold's concerns about the pressures on athletes by clubs, such as the Berlin Gymnastics and Sport Club, either to conform or to leave top-level sport. One answer, as he suggested to his Stasi controller, was for female athletes in particular to be kept off steroids for at least two years until their bodies had "normalized."[23] Höppner raised this issue at a meeting with Ewald, Professor Edelfried Buggel, the deputy state secretary for Physical Culture and Sport, and other high-ranking officials. When he pointed out that outstanding results required the use of anabolic-androgenic steroids, especially among young female swimmers, Ewald, unusually for him, kept silent. Buggel could only counter weakly that "it is problematic." Ewald did, however, respond with his usual abrasiveness when Höppner sought assistance with the media in ensuring that female athletes with pronounced voice changes should be kept in the background during interviews. Why, Ewald asked, should they be held back when Höppner himself had given them anabolic-androgenic steroids? Höppner could only reiterate that no easy solution was possible while performance targets remained so demanding and material stimuli for trainers and athletes encouraged the maximum application of supportive means.[24]

Höppner similarly made no headway when, at the national training camp in Kienbaum in 1976, he expressed concern for young swimmers who were kept in the dark about substance application. Ewald and Rudi Hellmann, head of the SED Central Committee Department of Sport, countered that because of their age, they did not need to know.[25] More than ten years later, the situation had changed little, as is apparent from a statement by Michael Regner after the collapse of the GDR. A former swimming trainer at ASK Vorwärts Potsdam, Regner admitted that he had supplied Oral-Turinabol tablets to teenage girls as part of a program of doping and out of conviction that such substances were absolutely necessary to outdistance the hostile West. He did, however, profess alarm that trainers had administered excessively high levels of drugs and STS 646 to youngsters.[26] STS 646 was one of several experimental steroids; others included STS 482, STS 648, and Substance XII, which scientists at Jenapharm, the Central Institute for Microbiology and Experimental Therapy, and the FKS had been developing since the late 1970s to find less harmful and more powerful performance enhancers than Oral-Turinabol.[27]

While STS 646 became the main anabolic-androgenic agent during the 1980s, its use can be classified as a form of wild doping not only because dosages sometimes exceeded prescribed levels but also because it was never formally approved by the appropriate medical and health authorities, such as the Institute for Drug Use, for application in top-flight sport. As late as January 1988, at a meeting of SMD, FKS, Jenapharm, and government representatives, when Höppner queried why STS 646 had yet to be authorized and explained that he was being put in a difficult position by athletes basing their case for a pension in relation to this drug, discussion was cut short by Buggel: "Work on the substance should proceed as planned."[28] His blunt intervention underscores the primacy of politics over ethics.

Weightlifting was another sport notorious for the doping of minors and for excessive levels of doping with steroids. The chief medical officer of the GDR Weightlifting Federation, Hans-Henning Lathan, was one of the country's most experienced doping researchers, a member of the FKS Research Group on Additional Reserves, a GDR representative on the Medical Commission of the International Weightlifting Federation, and a Stasi informer (IMS, Inoffizieller Mitarbeiter für Sicherheit; "Klaus Müller").[29] His reports to his Stasi controller are a mine of information on the distribution of drugs and their side effects, the doping of young weightlifters, and unregulated doping. He was an avid proponent of doping young weightlifters with anabolic-androgenic steroids in which, according to Lathan and a coresearcher Dr. Ulrich Kämpfe, the Soviet Union and Bulgaria had, as pioneers, seized an early advantage. In preparation for the 1984 Olympics, the two conducted research into the impact of Oral-Turinabol on the physical and sporting development of young weightlifters, among them forty with an average age of fifteen years from four top Children's and Youth Sports Schools.[30]

One tragic case of overdosing concerns Gerd Bonk, the Karl-Marx-Stadt Sports Club super heavyweight lifter, world-record holder, and winner of Olympic bronze in 1972 and silver in 1976. In 1979, he took 12,775 mg of steroids, especially Oral-Turinabol; even when he was later diagnosed with diabetes, he was still administered harmful substances such as hCG (human chorionic gonadotropin) and Depo-Testosterone injections in preparation for the 1980 Moscow Olympics. As a result of two urine tests by the Kreischa laboratory, he was withdrawn from the squad because he was regarded as a security risk and would therefore place Ewald, in the latter's opinion, in the hands of the Soviet sports leadership.[31] After the end of his active career, Bonk was diagnosed with serious organ damage, collapsed kidneys, diabetes, and other illnesses. While Bonk was top of the GDR weightlifting doping pyramid, many others were close behind—such as Mantek, Heuser, Käks—and were taking Oral-Turinabol, hCG, Depo-Testosterone, testosterone propionate, and Clomiphene. Paradoxically, Lathan sought to curb already high dosage levels by carrying out urine and other tests outside the official doping control system.[32]

The situation was little better in *Körperkulturistik*, a term covering sports such as bodybuilding and powerlifting, which were frowned on by officialdom, partly because such terms had capitalist connotations and partly because they enjoyed a high level of contested autonomy from overarching bodies like the DTSB. By 1990, about fourteen thousand practitioners were involved in bodybuilding, powerlifting, and fitness sports. Andreas Müller has shown that wild doping was the norm, with heavy dosages of anabolic-androgenic steroids, especially Oral-Turinabol, commonplace in bodybuilding since the 1970s and accelerating during the 1980s as both males and females strove to cope with onerous training regimes.[33] As bodybuilders made no secret of their use of steroids and were not under medical supervision, they represented a threat to the GDR's international reputation and to their own health. In 1980, Lathan informed his controller of the prevalence of totally unregulated anabolic doping in the world of *Körperkulturistik* and said that it was widely believed that two athletes had died as a result of taking too many pills.[34] By the early to mid-1980s, growing concern in strength sports circles over the health risks and the spread of doping among youngsters, together with the authorities' fears of the leakage of information, led to the introduction of some doping controls in competitive sport. The measures made little impact, as they were ill conceived, even failing to clarify which substances were to be banned.

That doping was practiced openly in strength sports is indicative of the difficulties faced by the authorities in keeping the lid on the Pandora's box of doping secrets despite the many elaborate security measures permeating the elite sports sector. Although minors could be kept in the dark because of their lack of maturity and dependence on their coaches and teachers, many older performers might not have asked sufficiently critical questions and, in some cases, were willing to cooperate with trainers and sport physicians in doping practices. Their actions can partly be explained by the political and social pressures underpinning GDR elite sport, as well as by the personal drive to outperform rivals both at home and abroad and by the status enhancement and the material rewards obtainable in such a well-funded area of society. It should, however, be stressed that athletes' level of awareness of doping cannot be gauged with exactitude, and probably only a minority of experienced performers, especially those with a scientific background, had an insight into the benefits and the appreciable risks of performance-enhancing substances.[35]

GDR Perceptions of Doping and Sports Ethics: Medals Before Morals?

The many risks associated with doping were a matter of great concern to some GDR scientists. For example, harm to young athletes is an issue frequently raised at meetings between Stasi controllers and numerous informers with a scientific background. Dr. Kurt Franke (IM "Philatelist"), an expert in sports medicine and surgery at the Surgical Clinic of the Berlin-Pankow Hospital, warned on various occasions against doping young children because the re-

sultant overload could damage connective and supportive tissue, with serious consequences for the spinal column and knee joints.[36] Franke's strictures
underline the acute anxiety among many East German sports physicians over
the high risks of doping in elite sport, especially of youngsters and females
with anabolic-androgenic steroids, a deep-rooted problem that could be significantly exacerbated by widespread wild doping. They attributed the excessive
use of steroids and the disregard for ethical issues to the fierce rivalry between
trainers in the pursuit of financial rewards and success for their charges.[37]

While sports scientists might express serious misgivings to their Stasi controllers, many remained central to research projects and to the administration of drugs, whether at the Dynamo Sports Association, Jenapharm, or the
FKS. The Dynamo sports physician and Stasi informer Dr. Bernd Pansold (IM
"Jürgen Wendt") emphasized the dangers of virilization and the possibility of
grave long-term effects, such as liver damage and prostate cancer, if appropriate
dosages were not observed and regular health checks not carried out.[38] In 1977,
he even informed his controller that ethical problems were greater in Socialism
than in capitalism and that victory at any price by females and in swimming
might ultimately have a detrimental effect.[39] Despite his many reservations,
he remained pivotal to the doping program at Dynamo and continued as a
member of Höppner's Working Group on Supportive Means. In 1998, he was
found guilty of being an accessory to the bodily harm of minors, some aged
thirteen to sixteen years, between 1975 and 1984.

The questioning of the doping program reached the higher echelons of
the sports system in the person of Professor Hans Schuster, the rector of the
German College for Physical Culture in Leipzig (1965–1967), director of the FKS
(1969–1990), and a longtime Stasi informer. In several internal papers between
1975 and 1985, including one submitted to Mielke in 1976, the depth of Schuster's
concern over doping in general and the androgenization of young females,
especially in swimming and athletics, persuaded him of the need for a long-
term alternative appropriate to the GDR's resource base even though this would
entail a fall in the country's world ranking.[40] Schuster's position is not free from
hypocrisy, as he had urged Mielke as early as 1964 that hormone doping, notably
with testosterone, should be implemented in the Dynamo Sports Association.
Among Schuster's other misgivings were the illegality of STS 646, unregulated
doping, the possibility of addiction, and the increased risk of injury to young
males from overloading in training. Ewald in particular came under fire for
what Schuster deplored as his "pathological ambition." The angst among sports

scientists over the abuse of supportive means questions the argument that the GDR showed "at least some concern for the minimization of risk" by permitting, under medical supervision, only drugs from official sources.[41] Ewald, Buggel, and many other sports officials, as well as high-ranking Politburo members like Erich Mielke, regarded risks as very much secondary to results and pressured doubters into silence.

How the scientific community might rationalize the continuation of doping emerges from a 1979 tract by Professor Siegfried Israel.[42] A specialist in internal medicine, Israel held posts at the FKS and Kreischa and was also the GDR cycling team doctor at several Olympics and World Championships in the 1960s. While recognizing that overdosing was widespread and undertaken without sufficient regard for side effects as a result of the ambition of trainers, physicians, officials, and athletes, Israel defended biological supportive means as part of the inexorable development of scientific-technical progress. Flaying "antiquated Coubertinism" and the "performance defeatism" of sports doctors, he advocated the replacement of the Hippocratic Oath by a new understanding of the doctor's profession in which the treatment of illness is expanded to a more effective combination of the interests of the individual and society. In the bipolar world of the Cold War in which meaningful sporting activity is not value free, Israel contrasted the aggressive application of doping in capitalism with the compatibility of the medical activity of doctors—including the use of anabolic steroids—with their social mission in the supposedly morally superior socioeconomic order of Socialism.

Cold War and Beyond

While Israel's criticism of aggressive doping in capitalism is entrenched in Cold War rhetoric, his advocacy of biological doping is located within a general cultural context that embraces the application of science and technology to society and sport for the enhancement of pleasure, health, economic activity, and sporting prowess. The application is not, of course, free from ambivalence and contradictions, giving rise to fundamental questions about what is "artificial" and what is "natural" and, linked to sport's constant striving for *citius, altius, fortius*, challenges existing legal and moral codes and poses risks to the health of athletes. While the GDR was particularly ruthless in striving to reach the summit of global sport, its recourse to doping was by no means unique. Recent studies have revealed that, while not on the same scale as that of the GDR, doping in West Germany was more widespread and systematic than originally thought—or admitted—and that from the early 1970s bodies such as the Ministry of the Interior were increasingly active in the promotion of elite sport and in funding research projects into the use of testosterone and anabolic-androgenic steroids.[43] East German centralization and advanced scientific application notwithstanding, the prevalence of wild doping shows that the Manhattan Project was not the orderly mechanism often associated with the Communist dictatorship. Even in the ten years that SPT 14.25 was implemented with the utmost rigor, the elaborate regulations concerning the administration of drug dosage were frequently infringed in the pursuit of myriad internal and external rewards, and wild doping remained pervasive in the niches of powerlifting and bodybuilding. Moreover, political imperatives, a seeming addiction to the use of performance-enhancing substances, and an increasingly competitive global sports environment led to the widespread application of experimental steroid substances such as STS 646 and to the universal doping of minors after the Munich Olympics, perhaps the bleakest chapter in the whole doping story.

The relative ease with which the GDR circumvented international doping controls highlights the countless intractable problems in the implementation of any antidoping policy, global or national. Even the GDR's own elaborate internal monitoring, including surveillance by the Stasi, was far from successful in preventing the violation of official guidelines as individuals and groups pursued status and material rewards in such a highly prestigious and hard-nosed sector as elite sport. Indeed, the often bitter rivalries and jealousies among top sports doctors in the Dynamo Sports Association were referred to in a Stasi report as a *Kleinkrieg*.[44] It is also extremely disconcerting that sports physicians and officials knowingly put the health of their charges at risk, a phenomenon that indicates that an international antidoping policy founded not in ethical codification but rather on the health of the athlete is at worst a chimera and at best a costly struggle with an uncertain outcome.[45] In short, given the political kudos attached to elite sport both during and after the Cold War, as is apparent from the recent tribulations of the World Anti-Doping Agency (WADA) over state doping in Russia and elsewhere, GDR political and sports leaders are not unique in instrumentalizing risk-inherent pharmaceutical and technological means to create fragile "mortal engines." GDR experience, however, is also a reminder that even the highly elaborate surveillance of top-level sport failed

to curb widespread wild doping and that the social and political benefits of
the "sports miracle" would prove totally inadequate in stemming the tide of
popular unrest that subverted the foundations of SED hegemony. Indeed, in
the year after the GDR finished an impressive second to the USSR at the 1988
Seoul Olympics, the fall of the Berlin Wall presaged the collapse of the East
German Communist state and the end of the Cold War.

9

"THE MOST BEAUTIFUL FACE OF SOCIALISM"

Katarina Witt and the Sexual Politics of Sport in the Cold War

Annette F. Timm

No one really seems to know who first called East German figure skater Katarina Witt "the most beautiful face of Socialism." The quote is usually attributed to *Time* magazine, though it also circulated in East Germany—in a form ("Socialism with a beautiful face") that made it a cynical play on Alexander Dubček's famous description of the Prague Spring: "socialism with a human face."[1] Yet the phrase's anonymity lends it more power, and its constant repetition in both the German and English press testifies to an obsessive fascination with the impact of Katarina Witt's attractive face and shapely form on her success as an athlete. Since many commentators on her fame seem to forget this, let me begin by underlining her athletic accomplishments. She remains only the second female figure skater after Sonja Henie to repeat a gold-medal victory at the Olympics. Henie won three gold medals—Witt won two: first in Sarajevo in 1984 and again in Calgary in 1988. Witt also won four World Figure Skating Championships between 1984 and 1988 (placing second in 1982 and 1986), and she was European champion every year between 1983 and 1988 (tying with Henie's six consecutive titles).

This success was no accident. She was a voluntary and successful pupil of the East German program for developing elite athletes. She began to skate at age five, entering the Kinder- und Jugendsportschule (Children and Youth Sport School) in Karl-Marx Stadt (now Chemnitz) at the age of eight, and she completed her first triple jump at age eleven.[2] At least up until 1987 and 1988, when she started to face challenges from Debi Thomas, Elizabeth Manley, Caryn

Kadavy, and Midori Ito, Witt's winning performances were generally the most technically difficult programs on the ice. Clearly, she was one of the most focused and successful athletes of her day, so it is striking that her enduring legacy has been the various sexualized labels attached to her—"glamour girl of the GDR," "the red princess," "the Brooke Shields of Sarajevo," or the "Hollywood-ready . . . system-crossing symbol of lust."[3] On the surface, this is not surprising to anyone who remembers her costumes and the conscious effort that her trainer, Jutta Müller, clearly made to heighten Witt's already substantial sexual allure through less-than-demure cutouts and the careful placement of feathers and sequins. Figure skating in general has had its fair share of controversies surrounding attention to the appearance of athletes who must look graceful as they are performing gravity-defying and extremely technical maneuvers on the ice. This is a made-for-TV sport story if ever there was one, and Witt attracted the kind of media attention that only a combination of photogenetic qualities and athletic tensions could create. From drab, gray Communism, wrote Rick Reilly in *Sports Illustrated* in 1986, comes an athlete "so fresh-faced, so blue-eyed, so ruby-lipped, so 12-car-pileup gorgeous, she makes a lousy enemy of capitalism. Forget Raisa Gorbachev; here's Katarina, 5′5″ and 114 pounds worth of peacekeeping missile."[4]

But this focus on the superficial reasons for Witt's fame can easily obscure much more interesting aspects of her role as the pretty ambassador of Communism during the Cold War. Underneath the crass sexualization and Iron Curtain symbolism that so fascinated the English-speaking press, Witt's role as the Socialist darling—she was almost always referred to by her nickname, "Kati"—tells us something more important about the role of sport and sex in the Cold War. I begin by investigating the surface layer—how beauty and sex appeal supposedly turned Cold War rhetoric on its head. But I ultimately argue that we cannot quite understand Kati Witt's story if we stick to the comfortable trope of the conflict between femininity and athletic prowess or if we remain fixated on the thesis that capitalism wins because sex sells. Probing beneath this surface, we find that the regime's deployment of Witt as a Socialist symbol had links to broader aspects of sexual culture in the German Democratic Republic (GDR), and it played—in ways likely unconscious and unintentional on the part of her handlers—on subterranean Western imagery of totalitarian female sexuality.

From the beginning of her athletic success on the international stage, Witt seemed to represent the precise opposite of what had up to this point become the image of East German female sport. Particularly after the 1976 Montreal

Summer Olympics (where the swimmers alone earned eleven gold medals, six silver, and one bronze), the enormous success of East German athletes came with an asterisk. GDR swimming coach Rolf Gläser's insistence that "the girls are supposed to swim not sing" could not quell international suspicions that the muscle mass and deep voices of the female swimmers were products of more than just advanced training techniques and that banned substances had been used.[5] Similar suspicions of doping followed female speed skaters and track athletes. In this context, Witt's appearance on the international stage presented East German sports officials with an opportunity to revise the impression that only masculine women could be successful in GDR sport. It helpfully counteracted the dour image of masculinized female East German athletes.

One context for these conscious attempts to use sport as national propaganda for the GDR was the growing importance of television in the marketing of international sporting events. As Christopher Young argues, to understand the importance of sports culture in Europe in the 1980s and 1990s, we have to explore how satellite television transmissions transformed the relationship between states, markets, and media not only in the capitalist West but also in Communist countries.[6] By the end of the 1980s, more than forty satellite television services had become available in Europe, which dramatically curtailed the monopolies of individual national broadcasters but also sparked a worldwide interest in international sporting events, which were now much easier to broadcast live.[7] Of all the Eastern Bloc countries, this new technological situation affected the GDR most directly, because there were no linguistic barriers to access when Western transmitters were quite deliberately positioned on the German-German border.[8] Having long seen themselves in direct competition with West German TV, particularly in the field of sports coverage, administrators at the Deutscher Fernsehfunk (DFF), the official East German state broadcaster, initially believed that they would benefit from the fact that after 1964 in Tokyo, Olympic and world championship events could rely on direct satellite feeds.[9] Enormous efforts were made to compete with the West to cover the Olympics, and East German coverage of the 1968 games in Grenoble was ranked even higher than West German coverage by the viewers of Germany's largest public broadcasting channel, the Arbeitsgemeinschaft der öffentlich-rechtlichen Rundfunkanstalten der Bundesrepublik Deutschland (ARD).[10] However, with the emergence of the dual (public/private) broadcasting system in the Federal Republic in 1984 (after a 1981 decision of the Federal Constitutional Court to allow it), East German television officials realized that they were unlikely to be able to compete with this suddenly more diverse competition from the West.[11] This capitulation in terms of overall coverage of events like the Olympics made individual athletes all the more symbolically important, and those who won medals were elevated to star status. As Lothar Mikos has argued, Witt performed a central role in this noncommercial star system, and by the late 1980s, she was regularly featured in television documentaries that glamorized her family life and her relationship with her trainer, Jutta Müller, in ways that directly aped Western sports coverage.[12]

Witt was very self-aware about how her international fame might influence GDR citizens, and she was a willing participant in the glamorization of her image for political purposes. In a speech to the Eleventh Congress of the Free German Trade Union Federation in April 1987, having just returned from her gold-medal performance at the Worlds in Cincinnati, she addressed the phenomenon of her paradoxical stardom in the capitalist West:

> I have been asked many times how it was that my appearance at Worlds and the subsequent exhibition skating tour led to what journalists called the "stage tour of cheers [*Etappentour des Jubels*] through America." This is perhaps not so normal for a GDR citizen in the mainland of imperialism, after all. I have been reflecting about this for a long time and often spoke about it with my trainer and adviser Jutta Müller. . . . We arrived at the conviction that effort [*Leistung*] paired with the self-conscious but also openhearted demeanor that we all possess will in the end receive recognition in the whole world. During the Worlds and the exhibition skating tour, and particularly on television, Americans learned about the existence of our Socialist homeland. . . . Through the politics of our party and our government, the German Democratic Republic has made a name for itself across the globe as a state of peace where the Olympic idea has a home. It is my great luck to live in this country, my Socialist fatherland.[13]

There is little doubt that this speech would have been influenced or even written by Witt's political handlers. Nevertheless, this quite self-consciously articulated pairing of support for Socialism with an appreciation of how her own attractive appearance and "openhearted demeanor" were at least partly responsible for her fame displays Witt's understanding of the role that her image was playing for the SED (the Socialist Unity Party of the GDR). She quite willingly served as an advertisement for her country and hoped that her success would convince Americans to look more favorably on a nation about which they knew so little.

That even the SED was aware of the propaganda power of Witt's sex appeal is demonstrated by the fact that the party's Central Committee gathered and commented on international press reports on the subject, such as a February 1988 article about Witt in the *Christian Science Monitor*. A party memo on this quotes the article's description of Witt's "phenomenal beauty" and its argument that the skater's devotion to Socialism was single-handedly defeating the rumors about drug programs out to create East German *Supermenschen* (super people).[14] As Witt pointed out in a 2013 interview with the German newsmagazine *Der Spiegel*, the importance of her sexy media image was also recognized by trainer Jutta Müller, who was responsible for the skater's costumes and hairstyles and who was allowed to travel to West Berlin just to buy fabric. "We always had the feeling: there have to be more feathers, more rhinestones; it has to be more colorful; most important, there just has to be more, just so that we even have a chance against the Americans, the West Germans, and the Canadians, since this is exactly what they thought we couldn't do. We in the GDR were in an underdog situation; this really spurred us on."[15] It is thus no accident that Witt's costumes always pushed the boundaries of propriety.

In March 1988, Müller was forced to add some extra feathers to cover up the high-cut leg holes of Witt's short-program dress at the World Figure Skating Championships in Hungary after Canadian skater Elizabeth Manley's coach, Peter Dunfield, complained that she was "exploiting" herself: "We're here to skate in a dress, not a G-string."[16] This prompted what became known as the International Skating Union's "Katarina rule," which allowed skaters to wear only skirts "covering the hips and posterior."[17] While feminist sport scholars have often and quite justifiably lamented the sexualization of female athletes,[18] there can be little doubt that Witt's sex-symbol status was consciously created, that it was not solely motivated by economic interests, and that she willingly participated in juxtaposing her obvious athletic talent with her feminine allure. Having said this, the complaints against her were also calculated to influence the competition. It was often other coaches who complained that her victories came partly as a reward for her looks instead of her talent.[19]

Both the archival evidence and Witt's own self-aware reflections make it clear that both she and her handlers focused on her appearance as a politically symbolic weapon. "We of course had this ambition," she told the *Spiegel* reporter, "coming out of this small, gray, supposedly joyless country to show that there was also a zest for life [*Lebenslust*] where we came from."[20] In her memoir, Witt notes that she chose Georges Bizet's *Carmen* for her gold-medal long-program performance at the 1988 Calgary Olympics because she knew that she "had the right body language" to interpret this "spirited music from Spain." "Passion, pain, mourning, and the erotic—I can convincingly convey these things on the ice. And then there is the story of Carmen, the woman between two men, a subject that interested me, that I can comprehend and understand."[21] Witt's coy allusion to how her own romantic involvement with two men provided her with the insight to intensify her artistic performance leaves little doubt that she saw her sexual attractiveness as an advantage. She also viewed the controversies about her skating costumes as part of the competition, countering the charge that she was the one playing directly to the seven male judges at Calgary with the observation that Debi Thomas's black bodysuit, with its plunging back, would "not exactly have led the men to think about their toy railways."[22] It is thus difficult to disagree with Allen Guttmann when he argues that sex appeal and athletic performance were rather inextricably and self-consciously intertwined in the creation of Witt's image.[23] Guttmann argues against scholars such as Mary Jo Kane and Susan L. Greendorfer, who insist that in "portraying female athletes as feminized and sexualized others, the media trivialize and therefore undermine their athletic achievements."[24] Of course, Witt does not provide a particularly good example for the larger and still very pressing issue of how women are mistreated in sport. As Catriona M. Parratt has noted, "We are still living in a world in which sport is deeply implicated in denying women and many men the 'opportunity fully [and safely] to realize their humanity,' in which sport systematically denies them their full humanity," a fact that "every female soccer player in the dark empire that is Sepp Blatter's FIFA" knows only too well.[25] But one does not have to deny the trivializing and misogynistic tendencies of modern sports media to acknowledge that "Katarina Witt *intended* to present a fusion of the athletic, the aesthetic, and the erotic" in her performances.[26] Aside from granting her agency, however, recognizing the conscious intent behind the creation of the sex-bomb image requires specific historical contextualization and a recognition of the Cold War political background.

Witt's media image was part of a calculated SED plan to present her and other successful athletes as international representatives of Socialism—as "diplomats in tracksuits" (*Diplomaten im Trainingsanzug*).[27] Witt played along with the image, often telling the Western press that her parents could not have afforded skating lessons in a capitalist country. This response thrilled East German sports officials, who set out to capitalize on the fact that Witt had become a star in the American press and who sought ways to control the message that she was a successful "Socialist personality."[28] Politburo member Egon Krenz, the SED secretary responsible for sport after 1983, carefully examined all foreign requests for performances and media interviews, and he vetted GDR sports journalists' articles and books extolling the skater's exemplary service to her nation.[29] By the mid-1980s, the GDR's Ministerial Council (the highest executive office of the state) had recognized the vastly increased "political, ideological, and economic value of elite sport within the international class struggle" and had begun to consider ways it could be used to influence public opinion and morale in the country.[30] Internal documents of the Ministerial Council discuss how the *Ausstrahlung* (the radiance, charisma, or charm) of sports stars could be used for political purposes and how the state could literally cash in on this appeal. Particularly during the Calgary Olympics, the SED sold images of Witt to magazines like *Time* and West Germany's *Stern*.[31] The attention to Witt's sexual presentation fed the kind of interest that produced the first mass press conference for an East German athlete (with approximately six hundred journalists in attendance) after her gold-medal victory in Calgary.[32] As an East German sports organization put it in a glowing pictorial account, "her beautiful face and her golden successes are two sides of the same medal."[33]

The SED also lobbied to make sure that Witt received honors that would improve her selling price in the West. They carefully courted the International Olympic Committee (IOC) chairman Juan Antonio Samaranch by inviting him to a June 1988 antinuclear meeting in Berlin. In July, Witt flew to Switzerland to receive her "Olympic Order" in Lausanne, becoming the first recipient to receive the award at IOC headquarters.[34] This was a carefully staged series of events—an instrumentalization of sport for political purposes—as was demonstrated when the famous East German sports reporter Heinz-Florian Oertel, who accompanied Witt to Lausanne, specifically asked Samaranch to comment on his visit to the antinuclear meeting in East Berlin. Although Samaranch quickly deflected Oertel's question by once again thanking Erich Honecker for being "a great friend and supporter of sport and Olympianism," this event nonetheless demonstrates how focused GDR sports officials were on using sport to highlight political achievements.[35]

The SED's intention to turn Witt into an international diplomat is best exemplified by the achievement of having her named sports and goodwill ambassador to the United Nations International Children's Emergency Fund (UNICEF) in September 1988, an honor that the foreign ministry viewed as a means of "raising the international reputation of the GDR."[36] In the press conference in New York, she linked the GDR's exemplary policies to combat child poverty and to provide maternal health and welfare policies, noting that despite her youth she could "imagine what it would be like to be a mother and to hold a small wriggling child in her arms." Quickly bridging the gap from symbolic motherhood to her own fame, she then pointed out that the women's skating competition at the Calgary Olympics had had the highest American ratings since the TV series *Roots*.[37] The creation of a marketable international ambassador for East German Socialism seemed complete.

But the image was deceiving. For one thing, Katarina Witt never expressed any maternal or familial instincts. Her autobiography is full of pride at her conquests of married men, her short love affair with *MacGyver* star Richard Dean Anderson, and her self-confident rebuffing of the advances of one Donald Trump.[38] So placing her in the role of advocating for the child welfare and population politics of the GDR was certainly a calculated public relations move on the SED's part. Trying to establish her as the champion of charity work was also an attempt to downplay Witt's true political value to the regime, which even encouraged SED functionaries to compromise their ideological principles. Desperate to prevent her defection, Krenz made a deal with her before the Calgary Olympics. If she won gold again, she could skate as a professional in the American revue *Holiday on Ice*, thus becoming the very first East German athlete to be allowed to accept cash from the West. Eighty percent of her earnings went directly to the German Gymnastics and Sports Federation (DTSB).[39] Despite concerted efforts to paint Kati as just like every other GDR girl, this feminine icon of Socialism was not the product of mass-participation sports who would now retreat to fulfill her motherly duty. This was simply a different form of professionalization of sport framed in the guise of late Communism, and Witt certainly did receive benefits from having perfectly fulfilled the regime's plan to turn gold medals into hard currency.[40]

So on the surface, the notion that Katarina Witt and her political handlers had carefully sold her sexuality to a Western public to increase the prestige of the Communist system certainly has some merit. But this is only one of the dimensions of the Kati phenomenon, and it misses key nuances in the story of what sex meant in East Germany and how it was coded in the conflict between democracy and totalitarian systems. The sex that the GDR was selling was not the crass commercialism of the Western world, even if it was dressed up in that costume. While Jutta Müller and other skating officials certainly played the sex card in their quest for GDR Olympic glory, they could also rely on the fact that the GDR's unique sexual culture would allow Witt to frame her sexual allure in ways that were quite compatible with her image as a Socialist personality. Beneath the surface of the conflict between a Western sex-sells approach and the supposedly sexless and gray world of the Worker and Farmer State, Witt saw herself as embodying a natural attitude toward sex and nudity that by the 1980s had become, as Josie McLellan has argued, "one of the most visible markers of East German difference."[41] Nowhere in Europe was nudism as common as in the GDR, and by the time the Berlin Wall fell, the state had long given up trying to prevent what many viewed as a kind of "inner emigration" on nudist beaches and camping resorts. Initially viewed as a form of individual expression that represented an implicit challenge to the regime, by the 1980s, nudism—known as *Freikörperkultur* (FKK; free body culture)—was widespread and socially accepted in the GDR.[42]

This acceptance of nonsexualized nudism was central to Witt's self-understanding, as she makes clear in her autobiography. She insists that she had been "bewildered by the uptight attitudes toward sexuality" on her trips to the West during the Cold War, and she explicitly paints the more relaxed East German reaction to sex as an achievement of Socialist politics:

> Women's equality and self-actualization, including sexual liberation, are demanded with such militant slogans there. I cannot detect this problem at home in the GDR. Maybe it is because women at home had always been integrated into development—that there are practically no only-housewives and that the Socialist principle of equality for all and especially in the relationship between the genders had been in force since the Second World War. [Here] women are and understand themselves and their efforts and demands to be important. There are no marriages of dependence, which need to be kept together for survival reasons at the cost of the lifelong renunciation of love and pleasure [*Lust*].[43]

This "inner freedom" of uninhibited sexuality is only heightened, Witt argues, by the lack of consumerist compensations in a Communist country. She could even justify having two lovers at once, and she made sure that they did not find out about each other not because she felt guilty but only to avoid hurting them. This ability, she concludes, has something to do with the relaxed relationship that athletes have to their own bodies and to their sexuality. They view sex as uninhibited and natural, but this does not mean that they constantly and indiscriminately change partners. I also think that people who stand in a permanent situation of extremes, who are constantly in the public eye and under pressure to succeed, athletes and artists, for example, live and love much more intensely and spontaneously. This can strike some as amoral.[44]

Unless we wish to entirely ignore Witt's own agency in creating her public image, we must take these self-evaluations and their mixture of the broader cultural circumstances of her upbringing and her own self-understanding as a high-performance athlete into consideration. Her sex-symbol status was not merely a creation of Western media, and it meant something quite different to her than a Westerner—someone nursed in a culture saturated by highly sexualized imagery of female bodies—might expect.

Granting her this power of self-representation, however, should not obscure the dynamics of a specifically Cold War resonance in the creation of her media persona—a resonance that she was likely unaware of, that she could not control, and that we can understand only in historically contextualized ways that move beyond the simplistic sex-sells cliché and universalizing arguments about the sexualization of female athletes. Witt's depiction on the world stage as Communism's first sex symbol underlined a subterranean gendered tension that was unique to the Cold War divide: the suspicion that Soviet Bloc countries had purposely deployed seductive female agents to blackmail unsuspecting Western politicians, civil servants, or businessmen into passing on state secrets to Communist intelligence agencies. Perhaps first entering popular culture in the 1939 film *Ninotchka*, starring Greta Garbo,[45] but most obviously popularized by Ian Fleming's James Bond novels, by the 1980s the idea of the "honey trap"— a woman sent from a Soviet regime to seduce and trap a Western man—had begun to color all popular representations of Eastern Bloc female sexuality, and it was often coupled with the hint that hypersexual young women would eventually become hardened sadists.[46] In Fleming's novel *From Russia, with Love* (1957), Rosa Klebb, the hard-hearted and "sexually neutral" (in other words, bisexual) head of the Soviet counterintelligence agency SMERSH, directs her attractive underling Tatiana Romanova to seduce and then kill James Bond. Although the plan backfires when Tatiana falls in love with Bond, the initial presumption that women under Communism had to sacrifice their bodies is clear. Klebb instructs Tatiana:

> For the next few weeks you will be most carefully trained for this operation until you know exactly what to do in all contingencies. You will be taught certain foreign customs. You will be equipped with beautiful clothes. You will be instructed in all the arts of allurement. Then you will be sent to a foreign country, somewhere in Europe. There you will meet this man. You will seduce him. In this matter you will have no silly compunctions. Your body belongs to the State. Since your birth, the State has nourished it. Now your body must work for the State. Is that understood?[47]

In the 1963 film version of *From Russia with Love*, Klebb was played by the German actress Lotte Lenya, former wife of the famous composer Kurt Weill and star of one of the Weimar Republic's most famous Socialist films, *Die Dreigroschenoper* (*The Threepenny Opera*, 1928). This link to German Socialism, not to mention the emphasis on an older all-powerful woman and her younger and more beautiful protégé, explains why Jutta Müller was often nicknamed "Rosa Klebb," at least in the English-speaking world.[48] As a former Canadian figure skater who competed in this period told me, joking that Müller's elegant mink hats and her attractive yet severe demeanor made her look like she had herself once been a honey trap or that she and Witt had a sadomasochistic sexual relationship that mirrored Müller's extreme coaching methods was not unheard of in North American skating circles in the 1980s.[49]

These rumors of course tell us more about the impact of popular imagery on Western stereotypes about Communist female sexuality than they do about Witt and Müller's relationship or about the image that they wished to project. After all, Fleming and his Hollywood interpreters were less interested in accurate portrayals of spies' sexual encounters than in creating fantasies about obedient female bodies that would attract audiences. But the innuendo certainly did resonate in interpretations of Socialist female sexual power in this period, and some of it survived the collapse of Communism. Thomas Brussig's 1995 comedic and nostalgic novel about the GDR, *Helden Wie Wir* (*Heroes like Us*), contains a scene that intertwines sexual attraction for Kati with a kind of sexual awe for Müller. The main character, Klaus Uhltzscht, reacts to his Socialist mother's pestering questions about whether he finds Katarina Witt sexy ("6y") by falling into a sexual fantasy about Müller, whom he describes as "my mother's idol, and—in her capacity as the woman who always got her students to 'perform'—the doyenne of my sexual fantasies."[50] The novel's deployment of the dominatrix trope is clearly meant to underline that—at least in fantasy—the grayness of the Communist East had some sexual compensations.

These examples should serve to underline that the constant comments linking Katarina Witt's sensuality and attractiveness with her service to the state drew on already established tropes in Cold War culture. Titillating allusions to sexual deviance had become a common way of highlighting the political divide between East and West, and they drew from even older tropes in popular culture about the sexual nature of totalitarian evil. The link was explicit and obviously exploitative in the wave of Nazisploitation films and soft-core novels that were common in the United States, Italy, and even Israel in the 1970s and 1980s.[51] These pornographic descriptions of often sadistic female camp guards revealed an undercurrent of fascination with the sexual power of women under totalitarian regimes. Representations of Nazi and Communist women hardly differed in this regard, as is demonstrated by the fact that the most famous Nazisploitation film, *Ilsa, She Wolf of the SS*, was followed by a Communist-themed sequel: *Ilsa, the Tigress of Siberia*.[52] Taking the Bond-girl strategies to the extreme, these obviously pornographic films rely on the depiction of powerfully sexual women to transmit the thesis that sexual deviance is at the heart of totalitarian dictatorship.[53] Like the honey trap, the imagery of the totalitarian dominatrix served to both titillate and comfort: the sexual thrill was accompanied by the reassurance that the viewer was safe from dangerous Fascist and Communist vixens. While Witt was likely oblivious to these tropes, the contrast between them and the naturalistic and uninhibited sexuality that she thought she was projecting was an undercurrent of her fame in the West. The SED's insistence that she represented the future of East German motherhood—the epitome of the female version of the Socialist personality—contrasted with Western stereotypes that uninhibited female sexuality under totalitarianism represented a threat to the democratic West, and both fed the public's fascination with Katarina Witt as a symbol of the Cold War. The honey pot and the dominatrix lurked behind Western portrayals of "the most beautiful face of Socialism" whether this was explicitly stated or not.

That sexual morality served as a useful metaphor for Cold War tensions should not be particularly surprising. Historians such as Howard Chiang and Margot Canaday have stressed that American Cold War rhetoric commonly

cited the link between threats to the nuclear family and threats to national security.[54] It is thus not such a stretch to say that Kati Witt's Olympian sex appeal
played right into Cold War sexual tensions. Even as academic scholarship tended
to concentrate on the social-control mechanisms of totalitarian regimes, the
producers of popular culture in the West had noticed that a political focus on increasing the birth rate carried a certain promise of sexual liberation. Meanwhile,
the regime's goals could be met by affording citizens the opportunity to find
happiness in intimate spaces, distracting them from more ideologically threatening searches for consumer satisfaction. So while it is easy to read Witt's self-
presentation as an embrace of Western consumerism, there was much more
going on here. In presenting herself as a practitioner of uninhibited Socialist
sexuality, she was also demonstrating how the East German state had used the
gift of sexual freedom as a strategic weapon—how sexual freedom was being
instrumentalized for political purposes.[55] As McLellan has argued, "Sex was
a useful way of offering young people 'a bit of freedom,' allowing the regime
to appear to be on the side of the young while still pursuing its own agenda
of a peaceful population and a healthy birth rate."[56] Perched between Western
sexual commercialization and her symbolic role as the representative of "real
existing communism,"[57] Witt was vulnerable to those who sought to deploy her
natural attractiveness. As one of the Stasi agents who followed her every move
noted in 1983, "Witt . . . is very conscious of her attractive appearance. . . . She
likes it when men make efforts to please her, likes to flirt, and in no way sees
herself as a wall flower. . . . In my opinion this coquetry is normal and natural
for her age, because her appearance constantly places her in the limelight."[58]
When she read these words in her Stasi file, it must have become clear to Witt
that the regime had consciously capitalized on her flirtatious nature. But even
before the collapse of Communism, it had become clear that the appeal rested
on the Cold War divide.

Soon after earning her second Olympic gold medal, Witt's popularity within
East Germany began to wane. A March 1988 meeting in the State Secretariat for
Physical Culture and Sport revealed that complaints were being voiced across
the country about people who were allowed to travel abroad without ever having
worked a proper job. Witt's recent appearances in Western skating revues were
particularly resented,[59] revealing that the bargain she had struck with Krenz
was beginning to backfire. That summer, Witt dramatically miscalculated her
popularity by introducing the Canadian rock star Bryan Adams at a concert in

Berlin. Seen to be flaunting her privileges, she was booed off the stage.[60] A year later, the fall of the Berlin Wall and the impending collapse of Communism allowed these sentiments free rein, and there was an anti-Kati feeding frenzy. The conservative West German tabloid *Bildzeitung*, which had hailed Witt as a German Olympic princess in 1988, began publishing vicious denunciations of her involvement with the Stasi and the perks she had received as a GDR national hero. From one day to the next the "wunderbare Kati" became "die SED-Ziege" (the SED goat).[61] A constant string of revelations emphasized that Witt had refused to denounce her allegiance to the soon-to-be defunct GDR and had expressed mixed feelings and nostalgia about the collapse of the nation she still loved. "It was expected of me," she writes in her autobiography, "that I should act disgusted with myself [*daß ich mich jetzt in Abscheu ergehe*] and find everything about how it was with our system horrible. I am not ready to do this; I'm missing the information to come up with a final judgement."[62] When *Bunte* magazine declared her the "disappointment of the year," she returned the Bambi award—Hubert Burda Media's award for excellence in international media and television—that she had won in 1988, arguing that she had no reason to stop being proud of the country that had made it possible for a child of simple means (*Kind einfacher Menschen*) to pursue an expensive sport.[63] Although Communist newspapers like *Die Junge Welt* continued to write glowing testimonials and interviews with her in the year between the fall of the Berlin Wall and German reunification in October 1990,[64] and while her popularity soared in the United States (with advertising contracts for Coke and a successful HBO film, *Carmen on Ice*, with American figure-skating star Brian Boitano), Witt had at least temporarily become persona non grata in a united Germany. Trying to counter charges that she had spied on others, she asked to see her Stasi file in 1992. Although she was shocked at the extent of the file (twenty-seven binders with 3,103 pages), by the fact that the Stasi had begun monitoring her when she was eight, and by the long list of those who had informed on her,[65] she admitted that her relationship with the Stasi had been mutually beneficial and even friendly. The careful balancing act between East German folk hero and Western sex symbol had seemingly collapsed.

Yet Witt's insistence on a specifically German (and particularly East German) attitude toward sexuality endured well past her skating career and entered a new phase after the trauma of German reunification had subsided. Her decision to pose for the December 1998 issue of *Playboy* magazine, while clearly one step on the path to translating her former fame as a Socialist sports star into lucrative media contracts after German reunification, also provides insight into the attitude toward sexuality that she thought she had been representing during her skating career. Witt personally chose the celebrity photographer Lance Staedler for the photo spread of ten pictures,[66] and the style is notably different from the cover image (taken by frequent *Playboy* contributing photographer Stephen Wayda) and from the rest of the photos in the issue, which conform much more closely to the magazine's typically lurid style. There seems little doubt that Witt had considerable influence on the precise poses that Staedler created on set in Hawaii. She told a FOX sports reporter at a publicity event for the *Playboy* launch in November 1998 that she had said yes to *Playboy* only after the magazine had been asking her to do the shoot for years: "They have been very supportive in the way we wanted to do it," Witt noted, "and it turned out wonderful. I'm very happy with it, they're absolutely beautiful and there's nothing to hide about it."[67] These sentiments, along with her frequent statements about the relaxed nudist culture of the GDR, make it no accident, I argue, that the poses in the *Playboy* spread bear a remarkable resemblance to those typical of *Lebensreform* (life reform) movement during Germany's Weimar Republic, which had considerable influence on East Germany's FKK.[68] In stark contrast to the arched backs and pouting lips of other *Playboy* models, Witt is shown doing a split jump through the air or bending over to scoop up water for a drink in front of a water fall. The athletic body movements and the obvious attempt to naturalize sensual nudity through a beautiful natural setting are strikingly similar to Weimar-era *Lebensreform* photography. It is not difficult to find almost precisely the same poses in the pages of *Die Ehe*, a magazine published between 1926 and 1933 in Magnus Hirschfeld's Institute for Sexual Science that advocated uninhibited nudity and a science-based approach to sexuality and marriage.[69] Whether or not Witt consciously directed the photographer to make these visual allusions, her upbringing in the nudism-friendly GDR was clearly uppermost in her mind when she was engaging in this photo shoot. "Being nude on the beach, or nude in a waterfall—it's natural," she notes in her 2007 English-language memoir.[70] At least until her growing fame made it uncomfortable, she had often visited nudist beaches with her fellow teammates, seeing this as "absolutely not erotic . . . uninhibited and chummy [*unverkrampft und kumpelhaft*]"—completely natural.[71] Her *Playboy* spread was clearly an attempt to recapture a link to this more natural and uneroticized sexuality that had been threatened during the initial backlash against her after the fall of the Berlin Wall.

Despite the enormous popularity of this issue of the magazine—which seems to have sold around a million copies, quickly selling out in the United States and in its various translations across the world—Witt's image never quite escaped the salacious tendencies of Cold War popular culture. The tendency to link female sexuality with the power of the coercive state only grew with the revelations about Stasi activities after the collapse of Communism. Josie McLellan has described how her East German interview partners always assumed that the Stasi was deploying prostitutes to entrap Western sailors in the port city of Rostock and businessmen during the Leipzig exhibition.[72] After the fall of the wall, a constant stream of exposés in the popular press discussed the Stasi's use of prostitution and seduction for intelligence purposes, often in salacious tones.[73] This even affected the otherwise more sympathetic wave of *Ostalgie* (nostalgia for the East) that swept German popular culture after the success of Wolfgang Becker's 2003 enormously popular film *Good Bye Lenin!* Several public-interest shows about *Ostalgie* aired on German TV in the summer of 2003, and they contained numerous allusions to East Germans' attitudes toward sexuality and nudity. For instance, in an episode of the television variety show *Ein Kessel DDR* (A pot of GDR), which aired in August 2003, the hosts interviewed both the "art-house" photographer of nudes, Günther Rössler, and a former East German prostitute who had been instructed to seduce Western businessmen.[74] But this version of the *Ostalgie* documentary, perhaps because it was produced by MDR (Mitteldeutscher Rundfunk), the new public broadcaster created for the former East German states of Thuringia, Saxony, and Saxony-Anhalt in 1991, presented more of a balance between pure nostalgia and representation of Stasi repression than its counterparts did. In contrast, the four-episode television series *DDR Show*, produced by the private station RTL and cohosted by the Westerner Oliver Geißen and Katarina Witt herself, played directly on Witt's sex symbol status to reawaken old tropes about Communist sex bombs, with Geißen making frequent allusions to Witt's *Playboy* spread. Far more controversially, Witt appeared for her opening interview in pigtails and a form-fitting re-creation of her FDJ (Free German Youth) uniform, prompting considerable backlash from those who thought she was not appropriately distancing herself from the politics that these symbols represented.[75] In an article in the Berlin newspaper *Tagesspiegel*, Harold Martenstein criticized the way that Witt's appearance pri-

oritized sports and erotic memories over the Stasi's imprisonment of political
enemies and how the commodification of GDR history was diminishing the
regime's crimes. "What is remarkable about our system is its strong stomach,"
Martenstein lamented. "Capitalism digests everything. Right now it is digesting
the GDR."[76] Demonstrating how sensitive it had become to link Witt's status as
a sex symbol with her role as a representative of East Germany, the Christian
Democratic Union (CDU) politician Günter Nooke also tried, unsuccessfully, to
take her to court for violating a West German law against wearing the symbols of
an organization that threatened the German constitution.[77] Try as she might, in
other words, Kati Witt never entirely succeeded in rescuing her sexual image by
linking it to a supposedly more pure and commercially untainted East German
naturalness. In fact, she often played right into Cold War stereotypes by failing
to understand what it was that made her symbolic role as an East German sex
bomb so powerful and marketable.

The story of Katarina Witt is not simply the story of yet another woman
who caved in to market capitalism and sold her body for profit. If this had been
her only goal, she would have defected in 1988 and saved herself the wrath of
the anti-Stasi crusaders of postreunification Germany. Since the skeletons in
her Stasi closet were only what we would have expected to find—the gift of a
Lada and VW Golf, cheap rent on a nice apartment in Berlin, a house on the
city's outskirts, and an intense relationship with her Stasi minders—it was
only her refusal to deny her affection for the GDR, her *Ostalgie*, that prompted
her demonization in a united Germany. But while she was not prostitute, spy,
or victim, Witt was also not, as she claimed, "at most an object" of the East
German state.[78] Her fame rested, and to some extent still rests, on the specific
sexual tensions within her sport and the heightened politics surrounding this
tension in the Cold War. As other contributions to this book have made clear,
sport was a primary arena for Cold War competition—a kind of soft politics that
contributed to the cultural atmosphere of pitting one political system against
another. Achieving prestige in this realm was of almost obsessive importance
to the leaders of the GDR, whose "instrumentalisation of sport for external
legitimacy and internal 'national' identity" affected every decision made about
Katarina Witt's career and public persona.[79] But her fame and her symbolic
usefulness to the regime cannot be understood without attention to the cultural
resonance of an already well-established archetype in Cold War dramas: the
sexually alluring Eastern Bloc sex bomb, dangerous in her ideological ferocity

yet undeniably seductive and possibly open to the corruptions of the creature comforts that only Western men could offer her. The phrase "the most beautiful face of Socialism" must be understood as a shorthand for how sex, sports, and politics had collided in particularly powerful ways during the Cold War. Even while likely being unaware of some of the mechanisms of this collision, Witt masterfully capitalized on these tensions, demonstrating in the process that sex sells rather differently in each historical context.

PART IV

ASIA

LEARNING FROM THE SOVIET BIG BROTHER

The Early Years of Sport in the People's Republic of China

Amanda Shuman

When Soviet gymnast Nina Bocharova mounted the balance beam during an exhibition performance in Beijing in 1953, a Chinese team captured her impressive strength on newsreel. As she gracefully lowered herself onto the beam, the newsreel narrator introduced her by listing her most impressive accolades: "fifteenth Olympic team champion, fourth World Festival of Youth and Students absolute champion, merited athlete—Nina Bocharova."[1] Following her cartwheel dismount, the camera captured Bocharova's broad smile for the crowd of Chinese spectators. The same newsreel then presented several other top Soviet gymnasts in much the same manner; showcasing highlights from individual performances, the narrator listed each athlete's highest achievements. At the end, the Soviet athletes were paraded onstage to applause as their Chinese hosts brought them large bouquets of flowers.

Bocharova, who turned ninety-one in September 2015, may not have been aware of it, but her performance and that of a Soviet gymnastics team in China during 1953 helped usher in a new era in Chinese sport during the first phase of intense, nationwide efforts in Socialist construction. When Mao declared the establishment of the People's Republic of China (PRC) in October 1949, the country was in ruins from years of war. Embargoes imposed by Europe, the United States, and Japan on Chinese goods, combined with the advent of Chinese involvement in the Korean War, produced a society "stretched beyond its limits."[2] At the same time, Mao decided China would adopt the "lean to one side" policy, which accepted the Soviet Union as the leader of the international

Socialist movement and provided for a Sino-Soviet alliance in foreign affairs. It also included Soviet assistance to numerous Chinese domestic policies related to the arts, culture, education, and sciences.[3] PRC leaders sought Soviet advice from the beginning in building a centralized state structure for sports and physical culture (*tiyu*),[4] and they called on the entire Chinese sports world to "learn from the Soviet Union" (*xuexi Sulian*). Soviet sports models and athletes saturated the official Chinese media. Soviet experts went to China, and official sports delegations became conduits for those involved to forge new connections. Most sports historians of China today have little doubt that Soviet assistance in this period greatly influenced Chinese sport.[5] The Chinese sports world also acquired specialized knowledge from the Socialist Bloc. When leaders of the new People's Republic sought international recognition, sports exchanges helped improve political relations with these new allies.

Yet we need to rethink the role of these international sports exchanges in the context of a nascent Socialist state. How the new regime employed sport domestically as a means of establishing its legitimacy and building a new state from the ground up is often overlooked. Although national sports development in China was generally "controlled and managed by the state,"[6] I question the reach of this centralized rule in the early 1950s. The Communist Party was still in the process of consolidating its power in many localities,[7] and the State Sports Commission was not officially established until June 1952. Party leaders nevertheless saw sport as an important conduit for gaining legitimacy from the beginning because of its close connection to Chinese nationalism and its potential to reach the masses. For decades Chinese nationalists of all backgrounds had identified the weakness of China corporeally as a fragile, effeminate "sick man of East Asia."[8] The party leadership, Mao in particular, correlated this "sick man" image with the physical deterioration of the bodies of the Chinese population.[9] The immense population was considered the most valuable state resource for the future of the nation,[10] but its weakness could be overcome only by producing physically fit bodies. National sports development in China throughout the 1950s was thus not "largely elite pursuits."[11] Rather, it focused on establishing grassroots programs that would build a strong and healthy citizenry and a new Socialist state.

National sports development in the early 1950s, sports exchanges in particular, aimed to teach Chinese citizens the important connection between their own physical training, Socialist construction, and China's image worldwide. The leadership initiated large-scale "thought reform" projects across society in the early 1950s to teach citizens how to "interpret the world within the ideological framework favored by the Communist Party."[12] It stressed China's new position in the world, and cultural exchanges helped "reshape the nation's identity."[13] The saturation of official Chinese media with Soviet and Socialist Bloc sports models was part of the project to elucidate China's new position as part of the Soviet-led Socialist world. Glowing portrayals of foreign athletes in the media were often accompanied by introductions to broader sports developments in "fraternal countries," as Chinese sports leaders worked hard to implement Soviet-inspired sports programs like the "Ready for Labor and Defense" system—which emphasized all-round training for the masses and existed throughout the Socialist Bloc. One goal was to create a base from which competitive athletes could later be drawn, and Chinese media often directly connected the success of top Soviet and Socialist Bloc athletes to the development of this system at the grassroots level. Sports exchanges showcased the fruits of these Soviet sports programs to ordinary Chinese, demonstrating how through them individuals could transform their bodies for the purposes of building a strong Socialist state and improve its international reputation.

Leaning to One Side

Deference to the Soviet elder brother meant that Chinese leaders often copied Soviet models without significant adaptation, even though there had been a rich history of *tiyu* in China before 1949.[14] Most discussion on sports and physical culture in the early PRC likewise centered on how to learn from and implement Soviet sports models in the PRC rather than encouraged a locally built system.

Coverage of Soviet athletes and programs in Chinese sports publications increased following Joseph Stalin's death in 1953, as part of Nikita Khrushchev's mission to strengthen the Sino-Soviet relationship.[15] *Xin tiyu* (New sport) magazine often translated articles directly from Russian on topics ranging from political theory to mass sport in the Soviet Union and elite athletic achievements and international success. Articles on technical skills or movements within specific sports often taught readers through precise descriptions and depictions. In August 1953, *New Sport* covered the training of elite Soviet athletes in track and field, accompanied by photographs or hand drawings illustrating proper technique. One article depicts the Soviet national record holder for the women's eighty-meter hurdles in thirteen still shots.[16] A reader could put these skills into practice without much further guidance. Each issue of the magazine also included a section called "International Sports News in Brief" that highlighted recent elite athletic events in the Soviet Union and notable Socialist Bloc sports achievements worldwide. This section appeared in nearly every issue of *New Sport*; some months a reader would be hard pressed to find any article in the magazine that did not mention the USSR.

In *New Sport*, Soviet experts, techniques, theories, and models saturated the entire realm of sports and physical culture. Soviet documentaries and books were translated, and an official directive from the Ministry of Higher Education in April 1953 called for the recruitment and hiring of Soviet specialists. The Beijing Sports and Physical Culture Research Institute, also established in 1953, hired a Soviet theorist in sports and physical culture, as well as experts in physiology, athletics, soccer, gymnastics, swimming, anatomy, and hygiene.[17] These experts helped build what would become the nation's central training institute for athletes, coaches, and sports leaders.

Media coverage of athletes and officials from other countries in the Socialist Bloc reached its apex during this period. Such exceptional athletes as the great Czechoslovakian distance runner Emil Zátopek merited extensive coverage. Zátopek won three gold medals in track and field at the 1952 Helsinki Olympics,[18] setting the Olympic record in the five thousand–meter and ten thousand–meter races. He then decided to enter the marathon, having never run one in his life, and beat the reigning British champion while setting a new Olympic record.[19] He was frequently referenced in Chinese articles on running, including two prominent pieces in the January 1953 issue of *New Sport*. One of these included a photo of him in running gear and a detailed description of his innovative interval-training methods.[20] Ironically, a hand drawing of proper running technique accompanying the article does not seem to resemble Zátopek's style at all,[21] which was notorious in the running world for being sloppy and labored.[22]

Zátopek was also held up as a model athlete because of his dedication to the army and devotion to Communism. Accompanied by a photo of Zátopek in his military uniform, another article in the same issue of *New Sport* profiled his army background and noted his loyalty.[23] The Chinese Communist Party also considered the People's Liberation Army an important part of its continued success and often encouraged youth to join. Many Chinese competitive athletes in the 1950s came from the army,[24] a trend not unusual for Socialist Bloc sport. Articles like these on Zátopek thus forged a close link for readers between his athletic duties and obligations to the army, nation, and Communist Party.

Most central to this period of learning were regular sports delegation visits between China and the Socialist Bloc. Foreign visits featured prominently in the official newspapers, portraying hosts and guests as friends, comrades-in-arms, and seekers of common goals through international Socialism, offering tangible proof to the general public that there was a growing relationship between China and the Socialist world. When foreign delegations visited China, Chinese officials also often produced numerous classified reports exclusively for internal use. These ran the gamut from detailed preparations on receiving a specific delegation and their meticulously planned daily activities, to periodic summaries that noted competition results, issues that arose, and alleged comments made by guests. Less important than the veracity of every detail and comment are the choice of content and their very existence.[25] What officials chose to record unequivocally demonstrates the importance Chinese leaders placed on gaining recognition from and strengthening political solidarity with particular foreign guests—at whatever expense. From these reports, distributed to officials at municipal and national levels, we also see clearly the explicit attempt to connect foreign recognition and support for the new Chinese Socialist state to the implementation of Soviet-inspired sports programs nationwide.

In August 1950, less than one year after the establishment of the PRC, Chinese basketball and volleyball teams visited Hungary, Czechoslovakia, Romania, and the USSR. An article in *New Sport* by a Chinese volleyball player described his team's visit that summer to Czechoslovakia in glowing terms, recounting the overwhelming generosity that the team had experienced over the course of the visit in and out of competition. A large contingent of people had met them at the Ostrava airport and thrown a welcoming party before escorting the delegation downtown in a motorcade that included a broadcasting vehicle at the front and "three very new Czech cars" for the Chinese athletes.[26] Local news discussed the Chinese team for a week; people greeted them everywhere they went and shouted slogans like "Stalin, Gottwald, Mao Zedong!" The team competed in a brand-new facility built by the labor of Czech youth groups. The author seemed especially impressed by the Czech youths' "high level of internationalist warmth toward us" as well as their "labor spirit."[27] As far as volleyball itself was concerned, the team gained valuable playing experience against a factory team in an industrial city.[28] Following a grand welcoming ceremony that included a band playing and an audience of more than a thousand people, the Chinese team lost to the Czech factory workers. Nonetheless, they were honored with a banquet complete with song and dance and good wishes from the factory head, along with souvenir photos. Visits like these presented in such publications as *New Sport* and *People's Daily* taught readers about what international Socialist solidarity entailed and categorically positioned China within the Soviet-led world.

Chinese leaders tagged the 1953 Soviet gymnastics team visit as a significant opportunity to "study the Soviet advanced experience" and raise the nation's gymnastics skill levels.[29] The visit was also timed so that the guests could attend national track-and-field, cycling, and gymnastics competitions held in Beijing.[30] Presumably members of the delegation could offer pointers on improving sport in China. However, the visit also took place following the Soviet Union's decision to strengthen Sino-Soviet relations following Stalin's death.[31] Chinese leaders decided to follow the Soviet path of development and launch the first five-year plan.[32] In addition to boosting sports knowledge, Chinese leaders took advantage of the visit to convince their own citizens that strong relations existed between the two nations and that following in the steps of Soviet sport would be the best path for China's development.

Media coverage of sports delegation visits also often promoted Soviet sports programs as the correct path to follow through watching, reading about, or even interacting with champion athletes. Such visits offered the ideal method of directly showcasing model athletes and teams to Chinese audiences. This was especially true during the Soviet gymnastics team's visit and the Hungarian soccer team's visit in 1954, since both had done exceptionally well at the 1952 Helsinki Olympics. In addition to Nina Bocharova, the Soviet gymnastics delegation included other well-known gymnasts from the men's and women's gold-medal-winning teams at Helsinki, as well as rising stars and future Olympians.[33] Over the next month, they held exhibition performances in Beijing, Tianjin, Shenyang, Nanjing, Shanghai, Guangzhou, and Wuhan.[34] The visit was widely covered in the official media.

Chinese sports leaders hoped their athletes would gain invaluable technical skills and knowledge through practicing or playing against top athletes from the Socialist Bloc. Visits thus often included a component of hands-on learning. The main purpose of inviting the Hungarian soccer delegation to China for a month in February 1954 was to showcase and learn from one of the best soccer nations in the world. The Hungarian national team in the 1950s, famously known as the "Golden Team" and the "Magical Magyars," had recently beaten England 6–3 in what became an unforgettable match at Wembley Stadium.[35] Such a prominent team gained the attention of Chinese sports leaders who desperately wanted to improve national soccer skills. Although internal reports from Shanghai suggest that Hungary sent only third- and fourth-tier players, the skill level was far above that of any team in China. The visit was clearly important, as seating plans from some of the matches suggest the chairman himself was present. A study group of nearly one hundred people—from the State Sports Commission, the August 1 (army) team, the Central Training Institute team, and a group of referees and leaders—followed the Hungarian delegation to several cities. In each place, they played matches with the regional team (such as the Huadong team in Shanghai). In addition, the August 1 and Central Training Institute teams traveled from Beijing to play exhibition and practice matches against the Hungarians.[36] The State Sports Commission instructed local sports committees to set up formal discussion sessions with Hungarian leaders and players.[37] Occasionally this also happened less formally. In Shanghai over a meal between Chinese and Hungarian sports leaders, one of the Hungarians made specific comments about the lack of Chinese offensive tactics ("when near the goal [players] forget what they're doing . . . and bounce [around] without purpose"). He also suggested how to position defenders.[38] In April 1954 a Chinese delegation went to Budapest for a year and a half of intensive training and skills development.[39]

Even if Chinese soccer skills seemed lacking and there was no guarantee of Chinese success in competitive sport, leaders considered these visits important enough to their overall Socialist project to spend precious state resources on them. Payment for all expenses during visits between China and the Socialist Bloc was usually the responsibility of the host. When the Chinese soccer team went to Budapest in 1954, the Hungarian government covered their lodging and daily living expenses,[40] and when delegations visited China, the Chinese government paid. Beyond organizing sports activities, meals, and lodging, preparation for a delegation visit often required meticulous planning at the local level, with the participation and cooperation of a range of committees and subcommittees for evening activities, sightseeing, transportation, translators, small gifts, and the distribution of spending money to guests.

Extraordinary athletes such as the Soviet gymnasts and Hungarian soccer team also garnered more attention, and better treatment and facilities, than the average guests. Food and meals during the Hungarian soccer team visit required meticulous preparation, and these guests also received a few small extras. In addition to providing coffee, fruit, and sweets to the players, at breakfast every day each one was offered a lemon, one hundred grams of chocolate, and Zhonghua brand cigarettes.[41] The Soviet gymnastics team visit required "professional research" as well as cultural activities and sightseeing for the guests. Study groups were organized to watch the exhibitions and arrange for local sports workers to participate in question-and-answer sessions with their Soviet comrades.[42] Prior to the team's arrival, the State Sports Commission sent explicit instructions to municipal and regional sports committees regarding standards of gymnastics apparatus for the visiting team. The commission asked each locality to provide a detailed report regarding whether such standards could be met.[43] Such equipment was an impossible request to fulfill. It simply did not exist in China. Instead, the Soviet team brought a set with them and gifted it to their hosts when they left.[44]

Chinese leaders sought to impress their foreign guests in numerous ways. In addition to sightseeing, most visiting delegations received the grand tour of local sports facilities. Official delegation reports, written by Chinese sports leaders to be read by higher-ranking government officials, often recorded positive comments made by foreign visitors on new construction. The Hungarian reporter who accompanied the soccer delegation in 1954 to Shanghai was apparently "very satisfied" with the newly built pool and the sixty thousand–person capacity of the Jiangwan sports stadium.[45] From these visits he concluded that one could "see China's great construction, [and] China is making great achievements not only in politics and the economy but also in sport."[46] Comments from a foreign guest stating future sports possibilities on as grand of a scale as the Olympics supported the notion that Chinese sports development was headed in the right direction.

Nevertheless, these positive comments about sports stadiums stood in stark contrast to the general impoverished state of facilities and equipment in China at the time. Throughout the 1950s, Chinese sports leaders at all levels constantly complained that they did not have the resources necessary to carry out the demands made of them.[47] Local sports leaders used international delegation visits as leverage when asking for money from the municipal or central government for facilities and equipment. In October 1952 the Beijing Education Bureau complained to the municipal government that, although Beijing had thirty years of experience in sports and similar cultural activities, the city's facilities were still underdeveloped and the manpower and budget were incapable of bearing the burden of current needs—particularly in exchanges with fraternal countries. Officials cited the example of the "crash job" made for the Polish basketball team that visited Beijing in the summer of 1952. They argued that the event had resulted in a lot of time wasted on preparing living quarters for the athletes and maintaining sports grounds.[48] This apparently included an attempt to improve drainage facilities in the Xiannongtan stadium, requiring workers to spend entire mornings using pumps to remove storm water before afternoon competitions could take place.[49] Sports leaders estimated that at least ninety-eight hundred million yuan were needed to repair Xiannongtan stadium and add enough room for thirty thousand more spectators.[50] They also asked for another forty-nine hundred million to add approximately ten thousand bleacher seats and make improvements in Beihai stadium for basketball and volleyball.[51] Fearing that the Beijing municipal budget could not handle such a request, local sports leaders suggested that the report be submitted to higher authorities. Prior to the Hungarian 1954 visit, the Shanghai Sports Committee asked the State Sports Commission for eighty billion, ten thousand yuan to fix the locker room's heating stoves and the "somewhat serious contamination" in the showers and toilets. The committee decided to "paint over [the contamination] to clean [it]."[52]

Sports leaders stressed a visiting team's influence on the character formation of Chinese athletes. By interacting with model athletes, Chinese athletes had improved their sporting ethics. The final report on the Polish basketball delegation visit to Shanghai in 1952 stated that the visit had especially helped in the area of "ethical style" (*daode zuofeng*), decreasing the "bad habit of purposely injuring the opponent."[53] Furthermore, official reports often held Socialist Bloc athletes in the highest esteem as examples of how to be good citizens. The Hungarian players were regarded as "very lively" with an "upright and honest style."[54] They also loved "being near the masses,"[55] walking around the city to meet ordinary people and watch kids play. In fact, by the mid-1950s Chinese athletes at the national level were required to interact with ordinary people on a regular basis. According to a former captain of China's gymnastics team, who had also participated in the Soviet gymnastics team's visit, every Chinese sports team in the 1950s performed at the grassroots level many times each year, and it was considered "very important work."[56] Model athletes from the Socialist world were thus always portrayed as those who practiced good sportsmanship while living honest lives and devoting free time to the masses.

Official claims about the ethical values of the Hungarian visitors must have seemed questionable, however, given that some players did not always behave the way Chinese leaders would have liked. In Shanghai, for example, the Hungarians decided to skip a morning stroll in the park and go shopping instead. A report produced during the visit—and designated as "top secret"—

also noted that the guests had complained about not having enough spending money, even though each player had received five hundred thousand yuan; each leader, eight hundred thousand; and the doctor, seven hundred thousand.[57] These acts did not portray the guests as good model athletes—or good Communists for that matter—and thus went unmentioned in the official media.

Sports leaders and official media often used delegation visits to educate the masses on China's new international position and get them more involved in sport. When Poland sent a representative team of about thirty-five people from men's and women's basketball to China in the summer of 1952, leaders of the welcoming committee for the delegation in Shanghai aimed to show how the visit "further promoted friendship between the Chinese and Polish people, sports and physical culture workers, and athletes."[58] Leaders also intended to use the games during the visit to carry out a kind of "thought education" on internationalism and patriotism and promote among the masses "the ethical style of new *tiyu*." The committee called on local work units to develop "mass basketball activities."[59] Basketball had in fact already long been a popular sport in China, especially in urban factories. Yet official media made every effort to connect this high-profile visit of an internationally competitive sports team from the Socialist Bloc to sport at the grassroots level. The same day that *People's Daily* published a front-page article introducing the Polish delegation, it also ran a longer article that covered sports development in the eight years since the establishment of the Polish People's Republic.[60] Poland had made achievements in sport because the party had placed great emphasis on the promotion and development of sport, especially among workers and youth in factories, trade unions, schools, enterprises, the army, and rural areas. Although basketball was not as popular as soccer in Poland, basketball teams had proliferated and continued to improve through studying the techniques and "advanced experience of the Soviet Union."[61] Media coverage of the visit thus connected for ordinary Chinese citizens how sport at the highest level indicated solidarity and friendship with the Socialist Bloc.

In fact, the leadership believed the key to successfully building Socialism in China was the adoption of Soviet-inspired sports programs at the grassroots level, most notably the Ready for Labor and Defense system. This system aimed to extend sports participation and raise the level of all-round physical fitness among ordinary citizens. The system's main goal was ostensibly to cultivate physically fit individuals who in their spare time voluntarily engaged in regular exercise. To accomplish this, participants trained regularly to pass fitness tests and receive badges at various levels. But it was more than just fitness: the system included the development of paramilitary skills, as well as courses on hygiene, health, and first aid.[62]

Although the system's core provided a general fitness program that aimed to connect all-round bodily training to national labor and defense goals, its various levels also provided a way to build a nationally ranked system of competitive athletes.[63] By the 1950s, the Ready for Labor and Defense sports system had become a de facto marker of sports and physical culture in the Socialist Bloc. Chinese sports leaders had high hopes for adopting this model not only to show a reverence for learning from the Soviet Union but also to join the rest of the Soviet-led Socialist Bloc on the same playing field.

Chinese sports leaders and media often linked the implementation of this system at the grassroots level to national athletic achievements. A January 1951 article in *New Sport* outlined how the system extended across society from schools to workplaces, villages, and even to elite athletes.[64] These connections were reinforced during delegation visits. When the Hungarian delegation leader spoke to local Chinese sports leaders in Shanghai, he traced the history of soccer in Hungary back to British influence in the nineteenth century. Yet he ended his speech by crediting Soviet influence and the Ready for Labor and Defense system—rather than this previous history—as the main reason for recent athletic success.[65] A *People's Daily* article published during the Polish basketball delegation visit similarly connected the growing number of students receiving Ready for Labor and Defense badges to a twofold increase in extracurricular sports activities in one year.[66] Participation numbers in national competitions had also steadily increased, national records improved, and more athletes competed internationally. Following this trajectory from training at the lowest levels to international sports competitions, the Chinese reader learned how average citizens became connected to the larger Socialist world through individual athletic pursuits. This link was strengthened through actual participation in China at the grassroots level: in 1951 sports leaders rolled out trials of the Ready for Labor and Defense system in some urban schools, and beginning in 1954 the system was promoted nationwide through local work units.

Conclusion

In China, international sports visits in the early 1950s supported broader foreign policy goals by building relations with the Soviet-led Socialist Bloc.

Official media projected this new geopolitical position back to Chinese citizens as a priori Socialist solidarity and friendship. By the 1950s, most Socialist Bloc countries had adopted the Soviet sports structure in some form. They regularly participated in sports exchanges and competitions with one another. China became a member of this Socialist world of sport when PRC leaders decided to follow the lead of the Soviet Union in sports development at home. They also participated in regular competitions and exchanges with the Socialist Bloc under the banner of international Socialism.

Yet when the country was economically impoverished, early PRC leaders sought to emulate Soviet models in sports and physical culture for reasons beyond training competitive athletes for international competitions. The new regime saw sport as a crucial step toward gaining legitimacy and building a new Socialist state. Party leaders understood China's problems in corporeal terms and believed that one of China's chief assets and woes was its enormous population: the body politic was a "sick man" because the people's physical bodies were weak. They also firmly believed that sports and physical culture would transform the masses and create a strong and healthy populace. Out of these masses would emerge competitive athletes who could represent a strong Socialist nation on the world stage.

Regular discussions and direct interactions with the Soviet Union and Socialist Bloc thus served several purposes: they established the PRC's position among its allies, projected this new position and its meaning back to Chinese citizens, and demonstrated to ordinary citizens the connection of sports programs at all levels. The introduction of the Soviet-inspired Ready for Labor and Defense system, which was often cited in official media as vital for overall sports success, helped reinforce these connections in people's everyday lives. As the main PRC sport and physical education program in the 1950s, the system acknowledged Chinese deference to Soviet knowledge on training the entire citizenry in transforming their bodies through sport while also teaching them how their individual participation linked to the construction of a Socialist state.

"THE COMMUNIST BANDITS HAVE BEEN REPUDIATED"

Cold War–Era Sport in Taiwan

Andrew D. Morris

On September 7, 2007, the Dacin Tigers of Taiwan's Super Basketball League played the Jiangsu Dragons of the Chinese Basketball Association during the Straits Cup Basketball Invitational Tournament. During the second quarter, Tigers fans began waving large flags of the Republic of China (ROC) but were quickly ordered by ROC Basketball Association personnel to stop doing so. Several fans assembled at a corner of the court in protest and taunted ROC Basketball Association officials by demanding, "We're in Taiwan; why can't we fly our own national flag?! Are we supposed to fly the [People's Republic of China] five-starred flag or something?!"[1]

This was not the first time that pressures from People's Republic of China (PRC) sports organizations had led to this strange circumstance. Fans of Taiwanese athletes participating in a host of major international sporting events held in Taiwan's capital between 2001 and 2005 were also urged by the Taipei city government to eschew the display of even the most basic national symbols.[2] National recognition of the ROC, even inside the island republic itself, could lead PRC sports authorities to charge Taiwan with contravening the historic "Olympic formula," designed in 1979 to keep both China and Taiwan in the Olympic Movement. This agreement limited the small island to regional status as "Chinese Taipei" instead of national status as "Taiwan" or the "Republic of China."

The International Olympic Committee (IOC), Beijing, and Taipei had all worked from 1977 to 1979 to produce this formula after three decades of boycotts, dirty tricks, name-calling, and power politics.[3] In Taiwan, the crucial arena of international sport was demarcated during the 1950s–1970s by its war with the mainland's "Communist bandits" to represent China and achieve official recognition from worldwide sporting bodies. The usefulness of sport to the Guomindang (KMT; Chinese Nationalist Party) one-party state was measured by its ability to demonstrate the centrality of Chinese culture on this small island "province" of Taiwan. Sport's purpose was to buttress the ROC's legitimacy and, by extension, to show Chinese Communist Party (CCP) rule in China to be unlawful and immoral. This history is little understood by scholars. Taiwan's Olympic program has been best covered by Liu Chin-ping in two Chinese-language books.[4] The PRC's approach to Olympic sport has been much more thoroughly studied in English-language scholarship, with work by Susan Brownell and Xu Guoqi that explains well China's engagement with Olympism and the logic behind its insistence on the "Olympic formula."[5]

The history of sport in Taiwan is more complicated than this two-dimensional, cross-strait struggle. Fifty years of Japanese colonial rule (1895–1945) deeply influenced all aspects of Taiwanese culture, even as those influences were dismissed by the Nationalist conquerors. Baseball was perhaps the longest lasting of these remnants. Despite its clear Japanese heritage, it ended up as the sport most closely identified with Taiwan. Official ROC sporting discourse was meant to establish Taiwan's teams and athletes as representative of a "Free China" regime and populace that could inspire a recovery of the mainland for the forces of liberty and democracy. Nevertheless, many Cold War–era sporting developments in Taiwan resembled those in the PRC. The rival Chinese regimes engaged in what Michael Szonyi has called "mirror-imaging." Each side engaged in "active fashioning of the self in contrast to the enemy," borrowing from each other "to ensure that the other side did not gain an advantage."[6] The Chinese sporting rivalry raging across the Taiwan Strait followed this model. Both Taiwan's Nationalists and the mainland's Communists used sport and physical culture to establish their own regime as the rightful modern revolutionary government of China. During the Cold War era, both sides attempted to use sport to exhibit and enforce models of disciplined citizenship and produce "healthy" bodies to end long-standing assumptions of Chinese weakness and degeneracy. Each hoped to keep up with the world of international sport as regional allies and competitors like Japan and the Soviet Union continued their excellence on the highest international stages. Each needed to make the case here for the superiority of its own not entirely distinct form of Chinese modernity. These tensions played out in three arenas: the Olympic Movement, the mass physical culture displays of Taiwan's provincial games, and the culturally hegemonic sports of baseball and basketball.

"China" and the Olympics

Nationalist-Communist fighting on the mainland had barely ceased when the competition turned to another battleground. Beginning in 1951, the two Chinese Olympic Committees began making their respective cases for the exclusive right to represent "China" at the 1952 Games in Helsinki. The ROC had sent delegations to the Olympic Games of 1932, 1936, and 1948 and even had planned to bid for the 1952 Games of the XV Olympiad,[7] an effort shelved because of the Nationalist-Communist civil war. In July 1952, the IOC naïvely ruled to allow both Chinese teams at Helsinki. ROC Olympic Committee chief Hao Gengsheng declared that his athletes would never compete against Chinese Communists and announced the ROC's withdrawal from the Games. After ensuring that Taiwan would not send a delegation, the PRC team left Beijing six days after the Games had actually begun. Premier Zhou Enlai dismissed any who would quibble over such minor details, declaring, "Raising the five-starred red [PRC] flag at the Olympic Games is in itself the victory." That flag was raised, and a single Chinese male swimmer was able to join a backstroke preliminary race before the Games ended.[8] Four years later at Melbourne, the situation was reversed when the PRC boycotted.[9]

The 1960 Olympics at Rome saw no sign of the PRC, which had indignantly withdrawn from the IOC two years previously as a reaction to what it saw as President Avery Brundage's role as "a faithful menial of the U.S. imperialists bent on serving their plot of creating 'two Chinas.'"[10] The ROC's participation was still controversial. Now labeled by the IOC as simply "Taiwan," the ROC delegation carried a large "UNDER PROTEST" sign during the opening ceremonies.[11] The Winter Olympics at Squaw Valley earlier that year witnessed what even ROC Olympic Committee member Tang Mingxin called a "political show." Desperate for a way to join the Winter Olympics, the ROC Olympic Committee constructed an impromptu "ice rink" on the Shao Mei Ice Cream Company factory grounds—the coldest place in tropical Taiwan—where it held an Olympic selection meet. Four of the very few ice-skaters in Taiwan thus became Olympians in name only, as the ROC was not recognized by the International Skating Union. They technically constituted an observation delegation, but the ROC flag flew in the Olympic Village.[12]

Cross-strait Olympic intrigue reached a much more serious level in Tokyo in 1964. C. K. Yang (Yang Chuanguang) was an Amis Aborigine from eastern Taiwan who had grown up playing baseball under Japanese rule. He won a silver medal in the decathlon at the Rome Olympics in 1960; his epic battle there with close friend and UCLA (University of California, Los Angeles) teammate Rafer Johnson to this day is one of the most memorable moments in Olympic history.[13] Yet after that great competition, Yang felt obliged to compose a classically inflected apology to Chiang: "I was not able to achieve first place, a fact that is both very moving and very shameful. The only fortunate thing is that the Soviet [bronze medalist Vassily Kuznyetsov] finished behind me; the Communist bandits have been repudiated."[14] This clumsy political posturing contrasted directly with the public and sincere Olympic sportsmanship exhibited among Johnson, Yang, and Kuznyetsov.

As the Tokyo Olympic Games approached, all observers expected Yang to take decathlon gold. He had set the world record in 1963, pole vaulting so high that the official decathlon tables did not have a score for his feat. *Sports Illustrated* called him "the first truly great Chinese athlete of modern times" and by year's end named him the "World's Best Athlete."[15] In a *New York Times* article, Yang's UCLA coach described the obligations that the "Asian Iron Man" felt to represent the Chinese people: "He carries a load nobody knows about."[16] Indeed, just before these Olympics began, President Chiang informed Yang that he *had* to win a gold medal for the sake of Chinese pride.[17]

ROC Olympic Committee chief Hao Gengsheng had called Yang "the model of the 'modern Chinese man.'"[18] This high praise was also demonstrative of the many accidents of history that had led to the geopolitical reality of 1960. The island of Taiwan had been seen as marginal for centuries; the Amis Aborigines of the eastern coast of Taiwan also occupied a minimal place in modern Taiwan under Japanese and then Chinese rule. This double marginalization made Yang's case as the model for half a billion Chinese men quite compelling. There was virtually no ideological space in Chiang's Taiwan for talking about Yang as anything but "Chinese." But one element of the ROC's narrative about its rule of Taiwan had to do with its benevolent treatment of the once-"savage" Aboriginal populations. What better proof could there be to all the diverse peoples of mainland China of the ROC's wise embrace and competent command of this diversity than an Olympic triumph by a "model Chinese man" raised from his humble Japanese/Aboriginal beginnings? Indeed, Yang's every motion would be interpreted as a signal of the strength or weakness of "Free China." What happened at Tokyo, however, was stunning. Before the competition began, Yang's traitorous teammates Ma Jingshan and Chen Jue, bought off by PRC agents promising a long-awaited defection back to mainland China, spiked his morning orange juice.[19] An out-of-sorts Yang was in ninth place after the first day of competition. Remarkably, he won three events the next day but finished in fifth place overall, shocking and puzzling the sporting world. The failure of ROC intelligence operatives to create unity among their athletes was kept secret and not made public for more than three decades.

The PRC's withdrawal from the IOC, its participation in the anti-imperialist sporting Games of the New Emerging Forces, and Mao Zedong's Great Proletarian Cultural Revolution took China off the international sporting stage until the late 1970s. The ROC participated in several consecutive Olympic Games without fear of PRC participation, but this ease started to fade with the Asian Games Federation's (AGF) desire to expel the ROC and enroll the PRC before the seventh Asian Games in 1974 in Tehran. The PRC's All-China Sports Federation was aggressive in its condemnation of the AGF's ongoing recognition of "the illegally appropriated membership of the Chiang Kai-shek clique."[20] The Iranian organizers relished the chance to curse the "superlords, these great gnomes of sports . . . these remnants of the old colonial policies of Europe" who hoped to disregard the newfound "Asian solidarity" and to control matters of AGF membership.[21]

The 1976 Olympic Games at Montreal, one year after Chiang Kai-shek's death, were the last chance for the ROC to "represent China" at the Olympics before the PRC rejoined the movement in 1979. This development may have seemed unlikely with Mao and his Great Proletarian Cultural Revolution still alive, but the trend toward inclusion of the PRC should have led Taiwan's sporting authorities to treat this precious opportunity on the international Olympic stage with great care. Instead, Montreal 1976 became one final example of an ROC boycott over questions of official nomenclature.

Very few people in mid-1970s Taiwan could believe an ROC "recovery of the mainland" was likely by this point. As early as 1953–1954, Chiang was talking publicly about "counterattacking" the mainland purely for the purpose of manipulating American military and diplomatic support for the ROC.[22] By 1955, even he was admitting to American political leaders his repeated talk of invading the mainland was more for "domestic propaganda" than anything else.[23] Two decades later, it was ludicrous to imagine the ROC military retaking the mainland, but an ongoing militarized "state of emergency" in Taiwan was still useful in justifying the KMT's authoritarianism.[24]

Even though Canada had recognized the PRC as China's sole legitimate government in 1970, Taiwan's Olympic Committee still pressed forward with its unrealistic demand that its delegation compete at Montreal as representatives of the ROC. The IOC supported Taiwan's bid for "ROC" status at Montreal, but even with this pressure, Canada's Department of External Affairs, citing the 1960 "Rome formula," maintained that athletes from Taiwan could compete only as "Taiwan."[25] As Prime Minister Pierre Trudeau said more vividly, "We Canadians love the Taiwanese. We just don't call them Chinese."[26] This time, orders came from Chiang Ching-kuo, the generalissimo's son now serving as premier, to withdraw.[27]

Three years later, when the IOC-China-Taiwan "Olympic formula" was finalized, "Chinese Taipei" had become the only ground that still remained for the ROC sporting community. In just a matter of years, the ROC on Taiwan had fallen from World War II victor and UN Security Council member to the status of a pariah nonstate able to exist only as a pretend fragment of its mortal enemy's totalitarian regime.

"Everyone Here Is an Athlete": Taiwan's Provincial Games

The prevalence of the Olympic Games as a worldwide ideology of national modernity, strength, and progress made the language of sport an attractive site for the discussion of the national crisis of the ROC. These categories were all that Taiwan's government had as it tried to make its case for its fitness to rule the people of the mainland who had seen it off in 1949. Even after the misery of eighteen combined years of Japanese invasion and civil war, it was still possible to imagine the power and exertion of disciplined Chinese bodies representing Taiwan's fitness to claim a modern mandate for the ROC.

The most visible form of ideologically centered physical culture in KMT-ruled Taiwan was the Provincial Games.[28] These were held every year in late October to mark "Retrocession" (*Guangfu*, literally "glorious return"). The first Taiwan Provincial Games, held in October 1946 at Taiwan National University, were attended personally by Chiang Kai-shek and his wife, Soong May-ling, to commemorate the first year of glorious KMT rule of the island. There was much at stake in what Chiang saw as his new "model province." The newspaper *Minbao* (People's news) stated,

> The goal of the meet is to make the compatriots of all of Taiwan understand the importance of national and racial health—and not for the purpose of producing athletes for specific competitive events, which is the same as just as meaningless as circus performances.[29]

With civil war against the Communists under way by late 1946, the new Taiwanese citizens of the ROC could not afford to see sports only for their entertainment value. While many Taiwanese subjects had prospered under colonial rule, Chiang and his properly Chinese compatriots had sacrificed greatly to defeat the Japanese. Physical culture would be one more way of reminding the people of Taiwan of their real "national and racial" heritage.

In his speech at the 1946 Provincial Games Chiang expressed his happiness that Taiwan was returning to a state of freedom and equality in the Chinese motherland after the half century of Japanese imperialism. But Chiang's address took on a harder edge, as he reminded the Taiwanese people that their privilege of being ROC citizens also came with the responsibility to follow the classic virtues of the Chinese people.[30] With the fate of China on the line, Chiang and his Nationalist Party, as they had for two decades, hoped to marshal the discipline and vigor of sport toward another decisive triumph. Even in October 1949, just three weeks after the establishment of the PRC on the mainland, Taiwan's fourth Provincial Games stood as an inspiration, in the words of KMT stalwart Yu Youren, "to encourage youth to advance bravely, to work hard to open up a new age, to oppose extremism and aggression, and to strive for the independence and freedom of the nation and the [Chinese] people."[31]

The PRC, which inherited an impressive urban sporting culture and infrastructure from the Nationalists, is much better known for its sporting successes. The CCP's commitment to modern sport as a reliable agent of health and discipline and to Soviet models of training and sports bureaucracy, as well as the party's unprecedented reach into local life, all allowed PRC sports and physical culture to eclipse quickly the scope and ideological significance of KMT sporting practices.

Yet the PRC sports project was not entirely novel. The Communists' early programs to popularize, organize, systematize, and politicize martial arts surely would not have offended the Nationalist *wushu* (martial arts) advocates now on Taiwan who had worked so hard in these same directions in Republican China.[32] Early work to organize a "Ready for Labor and Defense" system of mass physical culture in the PRC, though based on the Soviet Union's Gotov k Trudi I Oborone (GTO) program founded in 1931, also resonated closely with 1930s Nationalist models of Fascist-style "militarized sport."[33] While the PRC and ROC used the harshest terms to describe the "Fascist clique" or the "Communist bandits," their prolonged Cold War confrontation led to each side "mirroring" elements of the other. Despite Chiang Kai-shek's half-century-deep loathing of the CCP, he hoped to learn from the victors' effective internal security, enforcement of party discipline, commitment to serving the masses, and even their grasp of Marxist-style dialectical thinking.[34] Between their shared May Fourth roots as parties dedicated to nationalism and social revolution, the Nationalists and Communists were working in parallel political directions in the sporting world as well.

By October 1953, the Cold War split between the PRC on the mainland and ROC on Taiwan had already been decided, but there was still a domestic disciplining, focusing, and legitimizing use to Chiang's talk of counterattack. Provincial chairman Yu Hongjun found himself addressing the athletes and spectators of the 1953 Provincial Games. A competent technocrat brought in to help rebuild after the destruction brought by the recent Super Typhoon Kit, Yu found himself engaging in very promiscuous counterattack talk. As the *United Daily News* summed up,

> Chairman Yu hopes that when everyone goes back [to the mainland,] they will serve as models for the propagation of sport. He said, "Everyone here is an athlete, and athletes' responsibility is to lead, to induce everyone to take part in exercise and sport, and to let every single compatriot be able to enjoy the joy of sport and the goal of strengthening one's body."[35]

In the new Cold War era, the camaraderie, strength, and sacrifice at the heart of modern sport figured heavily in official KMT discourse. These Provincial Games' athletes did not represent the elite Olympic level of training and achievement. The common citizens competing at the Provincial Games instead played the role of postconquest models of the properly Chinese sporting spirit. These experiences, Chiang later argued, would allow "every athlete present to serve as a model after we get back [to the mainland], teaching all of your colleagues in your organizations to become involved in exercise and train their bodies for health, making for a rich and strong nation."[36]

If Chiang's fantasies of a renewed civil war against the Communists were more and more remote by the mid-1950s, he did understand that his Nationalist Party still had to solidify the loyalties of the Taiwanese people in this new model province. Chiang's anti-Communism could be a compelling justification for one-party rule in Taiwan only if it could be based on an accounting of how his Nationalists were improving the lives of the Taiwanese people after half a century of Japanese colonial rule. Yet Chiang and his regime had for several years been criticized in a public and sophisticated fashion by dissenters such as those at the journal *Free China*. On the occasion of the January 23 Freedom Day holiday in 1954, *Free China*'s editors made a clear, if polite, appeal for a new societal emphasis on "freedom of the self," as opposed to the "national freedom" favored by authoritarians like Chiang.[37] A year later, to commemorate 1955's Freedom Day, *Free China* cited sources ranging from Song-dynasty poetry to the US Constitution to make a case for freedom of speech in Taiwan and rule by law.[38]

In 1955, the tenth anniversary of Retrocession and the vigorous, nationalistic occasion of the tenth Provincial Games gave Chiang a public chance to answer critiques like these. To those who emphasized inconveniences under Nationalist rule, Chiang declared,

> At this time we should think back to the mainland compatriots[, some of whom] rescued Taiwan at that time [at the end of World War II]. Today their suffering under the Communist bandits' tyrannical rule is hundreds and thousands times greater than the suffering of the Taiwan compatriots ten years ago [under Japanese rule]. Their only hope is to hope that we can go rescue them.[39]

The Provincial Games offered a chance every year for government leaders like Chiang to help Taiwan's athletes and sporting community understand their roles in the future development of all China. A newsreel of the games included footage of "anti-Communist national salvation calisthenics" (*fangong jiuguo cao*) performed by several hundred children during the opening ceremonies, clearly incorporating the ideological power of youth and movement to make a case for the coming Nationalist reconquest of the mainland.[40] For more than half a century, since the late Qing dynasty, calisthenics had been imagined in China to provide a healthy, educational, and enlightened experience, especially for children who were not yet ready for the ideologies of competition and sacrifice at the heart of sports proper.[41]

Even two decades later, when President Chiang had passed most of his responsibilities to his son Ching-kuo, the latter still used the pulpit of the re-branded 1974 Taiwan Regional Games to channel vividly his elderly father's faithless counterattack sensibility.[42] He urged the athletes and audience of Free China

> not to forget the seven hundred million compatriots on the mainland, who at this instant are being enslaved and oppressed and who have lost their freedom. . . . After the Eight Years' War of Resistance [against Japan], we shed blood and sweat under the president's leadership to recover Taiwan. The triumphant spirit of solidarity, progress, and struggle that we see today at these games makes us resolutely believe that under the president's leadership, the people of Free China will surely rescue the seven hundred million unfree Chinese people on the mainland and allow them to enjoy the life of freedom.[43]

If the Olympics and international sport were becoming domains of shrinking possibility for Taiwan, the Provincial Games and the ideological realm of mass sport continued to provide an important site for the imagination of Chinese and Nationalist triumph. By the 1970s, the younger Chiang had to use the specter of counterattack as a domestic gambit. Rising prosperity, exposure to the outside world, and dissatisfaction with three decades of martial law and one-party rule called once more for the subject-changing, conversation-ending discourse of the sixteen million people of Taiwan having to remember the great task of retaking the mainland.

Basketball, Baseball, and Fighting the "Commie Bandits" in Taiwan

Team sports, mainly baseball and basketball, were the final realm that held Cold War significance in Taiwan. Baseball is still considered Taiwan's national game, despite or perhaps even because of its association with the departed Japanese colonial power.[44] Basketball was introduced to China via the Tianjin YMCA between 1895 and 1898 and spread quickly throughout late-Qing and early-Republican China, and soccer had made its way into China via the European colonies of Hong Kong and Southeast Asia. During the ROC era, these two sports were known as conational pastimes;[45] after they arrived with the ROC government in Taiwan, basketball remained relevant, while soccer became more marginal.

If baseball lives on today in Taiwan as a palpable reminder of the influence of Japanese culture in Taiwan, the game of basketball carries almost as palpable a sense of its mainland origins. During the 1950s–1960s, especially, as Taiwanese/mainlander identities were being defined and resolved in Taiwan, basketball was understood to have an almost totalizing KMT/mainlander character. While Taiwanese people played baseball, and still dared to use Japanese terminology for what they had experienced as a Japanese game, basketball was played by mainlanders, largely the million-plus soldiers who had arrived with the KMT as young men and, until the late 1980s, were in Taiwan to stay. Besides the obvious linguistic, musical, or cuisine-related divergences, the baseball-basketball split was definitively marked as being Taiwanese versus mainlander.

Basketball, both more Chinese and American and not complicated by an overwhelming colonial heritage as was baseball, thus simply became a more useful symbol in the KMT's efforts to fight Communism through sport.[46] Early ROC-era Taiwan basketball teams performed well in the regional East Asian competitive circuit, which included Japan, Korea, Hong Kong, and the Philippines. These countries and territories clearly shared Cold War–era American influence in common, but the various competitions held throughout this anti-Communist crescent were meant to evoke much more specific nationalisms. During the mid-1950s, Taiwan hosted six cup tournaments, on the occasion of Chiang's birthdays, featuring their Asian rivals. Taiwan also held large Freedom Cup tournaments every January commemorating the anniversary of their historic recovery of fourteen thousand Chinese prisoners taken during the Korean War in 1954. During the 1960s, they also participated in several Park Chung Hee Cup basketball tournaments named for the autocratic president of the Republic of Korea, Taiwan's close anti-Communist ally.[47]

The Nationalist Chinese spirit of sport and moral toil can be seen in one of the most successful basketball squads in Taiwan at this time—Team Kenan (Overcoming difficulty), founded in 1951. The Nationalist government and military had formally inaugurated a Kenan Movement to defeat and distract from the material shortages and feelings of doubt, decadence, slack, longing for home, and dependence that affected so many displaced mainlanders during the years of early Nationalist rule.[48] Basketball seemed just the activity to metonymize the mainland Chinese culture that the KMT hoped could sustain these émigrés.

Because basketball by the 1960s and 1970s was closely associated with mainlander culture and an age of defeat and anomie, Taiwanese people still felt their true spirit could be demonstrated more authentically through baseball. Baseball had a unique status as one of the very few elements of Japanese culture that was allowed to continue under Chinese Nationalist rule. The Nationalists tried to sinicize the game, and the Free China Baseball Team traveled abroad to locales like South Korea, where their shared Cold War ideology and Japanese colonial heritage overlapped. In July 1955, the Free Chinese played an eight-game Korea-China Goodwill Baseball Series against six Korean teams in four different cities. The official program featured four prefaces by high-ranking politicians and the head of the sponsoring *Korean Free Press*. All were clear in invoking the shared bloody anti-Communist struggle and the ancient cultural and political ties between the centuries-long allies.[49]

Another rich source of Chinese and anti-Communist context for the otherwise Japanese game of baseball came in the person of Sadaharu Oh, the legendary Yomiuri Giants first baseman and home-run king who faced ethnic discrimination for decades in Japan because his father was Chinese. During the mid-1960s, the Nationalists took advantage of this ethnic impasse and made Oh a close friend of the regime. His introduction to fame in Taiwan also included an anti-Communist gauntlet through which Oh had to pass. His first press conference in Taiwan included the sincere claim, made by the head of his fan club, that Oh was a loyal Chinese young man who in the past had "resolutely refused the [PRC] Commie bandits' shameless seduction" and their invitations to visit the mainland.[50] In 1965, Oh simply seemed to become a much more believable Chinese patriot if he had some anti-Communist accomplishment to advertise in Nationalist Taiwan.

Even Little League Baseball—which Taiwan dominated from 1969 through the early 1980s—became a site for the imagination of the defeat of the Chinese Communists and the recapture of the mainland. Taiwan's skilled twelve-year-olds were sent off yearly to rule the Little League World Series in Williamsport, Pennsylvania, with orders from the elder and younger Chiangs to win and therefore help "quickly retake the mainland and restore glory to the motherland" and "exterminate Communism."[51]

The experiences of the first Taiwan team to win the Little League World Series, the Taizhong Golden Dragons in 1969, represented the climax of this intersection between Little League skill and Cold War hubris. On September 18, 1969, after the conclusion of the young champions' exhausting victory tour of Taiwan, the team was taken to Jinmen (Quemoy), the island held by the ROC military just a mile and a half off the coast of China's Fujian Province and a potent "symbol of the government's commitment to national recovery and anti-Communism."[52] There, on the island that had been shelled by the PRC military every other day since the 1958 Taiwan Strait Crisis, the government staged a surreal meeting of the Golden Dragon players and several ROC troops, two groups of young men fighting on different front lines of Chiang Kai-shek's struggle for Chinese supremacy.

Two particular details of the trip made it even more symbolically powerful. First, Golden Dragon catcher Cai Songhui's older brother Cai Songchuan was among the troops stationed on the ROC's most forward position at Jinmen. The synchronicity of their dramatic meeting was chronicled proudly by a Nationalist media eager to justify the regime's pretensions to work toward reconquering China.[53]

A second fantastic element of this trip came at Horse Mountain Observation Point, the northern station closest to PRC territory. Showing that ROC army officials took seriously their rhetoric about sharing the news of the victory with "the compatriots of the entire [Chinese] nation," they used massive speakers to make a special broadcast to the people of Xiamen on the opposite shore:

> Our ROC youth baseball team recently took part in the twenty-third youth baseball world championships in America and beat teams from Canada and the United States to win the world title. This is not only the glory of the entire populace of the Republic of China but represents a mission of glory accomplished for all the countries of the Pacific region. Mainland compatriots, the ROC youth baseball team's world championship is the [Chinese] nation's greatest sporting accomplishment in history and is the result of a superior educational system, allowing all of us Chinese people to enjoy this glory together. Just think, what kind of lives are your children living now?[54]

Most ROC officials had very little experience with baseball, a game that had rarely been played on the mainland. Basketball, with its American roots, seemed to be made for the Cold War. Despite its Japanese heritage, baseball became the sport that won the most attention for the ROC and its claims of representing the superior Chinese system, indeed the site of virtually the only diplomatic triumphs for Taiwan over the next two decades.

Conclusion

During the Chiang era, the ROC could boast about the great discrepancy in living standards between those living under Nationalist and Communist rule, but the incredible wealth in China today has taken away even this final plank of confidence as Taiwan experiences a prolonged economic slowdown. The realm of sport, despite the efforts of C. K. Yang, hundreds of Taiwanese Little Leaguers, and thousands of Provincial Games participants, was never successful in buoying Taiwan's status as the world became hypnotized by the PRC's sporting achievements. The hard-edged soft power of mass sports was much more effectively harnessed by the PRC's ideology of class struggle than by the ROC's attempts to define itself within categories of Confucian harmony and representative democracy. The fitness generated through Provincial Games was fastened to a militarized discourse of "counterattack" that its authors barely believed in. It was, however, great theater for the folks at home. International political prestige contested at the Olympic Games was thoroughly intertwined with the KMT's domestic agenda. Popular team sports enabled Taiwan to place a patina of fun on its most serious goals.

Elite athletes whose efforts could equal those of the world superpowers provided confirmation that the ROC regime still could claim legitimacy on the world stage, while the children whose efforts graced the fields of Williamsport or Gaoxiong could evoke the promise of a strenuous and competitive Chinese future. Sports never ended up saving Taiwan on any international stage. It was the Olympic world where Taiwan first was demoted to "Chinese Taipei." Domestically, however, this was finely organized propaganda that helped construct an ROC polity that, if it would never retake the mainland, could still unify the people of Taiwan.

NEW REGIONAL ORDER

Sport, Cold War Culture,
and the Making of Southeast Asia

Simon Creak

Southeast Asia may seem an unlikely place to examine sport and the Cold War. Athletes from the region won few Olympic medals during this period, and no country in Southeast Asia entertained an Olympic bid. In political terms, however, sporting performance often matters less than participation. This can be seen in a number of well-known examples in Asia from the Cold War, including the "China issue," Indonesia's politicization of the 1962 Asian Games, and the same country's founding of the short-lived but politically significant Games of the New Emerging Forces (GANEFO).[1] These contests and events demonstrated how sport, as a popular, performative, and embodied field of culture, operated to produce social and cultural meaning during the Cold War in a way that eclipsed the on-field feats of individual athletes and nations.

This essay turns to the South East Asia Peninsular (SEAP) Games—the precursor of today's Southeast Asian (SEA) Games—founded in 1959 by key US ally Thailand. Emerging from regional experiences of decolonization and the Cold War, this event promoted popular understandings of international relations in Southeast Asia and specifically embodied defining tropes of Cold War culture in Thailand, including militarism, social order, development, and the resurgence of the monarchy. Treating this event as an important element of Cold War culture, I examine the Thai military junta's objectives in founding the SEAP Games, the effectiveness of the inaugural SEAP Games in achieving these aims, and the cultural and semiotic features that reinforced the games' major themes.

Cold War Culture in Thailand
and Southeast Asia

Although the social and cultural features of the Cold War have attracted much attention in the past decade, there are multiple ways to study this subject. For instance, Cold War culture can be distinguished from the cultural Cold War. While the latter has a rather specific meaning—the battles for hearts and minds waged through art, literature, propaganda, and other forms of culture—Cold War culture has a broader and "more anthropological sense," referring to the values, mentalities, and emotions that created the Cold War as a contested and locally differentiated experience. In this respect, Cold War culture was "a logical extension of, but . . . transcends, the cultural Cold War."[2] Historian Masuda Hajimu argues similarly that the Cold War did not simply exist, a priori, as an objective reality in people's lives but was created through social and cultural experiences as "an imagined reality that came to be shared and solidified in the postwar era."[3] A key concern when approaching the Cold War in this way is to understand how social realities were "produced and consolidated, and why numerous people joined in."[4] In other words, what made a particular Cold War culture hegemonic within a specific social, cultural, and geographic context?

In Southeast Asia, more than anywhere else in the world, Cold War culture was profoundly shaped by decolonization.[5] By 1958, when the SEAP Games were first mooted, most countries had obtained independence: the Philippines from the United States; Burma and Malaya (later renamed Malaysia) from Britain; Indonesia from the Netherlands; and Cambodia, Laos, and North and South Vietnam from France. These new countries joined Thailand, which had not been formally colonized, and Singapore, which obtained full self-government from Great Britain in 1959, in forming a new regional order of independent (or de facto) nation-states in postcolonial Southeast Asia.

The intersection of decolonization and formation of a new regional order with the Cold War left deep ruptures throughout the region. Domestically, deep political cleavages including violent Communist insurgencies divided most societies while, diplomatically, the states of Southeast Asia fell into all three Cold War camps. In response to the Geneva Accords of 1954, which recognized the Communist Democratic Republic of (North) Vietnam, Thailand and the Philippines joined the United States and five other countries in the Southeast Asia Treaty Organization (SEATO). Among the neutralist nations, Indonesia and Burma were instrumental in planning the Asia-Africa Conference in

Bandung (Indonesia). Ironically, the Cold War thus reinforced the idea and "semantic unity" of Southeast Asia as a politically and geographically coherent region, despite the domestic and international disunity that brought this region to attention.[6]

Given the complexity of these dynamics, Southeast Asia experienced the Cold War not simply as site of superpower interventions and so-called proxy wars but as a profoundly significant historical period that helped create the modern nations and region of Southeast Asia.[7] In this respect, nationalism, nation building, and competing models of modernity and socioeconomic development were as important to local and regional experiences of the Cold War period as were new modes of imperialism, militarism, and ideological diffusion.[8] This perspective highlights the agency of local leaders, who used Cold War alliances for their own political purposes; the subjective experiences of local populations; and the interpenetration of local, national, regional, and global dynamics.

Despite having avoided direct colonization by the West, Thailand was similarly subject to these dynamics. The Thai-US relationship took shape after the war, when Washington blocked British efforts to punish Thailand for its alliance with Japan. It was then bolstered by the return of military rule in 1947. Although the local Communist Party of Thailand (CPT) did not pose a major threat, the military's anti-Communist inclinations and the advance of Communist forces in China, Korea, and parts of Southeast Asia propelled the United States to embrace the country as its key ally and "anti-communist bastion" in the region.[9] Accessing vast amounts of US aid, Thailand's military junta recognized the Western-backed Bao Dai regime in Vietnam, sent troops to Korea, banned the CPT, and offered Bangkok as the base of SEATO. By the mid-1950s, Thailand was a "US client-state under military rule."[10]

Successive coups in 1957 and 1958 by Field Marshal Sarit Thanarat, the charismatic and ruthless dictator, ushered in the "American era" of Thai history.[11] Sarit shelved the constitution and launched a self-styled "revolution" (*patiwat*).[12] He banned political parties; clamped down on unions; arrested Communist sympathizers; and cracked down on beggars, vagrants, and prostitutes.[13] Backed by ballooning US aid, Sarit invited the World Bank to develop capitalist plans for "development" and, in the social sphere, promoted militarist values of discipline, unity, and social order. Rejecting existing democratic institutions as "foreign," he also promoted indigenous political principles of orderliness, decisiveness, and benevolence as the basis of traditional charismatic leadership or "Thai democracy."[14] In addition, Sarit restored the symbolic centrality of the monarchy, which had been sidelined since the 1932 coup, seeking to latch on to the royal charisma or symbolic power (*barami*) of young King Bhumibol (r. 1946–2016).[15] Sarit's political biographer memorably dubbed this authoritarian concoction "despotic paternalism."[16] The Americans, viewing Buddhist kingship as an antidote to Communism, encouraged these developments and helped commoditize Thai national culture.[17]

Thailand's Cold War culture was framed by the resulting struggles, both violent and intellectual, over the US presence, anti-Communism, militarism, monarchism, and developmentalism.[18] Yet Thailand's Cold War culture also had dramatic ramifications beyond national frontiers. Thai leaders and their American backers promoted Thailand, a putatively peaceful country situated in the heart of a chaotic region, as a "center of the free world surrounded by suspicious enemies and bases of communist infiltration."[19] This leadership role, reflected most tangibly by the headquartering of SEATO in Bangkok, stemmed not only from the anti-Communism of the military and monarchy but also from Thailand's distinction in having avoided direct colonization.[20] Both the regional and domestic features of Cold War culture in Thailand informed the establishment of the SEAP Games in 1958–1959. As a popular and officially sanctioned cultural form, the SEAP Games promoted popular understandings of international relations in Cold War Southeast Asia, including emotions of regional friendship and antagonism, while also embodying the domestic Cold War culture of Thailand.

Postwar Sport in Thailand and Southeast Asia

Amateur sport and physical education had been introduced to Southeast Asia by colonial powers to promote discipline, physical well-being, and civilization.[21] Siam, as Thailand was known until 1939, was much the same. The modernizing regime of King Chulalongkorn (Rama V, r. 1868–1910) introduced popular British sports, conducted drills and basic gymnastics in schools and the military, and codified such violent traditional practices as Thai boxing (*muai thai*) and kite flying to counter Western perceptions of the Siamese as barbaric.[22] Although some sports became popular for gambling, amateur sport and physical education became increasingly institutionalized after the 1932 coup when the postabsolutist state created the Department of Physical Education in the Ministry of Education. Before World War II, however, imperial divisions largely limited prewar sporting links between Siam and its neighbors.[23]

After the war, state and military support for sport increased. The newly formed Committee for the Promotion of Sports and the Olympic Committee of Thailand (OCT) were respectively headed by Field Marshal Sarit and his protégé, Lieutenant General Praphat Charusatian, who was a deputy prime minister and the interior minister.[24] Besides the prestige of such positions, the military embraced amateur sport as a means of promoting unity, order, and development. Formerly a skilled boxer and coach, Praphat commanded his officers to utilize sport because it would create unity, build understanding among the group, and lead to the unification of the nation.[25] He later recalled, "I always believed that before we could develop our country we had to first develop the people themselves. . . . [Besides education] we also had to develop sport as well because it encourages health and stimulates the spirit. . . . [It] improves people's conduct."[26]

Decolonization and the Cold War also transformed international sport in Southeast Asia. By 1956, Thailand and all but one of its neighbors (Laos) had formed National Olympic Committees and joined the International Olympic Committee. As well as becoming part of the "imagined world" of Olympic geography,[27] Southeast Asian countries joined the Asian Games, which were conducted for the first time in 1951 in New Delhi. As a product of regional decolonization, the Asian Games were underpinned by a philosophy of egalitarian internationalism in which all countries in the region were formally represented as sovereign equals. The event also reinforced regionalism and nationalism. On the one hand, the Asian Games promised to reflect the Pan-Asian ideals of Nehru's Asian Relations Conference in 1947; on the other hand, they served "as platforms to showcase the host countries' rapid modernization and development processes."[28] From the Second Asian Games in 1954 in Manila, however, the principle of egalitarianism was reinterpreted according to the dictates of the Cold War. For the following two decades, Asia's Communist nations were sidelined. As Stefan Huebner writes, "The image of Asia . . . communicated was that of a community of countries either pro-American or neutral in the Cold War."[29] This image would be reproduced in the SEAP Games.

Establishing the SEAP Games

According to the event's foundational narrative, the SEAP Games were established in May 1958 on the sidelines of the Third Asian Games in Tokyo. At a series of meetings, the vice president of the OCT, Luang Sukhum Naipradith, gained agreement for a regional event from his Burmese, Lao, and Malayan counterparts.[30] Cambodia and South Vietnam did not attend those meetings but also accepted Thailand's invitation to join the games. Finally, Singapore—though initially overlooked—was added the following year on the basis that the causeway linking the island to Malaya made it part of the peninsula, thus bringing to seven the number of participating countries.

Referred to as the "Little Asian Games," Sukhum's initiative officially had two goals: to "strengthen the friendly relations that happily already exist among the countries that lie in the Peninsula" and "to improve the skills of our athletes so that they might reach the high level of competitive performance."[31] After the inaugural SEAP Games, scheduled for Bangkok in December 1959, subsequent SEAP Games were to be conducted biennially between the Asian and Olympic Games. Hosting duties would be rotated according to alphabetical order of the countries. The leadership of the SEAP Games Federation (SEAPGF), formed to oversee the event, would also rotate with the host nation. Thus, Praphat and Sukhum were, respectively, named the SEAPGF's inaugural president and vice president.

Less understood are the ways in which these developments emerged from the context of the Cold War in Thailand and Southeast Asia. The most immediate antecedent of the SEAP Games was not the Asian Games but sporting exchanges between Thailand and neighboring Burma, with which it shared its most intense traditional rivalry. The first of these events, a golf "friendship" tournament in 1955, was personally proposed by Burma's prime minister U Nu to improve relations after Burmese forces accidentally bombed a village in northern Thailand (while in pursuit of Chinese Nationalist forces). A few years later, while negotiating the Thai-Burmese Friendship Treaty (1957), U Nu proposed expanding the now-annual golf exchanges to a wider range of sports, based on the Olympics, with the additional aim of preparing athletes for the Asian and Olympic Games.[32]

Seemingly separate from these developments, the new honorary coach of the Thai national athletics team, an American named David Dichter, organized an athletics meet between the two countries in Rangoon. Like U Nu, Dichter stressed the twin goals of improving neighborly relations and preparing the teams for the Asian Games in Tokyo.[33] With several national records broken in Rangoon, the Thai Amateur Athletics Association sent Dichter to gauge interest in similar bilateral events in Cambodia and South Vietnam. These discussions evolved into the idea of a regional multisport event modeled on the Asian Games.[34] After Laos and Malaya added their support, Sukhum put the proposal into effect, and in March, two months prior to the Asian Games, Praphat (as interior minister) gained cabinet approval for Thailand to host the first SEAP Games in Bangkok.[35]

These developments reflected the appropriation of Olympic internationalism by Thailand and its neighbors. Supporters of the games promoted their regional or internationalist goals constantly. Praphat told the cabinet that the event would "cement friendly relations among the six neighboring countries . . . situated in the Golden Peninsula [mainland Southeast Asia], thus increasing closeness and intimacy." Sport, he stressed, was "one of the best means of cementing friendly relations."[36] "Only through these brotherly relations," he later noted in a letter to the US ambassador, "could peace and independence in this area be maintained according to the ideals of the United Nations."[37] Arguing similarly that the SEAP Games would promote "good understanding, goodwill and cooperation" in the region, Sukhum stated that "the various countries in the Peninsula [share] among them a great affinity in practically all respects, such as the way of life and climate as well as physical appearance."[38] Such idealism bore clear similarities to the internationalism of the Asian Games and, as Praphat indicated, the United Nations. Yet like the internationalism of the Asian Games, the regional spirit of the SEAP Games was circumscribed by the context of the Cold War. Specifically, the SEAP Games promoted "Thai-centric, anti-Communist regionalism in mainland Southeast Asia."[39]

Southeast Asia's only Communist nation, the Democratic Republic of (North) Vietnam, was not invited to join the SEAP Games and was not even mentioned in documentation. This omission was hardly surprising given Thailand's membership of SEATO and the de facto anti-Communism of the early Asian Games. But the implicit anti-Communism of the SEAP Games was crucial, as it made the event one of the largest anti-Communist institutions in the region. The US-dominated SEATO included only Thailand and the Philippines from the immediate region, but the SEAP Games included seven countries, including neutralist Burma, Cambodia, and Laos. Almost a decade before the formation of the Association of Southeast Asian Nations (ASEAN) in 1967, this gave the sporting event a degree of regional legitimacy SEATO lacked.

In addition to the anti-Communist criterion, the regionalism promoted by the SEAP Games was limited to the countries of mainland Southeast Asia, excluding the archipelagic states of Indonesia and the Philippines (which were also eager to join). According to Dichter, the goal was to keep regional games "small." This is possible, but the peninsular principle also reflected a local concept of the region with implications of Thai centrality. The best indicator of this was the attenuated Thai-language name of the games, Kila Laem Thong (literally Golden Peninsular Sport), in which *laem thong* (golden peninsula) is the vernacular form of the Pali-Sanskrit term *Suwannaphum* (golden land). This name connected the event to Thai irredentism of the 1930s and 1940s, which emphasized Thai territorial claims to "lost territories" occupied by neighboring colonial powers and to the status of Thailand as the "elder brother" of its colonized neighbors.[40]

Although the military abandoned its irredentist project after the war, the trope of Thai leadership in the golden peninsula was reborn as a security issue during the Cold War.[41] In this respect, the SEAP Games built on a number of Thai proposals to promote anti-Communist cultural cooperation with its mainland neighbors. Between 1954 and 1957, the Thai government discussed at least three separate proposals (which never materialized) for cultural or religious organizations in mainland Southeast Asia aimed at bringing together "free world" and neutralist nations to counter Vietnamese and Chinese Communism. One such group was called the Group of Buddhist Countries consisting of Thailand, Cambodia, and Laos to Resist Communism; another, consisting of these countries and Burma, was referred to as the Golden Peninsula Group; a third, based on the model of Scandinavia, included these four countries and Free Vietnam, as the Republic of (South) Vietnam was known among its anti-Communist allies.[42]

Like the SEAP Games, these organizations enjoyed a number of potential advantages over SEATO. First, the use of culture or religion to promote regional cooperation was less likely than political groupings to conflict with Thailand's obligations to SEATO. Second, the use of religion and culture and the absence of the United States highlighted the indigenous roots of regional cooperation. Finally, as a result of these factors, cultural associations permitted much broader regional membership than SEATO. While none of these proposed cultural organizations were formed, they did highlight Thai support for the use of cultural cooperation to promote regionalism among its non-Communist neighbors. This goal would ultimately receive its most concrete expression in government support for the SEAP Games.

Finally, the regional aims of the SEAP Games also reflected the goals of American cultural diplomacy in Southeast Asia. The American coach of the Thai track team, David Dichter, was based in Bangkok as a junior trainee officer with the US Information Service (USIS). Despite stressing the unplanned and out-of-hours nature of his involvement in athletics, Dichter's role personified the creative ways in which USIS officials were encouraged to execute the organization's objectives in Southeast Asia, which included boosting America's image, reducing the appeal of Communism, and promoting regional identity among non-Communist nations.[43] The USIS office in Bangkok actively promoted the SEAP Games on these terms.[44] In a report to the State Department, Dichter's superior argued that his work had increased "American prestige among the Thai general public. The Communists and leftist elements [in Thailand] will have great difficulty attempting to discredit American participation in the sports world of this region."[45] More specifically, the SEAP Games "promised also to further regional objectives through the unifying influence of amateur competitive sport."[46] The event would not just "help to create a greater mutual understanding among peninsular Southeast Asians," but it would also give "them greater strength to resist Communist subversion" and thus reduce the appeal of "propaganda-loaded all expense-paid tours offered by Red China." He concluded, "There are few cheaper or more effective ways than through the medium of sports to help achieve our policy objectives in peninsular Southeast Asia."[47] The US secretary of state, John Dulles, apparently concurred, offering departmental support for the provision of equipment and an American athletics official to help the Thais host the SEAP Games.[48]

Less obviously than Dichter, the SEAP Games' links to Cold War culture were also personified by Praphat and Sukhum. As minister of the interior, Praphat was intensely anti-Communist and had overseen a harsh crackdown on leftists in northeastern Thailand. He also enjoyed close connections to the American embassy. In terms of the development of the SEAP Games, Praphat's senior position in both the government and OCT was instrumental. As well as obtaining cabinet approval, he secured the initial budget of 2.5 million baht (around USD 118,000) for the inaugural games in Bangkok and leveraged his contacts at the US embassy to obtain American support for equipment and coaching.[49] In requesting this support, he cited Soviet funding of local sports in Burma and Indonesia, suggesting that he recognized the political issues at play.[50]

Sukhum also boasted lifelong ties to the United States. A cosmopolitan nobleman with impressive connections to the monarchy—his title "Luang" was bestowed by the king—Sukhum had been educated at the Gunnery and Boston University in the 1920s. Popular among his American peers, he fell in love with jazz and big-band music, excelled in gridiron and basketball, and developed a respect for what he perceived to be American values, including democracy. Recalled to Thailand to serve as a royal secretary and, later, as secretary general of the Office of the Civil Service Commission, Sukhum returned to the United States during World War II as an emissary of the anti-Japanese Free Thai movement. Appointed director general of the Public Relations Department after the war, he continued to work with the United States in such areas as psychological warfare, the Fulbright program, tourism, and the Peace Corps.[51]

In addition to its regional and international aspects, the founding of the SEAP Games reflected domestic Cold War culture in Thailand. In particular, sport was considered congruent with themes of Sarit's revolution—promoting moral rectitude and social order (*khwam riaproy*) in the face of crime and Communism.[52] In this context, sport represented a force for good that could build morality, discipline, and unity, as well as promote national development. Hosting the SEAP Games was seen as a means of boosting Thailand's standing in the region by showcasing national development and modernity. While such "nation-branding" objectives were characteristic of the Asian Games, especially the recent games in Manila (1954) and Tokyo (1958), they were also characteristic of the Cold War in Thailand, during which national culture was commodified as part of a free world culture centered on the United States.[53]

Cold War Culture in Practice

While the very formation and existence of the SEAP Games reflected links between sport and Cold War culture, the First SEAP Games in Bangkok also brought to light the ways in which these links could be contested. The greatest challenge to the official objectives of using sport to unite countries divided by political differences came with Cambodia's last-minute withdrawal from the games. The cause was a bitter diplomatic confrontation with Thailand over the Preah Vihear (or Phra Viharn) temple, an Angkorian ruin located on the border between the two countries. Ostensibly a nationalist dispute, this confrontation was also fueled by the two countries' Cold War rivalry, especially the personal enmity between anti-Communist Thai prime minister Sarit and his counterpart from Cambodia, the neutralist Sihanouk. Thailand took possession of the temple in 1953 after newly independent Cambodia adopted a neutralist foreign policy. Talks between the two countries collapsed in 1958 after Sihanouk visited Beijing and Cambodia recognized Communist China. Incensed, the Thai government declared a state of emergency in areas bordering Cambodia and did little to discourage popular protests and a press campaign against Phnom Penh in Bangkok.[54] In October 1959, just two months before the first SEAP Games, Sihanouk's government lodged a claim over the temple with the International Court of Justice, reigniting the anti-Cambodian press campaign and protests in Bangkok.[55] Cambodia withdrew from the SEAP Games the following month, citing concerns over the safety of its athletes and officials.[56]

In press coverage, themes of friendship and cooperation turned to visceral hatred. In explaining the government's decision, the Phnom Penh newspaper *Réalités cambodgiennes* cited the "extremely hostile atmosphere that currently reigns in the Thai capital against all things Khmer. . . . Hateful publications and anti-Cambodian slogans were in the cinemas, in the theaters, [and] on the street [in Bangkok]. [We] feared for [the safety of] our athletes."[57] On the other side, the Thai press contrasted the country's generosity in founding the SEAP Games with Cambodia's efforts to sabotage them because of the temple issue.[58] Reverting to national stereotypes, Sarit blamed the long history of conflict between the two countries, including the Cambodian belief that Thailand was a "barbarian country," speculating that Communists might have been behind the exaggerated perception of danger.[59]

Reception of the Games

If these events threatened to derail the regional objectives of the SEAP Games, this fear was soon dispelled by the effusive reception to the event itself. While the Thai athletes were said to have "brought fame" to Thailand by winning more than half the gold medals, the country's greatest achievement related to off-field matters.[60] According to Sukhum's cremation volume, the games showcased Thailand's capacity to hold such a large event and thus its level of development and modernity.[61] Likewise, the Bangkok newspaper *Siam Rath* argued, the games showed that "Thailand, which is a small country, can arrange a highly important event in an orderly manner [*duai khwam riaproy*]." In particular, the newspaper added, the games reinforced the positive work of the Sarit regime in the area of sport.[62]

More specifically, the Thai and foreign press highlighted the quality and cleanliness of the "modern stadiums," including the expanded capacity of the National Stadium (from twelve thousand to twenty-five thousand), floodlights for night football matches, a Thai-made electronic scoreboard, and a new indoor stadium. The games were also a popular success. While crowd numbers were not always reported, organizers had hoped to sell three hundred thousand tickets in total. The National Stadium was filled to capacity for Thailand's football matches, which made crowds "crazy with happiness," as well as for the opening and closing ceremonies.[63] The large and ebullient boxing crowds were also highlighted in reports.[64]

The press also acclaimed the event's success in achieving its regional aims. *Siam Rath* explained: "Traveling to compete in sport represents a good opportunity for athletes to socialize and become familiar with each other and to get along well. When the people have mutual understanding, increasingly friendly relations between countries will follow."[65] This showed the "good intentions of the people in the Golden Peninsula region" to cooperate with one another. *Siam Rath* also hoped that cooperation with Cambodia would improve in the future, as this would benefit that country and others "on this peninsula."[66] Interviewed by *Phim Thai*, another local newspaper, the managers of visiting teams echoed these regionalist sentiments. Burma's representative said the games would cement friendly relations and promote "better understanding of people in each country"; Malaya's representative thanked the Thai officials and people for "welcoming them as close friends"; and the South Vietnamese manager said Thailand had been a "good host and very welcoming."[67] There were isolated controversies over umpiring and other issues, but these did little to detract from the overall impression of goodwill. One report even suggested that these incidents were like an arguing husband and wife and could "build up meaningful friendship."[68]

Theatrics of the SEAP Games

As in similar events the world over, the opening and closing ceremonies, more than the sports themselves, brought to life the formal and informal themes of the games. These ceremonies attracted the most spectators, received the greatest attention in the press, and, most of all, represented the peak of national and regional myth making. The resultant theatrics did not simply reflect but effected the social forces underlying the SEAP Games.

Designed by Sukhum himself, the opening ceremony incorporated well-known rituals of the Olympic Games, including the athletes' march and assembly; official opening of the games by King Bhumibol, patron of the games; raising the SEAP Games flag; lighting the SEAP Games flame; and reading the SEAP Games Oath. As anthropologist John MacAloon argues of the Olympic opening ceremony, these "rituals are organized around the classic schema of rites of passage." They initiate a separation from "ordinary life" and a "period of public liminality" and effect the "transcendental ground" of the rituals, the idea of "humankind-ness."[69] In the SEAP Games, although the idea of humankind-ness was replaced by regionkind-ness, the structural features of these rituals remained similar. As during the Olympics, the opening ceremonies "stress[ed] the juxtaposition of national symbols and the symbols of the transnational [regional] . . . community," the latter being positioned hierarchically above the former.[70]

Adaptations to the familiar rituals reinforced these themes. Lacking the myth of the original Olympic flame in Athens, each delegation brought its own flame to Bangkok. After a series of elaborate rituals, a torchbearer from each country jointly ignited the SEAP Games flame in an homage to unity.[71] Likewise, in a modest addition to the athletes' march, each contingent was led by a young female shield bearer, dressed elegantly in that country's national costume.[72] Key symbols were similarly adapted. The SEAP Games flag positioned a rosette of six yellow-gold rings on a light blue background. Just as the background referred to "the water that surrounds or the sky that covers the South East Asia Peninsular countries," the rings, symbolizing the six original members of the federation, were "intertwined to denote friendship, brotherly love and unity of purpose."[73] In one of the most spectacular and joyous arrangements of the opening ceremony, the SEAP Games rings were formed on the stadium field by a group of young women performing traditional folk dances and, later, by massed service bands.

As MacAloon explains, the efficacy of these rituals and symbols depended on shared experience of *communitas*, the momentary collapse of social structures that occurs through rites of passage and constitutes participants as part of a new community. The popular experience of spectacle and *communitas* was evident from press reports. Just as Singapore's *Straits Times* dubbed the ceremony a "gloriously colourful spectacle,"[74] Bangkok's *Siam Nikorn* effused that it was "spectacular" (*teun ta teun chai*, literally "dancing eyes, dancing heart") and unforgettable, "the most impressive and grandiose image" created by the "biggest opening to a sports competition Thailand has ever seen."[75] Especially impressive, according to *Siam Nikorn*, was the march of athletes, "a strong and stable movement . . . driving us to think of close relationships among the six nations. . . . This has become a symbol of love, sportsmanship, [and] friendship of neighboring countries in the Golden Peninsula region." The absent Cambodia was also not overlooked: "This beautiful and impressive picture" would be recreated in future games in "every country in the Golden Peninsula, including

Cambodia." In such accounts, the spectacle and *communitas* of the SEAP Games not only reflected a regionalist ideology framed by the Cold War; it helped bring into popular experience the new regional order of Southeast Asia.

As well as regional themes, the opening ceremony animated the domestic Cold War culture in Thailand, especially themes of militarism, masculinity, and monarchy. The ceremony opened with massed service bands of the army, air force, navy, and police, which made formations on the field culminating with the Thai national flag. Like the regimented aesthetics of the athletes' march, such images embodied the ideal of orderliness (*khwam riaproy*) celebrated by the military regime. The country's military leaders played key roles. Prime Minister Sarit gave a speech on the benefits of sport for health and happiness, invoking notions of social purity at the heart of his "revolution."[76] General Praphat received the king and queen and raised the SEAP Games flag.

The performances also reinforced the Cold War gender order. Women were not absent, but their presence emphasized grace and femininity. Two examples have already been noted: the display of folk dancing performed by one thousand schoolgirls, which climaxed with their formation of the SEAP Games rings; and the female shield bearers in the traditional costume of each country, praised by visitors as "beautiful and meaningful."[77] The grace and beauty of these images could be contrasted with the image of order and regimentation of the male performers, including the massed service bands and a mass demonstration of physical exercise by one thousand schoolboys accompanied by a brass band from the elite Vajiravudh College. The sporting events held over the following five days reinforced this binary. Of 518 athletes representing seven countries in twelve sports, just thirty-eight women from four countries took part in only two disciplines (athletics and tennis).[78] If these figures were not especially unusual for the late 1950s, they nevertheless reinforced a somatic dichotomy characteristic of Cold War Thailand and Southeast Asia. Whereas the beautiful, graceful, and traditional female body was presented as a synonym of the Thai nation—and region—the regimented, masculine body of the soldier, athlete, and schoolboy was represented as its metonym, an image of the nation and region themselves.[79]

Finally, these performances took place under the gaze and presidency of the games' patron, King Bhumibol. The king oversaw a Buddhist ceremony at the start of official proceedings, officially opened the games with a short speech, and then released 2,502 doves (the year of the Buddhist Era), a dual symbol of international peace and acquisition of Buddhist merit. At all other times, he sat still and silently in the tribune of honor, the key actor in a newly invented theatrics of power that combined existing cultures of state ceremonialism with the modern genre of Olympic spectacle.[80] The central role of the king reflected not only Sarit's restoration of ancient and the invention of modern royal ceremonies in Thai symbolic life but also the way in which he latched on to the resurgent charisma (*barami*) of the monarch, capturing the mutually beneficial embrace of the military and monarchy in Cold War Thailand.[81]

Conclusion

The euphoric coverage of the SEAP Games reinforced a regional mode of idealistic internationalism borrowed from the Olympic Games, Asian Games, and even the United Nations. Tun Abdul Razak, the deputy prime minister of Malaya and president of the Olympic Council of Malaya, grasped this political significance. At a ceremony to farewell his athletes, Razak declared:

> Today, as a result of the rebirth of liberty in Asia, Asians are free to choose their own ways and it is particularly fitting that the Games should first take place in Siam which is the oldest free nation in this region. I am confident that as the years go by the S.E.A.P. Games will help bring this small family of nations even closer together, and so promote the spirit of goodwill, peace and harmony which we always cherish in this part of the world.[82]

Ostensibly, as Razak appreciated, the regionalist sentiment of the SEAP Games was a product of decolonization, which created a new regional order of nation-states and the demand for new forms of interaction between them. International sport, with its emphasis on both national and supranational identities, provided an ideal forum of this kind. Yet this was only half the story. The new regional order of Southeast Asia, reflected and celebrated in the founding of the SEAP Games, was created not only by national independence movements but their intersection with local and regional experiences of the Cold War.

The Cold War roots of the SEAP Games were made most obvious by those who were absent: the Communist DRV, despite being located on the Southeast Asian peninsula, and neutralist Cambodia, whose toxic relations with Thailand were inflamed not only by the temple dispute but by personal and ideological antagonisms arising from the Cold War. Underlying these absences was a complex association between the SEAP Games and the Cold War culture of Thailand. If Thailand's special distinction in the region had traditionally been its noncolonized status, its leadership in the SEAP Games owed as much to its Cold War identity as an anti-Communist bulwark of the United States. As a result, the regionalism of the SEAP Games was Thai-centric, anti-Communist, US backed, and limited to mainland Southeast Asia, circumscriptions that were inseparable from the context of the Cold War. While Razak hailed the "rebirth of liberty in Asia," the meaning of liberty had shifted, at least in part, from "freedom from colonialism" to "freedom from Communism."

The impact of the Cold War on the SEAP Games was probably inevitable, given the leading role of Thailand and the anti-Communist stance of the Asian Games. But more than simply mirror Cold War divides, the SEAP Games effected and embodied popular experiences and beliefs of the Cold War in Thailand and Southeast Asia, or what I refer to as Cold War culture. In the regional context, the games embodied the motif of regional friendship between the "free world" nations of peninsular Southeast Asia, consisting of both anti-Communist and neutralist countries, and of antagonism between rivals Thailand and Cambodia. Just as significantly, the SEAP Games embodied key themes in the domestic Cold War culture of Thailand: nationalism, developmentalism, the revival of the monarchy, and the militarization of life and politics. Adapted from the Olympics and Asian Games, the cultural production and practices of the SEAP Games—rituals, symbols, performance, and press coverage—reinforced these themes in a popular and participatory way.

Far from being a one-off, the establishment of the SEAP Games in 1959 had lasting consequences. In Thailand, the themes of the SEAP Games—paternalistic development under the military, the emergence of Thailand as a regional and global tourist destination, and the expanding personality cult of the king—reverberated on a grander scale in the Fifth Asian Games in 1966 and then the relocated Sixth Asian Games of 1970.[83] Regionally, an even more important legacy was the enduring nature of the SEAP Games themselves and the persistence of links between sport, regional politics, and Cold War culture. In 1975 Cambodia, Laos, and South Vietnam withdrew from the games because of the Communist revolutions in Indochina. Two years later, with the resultant addition of the archipelagic states—Indonesia, the Philippines, and Brunei—the word "Peninsular" was dropped and the SEAP Games became the SEA Games. Temporarily and controversially, the Coalition Government of Democratic Kampuchea returned to the renamed SEA Games in 1983–1987, but it was only after the thawing of the Cold War in the late 1980s and early 1990s that all ten countries in the region assembled on the same stage.[84]

PART V

THE POSTCOLONIAL

NEGOTIATING COLONIAL REPRESSION

African Footballers in Salazar's Portugal

Todd Cleveland

When superstar football (soccer) player Eusébio left the pitch following Portugal's 2–1 defeat to England in the 1966 World Cup semifinals, he was awash in tears, fiercely clutching his red-and-green jersey—the national colors of Portugal. Yet Eusébio was neither born nor grew up in the Iberian nation; instead, a Mozambican, he was one of many Africans who made their way from Portugal's colonial territories to the metropole to ply their athletic skills from the late 1940s to the end of the colonial era in 1975. Like Eusébio, many of these African players performed spectacularly on the field, significantly elevating the play of their respective clubs and vaulting the Portuguese national team to unprecedented levels.

While both Eusébio and Portuguese everywhere grieved following the squad's exit from the 1966 World Cup, the country was simultaneously engaged in far graver matters. Since the early 1960s, Portugal had been actively attempting to suppress armed insurgencies led by Socialist movements in three of its five African colonies: Mozambique, Angola, and Guinea. Unlike other European imperial states, Portugal's right-wing dictatorial regime intransigently resisted calls to decolonize. In this rejection, the country's authoritarian prime minister, António de Oliveira Salazar, enjoyed significant international support, touting Angola and Mozambique as key components in the bulwark against Communist expansion in Southern Africa. The Cold Warrior's insistence on the territorial—and thus racial—integration of Portugal and its African colonies was central to the country's public relations campaign intended to legitimize and thereby maintain the empire.

Yet, as the Cold War progressed, the Fascist government came under increasing pressure from the Socialist Bloc of nations, including the rapidly growing number of newly independent, left-leaning African states, regarding its imperial obstinacy and racially exploitative policies. The regime in Lisbon could ignore much of this criticism, as its lease of an air base in the Azores, dating back to 1943, was vital to American military capabilities and endeavors during the latter half of World War II and, even more prominently, during the ensuing Cold War. Moreover, Portugal had been a founding member of the North Atlantic Treaty Organization (NATO) and actively equipped its counterinsurgency forces with material funneled, at times illicitly, through this conduit. Eventually, even staunch allies such as the United States began to privately implore Lisbon to relax statutory controls in the empire, fearful that the resident populations would gravitate to the Soviet camp.[1]

This mounting pressure and attendant international isolation prompted Portugal to waive a host of travel and labor restrictions to facilitate the employment and relocation of African football players to the metropole. These integrative measures were intended to mollify foreign critics of all ideological persuasions, as well as Portugal's increasingly discontented colonial subjects. Lisbon was replicating France's earlier efforts to integrate its club and national teams by using players from its African colonies. The alleged benefits of colonialism were now fully on display.[2] Following these policy adjustments, Portugal could showcase a national football squad that seemed to evince a genuinely multiethnic nation of racial tolerance and acceptance. The inclusion of African players such as Eusébio on Portugal's national team (selecção) afforded the regime an opportunity to highlight the unity of the metropole and the colonies, the opportunities for social mobility for its African colonial subjects, and the racial harmony that this integration purportedly fostered.

Drawing on colonial archival sources, popular media, and interviews with former players and coaches, this essay examines the experiences of these African athletes as they relocated to Portugal and attempted to negotiate this politically charged environment from the late 1940s until 1975. The labor reforms that enabled these players to seek employment in Portugal were politically motivated, intended primarily to appease external critics—from Washington to Moscow and everywhere in between—and were, in practice, highly restrictive, while the regime's effusive, self-congratulatory propaganda regarding these players was largely spurious. The overt apoliticism that virtually all African players displayed in the metropole—a corollary of their long-term social improvement objectives—suggests that they actively and strategically sought to integrate socially, or at least cultivate this perception. Although these athletes were often internally conflicted, their professionalism and determination to improve their lives underpinned their conciliatory approach throughout this turbulent period. Thus, despite their allure as potential nationalist symbols for both African independence movements and the Portuguese regime, they failed to serve either the insurgencies or counterinsurgency while remaining widely respected and admired in both the colonies and the metropole.

The experiences of these footballers illuminate the largely cosmetic and limited nature of Lisbon's labor and social reforms. Nevertheless, they do show some of the ways that Africans could creatively exploit opportunities precipitated by Cold War politics in the waning decades of Portugal's dictatorial Estado Novo (New state) regime. Indeed, the government-sanctioned relocation of African football players to Portugal suggests that mounting international pressure significantly impacted the administration's operational ethos, especially after the outbreak of wars of independence in Angola, Mozambique, and Guinea-Bissau in the early 1960s.

The Origins of Football in Portugal's Colonial Empire in Africa

As in other colonized settings, football was introduced into Portugal's African empire by the standard agents of colonialism—missionaries, administrators, merchants, corporate officials, soldiers, and settlers. The game spread from port cities, such as Luanda, Angola, and Lourenço Marques (Maputo), Mozambique, to the hinterlands of these urban centers, often along roads and railway lines but also through missionary schools. Although Africans throughout the empire embraced the game, its introduction was anything but innocuous or inadvertent. Portugal's colonial regime intended football to "civilize" the indigenous populations as part of a broader program of physical education aimed to improve the bodies of the colonized masses. The game was also intended to subdue, discipline, inculcate, and even demean local populations. Football was more than just a game; it was a device used to establish and deepen both physical and psychological control of the subjects of empire. Thus, the sport was a key component in Portugal's campaign of cultural imperialism, an important pillar in the broader process of empire.

From these modest beginnings, increasing numbers of Africans were exposed to a game they would embrace. Local leagues were formed in the colonies, largely along racial lines. Players of European descent predictably enjoyed superior facilities and more structured playing environments. Even under less-than-ideal circumstances, Africans demonstrated considerable zeal for, and commitment to, the game. It was in these rudimentary leagues and in a variety of less formal, or even impromptu, matches that the African players who would one day showcase their skills in the metropole first learned, and subsequently mastered, football.

The Revised Rules and Strategies of an Established Game

For all of the latent talent in Portugal's colonies, only a particular set of historical factors and events prompted African players' eventual relocations to the metropole. In particular, the national team had long been an embarrassment. Between May 1949 and May 1955, the *selecção* had won only three times in twenty matches and failed to win a single game in the seven it played from 1957 to 1959. In the wake of these humiliations, Portuguese football officials began to consider utilizing African players to boost the prospects of both the metropolitan clubs and the *selecção*. Although footballers from South America and Eastern Europe had already featured in Portugal, talent in the colonies was yet to be mined. Yet for all of the concerns about competitiveness on the pitch, global political pressures were to prove even more influential in prompting the Portuguese government to alter both labor and migration policy concerning talented Africans.

By the 1950s, the drive for African independence was inevitable. Britain granted its Gold Coast colony (Ghana) independence in 1957. By the 1960s, a succession of colonies became independent. The British, French, and Belgians all abandoned their colonial projects, but the Portuguese regime clung ever more tightly to its empire, reinvigorating its "unholy alliance" with the entrenched white-minority regimes in Rhodesia (Zimbabwe) and South Africa as a barricade to thwart further Soviet influence in the region.[3] In a bid to stress the indivisibility of the colonies and the metropole, in 1951 the regime recast these possessions as "overseas provinces," suggesting that they were as integral to Portugal as areas of the metropole. Yet this obstinacy and artifice did not come without cost. Portugal's stance was becoming increasingly anachronistic, and the country increasingly isolated, just as its allies in Salisbury (Harare) and Pretoria were.

Co-opting Success: Capitalizing Politically on Footballing Accomplishments

Because the state had sanctioned the relocation of African players, it was keen to reap the political dividends their sporting success was sowing. The regime had long cast football as one of the three pillars of the Portuguese nation, alongside fado and Fátima (Christianity).[4] Moreover, by the 1960s, the country was enmeshed in three colonial wars and was hemorrhaging citizens because of severe domestic unemployment and the possibility of conscription for young men.

In this environment, the state moved aggressively to twin football and politics. As João Malheiro has argued, "In colonial-era Portugal, to make Eusébio—a black African—the grandest symbol of the country served perfectly the perverse intentions of the government officials. The fondness dispensed to our athlete of the century . . . had the intention of protecting the regime, of softening its racial intolerance, and of exhibiting to the world an artificial generosity."[5] State propaganda also linked Amália Rodrigues with Eusébio: the greatest Portuguese fado singer with the greatest "Portuguese" footballer. The most accomplished African players, including Eusébio, were regularly invited to state ceremonies, adorned with medals for their "contributions to the nation," and rendered "ambassadors" of the regime—official representatives of the nation both domestically and, perhaps more important, abroad.[6] As Eusébio later remarked, "I never was political and much less in that period. I was used by the regime, but only later did I realize that."[7]

These calculated measures commenced shortly after the African players began arriving in Portugal. One of the first, Matateu, a Mozambican who starred for Lisbon-based Belenenses, became an early example, and subject, of state propaganda. In 1951 Carlos Gomes wrote the following about an important domestic match in which the striker scored two goals to help his club defeat Sporting, 4–3: "Poor Matateu left the pitch on the shoulders of the (white) supporters, and, once again, the fascist apparatus took advantage of the popular happiness of the Belenenses supporters to publish his photograph on the shoulders of the whites, in order that they should be seen neither as racists nor exploiters: 'See how we treat the natives of the colonies!' "[8]

In another attempt to exploit politically the achievements of these players, following Benfica's successful European club championship during the 1961–1962 campaign, its second title in a row, the president of Portugal, Américo Tomás, presented the squad with state medals; publicly declared Eusébio and Mário Coluna, prominent Mozambican players on the team, to be "advertisements for the country"; and suggested that Eusébio's "actions and achievements dignified the club, the sport, and the country, itself."[9] Ana Santos has argued that this type of overt acknowledgment of these players' success and the associated media coverage that chronicled their accomplishments reinforced the "imagined community" that the regime was attempting to cultivate to bridge and unite the metropole and colonies.[10]

If Benfica's success in 1962 had provided the regime with an opening to intertwine football success, national pride, and imperial righteousness, the national team's third-place finish at the 1966 World Cup was even more pregnant with these sorts of propagandistic opportunities. After returning home, the government organized a parade through Lisbon's main arteries to celebrate the squad's success. The event featured four African players in the starting eleven. In appreciation of their efforts, high-ranking state officials formally honored the players and coaches with silver medals of the Ordem do Infante Dom Henrique, which essentially bestowed on them Portuguese knighthood for their efforts to promote "Portugal's good name and prestige."[11] On the occasion, the president of the Portuguese Football Federation declared, "The World Championship passes, but your effort and sportsmanship endure, making men speak of Portugal in the highest terms during those days when you were able to honor the country."[12]

Later that summer, Salazar invited Benfica player Mário Coluna, a Mozambican, and some of his African colleagues to the inauguration of the recently completed Salazar Bridge (now the April 25th Bridge). As Coluna shared with me during our interview, "Salazar gave the highest consecration of the country to me and my colleagues. After the 1966 World Cup in England, he honored me at the inauguration of Salazar Bridge. I went with him to cut the ribbon and to cross the bridge by foot."[13]

Perhaps the attention lavished on the squad was even more prodigious because of Portugal's 2–1 victory in the otherwise meaningless third-place game against an archenemy of the state. According to Hilário, a Mozambican defender and member of the 1966 squad, "In that World Cup we did something that no one in the world was expecting, and the Portuguese people and government presented us with medals and awards for what we had done; we were very well received. . . . In fact, the best gift we gave Salazar was beating Russia, because at that time we weren't allowed to play against Russia—only in the World Cup."[14] Indeed, one year earlier, Portugal's most famous club team, Benfica, had proposed to host an exhibition match against Russia's Dinamo Moscow, promising that a victory, "absolutely within our reach, would bring, without a shadow of a doubt, even greater reverberations for the honor and prestige of our country," only to be rebuffed by the regime.[15]

Metropolitan Constraints and National Treasures

Although African players could proceed to the highest levels of the Portuguese football firmament, this universe was, in practice, highly circumscribed. Although metropolitan clubs and the Portuguese government had coordinated their efforts to sign and relocate African players, these athletes were, almost always, prohibited from accepting subsequent employment beyond Portugal's borders. Having secured the services of players who were taking both their new clubs and the Portuguese national team to new heights, both the regime and the clubs were determined to keep them in the country. Perhaps no case illustrates this politico-sporting resolve better than that of Eusébio.

As a result of the star's success at the 1966 World Cup, he had attracted suitors from across Europe, only to discover that Salazar had classified him as a "national treasure," which precluded employment abroad. This decision cost both the club and the player dearly: Benfica had signed Eusébio for seven hundred contos, while the Italian giant, Turin-based Juventus, was reportedly offering more than twenty thousand contos.[16] Eusébio was understandably bitter about Salazar's politically motivated decision. Some years later, the Mozambican striker declared, "After the '66 World Cup, Italy made a big offer, one which would have made me the highest-paid player in the world. And yet I was not allowed to move. Why? Salazar was not my father and he certainly was not my mother. What gave him the right? The truth was that he was my slave master, just as he was the slave master of the entire country."[17] During my interview with Eusébio in 2010, he was apparently in a decidedly lighter mood but still harbored some of the resentment he had displayed some six years earlier, while underscoring the steadying influence and importance of his fellow Mozambican teammate Coluna: "Salazar told me not to think about leaving the country, because I was 'patrimony of the state.' Coluna and I would speak in dialect when we met with Salazar so that he wouldn't understand us. . . . Coluna would tell me not to say anything, to shut up, and he would explain everything to me later. . . . Afterward, Coluna told me that Salazar was the boss of everything in the current political regime."[18]

Negotiating a Politically Charged Environment

Eusébio's deference to his more senior countryman in the audience of Salazar—and ultimately to the head of state himself—exemplifies African players' strategic approach to navigating the political environment in Portugal during the Cold War, especially following the outbreak of the wars for independence in the colonies. Yet even as these footballers demonstrated prudence and caution, it was in the metropole that they developed their political consciousness, interacting with African students who had come to Portugal to study and, in some cases, engaging indirectly with the banned Portuguese Communist Party (PCP). Perhaps most acutely, those footballers who studied at the University of Coimbra and played for the university-sponsored club, Académica, found themselves operating in a milieu in which revolutionary ideas progressively circulated. Therefore, the vaunted state secret police, the Polícia Internacional e de Defesa do Estado (PIDE), kept close tabs on African players in Portugal, monitoring their personal interactions and traveling with them when matches took their teams behind the Iron Curtain. In response, most African players adopted a strategic apoliticism that facilitated their successful navigation of this highly charged environment. Consequently, these athletes were viewed neither as subversives by the Portuguese population nor as political stooges or collaborators by their African brothers who were fighting—and dying—for independence. They were also able to maintain an air of impartiality even though many African players donned both Portuguese national team jerseys and, as conscripts, military uniforms.

Although these African athletes were often internally conflicted, their professional approach to the game and to their new arrangements in Portugal underpinned their conspicuous apoliticism throughout this contentious period. There were exceptions; a handful of players returned to Africa to fight for independence, as was the case in the better-known Francophone context.[19] However, these Lusophone athletes–cum–freedom fighters numbered only four. Indeed, even if many of these players from Portugal's colonies harbored sympathies for the African independence movements, they remained outwardly detached. As Eusébio once famously declared, "I don't get involved in politics. I don't like politics. My only politics is football."[20]

Arrivals and Allegiances: Airing Their Devotion

As soon as these African athletes arrived in the metropole, their public statements suggested a disengagement from the continent and a commitment to football, family, and virtually nothing else. These comments disarmed potentially suspicious Portuguese, while endearing the players to the supporters of their new clubs and the regime.

Public remarks made by Matateu, who arrived from Mozambique to play for Belenenses in 1951, were typical: "I want to say with much pleasure that in spite of having come from African lands, I feel very 'Belenense' and that I will do the best that I can and know how to do."[21] Open admiration for their new country continued as they settled in, often heavily flavored with gratitude, respect, even obsequiousness. Three years after arriving from Angola to play for Académica, a club located in the city of Coimbra in central Portugal, Mário Torres effusively declared in an interview, "I was blessed at that time [1956] when destiny wrote in my life's book the beautiful chapter that I have been living in the beautiful city of the Mondego [Coimbra]. Here, I have lived the most beautiful moments of my existence—here. I encountered a future, glory, and happiness!"[22] Apparent sincerity aside, the Portuguese regime could hardly have crafted a more rapturous statement for Torres to recite.

Developing Political Consciousness

For all of the approbatory declarations these players made following their arrivals, it was in Portugal that they would begin to become more broadly aware, and critical, of Lisbon's imperial politics. Very few of these footballers, however, acted on their new, or heightened, political consciousness, remaining in the metropole rather than surreptitiously returning to the colonies to assist in the various struggles for political independence. Yet simply by congregating with subversive elements in Portugal and engaging in discussions about Cold War politics and the mere possibility of decolonization, these African athletes were rejecting, even if only selectively, the political roles assigned to them by the regime.

One of the African players who walked the fine line between sedition and collaboration was the Mozambican defender Mário Wilson. The Académica legend indicated that he regularly discussed African independence with teammates, classmates, and others, including Agostinho Neto, who would go on to become the head of Angola's Socialist MPLA (Movimento Popular de Libertação de Angola) party and the country's first president. "We [Neto and I] used to meet [in Lisbon, where Neto was studying]. . . . We came many times . . . to send correspondence to Angola and Mozambique. I began to perceive things that I previously had not, coming to see Mozambique with a new set of eyes."[23] Wilson indicated that over time players from Africa exchanged these ideas even when not in the presence of a political revolutionary such as Neto, while football afforded them the requisite cover. "After more African players started to arrive, we got together because we wanted the independence of the colonies. We enjoyed a lot of projection because of football; therefore, we were important elements for the decolonization of Africa. I played with guys from Angola who studied in Coimbra who did the same thing."[24]

As Wilson mentioned, this city was a setting in which many African players received their initial dose of political consciousness. Many footballers were motivated to attend the University of Coimbra, the country's premier institution, and simultaneously to play for Académica. During the colonial era, the squad was composed solely of matriculating students. This decision was primarily practical in nature, as these student-athletes were opting to pursue an education that would, in turn, serve them well long after their athleticism faded.

While Académica rarely recruited in Africa, leaving this endeavor to the major Portuguese clubs—Benfica, FC Porto, Sporting, and Belenenses—Coimbra became a target for many African footballers after they arrived in the metropole. To reach the city, they requested transfers or loans to Académica from their existing metropolitan squads. Although the clubs that lost players to Coimbra in this manner were understandably unhappy with this practice, the Portuguese regime saw the enrollment of Africans at its best university as valuable propaganda material and therefore sanctioned these players' strategic requests. The government would, however, come to rue this decision.

Coimbra students were much more radical than others elsewhere in Portugal, and as full members of the student body, Académica's African footballers were not immune to the leftist political sentiments circulating around campus. In fact, João Santana and João Mesquita have argued that the political tone within the squad was irreversibly set by its manager, Cândido de Oliveira, who oversaw the team from 1956 until his death in 1958. As an opponent of the regime, the player, manager, and football journalist had found himself incarcerated a number of times, including at the infamous Tarrafal political prison camp in the Cape Verde Islands. Uncurbed, de Oliveira's politics colored his interactions with his players. Regarding the political environment in the city and within the club, António Brassard, who arrived from Mozambique in 1964 to play and study in Coimbra, remarked:

> I started gaining political consciousness after my arrival in Coimbra and Académica. I started to understand the problems of the African colonies here in Portugal. I started to understand that Mozambique had an option to fight for independence. That opened my eyes about the problems of overseas countries. I also started reading books and articles about politics from our friends. They had to hide the books, but they provided them to us. We had a chance to learn about other realities and ideas about what Portugal's policy was in those overseas countries.[25]

If this type of political consciousness among players developed rather inaudibly, there were two flashpoints in the 1960s at Coimbra sparked by student opposition to the colonial wars and resultant crackdowns by the regime. The first came in 1962, during a time of general unrest that prompted the postponement of all football matches for one week. Due to face Sporting following the prospective resumption of the season, the Académica players gathered to vote whether to resume playing or boycott as an expression of their unity with the politically discontent student body. At the time, the Coimbra students had adopted an ardent leftist stance, accusing football players—among others—of being capitalists, "professionals in the service of Salazar," and thus insisted that the Académica squad refuse to play.[26] It was the Cold War playing out on the football fields of Portugal.

To address the unrest, troops were dispatched to the city, and for a brief moment it was not clear whether the club would continue to exist. As captain of Académica, Mário Wilson was thrust into an unenviable position. The Mozambican player recalled, "There was a serious student protest, which led to halting the league for a week, as a form of protest against colonialism. Soldiers appeared, and we were called in . . . to define our position. I was the first to be heard because I was captain. 'Are you playing or not,' they asked me. 'Sorry, but I need to speak with the players,' I replied. We all met in a room, and I spoke: 'We have time for our struggles; let's not commit collective suicide. I think we should indicate that we will play.' "[27] The decision by Wilson and his teammates was, ultimately, prescient: it would take a further twelve years before the nation, led by midlevel military officers weary of participating in the colonial conflicts, was ready for revolution, finally overthrowing the repressive regime in a reasonably peaceful coup d'état on April 25, 1974.

In 1969, about five years before that transformative event, Coimbra had again been at the forefront of political upheaval instigated by leftist university students in opposition to Portugal's ongoing imperial resolve. Student protests again boiled over, and, reactively, the regime cracked down, transforming the campus into a police state. Amid the chaos, Académica somewhat improbably advanced through the successive rounds of the annual Taça de Portugal (Portuguese Cup) tournament, and a victory over Sporting saw the squad poised to face mighty Benfica in the cup final, held annually following the conclusion of the domestic season in Portugal's national stadium just outside Lisbon. Ahead of the June 22 clash, members of banned, leftist political parties courageously circulated political flyers, while on match day opponents of the regime smuggled banners into the grounds and rapidly unfurled them before passing them back through the crowd to sympathizers. Even the Académica squad participated in the dissent: the team's players entered the stadium at a deliberately slow pace and wore their traditional black capes in a manner that suggested (political) mourning. Fearful of exactly these types of displays, the national television station, Rádio e Televisão de Portugal (RTP), decided not to broadcast the game, and the Portuguese president, who traditionally attended the match, stayed away to avoid embarrassment. The whole country was on edge, and the match consequently constituted much more than just a game. Ultimately, Benfica won 2–1, though many of its players later admitted solidarity with Académica and wished they had faced a different opponent in the final. As João Nuno Coelho and Francisco Pinheiro have argued, Benfica's win may well have "saved the regime" because, had Coimbra won, the victory likely would have grown into something larger and broader.[28]

Although the political turmoil of the 1960s eventually abated, even if only temporarily, Mário Wilson continues to insist on Académica's ongoing importance to the independence of the colonies. "We lived in a time and atmosphere that we took advantage of to . . . help the colonies achieve their independence through our study, because we, the ones who came here [to Coimbra] to study and play, were the ones who had to help the cause."[29] In fact, the only African footballers to flee the metropole to fight for independence in the colonies derived from Académica. These dissident athletes included Daniel Chipenda, Augusto Araújo, José Julio, and França. Indeed, as the former player Zeca Afonso rightfully declared: "Académica wasn't [just] a club, it was a cause."[30]

Subversive Spaces: The Casas dos Estudantes do Império

Left-wing elements hostile to the Estado Novo were present not only within the student body at the University of Coimbra but also at the Casas dos Estudantes do Império (CEI; Houses of the Students from the Empire). These centers, including the landmark entity in Lisbon as well as smaller versions in the cities of Porto and Coimbra, hosted and served as gathering sites for students from Portugal's colonies who had come to the metropole for varying periods of time.[31] The Lisbon CEI opened in 1944 and functioned until 1965, at which point the regime shuttered the houses, declaring them loci of anticolonialism and anti-Salazarism.

In this assessment, the government was accurate. The African members of these houses clandestinely consumed Marxist literature, interacted with members of the PCP, and eventually generated their own cultural-political output, much to the consternation of an increasingly observant and intolerant state. As Jorge Querido, a Cape Verdean engineer and activist member of the Lisbon CEI who was later imprisoned for his political activity, recalled, "The CEI was one of the few oases of democracy and liberty that survived in the vast colonial-fascist desert; it was a body alive, an authentic institution of informal education . . . and, above all, in us Africans, it awoke in us our own identity and taught us how to combat the mental and cultural alienation provoked by centuries of colonial domination."[32]

Given the CEI's role as an incubator and cultivator of leftist ideologies, it should come as no surprise that many of the African liberation movements' leaders, including Amílcar Cabral (Guinea), Agostinho Neto (Angola), Mário Pinto de Andrade (Angola), and Marcelino dos Santos (Mozambique), had transitioned through these houses, primarily the flagship center in Lisbon. Moreover, many other African CEI members daringly fled Portugal to return home to aid the leftist nationalist parties.[33] The African footballers present in the metropole were keenly aware of the revolutionary political bent of many of the members of the CEI, so many of them gave both the students and the centers a wide berth. Because the CEI students were among the only other Africans present in the metropole during the colonial period, other players engaged, openly and eagerly interacting, though these migrant footballers were also careful to avoid being too closely linked with these "intellectually radical" elements.[34]

Tomás Medeiros, a São Toméan who was studying in Lisbon and was a member of the CEI in the city from the mid-1950s until he fled Portugal in 1961, provided insights during our interview into the ways that African footballers in the metropole engaged with the Casa. In his testimony, he echoed sentiments discussed previously about the initial, effective absence of political consciousness among these athletes, the way they gradually developed this awareness, and the utility of these footballers to the regime. "The players who came from Africa did not have political consciousness. . . . They received it here from students and from the Portuguese Communist Party. . . . Many footballers who came from Africa were from poor social strata. . . . They were instrumentalized by the regime. One of the guys used by the colonial regime was Eusébio. He had offers to play in other countries, but Salazar refused. That was the policy of the regime."[35]

Agosto Matine, a Mozambican midfielder who arrived in Portugal just as the Lisbon Casa was being closed, confirmed the interactions between African footballers and students from the empire but also the precautions that the former took regarding these relations: "Yes, we interacted with students from the CEI, but we avoided being seen with them, so it was only on a few occasions. The most convenient place to meet was at the cinema. . . . We chatted a lot. In fact, we used native languages—Angolans or Mozambicans, this was the way we chatted. We also were careful, as if more than five of us were together, someone would be watching."[36]

The "someone" to which Matine was referring would have been a member of the PIDE. Members of this agency closely surveilled African footballers playing for metropolitan clubs, especially when these squads traveled abroad to Socialist nations, but also domestically when these athletes gathered with friends at cafés or attended movies. In particular, the state was keen to avoid embarrassment that any subversive activity—up to and including formal defection—could have generated, as many of the African players in the metropole had become the international faces of Portuguese football. Consequently, these migrant athletes were forced to exhibit judiciousness regarding when and with whom they congregated, both domestically and while abroad.

Although there was nothing comical about this surveillance, in my interviews these former footballers often chuckled as they recounted the PIDE's methods. The police service often dispatched agents to accompany the Portuguese national team and traveling clubs, impersonating journalists or even pretending to read newspapers in foreign hotel lobbies while not so covertly observing their targets' every move. António Brassard even discovered, some years after he had retired, that the PIDE had sent an agent to his wedding ceremony and that the undercover photographer had filed the pictures he took at the event at the agency's headquarters.[37]

Although African players were aware of, or at least suspected, this level of surveillance, they still occasionally drew unwanted attention. On more than one occasion, Mário Coluna was accused of exhibiting Socialist sympathies as a result of his interactions with African students and/or nationalists while traveling abroad for matches elsewhere in Europe. After his return to Portugal, the player was called in to the PIDE offices and aggressively interrogated, but in each instance, his celebrity endowed his explanations with sufficient plausibility—that the Mozambicans or Angolans with whom he had interacted were simply requesting tickets so that they could watch him play. According to Coluna, regarding an incident of this nature that occurred in Bratislava in 1965,

> Some Mozambicans called me and came to the hotel, and we talked. Meanwhile, some journalists that were traveling with the team were police informants. They saw me having a conversion with Marcelino dos Santos [a Mozambican nationalist] and others and then informed the PIDE in Lisbon. I was called in by the PIDE, and they said, "We know that you have contacts with FRELIMO [Frente de Libertação de Moçambique] guys, and the MPLA." I said, "They [the Mozambicans] came to meet me at the hotel to ask for tickets to go to the stadium to watch the match and to support Benfica. Our contact was about football, not politics, because I am not a politician." It was in this way that I saved myself.[38]

Coluna and others indicated, however, that when they did engage in conversations with fellow Africans that could be construed as subversive, they spoke in dialect, rendering their articulations beyond the comprehension of anyone who might be eavesdropping.

Regarding direct interaction with the PIDE, the Mozambican player Hilário indicated that often, prior to departure, players were brought into the agency's offices and menacingly "reminded" of their focus. "The only thing that the PIDE did to me was when the teams traveled to the Communist countries, the African players who were on the club or in the national team were called to the PIDE and asked, 'Do you know where it is you're going? Do you know what you're going to do?' And we would respond: 'Yes, I know, to play football.' For all of these trips, the Africans were contacted."[39]

Conclusion

Portugal and its colonies witnessed some of the most contentious struggles between East and West during the Cold War, as both the United States and the Soviet Union aggressively attempted to keep in or attract to their political orbits, respectively, the various leaders of these nations. From the late 1940s until 1975, a stream of African footballers entered the charged metropolitan environment, which featured a taut political climate further exacerbated by the commencement of the wars of independence in the colonies—these players' homelands. Each of these struggles pitted colonial against anticolonial forces, pitting Cold War ideologies against one another in proxy conflicts that saw armed Europeans and Africans engaged in the various arenas. Rather than be drawn into these ideological and, eventually, martial engagements, the overwhelming majority of these migrant athletes eschewed the political currents that daily circulated around them, determined instead to focus on football, their families, and, for some, their education to facilitate their integration into metropolitan society.

As they navigated this political minefield, their outward apoliticism served these African footballers well. Indeed, even as Portugal underwent a democratic transition in the aftermath of 1974, many of them continued to shun politics. Although both Portugal and these African nations attempted to claim these athlete-heroes as their own, even today most of these retired footballers consider themselves as dual nationals, resisting appropriation by Portugal or their respective African homeland. Despite their obvious political utility—then and now—Eusébio's self-protective declaration, "I don't like politics. Football is my politics," continues to characterize many of these former sporting luminaries.[40]

DEFLECTED CONFRONTATIONS

Cold War Baseball in the Caribbean

Rob Ruck

After revolutionaries surged into Havana, Cuba, on New Year's Day 1959, the island's sporting ties with the United States began to unravel. Within a year, the Cold War tore asunder the most enduring transnational relationship in baseball history. That alliance, however, was already troubled. Major League Baseball's color line, as well as its interference in the island game, had frayed Caribbean baseball's bonds with the United States long before Fidel Castro's seizure of state power. But the Cold War brought these problems to a head and redefined baseball's global balance of power. By the 1970s, the Dominican Republic had replaced Cuba as the center of Caribbean baseball and become the greatest new source of talent in the game. While Cuban baseball veered off on a noncapitalist tangent, the Dominican Republic pushed the game's capitalist boundaries.

Prior to 1947, Major League Baseball's color line was a jarring reminder to Latinos that their northern neighbor's racial codes and practices were far more pernicious than their own. The Cold War focused attention on baseball's racial contradictions. In many ways, race was America's Achilles' heel during the Cold War, especially as stories of police dogs attacking children, church bombings, and murder circulated in the Caribbean basin. Those incidents reinforced notions of the United States as a perilous country unwelcoming to people of color.

Because Major League Baseball (MLB) had adhered to segregation from the 1890s to 1947, darker-skinned players throughout the Caribbean basin gravitated to Cuba, not the United States. A few played in the Negro Leagues and often came back to the islands annoyed by the racial animosity and hostility they had encountered in the United States.

But in April 1947, Jackie Robinson ran on to Ebbets Field in Brooklyn to play first base for the Dodgers, reintegrating MLB. By 1959, the US leagues had grudgingly given ground on the racial segregation that had marred the US game and excluded most Latin players for more than half a century. Robinson's success allowed Latin players once unable to pass the major leagues' racial muster to follow in his footsteps. Among them was Saturnino Orestes Armas Miñoso, who became the first Afro-Cuban in the majors. Because most teams feared that integration would cost them at the gate, they integrated rosters slowly, and only a trickle of African American and Afro-Latin players debuted over the next decade.

Fans in the Caribbean scrutinized the efforts of these darker-skinned players to establish themselves in the major leagues, just as they followed the racial upheavals rocking the United States. Dominican Felipe Alou recalled his teachers talking about the civil rights struggle when the Brooklyn Dodgers visited Ciudad Trujillo for spring training in 1948. "I was shocked because we had always looked up to the United States. The word democracy meant a lot to us because we were living at the time under a dictatorship."[1]

"I got to see Jackie Robinson play," Alou recalled. "It was an incredible baseball game for a youngster who someday wanted to play the game. We knew what was going on with Jackie Robinson to an extent. We knew about the race problem, and I remember a teacher told us that the only reason the Dodgers were having spring training was because Jackie Robinson—they wanted to keep him away from the problems in the South." Alou had no idea that he would endure some of the same racial opposition that Robinson encountered.[2]

Robinson was extraordinarily successful both on and off the field, winning Rookie-of-the-Year honors and spurring record attendance for the Dodgers. "Baseball's Great Experiment," as Jules Tygiel dubbed it, entered the larger conversation about race and eased the way for integration in other arenas, including the 1954 US Supreme Court decision in *Brown v. Board of Education.* Major league owners gradually adjusted to integration and profited from the infusion of talented players they had once spurned. But they were unwilling to share power with Negro League or Caribbean teams, much less with their own players, who were seeking unionization and a greater say over the terms of their employment. After baseball's integration in 1947 and the Cuban Revolution in 1959, MLB sought even greater control over the Caribbean's sporting life.

Though Cuba had been an important source of talent and profit for major league owners and off-season wages for major league players since the early 1900s, Cold War politics meant that the island lost its place as Caribbean baseball's epicenter. It spun out of MLB's orbit while the other baseball-playing islands grudgingly accepted a subordinate role.

But race remained a sensitive issue within baseball and was the backdrop for post-1959 politics in both Cuba and the United States. Few matters exposed US rhetoric to greater scrutiny. MLB, which had long sought to anoint itself as the sporting incarnation of American democracy, was not immune to criticism. Struggles over segregation, fought in countless towns and cities during the decades after the end of World War II, frequently were over sport.

Although every MLB team had at least one non-Caucasian player by 1959, some teams countenanced segregated accommodations for players during spring training and on the road. Moreover, none hired African Americans or Latinos to front-office positions. Most minority players felt they were being treated with less respect and reward than white players. These racial conflicts played out in locker rooms, in the stands, on the sports pages, and on baseball diamonds during the Cold War and affected how people in the Caribbean looked at the United States.

At first, little suggested that the change of state authority in Cuba—albeit a revolutionary one—would rupture the island's long-standing connection with MLB. On July 24, 1959, just a little over seven months after Fidel Castro entered Havana, he led Los Barbudos, a team of comrades from the mountains, onto the field at Gran Estadio to play an exhibition game against a military police squad. Afterward, the Havana Sugar Kings and the Rochester Red Wings played their regular season International League game.

Cubans relished the presence of the Sugar Kings, who played in the International League, a top minor league affiliated with the majors. They were even more invested in the Cuban winter league, whose teams were Cuban owned. Both leagues featured Caucasian, African American, and Cuban players. The presence of Fidel and Los Barbudos on the undercard underscored a deeper common denominator—the appreciation for baseball that Cubans shared with the United States.

The next evening, however, festivities commemorating the July 26, 1953, attack on the Moncada Barracks—which revolutionaries considered the catalyst to their movement—spilled onto the field. As partisans outside the stadium fired celebratory shots into the sky, several bullets came down inside the ballpark, wounding Sugar Kings shortstop and Cuban native Leo Cardenas and Rochester's Brooklyn-born Frank Verdi, who was filling in as the third-base coach. The game was called and the home stand canceled after the Red Wings took flight the next day.[3] Though the rest of the Sugar Kings' season unfolded without further trouble, the incident foreshadowed MLB's exit from Cuba.

A few months later Fidel Castro threw out the first pitch before the seventh and deciding game of the 1959 Little World Series between the winners of the International League and the American Association, baseball's top minor leagues. With Che Guevara watching from the stands, the Sugar Kings captured the title. For a moment, the looming threat that US-Soviet rivalries posed to baseball seemed inconsequential. Island *fanaticos* rejoiced again that February when Cuba won its fifth consecutive Caribbean Series, a championship staged among the winners of the region's winter leagues.[4]

But as Castro edged closer to the Soviet Union, relations between the United States and Cuba collapsed. The International League, under State Department pressure, yanked the Sugar Kings out of Havana midway through the 1960 season and stuck them in New Jersey, despite Castro's offer to subsidize the team if that would keep them on the island. He even volunteered to pitch for the team. The Cuban winter league began play a few months later with only Cubans on the rosters, a comedown for fans accustomed to watching some of the best players in the game since the early 1900s. The league soon suspended play, and in March 1961, the revolutionary government abolished professional sport. Cubans were forced to decide if continuing their career in the States was worth exile from their homeland, and playing in the States was no longer an option for Cuban youth.[5]

The geopolitical context made rapprochement in baseball inconceivable. After Cuba nationalized US holdings, the Central Intelligence Agency (CIA) retaliated by trying to assassinate Castro. When that failed, the CIA backed the Bay of Pigs invasion, a military and political fiasco that buttressed Castro's power. The USSR then placed atomic weapons on the island in case the United States again intervened militarily. During a tense few weeks in October 1962, many feared that the Cold War would become hot. The Soviets removed their warheads in return for the removal of US missiles from Turkey, but the United States then embargoed the island, as Cuba moved even closer to the USSR.

Cuban baseball fell out of MLB's orbit, but Cuban fervor for baseball did not dissipate. The game did not disappear on the island. Instead, Cuban baseball created a parallel sporting world complementing its leaders' vision of revolution, race, and sovereignty. Baseball became a tool of domestic and international statecraft, freighted with ideology. It modeled the larger political division roiling the region and exposed deeper conflicts between the Caribbean and the United States over notions of race and sovereignty that continue to this day.

Baseball's Democratic Vision

By the early twentieth century, baseball in the United States had become the poster boy for a rising nation's democratic aspirations. "I see great things in baseball," Walt Whitman wrote in 1889. "It's our game—the American game." For John Tener, president of the National League and a future governor of Pennsylvania, baseball constituted "the very watchword of democracy." On the sandlots, Zane Gray gushed, "caste is lost. . . . Ragamuffins and velvet-breeched, white-collared boys stand in that equality which augurs well for the Stars and Stripes."[6]

Indeed, baseball modeled what many thought the United States represented at its best—a place where fair play and opportunity prevailed, a meritocracy in which performance trumped class, religion, and nationality. For immigrant boys from Europe, baseball was an arena where they could prove their worthiness of attaining citizenship.[7] But the men who came to control baseball's major leagues honored those democratic notions in the breach. Their leagues excluded more people than they included and imposed a color line that undercut the game's democratic rhetoric. As their control over baseball's commercial markets tightened, these owners sought absolute power over players and banded together whenever rivals threatened their monopoly.

Ironically, the democratic ideals that US baseball proclaimed, but did not attain, were already on display in Havana. There, players of all nations and races played with and against each other in the Liga Cubana. In the early twentieth century, baseball in the United States and Cuba reflected diametrically opposed notions of sport. The former implicitly embraced social Darwinism, and the latter sought to realize José Martí's radical vision of "a nation for all."[8]

As long as geography and race separated the United States from the Caribbean, baseball in these domains coexisted in mutually beneficial ways. But that did not free baseball from entangling politics or ongoing power struggles. MLB's hegemony was tested twice after World War II. Mexico's Jorge Pasquel mounted the first defiance when he tried to beat the majors at their own game.

Then, as the Cold War drove the United States and Cuba apart, Fidel Castro decided he would not play MLB's game at all. Pasquel's capitalist challenge ultimately proved more threatening than Castro's decision to eliminate professional sport and refashion baseball on the island along Socialist lines. Whether it was before, during, or after the Cold War, the question came down to who would control the game. That struggle did not begin with the Cold War; it preceded it.[9]

Baseball's formative years in Cuba under the Spanish Empire were laden with political baggage. While José Martí and other independence leaders considered bullfighting a barbaric vestige of Spanish colonialism, they lauded baseball as a sport where the distinctions of class and race could be overcome.[10] Baseball, like the United States, evoked a sense of modernity. For Cubans, Benjamin Cespedes argued, baseball was "a rehearsal for democracy."[11] The sport, historian Louis Pérez wrote, became "identified with the cause of Cuba Libre, fully integrated into the mystique and metaphysics of national liberation."[12] It was not simply a rhetorical linkage. *Independistas* staged games in Caracas and Key West to raise money and deepen commitment to the struggle against Spain, while Spanish authorities sometimes banned the game to suppress rebel activity.

Afro-Cubans had been central to the independence struggle, and postcolonial Cuba attempted to create a racially democratic society. Such a polity could not accept a color line in its national game.[13] That would have contradicted José Martí's vision of a democratic, egalitarian community and the presence of so many Afro-Cubans in island baseball. And because Cubans, not US sporting emissaries, spread the game to the Dominican Republic, Venezuela, Mexico's Yucatán Peninsula, and Puerto Rico, neither did these locales.

Geography and race limited contact and friction between MLB and Caribbean play until after World War II. The distance between Caribbean baseball venues and the United States and the timing of their seasons (one playing in the summer, the others in winter) meant that they did not compete for each other's players. Consequently, those involved with baseball beyond US borders operated with considerable autonomy. MLB did not seek to acquire the clout that United Fruit or the Hershey Company achieved in the region. Major league owners never built ballparks or operated island leagues. Dynamics between leagues and teams in the United States and the Caribbean settled into a fairly amicable, laissez-faire relationship, with little friction over who would define and control the game.

Nowhere was that autonomy more evident than in their respective racial policies. Baseball's contradictions were inescapable for those with roots in the

African diaspora. Latinos, especially Cubans, had played for US teams since the 1870s when Cuban Esteban Bellán debuted with the Troy Haymakers. But in the 1890s, after a color line eliminated the score of African Americans playing in the major leagues, only Caucasians or those who could pass as white continued to seek roster spots. Darker-skinned players from the Caribbean could, however, play in the Negro Leagues each summer, and during the winter, all players regardless of race or nationality could play in Cuba and elsewhere in the region.

These parallel baseball worlds benefited from an informal working relationship. Major league teams barnstormed in Cuba to generate revenue, and major leaguers made sorely needed money in winter baseball.[14] Latin fans, meanwhile, relished watching major leaguers in winter play and became invested in players they followed from afar during the major league season. MLB's color line kept these contradictory racial dynamics intact until after World War II.

A perfect storm confronted MLB after 1945, when racial integration, a union campaign, and Mexico's Jorge Pasquel challenged its power. As major league owners sorted out the consequences of integration and mobilized to squash organizing efforts, Pasquel blindsided them. A mogul deeply imbued with Mexican nationalism, Pasquel sought to put his country's league on equal footing with MLB. His audacity constituted the first international threat to its near-monopoly powers.

Mexican baseball lagged the Cuban game, but the country's population and booming wartime economy underscored its potential. So did Pasquel's willingness to spend his considerable wealth. Funding the Mexican League's transition to summer play during World War II, he signed scores of Negro Leaguers and Cubans to upgrade the caliber of play. Negro Leaguers Satchel Paige, Josh Gibson, and Leon Day and Cubans Martín Dihigo, Rámon Bragaña, and Lázaro Salazar were among those gracing wartime rosters.

Major league owners cared little that Pasquel's raids convulsed the Negro Leagues. Nor were they overly concerned that a few Cubans who might have played for them were no longer available. Negro Leaguers and Cubans, however, relished the higher salaries and racial atmosphere of Mexican play. But after the war, Pasquel went after major league players, including some of the sport's biggest stars. He signed eighteen white major and minor league players and sought even more, offering them far more remuneration than they were currently receiving. In all, more than half of the 180 players on Mexican League rosters during the 1946 season were foreigners, including twenty white major leaguers, twenty-seven Negro Leaguers, and forty-nine Cubans.

It was not just Pasquel's efforts to sign major leaguers that made his vision of baseball anathema to MLB. Though a capitalist, Pasquel was also a nationalist willing to place the league's success ahead of immediate self-interest. He instituted revenue sharing and player allocation to promote competitive balance among Mexican League teams, measures that MLB scorned.

Baseball's impending integration upped the ante for major league owners. After the Dodgers signed Jackie Robinson to a contract with their Montreal farm club in October 1945, the baseball world watched with a mix of hope and trepidation.[15] While African American and Afro-Cuban players waited to see what integration would mean for them, Mexico offered an alternative to the Negro Leagues, one that paid better and allowed players to avoid racial problems, especially in the minors. As Newark Eagles shortstop (and future Hall of Famer) Willie Wells said while playing in Mexico, "Not only do I get more money for playing here, but I live like a king. . . . I've found freedom and democracy here, something I never found in the United States."[16] The handwriting was on the wall—major league teams seeking to sign darker-skinned players could not ignore Mexican baseball.[17]

Unable to intimidate Pasquel but determined to crush him, MLB commissioner Happy Chandler banished for five years the eighteen players who had jumped to Mexican teams. Mexicans, who lamented that they were cursed to be so far from God yet close to the United States, relished the spat. Many saw the conflict with MLB as a struggle for national sovereignty.[18] The baseball battle, coming during the centennial of Mexico's disastrous 1846 war in which the United States seized a third of its territory, was a chance for symbolic payback.[19] When Pasquel did not meekly fold his hand, MLB escalated its counteroffensive. Owners could withstand the damages caused by a score of players heading to Mexico, but they feared that a comparable threat from Cuba would affect far more players.

The Cuban winter leagues were the best in the region, and men who played there and in Mexico earned salaries that compared favorably with major league paychecks. Thus, if the Mexican summer and Cuban winter leagues joined forces at a time when integration was changing the complexion of the industry's workforce, MLB would be faced with a rival that offered players a credible alternative.

To stave off such a threat, Commissioner Chandler extended the ban on players to anyone who participated in a game *with* a blacklisted player, on the barnstorming circuit or in the islands. That affected Cuba more than any other venue.[20] It meant that MLB was telling Cubans who could play in Cuba. Any player with major league aspirations, white, black, or Latino, could not ignore the edict. If even a few suspended players appeared in Cuban winter league play, virtually every player's future would be imperiled.

Cuban director of sport Luis Olmo Rodríguez fumed over MLB's heavy-handedness. "Since baseball has turned its back on us here," he declared, "there seems to be no alternative but for us to form a Latin American federation of baseball and compete as best as we can with the United States."[21] During the 1946–1947 winter season, two competing Cuban leagues fielded teams. One abided by MLB's dictates; the other did not. Though the league that included banned players was more popular, it feared permanent estrangement from MLB and made peace on MLB's terms after the season. By then, MLB had banned a score of players, including iconic Cuban managers Miguel Ángel González and Adolfo Luque. "We must heal the wounds," one owner said, admitting defeat. "We must get into organized baseball for our own protection."[22]

By surrendering, Cuban teams allowed MLB to determine who was eligible to play in Cuba and to regulate the flow of players to the States. These and other concessions reduced Cuba's winter league to a developmental league for MLB. Puerto Rico, Venezuela, and Panama quickly followed suit. So would the Dominican Republic, still an afterthought in Caribbean play in 1955. Baseball's center of gravity lurched northward toward Yankee Stadium.

MLB might have invited Pasquel into its cartel, adding Mexican franchises and boldly expanding its footprint. But its owners had never sought win-win relationships, whether with rival US leagues, the Negro Leagues, or their own players.[23] The Mexican League remained defiant, but not for long. Unable to generate sufficient revenues to pay for foreign players' salaries, Pasquel incurred substantial deficits. After he lost interest and left baseball, the Mexican League and MLB signed an accord agreeing to respect each other's contracts. If a major league team wanted a Mexican player, it had to compensate his Mexican club. While few Mexican players would head to the majors and Mexicans maintained control over their own leagues, it was clear to all that MLB had crushed the Caribbean challenge.

The Cuban Challenge

After banning professional sport in 1961, the Cuban government created INDER, the National Institute of Sport, Physical Education, and Recreation. It adopted a Soviet model for sport but with characteristic Cuban zeal. Although importing Soviet training methods in several sports, Cubans played baseball as they always had. Decidedly noncommercial and rhetorically nonprofessional, sport was redesigned to foster mass participation as well as develop elite athletes for international competition. Sport was a *derecho del pueblo*, a right of the people. It was also a way to make a bold statement on the global stage.

Cuba began punching above its weight at the Olympics. In Montreal in 1976, Alberto Juantorena became the first man to ever win gold in both the four hundred and eight hundred meters. With Cuban boxers, led by heavyweight Teofilo Stevenson, winning another eight medals, the small nation came in eighth overall in the Games. Though boycotts marred the next three Olympic competitions and Cuba did not attend either the 1984 or 1988 Games, Cuba surpassed its medal count in Barcelona in 1992, finishing fifth in the gold-medal tally.

Cuba did even better in baseball. With a 9–0 record, Cuba won the first Olympic gold medal awarded for baseball.[24] INDER, not private owners, now organized island baseball, creating leagues and competitions and directing the national squad's selection, training, and play abroad. Though the number of Cubans playing MLB slowly declined over the next thirty years, Cuba was virtually unassailable in international competition. It won every Pan American Games gold but one between 1963 and 2007. While Pan American and Olympic victories were cheered on the island, they also projected a positive image of Cuba abroad, especially in Latin America where the United States sought to isolate the specter of Socialism.

Cuban baseball, however, lost its major league connections. Older fans could reminisce about winter seasons featuring major and Negro Leaguers but could no longer watch US professionals playing in Cuba. Nor could they follow the US summer game anymore. A pause button had been hit, halting the flow of major league coverage. As the Cubans who had accepted exile to continue playing in the majors retired, no other island players took their place. Soon Cuban-born players had all but disappeared from the majors. Cuba's departure created opportunities for other Caribbean leagues to emerge in their own right. It did not take long for them to fill the void. While only fifty-five Latinos had played in the majors before 1950, sixty-five debuted in the 1950s, and well over one hundred began play in the 1960s. They were a harbinger of the future. Latinos constituted a tenth of all major leaguers by the 1970s, a number that has almost tripled since then.

While Roberto Clemente and Orlando Cepeda led a cohort of Puerto Ricans into the major leagues during the 1950s, Dominicans would surpass them. By the time the Sugar Kings decamped for Jersey City in 1960, Felipe, Mateo, and Jesus Alou; Juan Marichal; Manuel Mota; and Julian Javier were in the majors or about to arrive. By the 1980s, the Dominican Republic was baseball's Caribbean mecca. It currently accounts for a tenth of all major leaguers and a third of those on minor league rosters.

Cuban émigrés had introduced baseball to the Dominican Republic during the 1890s, just as they did elsewhere in the basin, and Cuba would remain its baseball touchstone until integration. Dominicans took their cues from Cuban play even more than the major leagues, listening to Cuban games on the radio and reveling when their countrymen played for Almendares or Habana in the Cuban league. After Dominican strongman Rafael Trujillo came to power in the wake of the US occupation, he modeled his country's amateur sports system after Cuba's Dirección General Nacional de Deportes (National Sports General Directorate).[25]

Politics had infused Dominican baseball with symbolic significance since teams of US Marines and sailors played native squads during the 1916–1924 occupation. "Sometimes we felt humiliated by the occupation," scholar Manuel Baez Vargas remembered, "but in sport we fraternized. The crowds were full of this fervor and wanted us to win because we were their team and because we represented the Dominican flag." Juan Bosch, who became the first democratically elected president after Trujillo's assassination in 1961, only to be ousted by a military coup months later, countered: "These games were not a form of collaboration with the North Americans. They were a way to assert Dominican independence. The game was seen as [a way] to go beat the North Americans."[26] When popular forces sought to bring Bosch back from his Cuban exile in 1965, the US Marines occupied the Dominican Republic. President Lyndon Johnson, who had sent the Marines into Vietnam earlier that year, feared that Bosch would align his nation with Cuba and the Soviet Bloc.

The Dominican Republic, Cuba, and Nicaragua shared not only baseball but also US military occupation. A Dominican ball club in Santiago even adopted Sandino as its name in 1929 to express solidarity with Nicaraguan rebel leader Augusto César Sandino. "We had an empathy, a sympathy for Sandino and the Nicaraguans," baseball chronicler Pedro Julio Santana explained. "Here was this hero who was resisting the invasion of the United States, fighting patriotically for his country." Sandino was known as *el aguila del Chipote*, the eagle of Chipote, and the Santiago ball club's name became Las Aguilas.[27]

Political leaders across the spectrum and the region tried to shape baseball to their own ends. Although Trujillo enjoyed horseracing far more than baseball, he saw the game as a means of social control. As ex-major leaguer Winston Llenas remarked, "They say here '*Al pueblo hay que darle pan y circo.* To the people you must give bread and circus.' Baseball has been the fucking circus! Trujillo used baseball to buy peace. When we were playing, it deflected attention away from politics. But for me, rooting against *Escogido* was the closest you could get to rooting against Trujillo."[28]

Trujillo subsidized the construction of ballparks, and members of his family were partisans of Escogido, one of Ciudad Trujillo's two teams. Santo Domingo, the capital, had been renamed Ciudad Trujillo not long after Trujillo took power as a result of the US occupation. When to the dismay of Trujillistas, San Pedro de Macoris won the 1936 island championship, Escogido merged with Licey, the capital's other team, to create a powerhouse for the 1937 season. The club was called Ciudad Trujillo, and to ensure victory, its directors recruited a handful of Negro Leaguers, including Josh Gibson, Cool Papa Bell, and Satchel Paige, to play on the island that summer. Ciudad Trujillo's opponents countered with Negro League and Cuban reinforcements of their own.[29]

Ramfis Trujillo, the dictator's son whom he made a colonel in the Air Force of the Dominican Republic when he was fourteen, took a proprietary interest in Aviación, the ostensibly amateur air force ball club. He had Manuel Mota, Juan Marichal, Mateo Alou, and other players drafted into the air force so that they could play for his team, which rarely lost. Felipe Alou, one of the first and best Dominicans to enter the majors, played winter ball for Escogido, the team most closely linked to the Trujillos. Mixing blandishments with menace, ruling family members did whatever they thought would help Escogido win. Petán Trujillo, the *jefe*'s brother, once strode onto the field after Escogido's Bahamian-born shortstop Andre Rodgers committed an error and slapped him. "It was a regime of torture and death," Alou later reflected. "You had to keep your mouth shut. I believe at that time that the United States had the power to unseat [Trujillo], and he was allowed to tyrannize this country for thirty-two years."[30] Trujillo was omnipresent. "Even the air we breathed belonged to Trujillo," Winston Llenas said. "The ballparks were the lungs that allowed us to breathe freely, if only for a few hours."[31]

Dominicans, like Cubans and Puerto Ricans, had chafed over baseball's color line but saw Jackie Robinson's breakthrough as a clarion call. Youth throughout the Caribbean hoped that it meant that if they were good enough, they, too, could make it to the major leagues. Many cheered on the Dodgers, who went to Cuba for spring training in 1947 and the Dominican Republic the following year. Brooklyn's Dodgers, who fielded more black and Latin players than any other team in the 1950s, became their team, too. When they beat the New York Yankees, one of baseball's least integrated squads in the 1955 World Series, people danced in the streets throughout the Caribbean.

But anger over racism in US baseball lingered even after its integration. Puerto Rican Peruchin Cepeda, renowned throughout the Caribbean, refused repeated entreaties to join the Negro Leagues. "My father was a proud man," his son Orlando explained. "As a black man, he had neither the inclination to endure segregation nor the temperament to buck racism in the United States." Cuban Luis Tiant Sr. was so embittered by his experiences in the United States that he urged his son Luis Jr. to turn down an offer from the Cleveland Indians after the color line collapsed. "I didn't want him to come to America," Tiant Sr. said after watching his son pitch for the Boston Red Sox in the 1975 World Series. "I didn't want him to be persecuted and spit on and treated like garbage, like I was."[32]

Ballplayers largely kept their heads down about politics and often turned the other cheek when dealing with American racism. But sometimes it was unavoidable. After Felipe Alou arrived in the United States to play in the New York Giants organization in 1956, the Giants sent him to Lake Charles, Louisiana. "I had no idea why they sent me there," he later explained, but "right away, I began to see the difference." He was not allowed to play, and an interpreter told him that "they were going to try to play me in some city that was more friendly to the black." Alou learned that the state legislature was debating whether to outlaw interracial play. Sent to Cocoa, Florida, he endured a two-and-a-half-day bus trip in which he encountered Jim Crow whenever the bus stopped to allow passengers to eat. In Florida, opposing pitchers tried to hit him when he batted. In West Palm Beach, he was threatened by police for refusing to leave a car where he sat with three black players in the parking lot of a diner while their white teammates were served. "That, I say, was my first act of rebellion against racism." It was not his last.[33]

Darker-skinned players faced abuse daily while in the minor and major leagues. Winter league play also did not escape interference from MLB and the US government. After Cuban major leaguers were left in limbo because of their country's break with the United States, Felipe Alou commiserated with Cuban pitcher Orlando Peña on the field before a Giants-Reds game. National League president Warren Giles quickly fined him for breaking a rule against fraternizing with an opposing player on the field. Alou indignantly refused to pay the fine, and Giles backed down. But Alou soon found himself in another conflict, this time with MLB commissioner Ford Frick.

After Rafael Trujillo's assassination, the Dominican Republic teetered on the abyss. Though many sought a more democratic future, the country had scant democratic tradition to tap as it moved forward. The Consejo de Estado, a ruling junta that included figures from across the political spectrum, organized elections for December 20, 1962. They promised to be the fairest and most democratic elections yet in Dominican history, but the political situation was fragile. Baseball, April Yoder argued, gave the consejo a degree of legitimacy it had yet to achieve with a restive population. The consejo welcomed back Juan Marichal and the Alou brothers after they appeared in the 1962 World Series, the first in which Dominicans participated.[34] Although the 1962–1963 winter season was suspended because of unrest, the consejo organized an eight-game goodwill exhibition of Cuban and Dominican professionals in 1962.[35]

"Because of the political unrest in my country," Felipe Alou wrote, "the government felt that it had to do something to calm down the people [and] divert the minds of the Dominican people from thoughts of revolution, riot, and mayhem." The players were caught between an imperious major league commissioner and political exigencies. Besides, Alou was mindful of who was asking him to participate. "When the military *junta* 'asked' you to do something," he said, "you did it."[36]

Although Ford Frick had no jurisdiction in the Caribbean, he told the Cuban and Dominican major leaguers they could not participate. Frick knew little and cared less about Dominican realities. He was focused on exercising MLB's authority. The series was hardly a pro-Castro, leftist affair; the Cuban ballplayers were men who had accepted exile to continue their careers, and anti-Castro incidents punctuated the games. Frick, however, fined Alou and other players for participating and threatened to suspend Alou for the 1963 season when he did not pay the fine. Alou refused, relenting only when his team, the San Francisco Giants, intervened (and, some think, paid the fine).

Alou, one of the most thoughtful players to emerge from the Caribbean, spoke about MLB interference in his country as well as its treatment of Latin ballplayers in a *Sport* magazine cover story after the 1963 season titled "Latin American Ballplayers Need a Bill of Rights": "If I had not played, it would have been a slap in the face of the people of my country. . . . It is unthinkable to many Dominicans that someone from a foreign country would tell other Dominicans who they can play with and who they can't." Alou vented about the racial indignities that Latin players experienced in the United States. Though an All Star and premier rightfielder, the Giants traded him months later. Among Latino ballplayers, only Roberto Clemente was as forthright and willing to take political stands.[37]

While the flow of Cubans to the majors all but ceased, Puerto Rico, the Dominican Republic, and Venezuela collectively eventually contributed more than a thousand native sons to the majors and several thousand to the minors. As that played out, winter leagues became increasingly dependent on the needs of major league teams, who saw them as a means to develop players. Because clubs preferred that established players not risk injury by playing winter ball and jeopardize their investments, they began sending minor leaguers on the cusp of the majors to winter teams with instructions to focus on aspects of their game and place less emphasis on their winter teams' success. Also, winter league salaries did not matter much to ballplayers after major league salaries began rising into the stratosphere. Though many Latin veterans played anyway because they felt they owed it to the fans, winter play lost its luster. Baseball in the Caribbean, especially in the Dominican Republic, became a multi-billion-dollar industry that served as a crucial source of young talent.

The history of Cold War baseball in the Caribbean can be divided into two clearly different periods—before and after the Cuban Revolution. Between 1945 and 1959 the various Latin American leagues carefully interacted with MLB. The slow reintegration of baseball in the United States was carefully watched in Cuba and elsewhere where the game had long been a multiracial enterprise. Organized baseball had been able to cherry-pick the islands' best talents, and a sizable number of players of African ancestry made it onto US rosters. When in the north, many of those athletes experienced the remnants of segregation. Their assimilation was not simple. Race, the greatest handicap in the US Cold War struggle for the minds and hearts of the postcolonial world, was an inescapable part of the fraught relationship with organized baseball.

The Cuban Revolution ended the flow of talent to the majors for decades. Professional sports were abolished, and the Soviet version of amateurism was adopted. Scouts, agents, and team owners turned instead to other territories, most notably the Dominican Republic. A large labor pool was then trained and delivered to major and minor league teams in the United States. Much of this activity was supported and organized by big league clubs, which established a number of academies that produced commodities (players) that were bought and sold in a market. Throughout the last two decades of the Cold War, the Communist Cuban and capitalist Dominican models coexisted, but the two nations rarely played against each other. Cuba dominated the formally amateur Pan American Games, while Dominican and other Caribbean leagues fed scores of athletes to the various outposts of the professional game. By the late 1980s when the USSR could no longer afford to subsidize the Cuban economy, many of its very best players chose the path of exile and defected. Not race but ideology divided Cold War baseball in the New World during what came to be called the "Second Cold War."

AMBIVALENT SOLIDARITIES

Cultural Diplomacy, Women, and South-South Cooperation at the 1950s Pan American Games

Brenda Elsey

The Cold War profoundly shaped the political landscape of Latin America in the 1950s. The anti-Communism of the United States endangered even democratically elected reformist movements, such as the one led by Jacobo Árbenz in Guatemala. At the same time, Latin American leaders hoped for development funds and trade with the superpower to their north. The cultural influence of the United States steadily increased, while Soviet interest in Latin America was largely limited to cultural exchange and sporadic interest in alternative models of Socialism.[1] Thus, the 1950s represents an interesting and often paradoxical period in Latin American relations with global politics. The Cuban Revolution of 1959 limited the possibilities of diplomats who sought to avoid the polarization created by the United States and USSR. The Cold War changed the way in which politicians and their constituents understood both Pan-Americanism and cultural diplomacy. Sports tournaments, in particular the Pan American Games, offer a unique opportunity to analyze how those changes affected everyday relationships among Latin American countries.

In the early twentieth century, Pan-Americanism replaced the Monroe Doctrine as the dominant diplomatic vision of many Latin American and US policy makers. The Cold War, however, politicized cultural events as battlegrounds between the Soviet Union and the United States—complicating the terrain that Latin American politicians had to navigate. The US State Department sent talented performers abroad to build goodwill and showcase the innovation of its free-market democracy.[2] However, US interference in Latin American politics undercut the respect for mutual sovereignty on which Pan-Americanism was predicated. While the Pan American Games failed to dispel suspicion of the US interventionist role in the hemisphere, athletes shared experiences beyond diplomatic agendas.[3] Recent research has examined how international events such as expositions, scientific conferences, and performances shaped participants' understanding of national, racial, and gender identities.[4] The effect of these exchanges was not always what officials planned. In fact, scholars have shown the variety of local adaptations to events intended to push particular agendas in international diplomacy.[5] This type of scholarship entails considering actors beyond formal diplomats, including groups outside, or subjugated by, state-driven projects. Furthermore, the Cold War cultural exchanges generated important conversations about *who* could serve as ambassadors. By focusing on women athletes, who historically occupied precarious positions as representatives of the nation, and examining interactions among Latin American delegations, this essay seeks to understand the significance of the Pan American Games as a site of grassroots diplomacy.

The preliminary hemispheric sports tournament took place in Dallas, Texas, in 1937, accompanying that year's Pan American Exposition.[6] The directors of sports clubs and sports journalists firmly believed that the games would generate goodwill between nations. Their framing of sport ambassadorship elided and obfuscated important realities of US–Latin American relations. First, cultural diplomacy, whether from the United States or Latin America, was of secondary importance to trade relations. Second, the planning of the games presented the obvious fallacy that nations operated with equal resources. Moreover, the boosters of sport as diplomacy reduced international conflict to a problem of familiarity rather than political or economic factors. Finally, when politicians and journalists discussed sports as diplomacy, they marginalized women as ambassadors. Since the nineteenth century, feminists had fought to place women's rights on a hemispheric agenda.[7] They refused to be shut out of the Pan-American Union and its cultural activities. Women athletes set precedents when they participated in the Women's Olympics of the 1920s and the Central American and Caribbean Games, which helped legitimate their presence at the Pan American Games.[8]

The International Olympic Committee (IOC), important in the region's conception of sport and diplomacy, wielded great influence, in part because of its considerable wealth but also because of its ties to the Young Men's Christian Association (YMCA).[9] The YMCA had established centers in Argentina, Brazil,

Chile, and Uruguay by the early 1900s and played a crucial role in the development of a number of sports, including women's basketball. The YMCA organized a precursor of the Pan American Games in 1922 during the centennial celebrations of Brazilian independence. At the tournament, YMCA directors encouraged Brazilian sports associations to accept official IOC tutelage and state support, which threatened their autonomy.[10] Once the Confederação Brasileira de Desportos (CBD; Brazilian Sport Confederation) secured official recognition from the Brazilian government, YMCA directors called on the government to intervene and provide funding for the 1922 Brazilian games.

Sports directors' interest in organizing a major Pan-American sport tournament dovetailed with a renewed interest in Pan-Americanism in the interwar period. Violence in Europe prompted public appreciation for the relative peace in the Americas. According to Barbara Keys, it was in the 1930s that sport synced fans around a common calendar, a pantheon of heroes, and a set of rules. According to Keys, "The world of sports was built on a fundamental dualism: based on the principle of national representation, it nevertheless claimed a universalism that transcended nationalism."[11] In the original 1937 iteration of the Pan-American tournament, athletes traveled to Dallas from Argentina, Brazil, Canada, Chile, Cuba, Paraguay, and Peru. Following this tournament, the Argentine Olympic Committee hosted a meeting of sixteen delegations to form the Pan American Sports Committee (PASO).[12] Delegates elected the notorious Avery Brundage, who already presided over the Amateur Athletic Union and US Olympic Committee, as PASO's first president. At the 1948 London Olympics, PASO delegates selected Argentina as the first host nation for the Pan American Games.[13]

Buenos Aires, 1951

Much had changed between the 1937 games and the 1951 tournament in terms of Latin America's relationship with the United States. Many Latin American politicians watched with distress as the Marshall Plan marginalized them from US economic support. Argentine president Juan Perón hoped the 1951 Pan American Games could help strengthen Argentina's economic and political ties in the region. In developing his "third position" in the early Cold War, Perón hoped to convince his neighbors to reject US imperialism, as well as the Communism of the Soviet Union. The year 1951 marked a shift, albeit an uneven one, between the staunch anti-imperialist rhetoric of Perón's first term and a more business-friendly approach of his second term. Historian Eduardo Elena has pointed out that Perón "stressed the benefits of doing business in the 'New Argentina' lauding 'social peace' and an orderly union movement as a boon for would-be investors rather than as signs of victory over capitalist injustice."[14]

The 1951 games were intended to showcase the modernity of Peronist Argentina, and women's status was part of that image. Perón's "New Argentina" sought to incorporate women as citizens, workers, and, of course, Peronists. This concern was reflected in efforts, spearheaded by Perón's wife, Eva, to secure women's suffrage, which was passed in 1949. The Pan American Games demonstrated Juan Perón's skill at orchestrating cultural spectacles and mobilizing workers' support.[15] Perón spared no expense in the games and assured sports directors that they could rely on a steady flow of funds for their preparation. Eva sponsored amateur tournaments and equipped youth clubs. In preparation for the Pan American Games, Perón promoted sports other than football, including traditionally elite sports such as fencing. He encouraged workers to participate in these sports as an incursion into the privilege of Argentine aristocracy.[16]

At the opening and closing ceremonies of the games, Perón positioned Argentina as a continental leader, one that collaborated in trade and respected ideological differences—all the more important given Cold War pressures. In the closing ceremonies, Eva promoted Peronism as a Pan-American movement that promised economic independence, political sovereignty, and social justice. She told the visitors, "We have defeated the hate that divides humanity . . . illuminated by the star of the Peronist doctrine that hopes to offer the world a new solution."[17] The Chilean and Mexican press reported favorably on the speech and appeared receptive to Peronism as an alternative to East-West bipolarity.

The constant refrain that sports transcended politics, echoed by journalists, politicians, athletes, and fans, short-circuited conversations about their use for political propaganda. Avery Brundage prefaced PASO's reports with reminders that the Olympic Games were "beyond the most powerful political manipulation."[18] However, Mexican journalists reported that Perón censored the press ruthlessly.[19] The popular Mexican sports magazine *La Afición* ran stories from the Newspaper Enterprise Association, whose sportswriters included Harry Grayson and Buck Canel. Grayson wrote an editorial arguing that the United States should have boycotted the Games because Perón was a dictator on par with Hitler, while Canel, who became a legendary Spanish-language sports radio star in the United States, described the environment as energetic and friendly.[20]

As the tournament progressed, the Mexican paper *El Universal* became involved in solidarity activities with the editors of the Argentine newspaper *La Prensa*, which had been closed by Perón for its criticism of his administration. The editors placed a prominent editorial on the sports page recommending that Mexico withdraw its delegation.[21] Criticism from Mexican officials was muted when the Pan-American Sports Organization awarded Mexico City the 1955 Pan American Games. In response, the Mexican delegation presented Juan and Eva Perón with a stallion sent by former president Manuel Ávila Camacho.[22] The Guatemalan delegation offered a mixed analysis of Peronism in Argentina, admiring the great number of public works that benefited the working class while commenting on the repressive political atmosphere.[23]

The Pan American Games in Buenos Aires generated antagonism rather than goodwill with the US State Department. Assistant Secretary of State Edward Miller arrived during the tournament to discourage the Peróns' criticism of US corporations.[24] The visit was lost on the Argentine public, as none of the major media picked up the story, because of either disinterest or censorship.[25] US sportswriters relentlessly criticized Juan Perón. The *New York Times* lamented, "It is indeed unfortunate, though, that the first Pan-American Games had to encounter the same political hobgoblins that haunted the 1936 Olympic games at Berlin. Today we have Perón. A decade and a half ago it was Hitler."[26] This sort of gross caricature spilled into coverage of the events as well. Sportswriters and directors fumed when Argentina took the lead in the tournament, describing it as "one of the blackest days in the long illustrious history of the United States track."[27] Despite the negative press coverage, Argentine crowds cheered US athletes. They responded with particular enthusiasm to African American athletes in track and field, like Jean Patton and Mal Whitfield.[28]

US journalists and athletes recalled the Pan American Games of the 1950s as full of "anti-Americanism." However, as Greg Grandin has pointed out, "What is often taken for Anti-Americanism in Latin America is, in fact, a competing variation of Americanism."[29] The hemispheric sports tournament undercut the insistence of US politicians on the Cold War polarizations. Memories notwithstanding, there was clear praise for US athletes in the Argentine press. A laudatory article on the US cycling team appeared in the Argentine sports magazine *La Cancha*.[30] Complimentary articles on US athletes also appeared in *El Gráfico*, which described US marksmen as "Olympians with long and fruitful careers and whose presence among us is very welcome."[31] Argentine writers present at the opening ceremonies reported that audiences cheered for the North Americans when they entered the stadium.[32] The Peronist government did not, however, outwardly promote the anti-US sentiment that the US press claimed. If it had, certainly the Peronist party's sports magazine *Mundo Deportivo* would have articulated such a position, but the reporting on the US delegation was quite complimentary, though not at the center of the press coverage. In contrast, the boxing coach Patrick Duffy boasted that US boxers refused to shake hands with the Peróns.[33] Duffy blamed the judges for all of the US losses. Fighter Norvel Lee complained that his fight with a Chilean had been rigged so that he would not advance to face an Argentine boxer. However, the former world heavyweight champion Gene Tunney declared the officiating to be excellent.[34] Accusations against Argentina frequently rested on gross generalizations of their supposed psychology. For example, writer John Cassidy explained, "Argentines admire and try their level best to emulate the British ideal of sportsmanship, but it is an imitation of a product whose basic ingredients are lacking." The problem, according to Cassidy, was that "Latin Americans do not worship law and order as Anglo-Saxons do. . . . They enjoy revolutions, disorder, emotion, leaders, national sovereignty, noble speeches, and themselves."[35]

The 1951 games were perhaps most remarkable from the perspective of the women's delegations. Women had endured significant financial and cultural obstacles to participate in the Pan American Games. When women track-and-field athletes requested inclusion in the tournament, one reader wrote to the *New York Times*: "Women foot racers—and what a rare exception they are—are interesting to watch until they move. Then their ungraceful waddles destroy all illusions and make men turn to the dainty gals who walk, and do not run, to the nearest beauty parlor."[36] Eva Perón played a significant role in highlighting women's presence. She also insisted that a female athlete recite the Olympic Oath alongside a male athlete.[37] Moreover, she ensured that women athletes' accommodations were equal to those of the male delegations. The Argentines housed the US women athletes together at the Eva Perón Foundation, without racial segregation. Of all US delegations, track and field was the most racially diverse and included many runners from the southern United States. Although the women's track-and-field manager, Evelyne Hall, claimed that racial segregation was insignificant in women's track and field, historians have demonstrated otherwise.[38] The Amateur Athletic Union (AAU) organized white-only tournaments in the 1950s, leaving prominent, historically black university teams with fewer opportunities to compete.[39] The experience of integrated housing was an abrupt change for the African American women.

Women athletes received attention, support for travel, and spaces of transnational solidarity when they competed in the Pan American Games. The women's track team made friends with a Texan athlete representing Mexico who translated the announcements into English for the group. The delegation extended their travel when the Chileans invited them for a friendly tournament. Women athletes recalled that the opportunity to travel was among the greatest gifts international play offered them. Participation in the Pan American Games in the 1950s landed women runners on the cover of Chile's sports magazine, *Estadio.* One of the Chilean track stars, Betty Kretschmer, explained that her success in track and field was important to her life primarily because it allowed her to travel, which was impossible otherwise.[40]

A lack of financial support especially challenged working-class female athletes. The eight athletes of the US track-and-field women's delegation had to raise their own funds to compete.[41] They had stood on street corners with cans, sold candy, and held fund-raisers in their local clubs. Those who managed the trip relished the opportunity to watch other women athletes. Mexican javelin thrower Hortencia García made such an impression that she lost her glasses to a member of the Chilean delegation who sought a souvenir of the great thrower.[42] Yet these exchanges were rarely featured in press coverage of the games. In political rhetoric, women did not constitute potential ambassadors.

The Pan-American tournament gave an unprecedented boost to women's athletics in Latin America. There were nine women's events in the 1951 games and fourteen men's events. This was a far greater percentage than had ever been included in a continental tournament. It motivated national Olympic Committees to seek out female athletes. Competitors then hoped to showcase their talents to receive support for the Helsinki Olympics in 1952. This, however, proved disappointing. Argentina sent only eight women among its 123 athletes to Helsinki. Brazil sent only five women of 92 athletes, Guatemala sent one woman of 22, and Mexico sent three of 64.[43] Most Latin American countries did not send any women, although there were important exceptions. Dolores Castillo, a diver who won Guatemala's only medal in the 1951 Pan American Games, competed at the Helsinki Olympics in 1952 as the only female athlete included in Guatemala's first trip to the Olympics.[44] Sports journalists covered Castillo's performances and reported on her regularly.[45] Thus, the Pan American Games became the premier international tournament for women athletes in the region.

Sports associations demarcated specific ways in which women's participation was welcome. During the equestrian events, the Mexican team included a woman, Eva Valdés, who was the sister of the team's captain, Alberto. The Argentine delegation protested her participation, and she was barred from competing. In the aftermath of the controversy, *La Afición* published a letter from an anonymous source ashamed of the attempt to include Valdés. The letter explained that this violated International Equestrian Federation rules that prohibited "Amazons" from the competition.[46] Thus, we see international sporting bodies preventing women from participating and from representing their nations.

During the games, the Peróns hoped to showcase working-class men and their ties to the industrial power of Argentina.[47] The press featured the amateur athletes who worked as butchers and construction workers. *Campeón* covered Perón's visit to the Confederación Argentina de Deportes (Argentine Sports Confederation), during which he explained that to democratize sports, working-class fans' attendance had to be subsidized.[48] Perón's narrative of his own political career was also intended to display the power and authority of the new Argentine man to visitors. The sub-secretary of information published a pamphlet in Spanish titled "Buenos Aires, capital del *justicialismo* [justicialism]," with maps marked for visitors to follow the history of Perón's rise to power.[49]

The near-universal applause for cultural diplomacy that placed everyday people in an ambassadorial role was at odds with the reality that most participating countries afforded only restricted political rights to citizens. The Venezuelan writer Napoleon Arraiz stated, "It has always been my opinion that one sports exchange between two brotherly nations is worth one hundred speeches from jacket and tie gentlemen."[50] Sports directors from across the continent practiced a low-stakes diplomacy during the meetings of each sports section. They met for hours to build a viable structure to the Pan-American Sports Organization. Delegates established rules, wrote procedures in the case of disputes, and elected officials within each sport. On the whole, visiting Latin American delegations expressed satisfaction with the organizational meetings. Arraiz wrote home, describing Argentina as a "great country, that is yours and is all of ours, that is fundamentally Argentine and profoundly global."[51] Only the US delegation seemed to express unhappiness. Although Gustavus Kirby admitted in his official report that the Argentine Organizing Committee went out of its way to provide the US delegation with comfortable transportation, as well as two interpreters, he stated that the food and language obstacles were insurmountable.[52] The assistant general manager of the US delegation complained, "The US menus were not followed and the native dishes were not very palatable or appetizing to our athletes. . . . Breakfast foods and cereals were practically unknown."[53] Thereafter, the US delegation traveled with its own chefs.

Mexico, 1955

The 1955 Pan American Games in Mexico City were perhaps the most successful in terms of organization, enthusiasm, and inter-American relations. The Mexican hosts provided state-of-the-art facilities and an athletes' village not more than twenty-five minutes from the site of competitions. The number of athletes doubled between 1951 and 1955, from two thousand to four thousand. The Pan American Games motivated women like Chile's Eliana Gaete to continue training at sports clubs, even when their lives became more complicated. After winning gold in the eighty-meter hurdles in 1951, Gaete married and gave birth to her first child, then repeated her gold-medal performance in 1955.[54] Mexican sports directors felt they had a special role in Pan-Americanism. They also built on the experience of hosting the Central American and Caribbean Games of 1954. As a result, organizers achieved full attendance at nearly every event. The director of the Mexican delegation, José de Jesús Clark Flores, spent months calming fears that the climate conditions and altitude of Mexico City would harm the games.[55]

In the years between the first and second Pan American Games, distrust of US foreign policy increased. There was growing criticism of proxy wars in Korea, the 1954 coup in Guatemala, and the exclusion of Latin America from foreign-aid packages.[56] Still, sportswriters, fans, and athletes claimed to believe fervently in the role of athletic competition in diplomacy. A *New York Times* reporter wrote, "There have been more breaches in the Iron Curtain for sports than in any other phase of activity. At a Government level there is little understanding. At the athletic level, however, all speak the same language."[57] This proved literally and metaphorically incorrect. The US sports community felt the sting at placing second in the previous tournament and arrived with a disproportionately large delegation. In response to the complaints of the US delegation in Buenos Aires, Mexican state officials decided to house the English-speaking delegations in separate dormitories.[58] The linguistic separation of Anglophones was rarely mentioned in official speeches and journalistic accounts. Friction over rules erupted frequently during the competition, and representatives of the US Olympic Committee, notably John McGovern, responded with bigotry and provincialism. According to McGovern, "Our Southern friends had not yet discovered that we knew best from our superior experience what to do and how to do it and that our aggressive approach was animated purely by a wish to be useful and helpful to them."[59] In spite of McGovern's attitude, many in the US delegation identified with Latin America, notably Miguel de Capriles. The Mexican-born Capriles represented the United States and directed the Inter-American Institute of Law at New York University. His appointment as head of the fencing team gave Mexican sports officials hope that the games would serve a positive diplomatic purpose.[60]

The 1955 tournament fit within President Adolfo Ruíz Cortines's agenda to strengthen Mexico's role in regional cooperation, particularly in the Organization of American States. His administration also saw an opportunity to blend ethnic nationalism with transnational goodwill. Interestingly, many of the delegates complimented Mexico on not using the games for political propaganda.[61] One could assume this was a jab at Perón, but it is rather unclear what was apolitical about the games. The head of the organizing committee, Manuel Guzmán Willis, a one-time discus champion, was a senator from Tamaulipas. Formerly the mayor of Tampico, in 1955 Guzmán was a rising star of Mexico's ruling party, the Partido Revolucionario Institucional (PRI; Institutional Revolutionary Party). He was experienced in mobilizing and controlling massive audiences. Journalists described the atmosphere at the opening ceremonies in Estadio Olímpico Universitario as electric. The new stadium featured a mural of the Mexican family with a peace dove and pre-Columbian imagery. Reporters described the torch ceremony as a combination of an ancient Aztec ritual with an Olympic tradition.[62] An indigenous runner, Eligio Galicia, was selected to carry the torch.[63]

By the start of the 1955 games, the Pan-American Sports Organization was headquartered in Mexico City, so reports included budgets in Mexican pesos and its official communications were published in Mexico City.[64] As an explicit rejection of US politics of segregation, PASO's constitution stipulated that the organization's policies must be "non-racial."[65] The diminished role of soccer hindered the popularity of the Pan American Games in Mexico, where the sport's popularity increased throughout the 1950s. With the professionalization of Latin American clubs, salaried players became ineligible. The Federation of Mexican Football sent a memo to its Sports Confederation objecting to its exclusion from the first Pan American Games.[66] The Argentine Football Association even sent a special request asking that Mexico reconsider sending a football team.[67] In 1955, only four teams participated, including Argentina, Venezuela, Netherland Antilles, and Mexico.[68] In 1956, the Pan-American Sports Organization wrote to the Fédération Internationale de Football Association (FIFA) requesting recognition for the Pan-American Football Federation. As evidence of the stop-and-start nature of this venture, FIFA responded that indeed it had already recognized the organization ten years earlier.[69] Despite FIFA's official recognition of the games, the growing importance of the World Cup worked against football at the Pan American Games and Olympics.

During the Pan-American Congress of the 1955 games, the United States proposed to host the games. The large attendance in Mexico City must have convinced US delegates that it was worth organizing the tournament. Perhaps the US leadership felt that by hosting, sports organizations would become more invested in it. In preparing for the 1955 games, Lyman Bingham, manager of the US delegation, explained that the amateur athletic organizations did not care about the exchanges with Latin America.[70] The United States was unique in the number of facilities available for major sporting events. Mexican delegates described the US presentation as a demonstration of "Yanqui" efficiency and organization.[71]

As happened with the first Pan American Games in Buenos Aires, women jumped at the chance to compete in the tournament. The 1955 delegations included an even greater number of women, particularly in track and field. Despite reporting a surplus of fund-raising for the 267 men and 86 women of the US delegations, women still had to raise their own funds for the 1955 games.[72] The demand of women athletes to participate challenged PASO, which encouraged Latin American delegations to bring women to round out events. Countries like the Dominican Republic sent female athletes to the 1955 games, which represented the most important tournament for women until that point. Dominican officials explained that previously women lacked sufficient preparation.[73] Two female athletes from track and field traveled with the volleyball team to Mexico. The women's contingents in the United States benefited from their participation in university athletics, which provided competition beyond sports clubs.[74] The constitution of the Pan American Games requires fifteen sports to be represented, but there is no explanation of why fewer number of female representatives are required or why particular sports have been chosen for women's inclusion.

The 1955 Pan American Games incorporated women's basketball and volleyball for the first time. Both were enormously popular in Latin America. As a result, players received increased attention in the lead-up to the games. A media campaign in Mexico lured volleyball player Susana Gómez, who had left the sport to focus on her job at a bank, back to the game to compete in the tournament.[75] Brazilian basketball player Neucy Ramos da Silva won a bronze medal with her team and subsequently became a star at her club in Rio, Botafogo. In the buildup to the Mexico games, the Brazilian press hinged its hopes on Neucy, just sixteen years old, after she won a free-throw contest.[76] However, Mexico did not have a counterpart to Eva as an advocate for women athletes. Like Perón in Argentina, Mexican president Adolfo Ruiz secured women's suffrage. However, his wife did not show the same interest or have that level of popularity among sports clubs.

National associations responded to women's complaints harshly, often dismissed sexual harassment, and provided little financial support. Chilean javelin thrower Marlene Ahrens was suspended for one year at the height of her career, preventing her from competing at the Tokyo Olympics of 1964. Ahrens had made remarks about the national association that Alberto Labra, head of the Chilean Olympic Committee, considered inappropriate. Yet Ahrens had refused Labra's sexual advances in the past. Despite her appeal and an investigation that supported Ahrens, the committee suspended her for a year, which prompted Ahrens's retirement.[77] The US women's track-and-field delegation vocally complained about the inequity of support they received. Despite the women's record-breaking performances, the US Olympic Committee allowed for only ten women in the delegation, up from eight in 1951, which frustrated the women who sought to achieve a medal in every event. The women included this criticism in their official report.[78]

The Pan American Games served as a flashpoint for critics of their own national sports associations. Those who valued amateur sports felt slighted in the 1950s by the increasing commodification and power of professional sports. The Brazilian sports community was very disappointed with the results of its track-and-field team at the 1955 Mexico City games. Athletes, fans, and journalists blamed the Brazilian Athletics Federation for poorly organizing travels. The flight arrangements to Mexico kept Brazilian athletes in transit four days.[79] During that time, athletes were given a dollar and a half for meals, which barely saved them from hunger. They also did not arrive with time to acclimate to the altitude of Mexico City. Sports directors and journalists complained that public support had inordinately benefited professional clubs.

The Cold War shaped the potential for diplomacy in the Pan-American tournament of 1955. When Brazilian triple jumper Adhemar Ferreira da Silva broke a world record set by a Soviet athlete, the PASO set up a tour of the United States for him and advised that all Americans should view his victory as theirs.[80] Da Silva was vocal in his criticism of the Soviet system of athletic training.[81] He had grown up impoverished and resented the benefits that Soviet athletes received from the government. Without irony, the reporter explained that Adhemar da Silva held a position with a government-subsidized recreation program. Da Silva's tour reflected the desire of Brazilians in PASO to promote the image of Brazil as a racial democracy and demonstrate its strong anti-Communism. In regard to da Silva's African heritage, *Sports Illustrated* explained, "Brazil is one of the most tolerant nations on Earth."[82] Da Silva experienced the violence of segregation while in the United States. At an AAU invitational tournament, Adhemar recalled, "Everybody was as nice as could be and I had no trouble, except I just had to stay away from where white people went. I felt pretty bad. I'm never again going any place where I have to worry about color."[83]

The coverage of the Pan American Games within Mexico constituted a foundational event for televised sports coverage.[84] It persuaded advertisers of the potential of television, paving the way for Mexico's Olympic and World Cup bids. It was at the 1955 Pan American Games that the delegates from Argentina and Brazil were so impressed with the Mexican sports facilities that they pushed for Mexico to bid for these tournaments.[85] The Argentine team did not dominate the second games as they had the first, but they came in second to the United States and beat out the host, Mexico. According to historian Raanan Rein, athletes felt pressured by the Peronist government to bring home medals and exhibit loyalty to the Peronist government when abroad.[86] The Argentine news agency Agencia Latina de Noticias collapsed following the event, leaving its representative at the games, Ernesto "Che" Guevara, unemployed. When a military coup overthrew Perón a few months after the 1955 games, the faction that assumed power displaced many of the sports directors who had been leaders in the Pan-American movement. The influence of military personnel increased within continental sports organizations, in ebbs and flows, as the Cold War dragged on through the 1980s.

Chicago, 1959

The next edition of the Pan American Games at Chicago in 1959 convinced many Latin American sports directors that a stronger relationship with their US counterparts was not only impossible but indeed undesirable. Despite the best intentions of its organizers, the Pan American Games in Chicago exposed how little the US public cared for hemispheric exchange. The dominance of the US athletes at the 1955 games in Mexico City had been muted by the focus on Mexican–Latin American relations. In the 1959 games, however, Cold War rhetoric and US anxiety over Latin America's politics heightened tensions. Furthermore, the US distrust of the new revolutionary Cuban government compromised the goodwill mission of the games for the next thirty years. However, the emergence of a nonaligned movement in the developing world meant that certain Latin American nations expressed an intense desire to strengthen their relationships with one another, and the Pan American Games afforded sports delegations that opportunity.

Visiting athletes had expected a better reception, given the economic climate of the United States. However, the US government showed little concern for "soft diplomacy" with Latin America. *Sports Illustrated* explained, "While 2,200 athletes from 24 nations tugged and ran and sweated and strained for two weeks in the third annual [*sic*] Pan-American Games, hardly anyone bothered to look."[87] Latin American delegations complained about the hostility of crowds toward the Cuban athletes, by fans, the press, and officials.[88] Furthermore, they were surprised by the poor accommodations. The seventeen women on Chile's basketball squad received only two hotel rooms, Ecuadorians complained that they were not given food, and the Brazilian athletes complained that hotels treated them rudely.[89] The Costa Rican newspaper *La Nación* felt the nutrition at the Chicago games to be a "grave problem."[90] Of course, the visitors noted the poor attendance at the games. Brazilians were shocked that the US Organizing Committee gave free admission to sports like water polo, and still nobody came.[91] Photographs of empty seats provided readers with visual evidence of US disinterest. The exception to the empty seats occurred when the Mexican squads competed. The Mexican American community in Chicago appeared in substantial numbers, sometimes intimidating the opposing teams.[92]

Despite the costly travel and public disinterest, Latin American athletes were still not ready to give up on the Pan American Games. The Argentine contingent, despite its anger over funding cuts, still maintained that the games created a sense of empathy among the delegations, regardless of the crowds.[93] The athletes wanted to compete at the highest echelon, regardless of the medal count.[94] For the reading publics at home, however, the message was clear—the US public simply did not respect or have interest in sports exchanges with Latin Americans. Therein lay a distinction between those who participated and those who consumed sport. Assumptions about what athletes experience are often created through the guideposts of consumer spectatorship, including advertisements and journalistic writing. These are often at odds with athletes' experiences, expectations, and hopes. Latin American sports directors and journalists felt duped by the US leadership, particularly Avery Brundage, who overstated the enthusiasm of the United States to host the games.[95] The US hosts did not construct an athletes' village in Chicago, which meant athletes were dispersed throughout the city. What the United States did not understand, according to the Latin American delegates, was the amount of socializing that occurred in the village, which constituted the grassroots diplomacy of the games.[96] Thus, the Pan-American Sports Congress was the site of significant animosity toward US sports officials.

Nevertheless, women's sports continued to thrive at the 1959 games, with particular growth among the Brazilian delegation. Given that Brazil had still banned certain women's sports, most notably football, it may be surprising that the women's basketball team nearly beat the US squad. The Brazilian women, however, won the volleyball tournament. Despite these accomplishments, the Brazilian delegation to the 1960 Olympic Games included only one woman among seventy-one men.[97] Women's basketball and volleyball were not yet in the Summer Olympics, so that perhaps reduced the number of female athletes. Yet Brazil did not send a women's team to the inaugural volleyball tournament at the 1964 Summer Olympics in Tokyo. Again, Brazil sent only one woman. Thus, the Pan American Games remained the premier international tournament for Brazilian women throughout the 1960s.

Women's tennis thrived at the 1959 tournament and featured the world's top players. At the Mexico City games, legendary US player Althea Gibson and Brazil's María Esther Bueno quickly recognized each other's talent. Bueno and Gibson paired to win Wimbledon doubles in 1958 and came in second at the US championships of 1959. Physical education instructors and sports clubs throughout the Americas encouraged women to play tennis and defined it as an elite, white, and feminine sport. Buenos's white identity helped her gain positive acceptance in Brazilian sporting circles and beyond.[98] When she was voted Female Athlete of the Year by the Associated Press in 1959, *Jet* magazine criticized the racial discrimination of such an award, given Gibson's performances that year.[99] *Jet* writers fairly criticized the racism of the Associated Press but missed the collaboration between the two women. Such neglect of women's potential as ambassadors stemmed in part from media coverage. Despite the prominence of women's athletics at the Pan American Games, journalists struggled to describe women's sports without emphasizing sportswomen's attractiveness.

After the debacle of the 1959 Chicago tournament, the games did not return to the United States until 1987. By then, US goodwill had become a subject of parody for Latin American audiences, particularly given support of military dictatorships across the continent. The ambassadorship that the architects of the Pan American Games hoped for had taken place, but almost always as a south-south, rather than a north-south relationship. Women athletes proved an important, and usually overlooked, exception. Many defied an easy nationalist categorization, as they were born, attended school, and trained in more than one country. Despite the coding of cultural diplomacy as masculine, and as emanating from the United States, women athletes created a Pan-American community that came closest to the goals of the tournament founders.

The neglect of women's contribution to the cultural diplomacy of the Pan American Games reflects a widely disseminated and transnational assumption that men could act as ambassadors. Moreover, the neglect of women's participation is part of a broader dismissal of female athletes. The tournament's inclusion of women appears to have been unintentional, but women athletes seized the opportunity regardless. The case of women's participation in the Pan American Games suggests that historical research of grassroots communities provides a more nuanced understanding of the relationship between cultural events, diplomacy, and politics. In the early Cold War, athletes showed little interest in abiding by the chauvinistic discourses of national political figures or the mainstream US media. The Cold War weighed more heavily on the games in the 1960s, after the Cuban Revolution, challenging athletes who had built relationships across borders on their mutual dedication to sport.

NOTES

INTRODUCTION

1. Keith Lowe, *The Fear and the Freedom: How the Second World War Changed Us* (London: Viking, 2017), 479.

2. See Richard Holt, Alan Tomlinson, and Christopher Young, "Sport in Modern Europe, 1950–2010: Transformation and Trends," in *Sport and the Transformation of Modern Europe: States, Media and Markets, 1950–2010*, ed. Alan Tomlinson, Christopher Young, and Richard Holt (London: Routledge, 2011), 1–17.

3. David Caute, *The Dancer Defects: The Struggle for Cultural Supremacy During the Cold War* (Oxford: Oxford University Press, 2003), 1.

4. Joseph Nye, *Soft Power: The Means to Success in World Politics* (New York: Public-Affairs, 2004), 5.

5. The following is an illustrative path through the US- and USSR-related literature. Alternative (and partly overlapping) routes can be found in Giles Scott-Smith and Joes Segal, "Introduction," in *Divided Dreamworlds? The Cultural Cold War in East and West*, ed. Peter Romijn, Giles Scott-Smith, and Joes Segal (Amsterdam: Amsterdam University Press, 2012), 3–4n3; and Annette Vowinckel, Marcus Payk, and Thomas Lindenberger, "European Cold War Culture(s): An Introduction," in *Cold War Cultures: Perspectives on Eastern and Western European Societies*, ed. Annette Vowinckel, Marcus Payk, and Thomas Lindenberger (New York: Berghahn, 2012), 2–5. The German experience can be read in David F. Crew, ed., *Consuming Germany in the Cold War: Leisure, Consumption and Culture* (Oxford, UK: Berg, 2003); and Tobias Hochscherf, Christoph Laucht, and Andrew Plowman, eds., *Divided but Not Disconnected: German Experiences of the Cold War* (New York: Berghahn, 2010).

6. Tony Shaw and Denise Youngblood, *Cinematic Cold War: The American and Soviet Struggle for Hearts and Minds* (Lawrence: University Press of Kansas, 2010); Christine Evans, *Between Truth and Time: A History of Soviet Central Television* (New Haven, CT: Yale University Press, 2016); and Travis Vogan, *ABC Sports: The Rise and Fall of Network Sports Television* (Berkeley: University of California Press, 2018).

7. Greg Castillo, *Cold War on the Home Front: The Soft Power of Midcentury Design* (Minneapolis: University of Minnesota Press, 2010).

8. Walter Hixson, *Parting the Curtain: Propaganda, Culture, and the Cold War* (New York: St. Martin's Griffen, 1998); Frances Saunders, *Who Paid the Piper? The CIA and the Cultural Cold War* (London: Granta Books, 1999); Giles Scott-Smith, *The Politics of Apolitical Culture: The Congress for Cultural Freedom, the CIA, and the Post-war American Hegemony* (London: Routledge, 2002); Nicholas Cull, *The Cold War and the US Information Agency: American Propaganda and Public Diplomacy, 1945–1989* (Cambridge: Cambridge University Press, 2009); Kenneth Osgood, *Total Cold War: Eisenhower's Secret Propaganda Battle at Home and Abroad* (Lawrence: University Press of Kansas, 2006).

9. Hugh Wilford, *The Mighty Wurlitzer: How the CIA Played America* (Cambridge, MA: Harvard University Press, 2008).

10. Yale Richmond, *Cultural Exchange and the Cold War: Raising the Iron Curtain* (University Park: Pennsylvania State University Press, 2003).

11. Penny M. von Eschen, *Satchmo Blows Up the World: Jazz Ambassadors Play the Cold War* (Cambridge, MA: Harvard University Press, 2004).

12. Campbell Craig and Frederik Logevall, *America's Cold War: The Politics of Insecurity* (Cambridge, MA: Belknap, 2012).

13. Scott Lucas, *Freedom's War: The American Crusade Against the Soviet Union* (New York: New York University Press, 1999).

14. For instance, see the pioneering work by Richard Stites, *Russian Popular Culture: Entertainment and Society Since 1900* (Cambridge: Cambridge University Press, 1992).

15. Elena Zubkova, *Russia After the War: Hopes, Illusions, and Disappointments, 1945–1957* (Armonk, NY: Sharpe, 1998).

16. Ethan Pollock, *Stalin and the Soviet Science Wars* (Princeton, NJ: Princeton University Press, 2006); Juliane Fürst, *Stalin's Last Generation: Soviet Post-war Youth and the Emergence of Mature Socialism* (Oxford: Oxford University Press, 2010); Muriel Dobson, *Khrushchev's Cold Summer: Gulag Returnees, Crime, and the Fate of Reform After Stalin* (Ithaca, NY: Cornell University Press, 2009); Steven V. Bittner, *The Many Lives of Khrushchev's Thaw: Experience and Memory in Moscow's Arbat* (Ithaca, NY: Cornell University Press, 2008); Alexei Yurchak, *Everything Was Forever Until It Was No More: The Last Soviet Generation* (Princeton, NJ: Princeton University Press, 2005).

17. Caute, *The Dancer Defects*, 20–22, 472–473.

18. Mervyn P. Leffler and Odd Arne Westad, eds., *The Cambridge History of the Cold War*, 3 vols. (Cambridge: Cambridge University Press, 2010); Richard Immerman and Petra Goedde, eds., *Oxford Handbook of the Cold War* (Oxford: Oxford University Press, 2016).

19. See, for example, David Crowley and Susan Reid, eds., *Style and Socialism: Modernity and Material Culture* (Oxford: Berg, 2000); David Crowley and Susan Reid, eds., *Socialist Spaces: Sites of Everyday Life in the Eastern Bloc* (Oxford, UK: Berg, 2002); and Douglas Field, ed., *American Cold War Culture* (Edinburgh, UK: Edinburgh University Press, 2005).

20. Scott-Smith and Segal, "Introduction," 3.

21. Tony Shaw, "The Politics of Cold War Culture," *Journal of Cold War Studies* 3, no. 3 (2001): 59.

22. This widespread view is put most succinctly by Patrick Major and Rana Mitter in three publications: Patrick Major and Rana Mitter, "East Is East and West Is West? Towards a Comparative Socio-cultural History of the Cold War," *Cold War History* 4, no. 1 (2003): 1–22; Patrick Major and Rana Mitter, *Across the Blocs: Exploring Comparative Cold War Cultural and Social History* (London: Frank Cass, 2004); and Patrick Major and Rana Mitter, "Culture," in *Palgrave Advances in Cold War History*, ed. Saki R. Dokrill and Geraint Hughes (Basingstoke, UK: Palgrave Macmillan, 2006), 240–262.

23. For more on this helpful difference in emphasis, see Jessica Gienow-Hecht, "Culture and the Cold War in Europe," in *The Cambridge History of the Cold War*, vol. 1, *Origins*, ed. Melvyn P. Leffler and Odd Arne Westad (Cambridge: Cambridge University Press, 2010), 398–419.

24. See Christopher Young, Anke Hilbrenner, and Alan Tomlinson, eds., "Forum: European Sport and the Challenges of Its Recent Historiography," *Journal of Sport History* 38, no. 2 (2011): 181–236, and *Journal of Sport History* 38, no. 3 (2011): 349–405; S. W. Pope and John Nauright, eds., *Routledge Companion to Sports History* (London: Routledge, 2013); Amy Bass, "State of the Field: Sports History and the 'Cultural Turn,'" *Journal of American History* 101, no. 1 (2014): 148–172; Richard Holt, "Historians and the History of Sport," *Sport in History* 34, no. 1 (2014): 1–33; and Robert Edelman and Wayne Wilson, eds., *The Oxford Handbook of Sports History* (Oxford: Oxford University Press, 2017).

25. Ten years have elapsed since the appearance of the only collection on the subject in English: Steven Wagg and David Andrews, eds., *East Plays West: Sport and the Cold War* (London: Routledge, 2007), which has a narrower focus on mega-events.

26. James Riordan, *Sport in Soviet Society: Development of Sport and Physical Education in Russia and the USSR* (Cambridge: Cambridge University Press, 1977), is the foundational work in English; based on a reading of published documents and secondary literature, it covers the pre–Cold War eras and then lays out the structure of the Soviet sport system in well-organized detail. The only academically engaged work on Cold War Soviet sport in Russian is Mikhail Prozumenshikov, *Bol'shoi sport i bol'shaya politika* (Moscow: Rosspen, 2004), which makes ample use of documentary materials in the archive of the Central Committee of the Communist Party of the USSR. The collection devoted to Soviet sport edited by Nikolaus Katzer, *Euphoria and Exhaustion: Modern Sport in Soviet Culture and Society* (Frankfurt am Main: Campus, 2010), contains several excellent essays on the Cold War period. Two works show how sport was both a blunt instrument in the hands of an authoritarian regime and a site of resistance to Soviet power: Robert Edelman, *Serious Fun: A History of Spectator Sports in the USSR* (New York: Oxford University Press, 1993); and Robert Edelman, *Spartak Moscow: A History of the People's Team in the Worker's State* (Ithaca, NY: Cornell University Press, 2009).

27. John Turrini undertook a pioneering study of "shamateurism" in US track and field during the 1950s and 1960s: *The End of Amateurism in American Track and Field* (Urbana: Illinois University Press, 2010). Kathryn Jay, *More than Just a Game: Sports in American Life Since 1945* (New York: Columbia University Press, 2006), shows how US sports in the postwar era were enmeshed with domestic and international politics.

Susan Cahn, *Coming on Strong: Gender and Sexuality in Twentieth-Century Women's Sport* (New York: Free Press, 1998), also devotes much attention to the postwar period. Michael Oriard, *Brand NFL: Making and Selling America's Favorite Sport* (Chapel Hill: University of North Carolina Press, 2007), studies the role of US professional football during the Vietnam War and the National Football League's interventions in the American political process. Two works analyze the struggle of African American athletes during the 1960s: Amy Bass, *Not the Triumph but the Struggle: The 1968 Olympics and the Making of the Black Athlete* (Minneapolis: University of Minnesota Press, 2002); and Douglas Hartmann, *Race, Culture, and the Revolt of the Black Athlete: The 1968 Olympic Protests and Their Aftermath* (Chicago: University of Chicago Press, 2003).

28. Two decades after reunification, details of the GDR's talent spotting, training methods, drug programs, and ideological manipulation of athletes have now been well established on the basis of a series of large-scale, archive-intensive studies financed by central government sources. The main works are Hans-Joachim Teichler, Klaus Reinartz, and Anke Delow, eds., *Das Leistungssportsystem in der DDR in den 8oer Jahren und im Prozess der Wende* (Schorndorf: Hofmann, 1999); Wolfgang Buss and Christian Becker, eds., *Der Sport in der SBZ und frühen DDR: Genese, Strukturen, Bedingungen* (Schorndorf: Hofmann, 2001); Hans Joachim Teichler, ed., *Die Sportbeschlüsse des Politbüros: Eine Studie zum Verhältnis von SED und Sport mit einem Gesamtverzeichnis und einer Dokumentation ausgewählter Beschlüsse* (Cologne: Sport und Buch Strauß, 2002); and Giselher Spitzer, *Doping in der DDR: Ein historischer Überblick zu einer konspirativen Praxis—Genese, Verantwortung, Gefahren*, 4th ed. (Cologne: Sport und Buch Strauß, 2012). An extensive bibliography is listed in Lorenz Peiffer and Matthias Fink, *Zum aktuellen Forschungsstand der Geschichte von Körperkultur und Sport in der DDR: Eine kommentierte Bibliographie* (Cologne: Sport und Buch Strauß, 2003); and an English-language synthesis appears in Mike Dennis and Jonathan Grix, *Sport Under Communism: Behind the East German "Miracle"* (Basingstoke, UK: Palgrave Macmillan, 2012). While highly valuable for their empirical strength, these works, with the exception of the latter, rarely stray from their narrow institutional focus and remain locked within the national framework. Uta Balbier, *Kalter Krieg auf der Aschenbahn: Der deutsch-deutsche Sport, 1950–1972—eine politische Geschichte* (Paderborn: Schöningh, 2007), goes further to reveal the considerable influence that this success exerted on structures and tactics in the Federal Republic. There is also a growing literature on East German soccer, with easiest access to non-German specialists found in Alan McDougall, *The People's Game: Football, State and Society in East Germany* (Cambridge: Cambridge University Press, 2014).

29. Chinese sport in the era has received comparatively less coverage but has been subject nonetheless to some excellent treatment. Andrew Morris, *Marrow of the Nation: A History of Sport and Physical Culture in Republican China* (Berkeley: University of California Press, 2004), provides essential background to the pre–Cold War era. Xu Guoqi, *Olympic Dreams: China and Sports, 1895–2008* (Cambridge, MA: Harvard University Press, 2008), has produced a wide-ranging general history of Chinese sport with special emphasis on the postrevolutionary period. A book by anthropologist Susan

Brownell, *Training the Body for China: Sports in the Moral Order of the People's Republic* (Chicago: University of Chicago Press, 1996), stresses body culture, covers the Communist period, and includes a historical chapter. Andrew Morris, *Colonial Project, National Game: A History of Baseball in Taiwan* (Berkeley: University of California Press, 2011), is the first major English-language work on sport in the Republic of China.

30. Laurent Dubois, *Soccer Empire: The World Cup and the Future of France* (Berkeley: University of California Press, 2010), explores race and national identity in France's imperial project. Lindsay Krasnoff, *The Making of Les Bleus: Sport in France, 1958–2010* (Lanham, MD: Lexington Books, 2013), studies the French attempt to formulate a "Third Way" for organizing sport that featured state involvement without the authoritarian overtones of Communist sport. Fabien Archambault, *Le contrôle du ballon: Les catholiques, les communistes et le football en Italie de 1943 au tournant des années 1980* (Rome: École française de Rome, 2012), gives an extensive account of the struggle between Catholics and Communists for the control of Italian football in the early phase of the Cold War. Excellent biographies are beginning to emerge—for example, Rick Broadbent, *Endurance: The Extraordinary Life and Times of Emil Zátopek* (London: John Wisden, 2016); and David Bolchover, *The Story of Béla Guttmann: The Greatest Comeback—from Genocide to Football Glory* (London: Biteback, 2017).

31. See Hallvard Notaker, Giles Scott-Smith, and David J. Snyder, eds., "Sports Diplomacy Forum," *Diplomatic History* 40, no. 5 (2016): 807–892; and J. Simon Rofe, "Sport and Diplomacy: A Global Diplomacy Framework," *Diplomacy and Statecraft* 27, no. 2 (2016): 212–230.

32. Mario del Pero, "Commentary," *Diplomatic History* 40, no. 5 (2016): 887.

33. Caute, *The Dancer Defects*, 617.

34. Odd Arne Westad, *The Global Cold War: Third World Interventions and the Making of Our Times* (Cambridge: Cambridge University Press, 2007).

35. For an argument advocating a broad approach to the study of the Cold War, see Pierre Grosser, "Looking for the Core of the Cold War, and Finding a Mirage?," *Cold War History* 15, no. 2 (2015): 245–252. For greater focus, see Frederico Romero, "Cold War History at the Crossroads," *Cold War History* 14, no. 4 (2014): 683–703, which builds on Holger Nehring, "What Was the Cold War?," *English Historical Review* 127, no. 537 (2012): 920–949; Lawrence Freedman, "Frostbitten: Decoding the Cold War 20 Years Later," *Foreign Affairs* 89, no. 2 (2010): 136–144; and David Caute, "Foreword," in "The Cultural Cold War in Western Europe 1945–1960," ed. Giles Scott-Smith and Hans Krabbendam, special issue, *Intelligence and National Security* 18, no. 2 (2003): n.p. For an argument that is skeptical of a broader approach to the Cold War and in favor of greater disaggregation, see Peter J. Kuznick and James Gilbert, "U.S. Culture and the Cold War," in *Rethinking Cold War Culture*, ed. Peter J. Kuznick and James Gilbert (Washington, DC: Smithsonian Institution Press, 2001), 1–13.

36. Allen Guttmann, *The Olympics: A History of the Modern Games* (Urbana: University of Illinois Press, 1992), devotes considerable space to International Olympic Committee politics in the Cold War period. Richard Espy, *The Politics of the Olympic Games* (Berkeley: University of California Press, 1979); and Christopher R. Hill, *Olympic*

Politics (Manchester, UK: Manchester University Press, 1992), have also produced useful, if hermetic, discussions of politics within the movement. David B. Kanin, *A Political History of the Olympic Games* (Boulder, CO: Westview Press, 1981), studied the Olympics from the viewpoint of a CIA analyst. Using new material and an additional two decades of history, Alfred Senn, a specialist on Lithuania, took on the same subject in *Power, Politics and the Olympic Games* (Champaign, IL: Human Kinetics, 1999). Most recently, Erin Elizabeth Redihan, *The Olympics and the Cold War: Sport as a Battleground in the U.S.-Soviet Rivalry* (Jefferson, NC: McFarland, 2017), looked at the Olympics specifically through a Cold War lens. Book-length studies of individual Olympic Games also provide a lens onto Cold War issues at significant junctures. See, for instance, David Maraniss, *Rome 1960: The Summer Olympics That Stirred the World* (New York: Simon and Schuster, 2008); Christian Tagsold, *Die Inszenierung der kulturellen Identität in Japan: Das Beispiel der Olympischen Spiele Tokyo 1964* (Munich: Iudicium, 2002); Keith Brewster and Claire Brewster, *Representing the Nation: Sport and Spectacle in Post-revolutionary Mexico* (London: Routledge, 2010); Kay Schiller and Christopher Young, *The 1972 Munich Olympics and the Making of Modern Germany* (Berkeley: University of California Press, 2010); Paul Charles Howell, *The Montreal Olympics: An Insider's View of Organizing a Self-Financing Games* (Montreal: McGill-Queen's University Press, 2009); Jenifer Parks, *The Olympic Games, the Soviet Sports Bureaucracy, and the Cold War: Red Sport, Red Tape* (New York: Lexington Books, 2016); Nicholas Sarantakes, *Dropping the Torch: Jimmy Carter, the Olympic Boycott, and the Cold War* (New York: Cambridge University Press, 2010); and Matthew Llewellyn, John Gleaves, and Wayne Wilson, eds., "The 1984 Olympic Games: Assessing the 30-Year Legacy," special issue, *International Journal of the History of Sport* 32, no. 1 (2015).

37. See David McDonald and James G. Hershberg, "1972 Summit Series," *Sport in the Cold War* podcast, episode 18, aired February 2016, http://digitalarchive.wilsoncenter.org/resource/sport-in-the-cold-war/episode-18-1972-summit-series.

38. Tsuyoshi Hasegawa, "East Asia: The Second Significant Front of the Cold War," in *The Cold War in East Asia, 1945–1991*, ed. Tsuyoshi Hasegawa (Washington, DC: Woodrow Wilson Center Press, 2011), 2.

39. On the Cold War as an "imagined reality," see Masuda Hajimu, *Cold War Crucible: The Korean Conflict and the Postwar World* (Cambridge, MA: Harvard University Press, 2015).

40. Michel de Certeau, *The Practice of Everyday Life*, trans. Stephen F. Rendall, 3rd ed. (Berkeley: University of California Press, 2011).

41. Stephen J. Whitfield, *The Culture of the Cold War*, 2nd ed. (Baltimore: Johns Hopkins University Press, 1996), 153.

42. See Robert Edelman, "Sport on Soviet Television," in *Sport and the Transformation of Modern Europe: States, Media and Markets, 1950–2010*, ed. Alan Tomlinson, Christopher Young, and Richard Holt (London: Routledge, 2011), 100–112.

43. See Robert K. Barney, Stephen R. Wenn, and Scott G. Martyn, *Selling the Five Rings: The IOC and the Rise of Olympic Commercialism* (Salt Lake City: University of Utah Press, 2002).

44. Vogan, *ABC Sports.*

45. Kuznick and Gilbert, "U.S. Culture and the Cold War," 6.

46. Rita Liberti and Maureen M. Smith, *(Re)Presenting Wilma Rudolph* (Syracuse, NY: Syracuse University Press, 2015).

47. Thomas Lindenberger, "Divided but Not Disconnected: Germany as a Border Region of the Cold War," in *Divided but Not Disconnected: German Experiences of the Cold War*, ed. Tobias Hochscherf, Christoph Laucht, and Andrew Plowman (Oxford, UK: Berghahn, 2010), 12.

48. Andrew Port, "The Banalities of East German Historiography," in *Becoming East Germans: Socialist Structures and Sensibilities After Hitler*, ed. Mary Fulbrook and Andrew Port (New York: Berghahn, 2013), 28.

49. The majority of authors in this book have contributed to the *Sport in the Cold War* podcast series, hosted and produced by Vince Hunt and curated by Laura Deal, which is available on the Woodrow Wilson Center website, at http://digitalarchive.wilsoncenter.org/theme/sport-in-the-cold-war/resources.

CHAPTER 1

1. See, for instance, Damion Thomas, *Globetrotting: African American Athletes and Cold War Politics* (Urbana: University of Illinois Press, 2012).

2. "Organizational Developments and Delineation of Psychological Warfare Responsibilities Since World War II," undated White House report, document number 3560, United States Declassified Documents Reference System.

3. "Report by the National Security Council on Coordination of Foreign Information Measures," NSC 4, December 17, 1947, http://fas.org/irp/offdocs/nsc-hst/nsc-4.htm; "Psychological Operations," NSC 4-A, December 9, 1947, http://fas.org/irp/offdocs/nsc-hst/nsc-4.htm; Gregory Mitrovich, *Undermining the Kremlin: America's Strategy to Subvert the Soviet Bloc, 1947–1956* (Ithaca, NY: Cornell University Press, 2000), 16–17.

4. Nicholas J. Cull, *The Cold War and the United States Information Agency: American Propaganda and Public Diplomacy, 1945–1989* (Cambridge: Cambridge University Press, 2008); Walter L. Hixson, *Parting the Curtain: Propaganda, Culture, and the Cold War, 1945–1961* (New York: St. Martin's Press, 1997), 35–55; Howland H. Sargeant, "The Overt International Information and Educational Exchange Programs of the United States," *Department of State Bulletin*, March 31, 1952, pp. 483–489.

5. Richard B. Walsh, "The Soviet Athlete in International Competition," *Department of State Bulletin*, December 24, 1951, pp. 1007–1010.

6. See, for instance, letter from George Kennan to Secretary of State, July 18, 1952, 861.4531/7-1852, Box 5167, Central Decimal File 1950–54, Record Group (RG) 59, National Archives (NA), College Park, Maryland.

7. "Evidence of Professionalism in Soviet Sports," June 16, 1955, "Intelligence Bulletins, Memorandums and Summaries, 1954–56" folder, Office of Research and Intelligence Box 2, RG 306, NA.

8. See, for instance, "Use of Sports Subjects in USIE Output," 800.4531/10-351, Box 4371, Central Decimal File 1950–54, RG 59, NA.

9. Laura A. Belmonte, *Selling the American Way: U.S. Propaganda and the Cold War* (Philadelphia: University of Pennsylvania Press, 2008), 6.

10. "Olympic Code Requires Athletes to Have Amateur Standing," *USIS Feature,* April 3, 1952, "USIS Features Via Airmail" folder, Box 3, RG 306, NA.

11. For policy guidance on this presentation, see, for instance, "Interim Report: Consideration of U.S. Position in Connection with 1956 Olympic Games," April 17, 1956, "OCB [Operations Coordinating Board] 353.8: Amusements and Athletics, June 1954–April 1956" folder, Box 112 (3), White House Office National Security Council Staff Papers, 1948–61 (WHO NSC Papers), Dwight D. Eisenhower Presidential Library (DDEL), Abilene, Kansas; and Kenneth A. Osgood, *Total Cold War: Eisenhower's Secret Propaganda Battle at Home and Abroad* (Lawrence: University Press of Kansas, 2006), 255–257.

12. "Comments with Regard to Soviet and Satellite Participation in the Olympic Games" (appended to letter from Walter Stoessel to Department of State), July 10, 1952, 800.4531/7-1052, Box 4372, Central Decimal File, 1950–54, RG 59, NA.

13. See, for instance, the cartoon of Karl Schwenzfeier in "#24: USIS Sports Packet, June 1956," "Feature Packets with Recurring Subjects, 1953–59" folder, Box 25, RG 306, NA. For Soviet propaganda on "immoral" and "uncultured" Americans, see Laura A. Belmonte, "A Family Affair? Gender, the U.S. Information Agency, and Cold War Ideology, 1945–1960," in *Culture and International History*, ed. Jessica C. E. Gienow-Hecht and Frank Schumacher (New York: Berghahn Books, 2003), 83, 85.

14. The idea of "People's Capitalism" came into force during the Eisenhower administration. For more on this strategy, see Andrew L. Yarrow, "Selling a New Vision of America to the World: Changing Messages in Early U.S. Cold War Print Propaganda," *Journal of Cold War Studies* 11, no. 4 (2009): 31–40.

15. For more on race and US propaganda, see Osgood, *Total Cold War*, 275–285.

16. Melinda M. Schwenk, "'Negro Stars' and the USIA's Portrait of Democracy," *Race, Gender, and Class* 8, no. 4 (2001): 125–127.

17. Belmonte, "A Family Affair?," 83.

18. "Carol Heiss Aims for World Figure Skating Title," "#19: USIS Sports Packet, January 1956," "Feature Packets with Recurring Subjects, 1953–59" folder, Box 25, RG 306, NA.

19. Allen Guttmann, *Women's Sport: A History* (New York: Columbia University Press, 1991), 190–206.

20. "U.S. Olympic Sports Carnival Sparks Drive for Funds," "#17: USIS Sports Packet, November 1955," "Feature Packets with Recurring Subjects, 1953–59" folder, Box 25, RG 306, NA. For more on US propaganda directed at the Olympic Games, see Toby C. Rider, *Cold War Games: Propaganda, the Olympics, and U.S. Foreign Policy* (Urbana: University of Illinois Press, 2016).

21. Letter from George V. Allen to all principal USIS posts, January 4, 1960, 800.4531/1-460, Box 2239, Central Decimal File, 1960–63, RG 59, NA.

22. "Terms of Reference for OCB Working Group on 1956 Olympics," February 20, 1956, "OCB 353.8: Amusements and Athletics, June 1954–April 1956" folder, Box 112 (2), WHO NSC Papers, DDEL.

23. "Hungarian Athlete Tells of Treatment Behind Iron Curtain," "#17: USIS Sports Packet, November 1955," "Feature Packets with Recurring Subjects, 1953–59" folder, Box 25, RG 306, NA.

24. Scott Lucas, "Mobilizing Culture: The State-Private Network and the CIA in the Early Cold War," in *War and Cold War in American Foreign Policy, 1942–62*, ed. Dale Carter and Robin Clifton (Houndmills, UK: Palgrave, 2002), 83–107; Liam Kennedy and Scott Lucas, "Enduring Freedom: Public Diplomacy and U.S. Foreign Policy," *American Quarterly* 57, no. 2 (2005): 313–314.

25. "The Inauguration of Organized Political Warfare," May 4, 1948, in *Foreign Relations of the United States, 1945–1950: Emergence of the Intelligence Establishment* (Washington, DC: US Government Printing Office, 1996), 668–672; Osgood, *Total Cold War*, 37–38.

26. "National Security Council Directive on Office of Special Projects," NSC 10/2, June 18, 1948, https://history.state.gov/historicaldocuments/frus1945-50Intel/d292; Sarah-Jane Corke, "George Kennan and the Inauguration of Political Warfare," *Journal of Conflict Studies* 26, no. 1 (2006): 111–113.

27. "New Group Formed to Assist Refugees," *New York Times*, June 2, 1949, p. 29; Katalin Kádár-Lynn, "At War While at Peace: United States Cold War Policy and the National Committee for a Free Europe, Inc.," in *The Inauguration of Organized Political Warfare: Cold War Organizations Sponsored by the National Committee for a Free Europe/Free Europe Committee*, ed. Katalin Kádár-Lynn (Saint Helena, CA: Helena History Press, 2013), 7–70.

28. Letter from Anthony Szápáry to C. D. Jackson, February 2, 1962, "Free Europe Committee, 1962" folder, Box 53, Alphabetical File, 1933–1964, Time Inc. File, 1933–1964, C. D. Jackson Papers, DDEL.

29. Toby C. Rider, "The Cold War Activities of the Hungarian National Sports Federation," in Kádár-Lynn, *The Inauguration of Organized Political Warfare*, 515–546.

30. André Laguerre, "Down a Road Called Liberty," *Sports Illustrated*, December 17, 1956, pp. 14–16.

31. Blanche Wiesen Cook, "First Comes the Lie: C. D. Jackson and Political Warfare," *Radical History Review* 31 (1984): 43–70; David Haight, "The Papers of C. D. Jackson: A Glimpse at President Eisenhower's Psychological Warfare Expert," *Manuscripts* 28 (Winter 1976): 27–37.

32. Hugh Wilford, *The Mighty Wurlitzer: How the CIA Played America* (Cambridge, MA: Harvard University Press, 2008), 225–232; Osgood, *Total Cold War*, 82.

33. Letter from Whitney Tower to Sid James, November 15, 1956, in *Documentary Chronology*, "Sports Illustrated—Hungarian Olympic Team Defectors" folder, Box 104, C. D. Jackson Papers, DDEL.

34. Letter from Tower to Szápáry, November 15, 1956, "HNSF, 1956" folder, Box 2, Private Papers of Count Anthony Szápáry (Szápáry Papers), Pound Ridge, New York.

35. Letter from Tower to Szápáry, November 19, 1956, "HNSF, Sports Illustrated, 1956–57" folder, Box 2, Szápáry Papers.

36. Olympic Games Organizing Committee of Melbourne, "Olympic Newsletter No. 19," 1956, Circulars, Communications, Organizing Program and Press Releases, 1954–56,

International Olympic Committee Archives, Lausanne, Switzerland; Harry Carpenter, "Hungary Out of Melbourne Olympics," *Daily Mail*, October 29, 1956, p. 11.

37. Robert E. Rinehart, "'Fists Flew and Blood Flowed': Symbolic Resistance and International Response in Hungarian Water Polo at the Melbourne Olympics, 1956," *Journal of Sport History* 23, no. 2 (1996): 131; Ian Jobling, "Strained Beginnings and Friendly Farewells: The Games of the XVI Olympiad Melbourne, 1956," *Stadion* 21–22 (1995–1996): 259.

38. Rider, *Cold War Games*, 114–116.

39. George Telegdy, "Operation Griffin," "Melbourne" folder, Box 2, Szápáry Papers.

40. André Laguerre, "Down a Road Called Liberty," *Sports Illustrated*, December 17, 1956, pp. 14–15.

41. Telegdy, "Operation Griffin."

42. Carl J. Bon Tempo, *Americans at the Gate: The United States and Refugees During the Cold War* (Princeton, NJ: Princeton University Press, 2008), 45, 65–66, 70; Michael Gill Davis, "The Cold War, Refugees, and U.S. Immigration Policy, 1952–1965" (PhD diss., Vanderbilt University, 1996), 128–133.

43. See, for instance, telephone conversation between Jackson and Tracy Voorhees, December 7, 1956, "Log—1956" folder, Box 69 (4), C. D. Jackson Papers, DDEL.

44. Cable from *Sports Illustrated* to Telegdy, December 18, 1956, "Sports Illustrated—Hungarian Olympic Team Defectors" folder, Box 104, C. D. Jackson Papers, DDEL.

45. Emese Ivan and Dezső Iván, "The 1956 Revolution and the Melbourne Olympics: The Changing Perceptions of a Dramatic Story," *Hungarian Studies Review* 35, no. 1–2 (2008): 16–17.

46. Letter from George Telegdy to John Matthews, ca. January–February 1960, "Free Europe Committee, 1960" folder, Box 53 (3), C. D. Jackson Papers, DDEL.

47. For more on US cultural infiltration, see Hixson, *Parting the Curtain*.

48. Letter from Leslie S. Brady to Elmer B. Staats, January 13, 1956, "OCB 353.8: Amusements and Athletics, June 1954–April 1956" folder, Box 112 (2), WHO NSC Papers, DDEL.

49. Tom Braden, "I'm Glad the CIA Is 'Immoral,'" *Saturday Evening Post*, May 20, 1967, p. 14.

CHAPTER 2

1. On boxing and early television, see Randy Roberts, "The Wide World of Muhammad Ali: The Politics and Economics of Televised Boxing," in *Muhammad Ali: The People's Champ*, ed. Elliott J. Gorn (Urbana: University of Illinois Press, 1995), 24–39. Carlo Rotella, *Cut Time: An Education at the Fights* (New York: Houghton Mifflin, 2003), is an excellent set of essays on the culture of the ring. See also Elliott J. Gorn, *The Manly Art: Bare-Knuckle Prize Fighting in America* (Ithaca, NY: Cornell University Press, 1986); and Elliott J. Gorn and Warren Goldstein, *A Brief History of American Sports*, 2nd ed. (Urbana: University of Illinois Press, 2013), 98–149.

2. Lewis A. Erenberg, *The Greatest Fight of Our Generation: Louis vs. Schmeling* (New York: Oxford University Press, 2005).

3. Quoted in Thomas Hauser, *Muhammad Ali, His Life and Times* (New York: Simon and Schuster, 1991), 28–30. Hauser's book, it should be noted, is a compendium of sources. Long passages from oral interviews and news stories are interspersed with Hauser's prose, the whole knit together as a biography of Ali and his times. While its depiction of the champ is a bit glowing, the book remains the single indispensable work on his life and times.

4. Ibid., 29–30; see also Michael Ezra, *Muhammad Ali: The Making of an Icon* (Philadelphia: Temple University Press, 2009), 10–13.

5. Ali often used the phrases "I'm the greatest," and "I'm king of the world," most notably on the night he won the Heavyweight Championship against Sonny Liston. Ali called his autobiography *The Greatest*, and David Remnick took *King of the World* for the title of his Ali biography. See Muhammad Ali with Richard Durham, *The Greatest: My Own Story* (New York: Random House, 1975), 120–123; and David Remnick, *King of the World: Muhammad Ali and the Rise of an American Hero* (New York: Vintage, 1998), xvi. For more on the fight, see Remnick, *King of the World*, 125–159; Hauser, *Muhammad Ali*, 56–80; and Ezra, *Muhammad Ali*, 80–89.

6. Hauser, *Muhammad Ali*, 81–83. For the larger context, see Randy Roberts and Johnny Smith, *Blood Brothers: The Fatal Friendship Between Muhammad Ali and Malcolm X* (New York: Basic Books, 2016), 1–21, 202–209; David K. Wiggins, "Victory for Allah: Muhammad Ali, the Nation of Islam, and American Society," in Gorn, *The People's Champ*, 88–93; Hauser, *Muhammad Ali*, 83–112; Remnick, *King of the World*, 125–135, 163–172, 205–218; and Mike Marqusee, *Redemption Song: Muhammad Ali and the Spirit of the Sixties* (London: Verso, 1999), 53–61.

7. Ezra, *Making of an Icon*, 62–66; Hauser, *Muhammad Ali*, 149.

8. Cannon, quoted in Hauser, *Muhammad Ali*, 104.

9. Ibid., 145–146; Marqusee, *Redemption Song*, 140–142; Hauser, *Muhammad Ali*, 161–166.

10. Hauser, *Muhammad Ali*, 82. For a discussion on how Ali became an emblem of the wider social, cultural, and political causes of the era, see Jeffrey T. Sammons, "Rebel with a Cause: Muhammad Ali as Sixties Protest Symbol," in Gorn, *The People's Champ*, 154–180.

11. Thomas R. Hietala, "Muhammad Ali and the Age of Bare-Knuckle Politics," in Gorn, *The People's Champ*, 125–142; Hauser, *Muhammad Ali*, 82.

12. Hauser, *Muhammad Ali*, 144–145. See also Remnick, *King of the World*, 285–287; and Wiggins, "Victory of Allah," 98–99.

13. Sammons, "Rebel with a Cause," 165; see also Remnick, *King of the World*, 285–288; and Marqusee, *Redemption Song*, 179.

14. Ali and Durham, *The Greatest*, 34; see also Hauser, *Muhammad Ali*, 89; Gerald Early, "Some Preposterous Propositions from the Heroic Life of Muhammad Ali: A Reading of *The Greatest: My Own Story*," in Gorn, *The People's Champ*, 70–87.

15. For an informal history of the 1950s, see David Halberstam, *The Fifties* (New York: Ballantine Books, 1994); for a broad synthesis, see James T. Patterson, *Grand Expectations: The United States, 1945–1974* (New York: Oxford University Press, 1997).

16. Mary L. Dudziak, *Cold War Civil Rights: Race and the Image of American Democracy* (Princeton, NJ: Princeton University Press, 2011); Peggy M. Von Eschen, *Race and Empire: Black Americans and Anticolonialism, 1937–1957* (Ithaca, NY: Cornell University Press, 1997); Tom P. Brady, *Black Monday* (Winona, MS: Citizens Councils, 1954).

17. Dudziak, *Cold War Civil Rights*, 79–114.

18. Ibid., 241–248.

19. Wiggins, "Victory for Allah," 90–102; Hauser, *Muhammad Ali*, 174–177.

20. Ezra, *Muhammad Ali*, 98–110.

21. Robert Lipsyte, "Children Bring Joy to World-Weary Champion," *New York Times*, February 20, 1966, p. S3; Robert Lipsyte, "Clay Says He Is a Jet Airplane and All the Rest Are Prop Jobs," *New York Times*, March 25, 1966, p. 49. Mike Ezra's *Muhammad Ali* takes up the issue of Ali as a race man on pages 120–129; see also Remnick, *King of the World*, 288.

22. Ezra, *Muhammad Ali*, 98–113.

23. Ibid., 125; Marqusee, *Redemption Song*, 213–216.

24. Ezra, *Muhammad Ali*, 125; Marqusee, *Redemption Song*, 215. A shortened version of this long quotation is in Hauser, *Muhammad Ali*, 167.

25. Remnick, *King of the World*, 289–291; Hauser, *Muhammad Ali*, 171–176.

26. Marqusee, *Redemption Song*, 226–227; Hauser, *Muhammad Ali*, 179–181.

27. Hauser, *Muhammad Ali*, 187–190.

28. Ezra, *Muhammad Ali*, 125–131; Hauser, *Muhammad Ali*, 167.

29. Hauser, *Muhammad Ali*, 177–179. See also Marqusee, *Redemption Song*, 225–226. On the Freedom Struggle and sport, see Othello Harris, "Muhammad Ali and the Revolt of the Black Athlete," in Gorn, *The People's Champ*, 54–69.

30. The literature on the Vietnam War and antiwar protests is enormous, but a few classic titles include Stanley Karnow, *Vietnam: A History* (New York: Penguin, 1997); Neil Sheehan, *A Bright and Shining Lie* (New York: Vintage, 1989); Michael Herr, *Dispatches* (New York: Vintage, 1991); and David Halberstam, *The Best and the Brightest* (New York: Ballantine Books, 1993).

31. Hauser, *Muhammad Ali*, 201–202. See also Michael Oriard, "Muhammad Ali: The Hero in the Age of Mass Media," in Gorn, *People's Champ*, 6–23.

32. Hauser, *Muhammad Ali*, 181–182, 186–187.

33. Ezra, *Muhammad Ali*, 137–197, presents an acute assessment of Ali after his fighting days.

CHAPTER 3

1. "Visit of Alexei Kosygin," November 16, 1971 (appended to letter from Arthur Laing [Minister of Public Works] to Mitchell Sharp [Secretary of State for External Affairs], November 23, 1971), File 20-USSR-9-KOSYGIN, pt. 4, vol. 9302, Record Group (RG) 25, Library and Archives Canada (LAC), Ottawa.

2. See, e.g., Bruce Muirhead, *Dancing Around the Elephant: Creating a Prosperous Canada in an Era of American Dominance, 1957–1973* (Toronto: University of Toronto Press, 2007), 123–244.

3. Robert Edelman, *Serious Fun: A History of Spectator Sports in the USSR* (Oxford: Oxford University Press, 1993), 140–141; Donald Macintosh and Michael Hawes, *Sport and Canadian Diplomacy* (Montreal: McGill-Queens University Press, 1994), 28–31; Donald Macintosh and Donna Greenhorn, "Hockey Diplomacy and Canadian Foreign Policy," *Journal of Canadian Studies* 28, no. 2 (1993): 96–112; Szymon Szemberg and Andrew Podnieks, "Protesting Amateur Rules, Canada Leaves International Hockey," 2008, previously available at http://www.iihf.com/iihf-home/the-iihf/100-year-anniversary/100-top-stories/story-17.

4. On the role of hockey in the Soviet crackdown ("normalization") following the August 1968 invasion of Czechoslovakia, see Oldrich Tuma, Mikhail Prozumenshikov, John Soares, and Mark Kramer, "The (Inter-Communist) Cold War on Ice: Soviet-Czechoslovak Ice Hockey Politics, 1967–1969," ed. James G. Hershberg, Cold War International History Project Working Paper 69, February 2014, https://www.wilsoncenter.org/sites/default/files/CWIHP_working_paper_69_soviet-czechoslovak_ice_hockey_politics_web_0.pdf; and Lawrence Martin, *The Red Machine: The Soviet Quest to Dominate Canada's Game* (Toronto: Doubleday Canada, 1990), 89–96.

5. "World Ice Hockey Championships (IIHF)," memorandum no. 125 from Berne (James A. Roberts) to Under-Secretary of State for External Affairs, Ottawa, May 3, 1971, File 55-26-HOCKEY, pt. 15, vol. 10920, RG 25, LAC; "Canada-USSR Hockey Relations," April 19, 1971, File 55-26-HOCKEY, pt. 15, vol. 10920, RG 25, LAC.

6. "Soviet Captain Wants Canada on Ice," *Washington Post*, March 31, 1971, p. D3.

7. Robert Bothwell, *Alliance and Illusion: Canada and the World, 1945–1984* (Vancouver: UBC Press, 2007), 313–314; see also Robert A. D. Ford, *Our Man in Moscow: A Diplomat's Reflections on the Soviet Union* (Toronto: University of Toronto Press, 1989), 119; and Charles A. Ruud, *The Constant Diplomat: Robert Ford in Moscow* (Montreal: McGill Queens University Press, 2009), 113.

8. Pierre Elliott Trudeau, *Memoirs* (Toronto: McClelland and Stewart, 1993), 206–208; see also Ford, *Our Man in Moscow*, 120–121; and J. L. Granatstein and Robert Bothwell, *Pirouette: Pierre Trudeau and Canadian Foreign Policy* (Toronto: University of Toronto Press, 1991), 193.

9. Granatstein and Bothwell, *Pirouette*, 193. On Kosygin, see Ford, *Our Man in Moscow*, 77–78; and Vladislav M. Zubok, *A Failed Empire: The Soviet Union in the Cold War from Stalin to Gorbachev* (Chapel Hill: University of North Carolina Press, 2007), 194–195.

10. Robert Ford, telegram 2339, August 19, 1971, quoted in "Kosygin Visit—Soviet Objectives," September 13, 1971, enclosed with V. G. Turner, "Kosygin Visit," letter to Canadian Embassy, Moscow, September 16, 1971, in File 20-USSR-9-KOSYGIN, pt. 1, vol. 9302, RG 25, LAC; see also Ford, *Our Man in Moscow*, 123–124.

11. "Kosygin Visit—Soviet Objectives," September 13, 1971, File 20-USSR-9-KOSYGIN, pt. 1, vol. 9302, RG 25, LAC.

12. Anatoli Tarasov, "Let a Puck Settle All Problems," *Sovetskii sport*, September 4, 1971, translated in R. Murray, "Soviet-Canadian Hockey Relations," memorandum no. 687, October 14, 1971, File 55-26-HOCKEY, pt. 16, vol. 10920, RG 25, LAC. On Tarasov

and the postwar rise of Soviet hockey, see, e.g., Edelman, *Serious Fun*, 110–117; and Martin, *The Red Machine*, esp. chaps. 3–9.

13. Murray, "Soviet-Canadian Hockey Relations."

14. "Visit of Premier Kosygin to Canada, October 1971: Canada-U.S.S.R. Hockey Relations," September 30, 1971, File 55-26-HOCKEY, pt. 16, vol. 10920, RG 25, LAC.

15. Letter from David Thomson to Ivan Head, September 13, 1971, File 150.3, vol. 150, MG 26 O 19, Pierre Elliott Trudeau Papers, LAC. I thank Alix McEwen at the LAC for this document.

16. Robert Ford, "Kosygin Visit Arrangements," telegram 2711, September 20, 1971, File 20-USSR-9-KOSYGIN, pt. 1, vol. 9302, RG 25, LAC.

17. Robert Ford, "Kosygin Visit: Itinerary," telegram 2841, September 30, 1971, File 20-USSR-9-KOSYGIN, pt. 1, vol. 9302, RG 25, LAC.

18. "Kosygin Visit-Arrangements," letter from Canadian Department of External Affairs, Ottawa (CDEA), to Canadian Embassy, Moscow, message no. PPRV 29, October 1, 1971, File 20-USSR-9-KOSYGIN, pt. 2, vol. 9302, RG 25, LAC; "Tough Old-Line Functionary," letter from CDEA to Canadian Embassy, Moscow, message no. GEA-794, November 4, 1971, File 20-USSR-9-KOSYGIN, pt. 4, vol. 9302, RG 25, LAC.

19. Canadian Embassy, Moscow, "Kosygin Visit," telegram 2863, October 1, 1971, File 20-USSR-9-KOSYGIN, pt. 2, vol. 9302, RG 25, LAC.

20. Canadian Embassy, Moscow, "Kosygin Visit—Arrangements," telegram 2869, October 1, 1971, File 20-USSR-9-KOSYGIN, pt. 2, vol. 9302, RG 25, LAC.

21. Canadian Embassy, Moscow, "Kosygin Visit—Program," telegram 2880, October 5, 1971, File 20-USSR-9-KOSYGIN, pt. 2, vol. 9302, RG 25, LAC. In 1973 Lunkov became Soviet ambassador to the United Kingdom.

22. "Kosygin Approves Canadian Itinerary," *New York Times*, October 7, 1971, p. 14; see also "Ottawa Outlines Kosygin Visit," *Washington Post*, September 28, 1971, p. A8.

23. Robert Ford, "Kosygin Visit—Arrangements," telegram 2942, October 7, 1971, File 20-USSR-9-KOSYGIN, pt. 2, vol. 9302, RG 25, LAC.

24. "Press Itinerary for the Visit to Canada of Mr. A. N. Kosygin, Chairman, USSR Council of Ministers," File 20-USSR-9-KOSYGIN, pt. 3, vol. 9302, RG 25, LAC. Reflecting the hockey game's perceived importance, an earlier, provisional internal itinerary had listed the Vancouver stop as follows: "22 Oct. Vancouver—visit lumber mill, port, general tour. Hockey Game in evening (highlight of tour Van-Montreal)." "Itinerary for Visit of Premier Kosygin to Canada," File 20-USSR-9-KOSYGIN, pt. 2, vol. 9302, RG 25, LAC.

25. Jay Walz, "Kosygin Attacked in Ottawa by Man Shouting 'Long Live Free Hungary!'" *New York Times*, October 19, 1971, pp. 1, 9; Tristin Hopper, "In 1971, a Canadian Rode the Soviet Premier like a Horse and Only Spent Two Months in Jail," *National Post* (Toronto), August 8, 2014, https://nationalpost.com/news/canada/in-1972-a-canadian -rode-the-soviet-premier-like-a-horse-and-only-spent-two-months-in-jail.

26. Paul Painchaud, ed., *From Mackenzie King to Pierre Trudeau: Forty Years of Canadian Diplomacy, 1945–1985* (Quebec City: Les Presses de l'Université Laval, 1989),

304. On aspects of Kosygin's visit not related to hockey, see Ford, *Our Man in Moscow*, 124–126.

27. Richard Jackson, "Kosygin Given Perfect Gift for 'Skating on Thin Ice,'" *Ottawa Journal*, October 20, 1971, p. 1; Jay Walz, "Hockey Breaks the Ice and Kosygin Smiles," *New York Times*, October 24, 1971, p. 3.

28. "Kosygin in Montreal as 1,200 Hold March," *New York Times*, October 22, 1971, p. 19.

29. "Visit to Vancouver Is Begun by Kosygin," *New York Times*, October 23, 1971, p. 7; Jack Brooks, "Kosygin Says Welcome 'Warmest,'" *Vancouver Sun*, October 23, 1971, pp. 1, 12.

30. "Visit of Alexei Kosygin."

31. "Notes on Informal Discussions Between Chairman Kosygin and Paul Martin," File 20-USSR-9-KOSYGIN, pt. 4, vol. 9302, RG 25, LAC.

32. Dusko Doder, "Kosygin Receives Big Warm 'Howdy' In Western Canada," *Washington Post*, October 24, 1971, p. A2.

33. Jack Wasserman column, *Vancouver Sun*, October 23, 1971, p. 39.

34. "Visit of Alexei Kosygin."

35. Brooks, "Kosygin Says Welcome 'Warmest,'" 1.

36. "People," *Sports Illustrated*, November 1, 1971, p. 54.

37. Brooks, "Kosygin Says Welcome 'Warmest.'"

38. Walz, "Hockey Breaks the Ice," 3; Doder, "Kosygin Receives Big Warm 'Howdy,'" A2.

39. Walz, "Hockey Breaks the Ice," 3; see also Doder, "Kosygin Receives Big Warm 'Howdy.'"

40. Jes Odam, "Canuck Fan Kosygin Gets Ovation," *Vancouver Sun*, October 23, 1971, p. 13; Hal Sigurdson, "A Script Written Just for Kosygin," *Vancouver Sun*, October 23, 1971, p. 21; Walz, "Hockey Breaks the Ice"; Doder, "Kosygin Receives Big Warm 'Howdy.'"

41. Brooks, "Kosygin Says Welcome 'Warmest,'" 1, 12; Doder, "Kosygin Receives Big Warm 'Howdy.'"

42. Odam, "Canuck Fan Kosygin Gets Ovation," 13.

43. Brooks, "Kosygin Says Welcome 'Warmest,'" 1.

44. Jack Brooks, "Kosygin Pleads to Canada for Hands Across Pacific," *Vancouver Sun*, October 25, 1971, p. 2.

45. Walz, "Hockey Breaks the Ice," 3.

46. "Notes on Informal Discussions Between Chairman Kosygin and Paul Martin."

47. "Visit of Alexei Kosygin."

48. Letter from Barnett J. Danson to Mitchell Sharp, October 28, 1971, File 20-USSR-9-KOSYGIN, pt. 3, vol. 9302, RG 25, LAC.

49. See, e.g., Jay Walz, "News Analysis: Kosygin and Trudeau's Polite First Steps," *New York Times*, October 28, 1971, p. 3; and "The Kosygin Visit—an Appraisal," telegram GEA790 from CDEA to Canadian Embassy, Washington, November 2, 1971, File 150.3,

vol. 150, MG 26 O 19, Pierre Elliott Trudeau Papers, LAC. I thank Alix McEwen at the LAC for this document.

50. William Thomas Warden, "Kosygin Visit/Conversations," telegram 968, October 29, 1971, FCO 82/20, National Archives, Kew Gardens, UK.

51. Macintosh and Hawes, *Sport and Canadian Diplomacy*, 30. Even Brundage, however, admitted that it "seem[ed] ridiculous" for the best Soviets, Czechoslovaks, and Swedes to participate in IIHF tournaments while the Canadians were deemed ineligible. John Soares, "'Our Way of Life Against Theirs': Hockey and the Cold War," in *Diplomatic Games: Essays on the International History of Sport and Foreign Relations Since 1945*, ed. Heather Dichter and Andrew Johns (Lexington: University Press of Kentucky, 2014), 261.

52. "Soviet Canada Hockey Relations," memorandum from A. Chernushenko to L. A. D. Stephens, November 19, 1971, File 55-26-HOCKEY, pt. 16, vol. 10920, RG 25, LAC.

53. Canadian Embassy, Moscow, "CDA-USSR Hockey Relations," telegram 4021, December 1, 1971, File 55-26-HOCKEY, pt. 16, vol. 10920, RG 25, LAC.

54. A. Chernushenko, "Canada/USSR Hockey Relations," November 22, 1971, File 55-26-HOCKEY, pt. 16, vol. 10920, RG 25, LAC.

55. Letter from CDEA to Canadian Embassy, Moscow, message no. FAI-2557, November 23, 1971, File 55-26-HOCKEY, pt. 16, vol. 10920, RG 25, LAC. The Canadian foreign ministry presumed Kovalski received his instructions from Sergei Pavlov, chairman of the Committee on Physical Culture and Sports, rather than Andrei Starovoitov, head of the Soviet Hockey Federation.

56. D. B. Hicks, draft memorandum, November 25, 1971, enclosed with letter from Under-Secretary of State for External Affairs to Canadian Embassy, Moscow, November 26, 1971, FAI-2605, File 55-26-HOCKEY, pt. 16, vol. 10920, RG 25, LAC.

57. Letter of agreement, enclosed with letter from L. A. D. Stephens to J. W. Willard (Deputy Minister, National Health and Welfare), April 19, 1972, File 55-26-HOCKEY-1-USSR, pt. 1, vol. 10920, RG 25, LAC.

58. Letter from Kosygin to Trudeau, October 10, 1972, File 55-26-HOCKEY-1-USSR, pt. 4.2, vol. 10921, RG 25, LAC; letter from Trudeau to Kosygin, September 29, 1972, enclosed with telegram GEA 956 from CDEA to Canadian Embassy, Moscow, September 29, 1972, File 55-26-HOCKEY-1-USSR, pt. 4.1, vol. 10921, RG 25, LAC. For the Canadian ambassador's more measured contemporary private analysis of the series' impact on bilateral relations, see esp. Robert Ford, "Hockey and Soviet-CDN Relations," telegram 2281, October 4, 1972, File 55-26-HOCKEY-1-USSR, pt. 4.1, vol. 10921, RG 25, LAC.

59. Red Fisher, "Summit Series 40th Anniversary: Clark's Game 6 Slash on Kharlamov Was Turning Point for Team Canada," *Montreal Gazette*, September 24, 2012, http://www.montrealgazette.com/sports/Summit+Series+40th+anniversary+Clarke+Game+slash+Kharlamov+turning+point+Team+Canada/7287054/story.html.

60. Jacob D. Beam (US Embassy, Moscow), "Soviet-Canadian Hockey—Blood on the Ice?," airgram A-577, August 30, 1972, CUL 13-3 USSR 1/1/70, Box 384, RG 59, US National Archives, College Park, MD.

61. Canadian Embassy, Moscow, telegram 2194, September 25, 1972, File 55-26-HOCKEY-1-USSR, pt. 4.1, RG 25, LAC.

62. Ibid.

63. Ford, "Hockey and Soviet-CDN Relations."

CHAPTER 4

1. Bureau of the Presidium of the CPSU Central Committee, "On L. I. Brezhnev," November 19, 1952, list (l.) 27, delo (d.) 1200, opis (op.) 1, fond (f.) 80, Russian State Archive of Contemporary History (RGANI), Moscow.

2. "Report of Administrative Bodies Department of the Central Committee of the CPSU on the Approval of Major General L. I. Brezhnev Deputy Chief of the General Political Department of the Ministry of Defense," May 1953, l. 109, d. 4, op. 108, f. 5, RGANI.

3. Note from Sports Committee of USSR to Central Committee of CPSU, March 30, 1956, , ll. 115–116, d. 29, op. 16, f. 4, RGANI.

4. Ibid. Formally, Brezhnev was not in charge of sport in the Central Committee of the CPSU, yet he frequently engaged in sports-political matters. For example, in early 1957, he had to resolve the issue when some European sports organizations refused to take part in competitions in the Soviet Union in protest against the Soviet invasion of Hungary in the autumn of 1956. See "The Information by Departments of the Central Committee of the CPSU on the Relationship with the Leadership of the Danish Athletic Union," February 1957, l. 15, d. 220, op. 47, f. 5, RGANI.

5. Commission of the CPSU Central Committee, "On the Preparations for the Participation of Soviet Athletes in the World Olympic Games, 1956," January 14, 1955, ll. 36–37, d. 192, op. 8, f. 3, RGANI.

6. Note from Sports Committee of USSR to Central Committee of the CPSU, l. 116.

7. Presidium of the Central Committee of the CPSU, "On the President of the Supreme Soviet of the USSR," May 4, 1960, l. 49, d. 1200, op. 1, f. 80, RGANI.

8. Plenum of the Central Committee of the CPSU, meeting minutes, June 21, 1963, l. 86, d. 1200, op. 1, f. 80, RGANI.

9. Plenum of the Central Committee of the CPSU, "On the Comrade L. I. Brezhnev," July 11, 1964, l. 61, d. 1200, op. 1, f. 80, RGANI.

10. Committee for State Security (KGB), report to Central Committee of the CPSU about preparation of XIX Olympic Games in Mexico, 1968, l. 28, d. 48, op. 62, f. 5, RGANI.

11. Ibid.

12. Departments of the Central Committee of the CPSU, report on attitude of the GDR to holding the XX Olympic Games in Munich, 1971, ll. 172, 174, 186–187, 190, d. 103, op. 63, f. 5, RGANI.

13. Quoted in CPSU Central Committee Propaganda Department, report on the Communist Party of Spain's position on the 1972 Olympic Games, April 19, 1966, l. 84, d. 2, op. 20, f. 4, RGANI.

14. Meanwhile, in 1970 the president of the Organizing Committee of the Summer Games 1972, Willi Daume, told reporters at a press conference that the Soviet Union was always positive about the idea of the Olympics taking place in Germany and voted for

Munich at the IOC session. See Willi Daume, transcript of press conference with Soviet and foreign reporters in Moscow, 1970, l. 141, d. 48, op. 62, f. 5, RGANI.

15. Record of conversations between USSR Sports Committee Chairman S. Pavlov and Hans-Dietrich Genscher, June 1971, l. 180, d. 103, op. 63, f. 5, RGANI.

16. Ibid. During his visit to the United States in 1971, federal chancellor Willy Brandt specifically discussed this issue with President Richard Nixon and the minister of internal affairs of Germany, Hans-Dietrich Genscher. Brandt reassured the Soviet Union that on this issue West Germany would make a decision "that will satisfy both sides; though you may not regard it as ideal." Ibid.

17. Record of conversations between CPSU and Ambassador Bittner, September 22, 1970, ll. 121–123, d. 1097, op. 20, f. 4, RGANI. See also Christopher Young, "Carrying a German Flame: The Olympic Torch Relay and Its Instrumentalization in the Age of *Ostpolitik*," *Historical Social Research/Historische Sozialforschung* 32, no. 1 (2007): 116–136.

18. Conversation between Koryukin V. D. (Soviet ambassador in Greece) and member of the new Greek leadership, April or May 1968, l. 17, d. 65, port. 3, op. 51, f. 167, Archive of Foreign Policy of the Russian Federation.

19. In particular, in 1967 the USSR and Greece had to face each other in the qualifiers for the European Football Championship. The first game was scheduled for the middle of summer in Moscow and the second in the fall in Athens. The Soviet leadership decided not to boycott the competition, but under the conditions that the first game would take place in Tbilisi rather than Moscow, there would be no preadvertising, and information about the match would be minimized. See Sports Committee of USSR, report to secretary of the CPSU on preparation for qualifying matches of European Football Championship, 1968, July 4, 1967, l. 31, d. 951, op. 20, f. 4, RGANI. The same attitude prevailed in subsequent competitions involving Greek athletes.

20. Note from Sports Committee of USSR to Central Committee of CPSU on participation of Soviet athletes in 1969 World Championships in Athletics, 1969, l. 89, d. 153, op. 19, f. 4, RGANI.

21. Repeated mention of Brezhnev's interest in sports can be found in the diaries, which he kept his whole life. For example, in the 1970s one can often read notes about hockey: "May 16 [1975]. I did not go anywhere—nobody called, I was the same. It looked like CSKA lost to 'Spartak.' Fine fellows, well played." Leonid Brezhnev, diary, May 16, 1975, l. 280b (verso), d. 985, op. 1, f. 80, RGANI. "April 10, Tuesday [1977]. I watched the hockey: team of the USSR—Sweden: the result of 4-2 in favor of the USSR." Leonid Brezhnev, diary, April 10, 1977, l. 200b, d. 986, op. 1, f. 80, RGANI.

22. In 1981 Brezhnev once again demanded that the hockey players be given state awards for their achievements. But this time, his colleagues in the Politburo expressed doubts, reminding him about the rewards the hockey players had received after the Games in Lake Placid. See Politburo of CPSU Central Committee, meeting minutes, September 17, 1981, l. 3, d. 47, op. 42, f. 89, RGANI.

23. Politburo of CPSU Central Committee, "On the Nomination of the City of Moscow to Host the XXI Olympic Games in 1976," l. 27, d. 153, op. 19, f. 4, RGANI.

24. Departments of the Central Committee of the CPSU, report on Summer Olympics, August 1970, l. 193, d. 699, op. 20, f. 4, RGANI.

25. Note from L. I. Brezhnev to K. U. Chernenko (Secretary of the CPSU), December 25, 1975, l. 55, d. 317, op. 1, f. 80, RGANI.

26. See Anatoly S. Chernyaev, "The Diary of Anatoly S. Chernyaev, 1976," trans. Anna Melyakova, https://nsarchive2.gwu.edu//NSAEBB/NSAEBB550-Chernyaev-Diary-1976-gives-close-up-view-of-Soviet-system/Anatoly%20Chernyaev%20Diary,%201976.pdf.

CHAPTER 5

1. N. Dumbadze, M. Karchava, Z. Bolkvadze, and G. Pirtskhalava, *"Dinamo" Tbilisi* (Tbilisi: Soiuz zhurnalistov Gruzii, 1960).

2. *Dekada gruzinskogo iskusstva i literatury v Moskve: Sbornik materialov* (Tbilisi: Zaria vostoka, 1959), 247.

3. Benedict Anderson, *Imagined Communities: Reflections on the Origin and Spread of Nationalism* (London: Verso, 1991).

4. Robert Edelman, "A Small Way of Saying 'No': Moscow Working Men, Spartak Soccer, and the Communist Party, 1900–1945," *American Historical Review* 107, no. 5 (2002): 1441–1474.

5. On Dinamo Kiev, see Manfred Zeller, "'Our Own Internationale,' 1966: Dynamo Kiev Fans Between Local Identity and Transnational Imagination," *Kritika: Explorations in Russian and Eurasian History* 12, no. 1 (2011): 53–82.

6. I am grateful to Robert Edelman for his observation regarding Dinamo Tbilisi's name.

7. On the history of Georgia's folk-dance ensembles, see Erik R. Scott, *Familiar Strangers: The Georgian Diaspora and the Evolution of Soviet Empire* (New York: Oxford University Press, 2016).

8. On the cultivation of football by Soviet and post-Soviet political leaders, see Régis Genté and Nicolas Jallot, *Futbol. Le ballon rond de Staline a Poutine, une arme politique* (Paris: Allary Éditions, 2018). The book's authors, French journalists, draw on an earlier, unpublished version of this essay, as well as a podcast interview I gave in 2015, in their discussion of Georgian football. For the interview, see Erik R. Scott, "Georgian Football," *Sport in the Cold War* (podcast), episode 8, aired December 2015, http://digitalarchive.wilsoncenter.org/resource/sport-in-the-cold-war/episode-08-georgian-football.

9. The term "beautiful game" entered international parlance with Brazil's victory in the 1958 World Cup. Richard Giulianotti, *Football: A Sociology of the Global Game* (Cambridge, UK: Polity Press, 1999), 26.

10. Eduardo P. Archetti, *Masculinities: Football, Polo, and the Tango in Argentina* (Oxford: Berg, 1999); Roger Alan Kittleson, *The Country of Football: Soccer and the Making of Modern Brazil* (Berkeley: University of California Press, 2014).

11. Archetti, *Masculinities*, 162.

12. Damion Thomas, "Playing the 'Race Card': US Foreign Policy and the Integration of Sports," in *East Plays West: Sport in the Cold War*, ed. Stephen Wagg and David L. Andrews (London: Routledge, 2007), 207–221.

13. Otar Gagua, *Boris Paichadze*, ed. D. Kvaratskhelia, trans. G. Akopov (Tbilisi: Ganatleba, 1985), 10.

14. Mindia Mosashvili, *Maradiuli dghesastsauli* (Tbilisi: Khelovneba, 1982), 25.

15. The term *chekist* came from a predecessor to the NKVD, the VChK (All-Russian Extraordinary Commission), and continued to be used to refer to those who worked for the NKVD's successor organizations, including the KGB (Committee for State Security).

16. "Otchety o rabote otdelov TsK KP Gruzii," 1936, delo (d.) 172, opus (op.) 8, fond (f.) 14, Sakartvelos shinagan sakmeta saministro arkivi [Archive of the Ministry of Internal Affairs of Georgia], Tbilisi; see also *Futbol'naia komanda "Dinamo" Tbilisi* (Tbilisi: Izdatel'stvo Gruzpromsoveta, 1940).

17. Nikolai Starostin, *Zvezdy bol'shogo futbola* (Moscow: Fizkul'tura i sport, 1969), 68–74.

18. *Nashi futbolisty: Dinamo Tbilisi* (Moscow: Fizkul'tura i sport, 1949), 8. On the Soviet goalkeeper, see Mike O'Mahony, *Sport in the USSR: Physical Culture—Visual Culture* (London: Reaktion, 2006), 140–144.

19. Gagua, *Boris Paichadze*, 100.

20. *Sovetskii sport*, September 8, 1953.

21. Drawing on his interview with Aksel' Vartanian, Robert Edelman advances this argument in *Spartak Moscow: A History of the People's Team in the Worker's State* (Ithaca, NY: Cornell University Press, 2009), 207–209.

22. The movies referenced are *Pirveli mertskhali* (The first swallow; 1975) and *Burti da moedani* (Ball and pitch; 1961).

23. "Chveni okros bichebi!" *YouTube*, June 14, 2013, https://www.youtube.com /watch?v=EpUKGOG51KI.

24. "Proekty postanovlenii po voprosam podgotovki sovetskikh sportsmenov k Olimpiade v Khel'sinki," February 21, 1952, d. 571, op. 132, f. 17, Rossiiskii gosudarstvennyi arkhiv sotsial'no-politicheskoi istorii [Russian State Archive of Socio-political History], Moscow.

25. "Materialy zasedanii prezidiuma Federatsii futbola SSSR," 1969, l. 75, d. 296, op. 31, f. R-7576, Gosudarstvennyi arkhiv Rossiiskoi Federatsii [State Archive of the Russian Federation] (GARF), Moscow.

26. See, for example, "Stenogramma otchetno-vybornogo plenuma Soveta Federatsii futbola," January 25, 1968, ll. 61–112, d. 87, op. 4, f. R-9570, GARF.

27. "Stenogramma plenuma Soveta Federatsii futbola SSSR," February 4, 1970, ll. 25–51, d. 660, op. 31, f. R-7576, GARF.

28. Robert Edelman, *Serious Fun: A History of Spectator Sports in the USSR* (New York: Oxford University Press, 1993), 136.

29. Lobanovksii is defended in Hans-Joachim Braun and Nikolaus Katzer, "Training Methods and Soccer Tactics in the Late Soviet Union: Rational Systems of Body and Space," in *Euphoria and Exhaustion: Modern Sport in Soviet Culture and Society*, ed. Nikolaus Katzer, Sandra Budy, Alexandra Köhring, and Manfred Zeller (Frankfurt am Main: Campus Verlag, 2010), 269–294.

30. Ibid., 283.

31. Edelman, *Serious Fun*, 175.

32. Valentin Bubukin, "Gody letiat bystree miachei," *Sportivnaia zhizn' Rossii* 8 (2005): n.p.

33. Avtandil Gogoberidze, *S miachom s trideviat' zemel'* (Tbilisi: Soiuz zhurnalistov Gruzii, 1965), 142.

34. Ibid., 48.

35. Federatsiia sportivnykh zhurnalistov Gruzii, *Voskhozhdenie kubku: Spravochnik* (Tbilisi: TsK KP Gruzii, 1981), 56–57.

36. Ibid., 104.

37. Starostin, *Zvezdy bol'shogo futbola*, 308.

38. Federatsiia sportivnykh zhurnalistov Gruzii, *Voskhozhdenie kubku*, 95.

39. Ibid., 91.

40. "Dinamo-dinamo," *YouTube*, October 24, 2009, https://www.youtube.com/watch?v=8lUX37PMw8o.

41. Guram Pandzhikidze, *Dinamo, Dinamo, Dinamo!*, trans. S. N. Kenkishvili (Rostov-on-Don: SKNTs VSh IuFU, 2011), 55–56.

42. "Stenogramma plenuma Soveta Federatsii futbola SSSR," January 25, 1971, l. 96, d. 1013, op. 31, f. R-7576, GARF.

43. Ibid., l. 94.

44. Anzor Kavazashvili, *Ispoved' futbol'nogo maestro* (Moscow: Ianus-K, 2010), 35.

45. Ibid., 49.

46. Alastair Watt, "Dinamo Tbilisi and the Quest for the Champions League," *Futbolgrad*, July 14, 2014, http://futbolgrad.com/dinamo-tbilisi-quest-champions-league.

47. Ibid.

48. Edelman, *Serious Fun*, 241–242.

49. Leonard Shengelaia, "O futbole, i ne tol'ko o nem," *Zaria vostoka*, November 28, 1990.

50. "Kak tbilisskoe 'Dinamo' kinulo 'Mrctcbi,'" *Tribuna*, February 27, 2013, http://www.sports.ru/tribuna/blogs/sixflags/427739.html.

51. David Clayton, *Everything Under the Blue Moon: The Complete Book of Manchester City FC—and More!* (Edinburgh, UK: Mainstream, 2002), 122.

52. "State of the Game: How UK's Football Map Has Changed," *BBC News*, October 10, 2013, https://www.bbc.com/news/uk-24464020.

53. See Lindsay Sarah Krasnoff, *The Making of Les Bleus: Sport in France, 1958–2010* (Lanham, MD: Lexington Books, 2013).

54. See Kittleson, *The Country of Football*, 165–211.

CHAPTER 6

Acknowledgments: I thank Robert Edelman, Uta Balbier, and Stefan Wiederkehr for their excellent comments and suggestions. I am also very grateful to Mita Banerjee, Brian D. Bunk, Damian Harrison, and Robert Kindler for their help.

1. Iurii Mikhailov (pseudonym), interview by the author, Evropeiskii Torgovlii Tsentr, Moscow, March 30, 2008.

2. In the former Soviet Union the supremacy of the Moscow teams was success-fully challenged by other clubs such as Dinamo Kiev. Thanks to its tremendous suc-cess Dinamo Kiev eventually grew to be more popular than Spartak in many Soviet republics. On spectator sports in the Soviet Union, see Robert Edelman, *Serious Fun: A History of Spectator Sports in the USSR* (New York: Oxford University Press, 1993); Robert Edelman, *Spartak Moscow: The People's Team in the Workers' State* (Ithaca, NY: Cornell University Press, 2009); and James Riordan, *Sport in Soviet Society: Develop-ment of Sport and Physical Education in Russia and the USSR* (Cambridge: Cambridge University Press, 1977).

3. John Bushnell, *Moscow Graffiti: Language and Subculture* (Boston: Unwin Hyman, 1990). On youth culture in the Soviet Union, see John Bushnell, "The History and Study of the Soviet Youth Counter Culture," *Soviet Sociology* 29 (1990): 3–10; Mark Edele, "Strange Young Men in Stalin's Moscow: The Birth and Life of the Stiliagi, 1945–1953," *Jahrbücher für Geschichte Osteuropas* 50 (2002): 37–61; Corinna Kuhr-Korolev, *Gezähmte Helden: Die Formierung der Sowjetjugend, 1917–1932* (Essen, Germany: Klartext, 2005); Jay William Risch, "Soviet 'Flower Children': Hippies and Youth Counter-culture in 1970s L'viv," *Journal of Contemporary History* 40 (2005): 566–584; and Sergei I. Zhuk, "Religion, 'Westernization,' and Youth in the 'Closed City' of Soviet Ukraine, 1964–1984," *Russian Review* 67 (2008): 661–679.

4. On globalization and modern sport, see Christiane Eisenberg, "Fußball Als glo-bales Phänomen: Historische Perspektiven," *Aus Politik und Zeitgeschichte* 26 (2004): 7–15; Allen Guttmann, *Games and Empires: Modern Sports and Cultural Imperialism* (New York: Columbia University Press, 1994); Barbara Keys, *Globalizing Sports: Na-tional Rivalry and International Community in the 1930s* (Cambridge, MA: Harvard Uni-versity Press, 2006); and Cornel Sandvoss, *A Game of Two Halves: Football, Fandom, Television and Globalization* (London: Routledge, 2003).

5. Richard Giulianotti and Roland Robertson, "Forms of Glocalization: Globalisa-tion an the Migration Strategies of Scottish Football Fans," *Sociology* 41 (2007): 133–152.

6. On public life in the Soviet Union, see Gábor Rittersporn, Malte Rolf, and Jan C. Behrends, *Sphären von Öffentlichkeit in Gesellschaften sowjetischen Typs: Zwischen partei-staatlicher Selbstinszenierung und kirchlichen Gegenwelten* (Frankfurt: Peter Lang, 2003); and Alexei Yurchak, *Everything Was Forever, Until It Was No More: The Last So-viet Generation* (Princeton, NJ: Princeton University Press, 2005), 29–65. On censorship in the Soviet Union, see Vladimir I. Malov, *Tajny Sovetskogo Futbola* (Moscow: Veche, 2008); and Nikolai N. Nikolaev, *Tass Upolnomochen . . . Promolchat'* (Moscow: Veche, 2008). On public life and historiography in general, see Jörg Requate, "Öffentlichkeit und Medien als Gegenstände historischer Analyse," *Geschichte und Gesellschaft* 25 (1999): 5–25.

7. For a discussion of similar trends in other youth cultures in Eastern Europe, see Sonja Häder, "Selbstbehauptung wider Partei und Staat: Westlicher Einfluss und öst-liche Eigenständigkeit in den Jugendkulturen jenseits des eisernen Vorhangs," *Archiv für Sozialgeschichte* 45 (2005): 449–474; and Frank Willmann, *Stadionpartisanen: Fans und Hooligans in der DDR* (Berlin: Verlag Neues Leben, 2007).

8. Sandvoss, *A Game of Two Halves*, 101.

9. Eric Dunning, "Zuschauerausschreitungen," in *Sport im Zivilisationsprozess: Studien zur Figurationssoziologie*, ed. Norbert Elias and Eric Dunning (Münster: LIT Verlag, 1984), 127.

10. Martin Albrow, *Das globale Zeitalter* (Frankfurt: Suhrkamp, 2007), 147–148; Phoebe C. Ellsworth, "Sense, Culture, and Sensibility," in *Emotion and Culture*, ed. Shinobu Kitayama and Hazel Rose Markus (Washington, DC: American Psychological Association, 1994), 23; Martina Kessel, "Gefühle und Geschichtswissenschaft," in *Emotionen und Sozialtheorie*, ed. Rainer Schützeichel (Frankfurt: Campus, 2006), 31.

11. Ramon Spaaija, "Football Hooliganism as a Transnational Phenomenon: Past and Present Analysis; A Critique—More Specificity and Less Generality," *Journal of the History of Sport* 24 (2007): 411–431.

12. On Soviet mass media and consumer culture, see Mariia Antonova, "Satira kak instrument distsipliny tela v epokhu khrushchevskikh reform: Formirovanie identichnosti sovetskoi zhenshchiny v 1950–1960-e gody," in *Sovetskaia sotsial'naia politika: Stseny i deistvuiushchie litsa, 1940–1985*, ed. Elena R. Yarskaia-Smirnova and Pavel V. Romanov (Moscow: Variant, 2008), 290–312; Susan E. Reid, "Cold War in the Kitchen: Gender and the De-Stalinization of Consumer Taste in the Soviet Union Under Khrushchev," *Slavic Review* 61 (2002): 211–252; Kristin Roth-Ey, "Finding a Home for Television in the USSR, 1950–1970," *Slavic Review* 66 (2007): 278–306; Monica Rüthers, "Kindheit, Kosmos und Konsum in sowjetischen Bildwelten der 1960er Jahre: Zur Herstellung von Zukunftsoptimismus," *Historische Anthropologie* 17 (2009): 56–74; and Oksana Zaporozhets, "Sovetskii potrebitel' i reglamentirovannaia publichnost': Novye ideologemy i povsednevnost' obshchepita kontsa 50-kh," in Yarskaia-Smirnova and Romanov, *Sovetskaia sotsial'naia politika*, 315–336.

13. Rüthers, "Kindheit, Kosmos und Konsum," 59–60.

14. Reid, "Cold War in the Kitchen," 214.

15. For a discussion of Soviet *kul'turnost'* (culturedness), see Vadim Volkov, "The Concept of Kul'turnost'," in *Stalinism: New Directions*, ed. Sheila Fitzpatrick (London: Routledge, 2000), 210–230.

16. C. Lee Harrington and Denise D. Bielby, "Global Fandom/Global Fan Studies," in *Fandom: Identities and Communities in a Mediated World*, ed. Jonathan Gray, Cornel Sandvoss, and C. Lee Harrington (New York: New York University Press, 2007), 181; see also Vamsee Juluri, *Becoming a Global Audience: Longing and Belonging in Indian Music Television* (New York: P. Lang, 2003), 119–121.

17. Zhuk, "Religion, 'Westernization,' and Youth," 679.

18. Requate, "Öffentlichkeit und Medien," 11. For discussions of gender and Soviet sport, see Julie Gilmour and Barbara Evans Clements, "'If You Want to Be like Me, Train!': The Contradictions of Soviet Masculinity," in *Russian Masculinities in History and Culture*, ed. Barbara Evans Clements, Rebecca Friedman, and Dan Healey (Basingstoke, UK: Palgrave, 2002), 210–222; and Anke Hilbrenner, "Auch in Russland 'ein reiner Männersport'? Zur Geschichte und Gegenwart des Frauenfußballs in der russischen Föderation," in *Überall ist der Ball rund: Zur Geschichte und Gegenwart des Fußballs*

in Ost- und Südosteuropa, ed. Dittmar Dahlmann, Anke Hillbrenner, and Britta Lenz (Essen: Klartext, 2006), 71–96. On masculinity and spectator sport in general, see Eva Kreisky, *Arena der Männlichkeit: Über das Verhältnis von Fußball und Geschlecht* (Frankfurt: Campus Verlag, 2006).

19. For a discussion of global impacts on Soviet and post-Soviet youth culture in general, see Hilary Pilkington, Elena Omel'chenko, Moya Flynn, Ul'jana Bliudina, and Elena Starkova, *Looking West? Cultural Globalization and Russian Youth Cultures* (Philadelphia: University of Pennsylvania Press, 2002).

20. On memory and nostalgia in post-Soviet Russia, see Serguei Alex Oushakine, "We're Nostalgic but We're Not Crazy: Retrofitting the Past in Russia," *Russian Review* 66 (2007): 451–482. On oral history and the Soviet past, see Donald J. Raleigh, *Russia's Sputnik Generation: Soviet Baby Boomers Talk About Their Lives* (Bloomington: Indiana University Press, 2006). On memory and oral history in general, see Maurice Halbwachs, *Das Gedächtnis und seine sozialen Bedingungen* (Frankfurt: Suhrkamp, 1985); Robert Perks and Alistair Thomson, *The Oral History Reader* (London: Routledge, 1998); Paul Thompson, *The Voice of the Past: Oral History* (Oxford: Oxford University Press, 1989); and Harald Welzer, *Das kommunikative Gedächtnis: Eine Theorie der Erinnerung* (Munich: Beck, 2001).

21. On Soviet Radio, see Tat'iana Goriaeva, *Radio Rossii: Politicheskii Kontrol' Sovetskogo Radioveshchaniia v 1920–1930 ykh godakh* (Moscow: Rosspen, 2000); and Tat'iana Goriaeva, *"Velikaia Kniga Dnia . . ." Radio v SSSR: Dokumenty i Materialy* (Moscow: Rosspen, 2007).

22. Mike O'Mahony, *Sport in the USSR: Physical Culture–Visual Culture* (London: Reaktion, 2006), 57–96.

23. "Khuligany na stadione," *Sovetskii Sport*, May 25, 1946, p. 3.

24. *Sovetskii Sport*, May 4, 1952, cited in Edelman, *Serious Fun*, 86.

25. Rüthers, "Kindheit, Kosmos und Konsum," 59–60.

26. Reid, "Cold War in the Kitchen," 214.

27. *Bolel'shchik*, the Russian word for "fan," is derived from the verb *bolet'* (to be ill, to suffer).

28. "Delo S-193-60," *Futbol*, August 21, 1960, p. 12.

29. Gilmour and Clements, " 'If You Want to Be like Me, Train!,' " 210.

30. Vladimir A. Kozlov, *Mass Uprisings in the USSR: Protest and Rebellion in the Post-Stalin Years* (Armonk, NY: Sharpe, 2002); Brian Lapierre, "In the Shadow of the Thaw: The Control of Marginals in Socialist Societies—Making Hooliganism on a Mass Scale: The Campaign Against Petty Hooliganism in the Soviet Union, 1956–1964," *Cahier du Monde Russe* 47 (2006): 349–376; Joan Neuberger, *Hooliganism: Crime, Culture, and Power in St. Petersburg, 1900–1914* (Berkeley: University of California Press, 1993).

31. "Kubok Evropejskikh Chempionov," *Futbol*, March 8, 1964, p. 14.

32. Luminita Gatejel, "The Common Heritage of the Socialist Car Culture," paper presented at "The Socialist Car" workshop at the Berlin School for the Comparative History of Europe, June 13–14, 2008.

33. Yurchak, *Everything Was Forever*, 25.

34. See the petition for the promotion of Azovets Berdiansk in 1962 that was signed by 768 "soccer enthusiasts" from the city of Berdiansk, delo (d.) 970, opis (op.) 1, fond (f.) 5091, Ukrainian State Archive (TsDAVO), Kiev.

35. See a complaint to the Moscow Committee of Sport by a group of Dinamo Kiev fans, list (l.) 24, d. 1323, op. 1, f. 5091, TsDAVO.

36. Record of the assembly of the Ukrainian referee council, December 1959, ll. 10, 13, d. 197, op. 1, f. 5091, TsDAVO.

37. See images 0-107729, 0-152212, and 0-152288, Tsentral'nyi Derzhavnyi Kinofoto-fonoarkhiv Ukrainy (TsDKU), Kiev.

38. Requate, "Öffentlichkeit und Medien," 13.

39. For the coverage of such events in the Soviet press, see Esther Meier, *Eine Theorie für "Entwicklungsländer": Sowjetische Agitation und Afghanistan, 1978–1982* (Münster: LIT Verlag, 2001); and Evelyn Mertin, "Der Boykott der Olympischen Spiele 1980 in Moskau in der Sowjetischen Presse," *Stadion: Internationale Zeitschrift für Geschichte des Sports* 19 (2003): 251–261.

40. Roth-Ey, "Finding a Home," 281.

41. See Häder, "Selbstbehauptung wider Partei und Staat," 450.

42. Robert Edelman, "Playing Catch-Up: Soviet Media and Soccer Hooliganism, 1965–75," in *The Socialist Sixties: Crossing Borders in the Second World*, ed. Anne E. Gorsuch and Diane P. Koenker (Bloomington: Indiana University Press, 2013), 272.

43. Ibid.

44. See, for example, *Ukraina Sportivna*, 1977, Nr. 2. k-z*, TsDKU.

45. Edelman, *Serious Fun*, 192.

46. Bushnell, *Moscow Graffiti*, 29–65.

47. Stefan Plaggenborg, "Konsum," in *Handbuch der Geschichte Russlands*, vol. 5, *1945–1991: Vom Ende des zweiten Weltkriegs bis zum Zusammenbruch der Sowjetunion*, ed. Stefan Plaggenborg (Stuttgart: Hiersemann, 2003), 813.

48. On fan chants, see Reinhard Kopiez and Guido Brink, *Fußballfangesänge* (Würzburg: Königshausen and Neumann, 1998).

49. Samotsvety was one of the most popular music groups among young people in the 1970s and 1980s. Aleksandr Alekseev and Andrei Burlaka, *Entsiklopediia Rossiiskoi Pop-Rok-Muziki* (Moscow: KSMO press, 2001), 339.

50. *Fanatskii Fol'klor* is a collection of fan songs compiled by Spartak fanatic Amir Khuslutdinov ("Professor"). Published in 1996, the first edition had a print run of two hundred copies.

51. Iurii Mikhailov, interview by the author.

52. "Horse stable" is a reference to the army team TsSKA Moscow. Bushnell, *Moscow Graffiti*, 87. In the 1970s, Haiduk Split won the Yugoslavian championship four times and the Yugoslav Cup five times.

53. Iurii Mikhailov, interview by the author. This fact is confirmed by other interviewees as well.

54. Iurii Zerchaninov, "Strasti vokrug Spartaka," *Iunost'* 12 (1977): 101.

55. Gilmour and Clements, "Soviet Masculinity."

56. Robert Edelman, "A Small Way of Saying 'No': Moscow Working Men, Spartak Soccer, and the Communist Party, 1900–1945," *American Historical Review* 107 (2002): 1441–1474.

57. Aleksandr Ponyrev (pseudonym), interview by the author, Kiev's Central Recreation Park, May 30, 2007.

58. The complex subject of fan violence cannot be discussed here at length. For an overview of the topic, see Eric Dunning, ed., *Fighting Fans: Football Hooliganism as a World Phenomenon* (Dublin: University College Dublin Press, 2002); and Richard Giulianotti, Norman Bonney, and Mike Hepworth, eds., *Football, Violence, and Social Identity* (London: Routledge, 1994). For a discussion of mass uprisings and violence in the Soviet Union, see, for example, Kozlov, *Mass Uprisings*.

59. Aleksandr Ponyrev, interview by the author.

60. Sonja Häder has traced the same phenomenon in the practices of punks in Eastern Germany. Häder, "Selbstbehauptung wider Partei und Staat," 460.

61. Amir Khuslutdinov, interview by the author, Moscow, April 9, 2008.

62. Iurii Mikhailov, interview by the author.

63. Bushnell, *Moscow Graffiti*, 38.

64. This fact is also confirmed by Kiev fanatics.

65. Amir Khuslutdinov, interview by the author.

66. Edelman, *Spartak Moscow*, 294–295; Manfred Zeller, *Sport and Society in the Soviet Union: The Politics of Football After Stalin* (London: I. B. Tauris, 2018), 200–209.

67. Oleg Skorobogatov, interview by the author, Moscow, April 7, 2008. For a discussion of punk youth culture in Eastern Europe, see Häder, "Selbstbehauptung wider Partei und Staat," 457–462.

68. Risch, "Soviet 'Flower Children,'" 566–584.

69. Iurii Mikhailov, interview by the author.

70. Ibid.

71. "Resheniia i rasporiazheniia Mosgorispolkoma otnosiashchiesia k deiatel'nosti stadiona za 1983 god," d. 382, op. 1, f. 3029, Tsentral'nyi Arkhiv Goroda Moskvy (TsAGM), Moscow.

72. Aleksandr Ponyrev, interview by the author; Iurii Mikhailov, interview by the author; Amir Khuslutdinov, interview by the author. The Young Pioneers is the official Soviet youth organization for children; teens were members of the Komsomol.

73. Edelman, *Spartak Moscow*, 294.

74. Aleksandr Ponyrev, interview by the author.

75. Iurii Mikhailov, interview by the author; Amir Khuslutdinov, interview by the author.

CHAPTER 7

1. Hanns Leske, *Erich Mielke, die Stasi und das runde Leder: Der Einfluß der SED und des Ministeriums für Staatssicherheit auf den Fußballsport in der DDR* (Göttingen: Verlag die Werkstatt, 2004), 518–529.

2. John Foot, *Calcio: A History of Italian Football* (London: Harper Perennial, 2007), 53.

3. Petition from Heiko H. to the DFV, May 5, 1986, private archive of Heiko H.

4. Leske, *Erich Mielke*, 525; Alan McDougall, *The People's Game: Football, State and Society in East Germany* (Cambridge: Cambridge University Press, 2014), 235.

5. Kay Schiller and Christopher Young, "The History and Historiography of Sport in Germany: Social, Cultural and Political Perspectives," *German History* 27 (2009): 326–327.

6. Alan Tomlinson and Christopher Young, "Towards a New History of European Sport," *European Review* 19 (2011): 503.

7. Christoph Dieckmann, "Nur ein Leutzscher ist ein Deutscher," in *100 Jahre DFB: Die Geschichte des Deutschen Fußball-Bundes*, ed. Wolfgang Niersbach (Berlin: Sportverlag Berlin, 1999), 319.

8. Tim E., interview by the author, Berlin, May 25, 2011; Holger F., interview by the author, Berlin, May 23, 2011.

9. On this process in Soviet football, see Robert Edelman, *Serious Fun: A History of Spectator Sports in the USSR* (Oxford: Oxford University Press, 1993), 221–223.

10. Jan Palmowski, "Between Conformity and *Eigen-Sinn*: New Approaches to GDR History," *German History* 20 (2002): 502.

11. Alan McDougall, "East Germany and the Europeanisation of Football," *Sport in History* 35 (2015): 552–525.

12. For a discussion on Chemie Leipzig's astonishing Oberliga triumph in 1963–1964, for example, see McDougall, *The People's Game*, 106–110.

13. Leske, *Erich Mielke*, 138–140.

14. See, e.g., letter from Rudolf H. to Dynamo Dresden, June 5, 1971, DO 101/079, Stiftung Archiv der Parteien und Massenorganisationen der DDR im Bundesarchiv [Foundation Archive of the Parties and Mass Organizations of the GDR in the Federal Archives] (SAPMO), Berlin.

15. McDougall, *The People's Game*, 147–149.

16. Petition from Wolfgang Q. to the DFV, February 23, 1977, Union Berlin Archive; petition from Klaus H. to the DFV, March 1, 1977, Union Berlin Archive.

17. Olaf S., email interview by the author, May 29, 2011.

18. On Italy, see, e.g., Foot, *Calcio*, 52–55.

19. "Attendances," European Football Statistics, http://www.european-football-statistics.co.uk/attn.htm (accessed January 12, 2016).

20. Leske, *Erich Mielke*, 92.

21. Heiko H., interview by the author, Toronto, October 13, 2011.

22. McDougall, *The People's Game*, 188–191, 226–234. The prize-winning author was Erik Neutzsch (for *Traces of Stones*, 1966).

23. Letter from the Brigade Marktforschung at VEB Kombinat Robotron to Dynamo Dresden, June 21, 1973, DO 101/079, SAPMO.

24. For a discussion on Dinamo Tbilisi, see Chapter 5.

25. McDougall, *The People's Game*, 224, 227.

26. Petition from Gerd R. to Rudi Hellmann, March 24, 1986, folio (f.) 35, DY 30/4986, SAPMO.

27. On CSKA's dominance, see Edelman, *Serious Fun*, 182–186, 207–208.

28. "Gemeinsam klapps!," May 14, 1988, f. 222, MfS HA XX/221, Bundesbeauftragte für die Unterlagen der Staatssicherheitsdienstes der ehemaligen Deutschen Demokratischen Republik [Federal Commissioner for the Records of the State Security Service of the Former German Democratic Republic] (BStU), Berlin.

29. Edelman, *Serious Fun*, 174–177.

30. Jörn Luther and Frank Willmann, *BFC Dynamo: Der Meisterclub* (Berlin: Das Neue Berlin, 2003), 141.

31. "Information über eine Beratung mit den Sportredaktionen der zentralen Medien am 30.10.1985," f. 245, DY 30/4964, SAPMO.

32. "Information zu Problemen im Fußballsport," June 26, 1985, f. 122, MfS HA XX/2669, BStU.

33. McDougall, *The People's Game*, 201–204, 221–222.

34. "Bericht zum negativen Fußballanhang des BFC Dynamo in der Spielsaison 1985/86 und die Ergebnisse der Arbeit des Hauptsachgebietes negativer Fußballanhang," July 11, 1986, f. 34, MfS ZOS/3212, BStU.

35. Leske, *Erich Mielke*, 525.

36. McDougall, *The People's Game*, 225, 234.

37. Robert Edelman, *Spartak Moscow: A History of the People's Team in the Workers' State* (Ithaca, NY: Cornell University Press, 2009), 94–95.

38. McDougall, *The People's Game*, 236.

39. Paul Betts, *Within Walls: Private Life in the German Democratic Republic* (Oxford: Oxford University Press, 2010), 186.

40. Petition from Günter D. to Rudi Hellmann, April 30, 1982, ff. 46–47, DY 30/4981, SAPMO; petition from Alfred I. to Erich Honecker, October 28, 1985, f. 2, DY 30/4983, SAPMO.

41. Anonymous petition to Rudi Hellmann, May 26, 1986, f. 4, DY 30/4980, SAPMO.

42. See, e.g., McDougall, "East Germany and the Europeanisation of Football."

43. Anonymous petition to the Central Committee (ZK), October 27, 1985, ff. 2–3, DY 30/4980, SAPMO.

44. See, e.g., petition from Günter Q. to Rudi Hellmann, March 23, 1987 [1986], f. 200, DY 30/4985, SAPMO.

45. Petition from Horst Z. to ZK, October 29, 1985, f. 377, DY 30/4988, SAPMO.

46. Petition from Alfred M. to ZK department of sport, June 11, 1985, ff. 103–104, DY 30/4984, SAPMO.

47. Anonymous petition to ZK, June 18, 1985, f. 137, DY 30/4987, SAPMO.

48. Hanns Leske, *Enzyklopädie des DDR-Fußballs* (Göttingen: Verlag die Werkstatt, 2007), 36.

49. Leske, *Erich Mielke*, 503–504.

50. "Zusammenstellung von Informationen zur Problematik der Schiedsrichterleistungen und-verhaltensweisen in Zusammenhang mit den Spielen des BFC Dynamo, der SG Dynamo Dresden und dem 1. FC Lok Leipzig in der Saison 1984/85," n.d., ff. 88–92, DY 30/IV 2/2.039/247, SAPMO.

51. "Protokoll der Videoauswertung des Endspiels im FDGB-Pokal vom 8. Juni 1985 zwischen dem BFC Dynamo und der SG Dynamo Dresden zur Beurteilung der Schiedsrichterleistung," July 3, 1985, ff. 195–196, DY 30/4963, SAPMO.

52. Petition from Günter D. to Rudi Hellmann, April 30, 1982, ff. 46–47, DY 30/4981, SAPMO; notes on a meeting with Günter D., June 16, 1982, ff. 51–52, DY 30/4981, SAPMO.

53. Petition from Hans-Jürgen H. to Rudi Hellmann, May 12, 1986, ff. 336–341, DY 30/4982, SAPMO; letter from Rudi Hellmann to Hans-Jürgen H., May 26, 1986, f. 335, DY 30/4982, SAPMO.

54. Letter from Rudi Hellmann to Alfred I., November 22, 1985, ff. 3–4, DY 30/4983, SAPMO.

55. McDougall, *The People's Game*, 237–238.

56. See Jonathan Wilson, *Behind the Curtain: Travels in Eastern European Football* (London: Orion, 2006), 185–190.

57. Ingolf Pleil, *Mielke, Macht und Meisterschaft: Die "Bearbeitung" der Sportgemeinschaft Dynamo Dresden durch das MfS 1978–1989* (Berlin: Ch. Links Verlag, 2001), 280.

58. Petition from Ralf R. to Egon Krenz, April 3, 1986, ff. 99–100, DY 30/4986, SAPMO.

59. Foot, *Calcio*, 52.

60. Andreas Gläser, *Der BFC war Schuld am Mauerbau: Ein stolzer Sohn des Proletariats erzählt* (Berlin: Aufbau Taschenbuch Verlag, 2003), 44.

61. "Attendances."

62. Patrick Major, *Behind the Berlin Wall: East Germany and the Frontiers of Power* (Oxford: Oxford University Press, 2010), 254.

63. Mary Fulbrook, *Anatomy of a Dictatorship: Inside the GDR, 1949–1989* (Oxford: Oxford University Press, 1997), 252.

64. Simon Kuper, *Football Against the Enemy* (London: Orion, 1994), 18; see also McDougall, *The People's Game*, 320.

CHAPTER 8

1. Klaus Latzel, *Staatsdoping: Der VEB Jenapharm im Sportsystem der DDR* (Cologne: Böhlau Verlag, 2009), 211.

2. Klaus Marxen and Gerhard Werle, eds., *Strafjustiz und DDR-Unrecht: Dokumentation*, vol. 7, *Gefangenenmisshandlung und sonstiges DDR-Unrecht* (Berlin: De Gruyter Recht, 2009); Ines Geipel, *Verlorene Spiele: Journal eines Doping-Prozesses* (Berlin: TRANSIT Buchverlag, 2001). Geipel, a fierce opponent of doping, withdrew her name from the list of members of the SC Motor Jena 4×100 relay squad that achieved a world record time in 1984.

3. Giselher Spitzer, *Doping in der DDR: Ein historischer Überblick zu einer konspirativen Praxis* (Cologne: Sportverlag Strauß, 2012), 427; Geipel, *Verlorene Spiele*, 32–34, 137–140.

4. René Wiese, *Kaderschmieden des "Sportwunderlandes": Die Kinder- und Jugendsportschulen in der DDR* (Hildesheim: Arete Verlag, 2012), 477–483, 552; see also Werner W. Franke, "Funktion und Instrumentalisierung des Sports in der DDR: Pharmakologische Manipulationen (Doping) und die Rolle der Wissenschaft," in *Materialien der Enquete-Kommission "Aufarbeitung von Geschichte und Folgen der DDR-Diktatur in Deutschland,"* vol. 3, pt. 2, ed. Deutscher Bundestag (Baden-Baden: Nomos Verlag, 1995), 941–947.

5. On the many power struggles within the sports system, see Mike Dennis and Jonathan Grix, *Sport Under Communism: Behind the East German "Miracle"* (Basingstoke, UK: Palgrave, 2012), 42–44, 78–80, 99, 146; and Hans-Georg Aschenbach, *Euer Held, Euer Verräter: Mein Leben für den Leistungssport* (Halle: Mitteldeutscher Verlag, 2012), 40, 44, 70–71, 81.

6. Honecker was responsible for sport from 1952 to 1958 and again from 1967 to 1971; he became party leader in 1971.

7. Steroid use and testing procedures are examined in Thomas M. Hunt, *Drug Games: The International Olympic Committee and the Politics of Doping, 1960–2008* (Austin: University of Texas Press, 2011), 24, 29–30, 44–45, 53–55.

8. Dennis and Grix, *Sport*, 96.

9. For the "master plan," see Spitzer, *Doping*, 270–279.

10. Extracts from East German research projects can be found in Brigitte Berendonk, *Doping: Von der Forschung zum Betrug* (Reinbek: Rowohlt Taschenbuch Verlag, 1992).

11. Ibid., 107.

12. On the distribution system, see Dennis and Grix, *Sport*, 102–105.

13. See Spitzer, *Doping*, 380.

14. Dennis and Grix, *Sport*, 146.

15. Mike Dennis, "Doping in East German Football Since the Mid-1960s," *Baltic Worlds*, June 19, 2012, pp. 3–5.

16. Michael Kummer, "Die Fußballklubs Rot-Weiß Erfurt und Carl Zeiss Jena und ihre Vorgänger in der DDR" (PhD diss., Potsdam University, 2010), 296–297, 417–418.

17. Berendonk, *Doping*, 155, 157, 209.

18. Ibid., 210–211.

19. "Treffbericht," August 5, 1976, p. 193, MfS ZA Teilablage A-637/79/II, vol. 2, Bundesbeauftragte für die Unterlagen der Staatssicherheitsdienstes der ehemaligen Deutschen Demokratischen Republik [Federal Commissioner for the Documents of the State Security Service of the Former German Democratic Republic] (BStU).

20. "Treffbericht," September 25, 1975, p. 260, MfS Außenstelle Leipzig AIM 5330/92, vol. 1, bk. 3, BStU; see also "IMV 'Rolf' vom 5.9.1978," September 9, 1978, p. 231, MfS Außenstelle Leipzig AIM 5330/92, vol. 1, bk. 4, BStU. In 2000, Kipke was given a suspended jail sentence of fifteen months and fined seventy-five hundred Deutsche Marks.

21. For examples of proven cases of causing bodily harm and for details on dosages, see Marxen and Werle, *Strafjustiz*, 161-174. In 1998, Gläser and Binus were sentenced and fined by the Berlin Regional Court for nine counts each of having administered harmful drugs to young female swimmers.

22. "Treffbericht," July 30, 1976, pp. 138-139, MfS AIM 9211/9, vol. 1, bk. 2, BStU.

23. "Treffbericht," August 5, 1976, pp. 193-194, MfS ZA Teilablage A-637/79/II, vol. 2, BStU.

24. "Kurzinformation über eine Beratung mit dem Vorsitzenden der LSK am 2.3.1977," pp. 247-249, MfS ZA Teilablage A-637/79/II, vol. 2, BStU.

25. "Treffbericht," August 5, 1976, p. 193.

26. Berendonk, *Doping*, 70-80.

27. Latzel, *Staatsdoping*, 130-139, 178-187; see also Werner W. Franke, "Nil nocere: Gutachterliche Stellungnahme zur Art und zum Ausmaß der Firma Jenapharm und ihrer Wissenschaftler beim verbrecherischen Doping-System der DDR," December 22, 2004, pp. 2-7, http://docplayer.org/6520381-Nil-nocere-heidelberg-22-12-2004.html.

28. Spitzer, *Doping*, 412.

29. On weightlifting in the GDR and the activities of Lathan, see Berendonk, *Doping*, 185-189, 377-381; Werner W. Franke and Brigitte Berendonk, "Hormonal Doping and Androgenization of Athletes: A Secret Program of the German Democratic Republic," *Clinical Chemistry* 43, no. 7 (1997): 1268-1269; and "Deutsche Ärzte und Doping: Dr. Hans-Henning Lathan," *cycling4fans*, March 2010, pp. 1-2.

30. "Deutsche Ärzte und Doping," 2-3. In a 1990 interview, one of the young athletes, Uwe, stated he had been aware that he was being doped.

31. "Abschrift: Bericht zum Vorkommnis um den DDR-Gewichtheber G. Bonk (SC KMSt) bei den Olympischen Spielen in Moskau," [1980], p. 129, MfS BV Leipzig AIM 5368/92, vol. 1, bk. 1, BStU; Thomas Purschke, "Gewichtheber Gerd Bonk: Opfer des DDR-Systems," *Frankfurter Allgemeine*, October 21, 2014, pp. 1-2.

32. Berendonk, *Doping*, 185-186.

33. Andreas Müller, *Kulturistik: Bodybuilding und Kraftsport in der DDR: Eine sporthistorische Analyse* (Cologne: Sportverlag Strauß, 2011), 12, 209-220, 304-309, 313-314.

34. "Information: Kraftsport in der Hauptstadt Berlin," March 30, 1988, p. 43, MfS ZA HA XX 1486, pt. 1, BStU; "Information zur Kraftsportsektion: 1071 Bornholmer Str. 81," June 29, 1989, p. 173, MfS ZA HA XX 1486, pt. 1, BStU.

35. For a discussion of athletes' awareness of doping practices, see Berendonk, *Doping*, 102-103; Aschenbach, *Euer Held*, 35-37, 171-172, 176-177; and Rob Beamish and Ian Ritchie, *Fastest, Highest, Strongest: A Critique of High Performance Sport* (New York: Routledge, 2006), 128-135.

36. "Tonbandabschrift IMB 'Philatelist' vom 18.4.1989," April 18, 1989, p. 237, MfS AIM 16572/89, vol. 2, bk. 7, BStU.

37. "Tonbandabschrift," June 18, 1976, pp. 182-183, MfS AIM 16572/89, vol. 2, bk. 4, BStU.

38. "Bericht," April 2, 1985, p. 82, MfS AIM 9211/9, vol. 2, bk. 2, BStU.

39. Marxen and Werle, *Strafjustiz*, 223.

40. See the documents in Spitzer, *Doping*, 355–357, 388–395, 400–405.

41. Thomas H. Hunt, Paul Dimeo, Florian Hemme, and Anne Mueller, "The Health Risks of Doping During the Cold War: A Comparative Analysis of the Two Sides of the Iron Curtain," *International Journal of the History of Sport* 17, no. 31 (2014): 2234, 2239.

42. Franke, "Funktion," 959–964; see also "Deutsche Ärzte und Doping: Professor Dr. Dr. Israel," *cycling4fans*, March 2010, p. 1.

43. Giselher Spitzer, Erik Eggers, Holger J. Schnell, and Yasmin Wisniewska, *Siegen um jeden Preis: Doping in Deutschland; Geschichte, Recht, Ethik, 1972–1990* (Göttingen: Verlag Die Werkstatt, 2013).

44. "Lage/Probleme innerhalb der Sportmedizin," November 3, 1987, p. 117, MfS ZAIG HA XX/3 26789, BStU.

45. The rationale for an international antidoping policy continues to be a highly contentious issue. The competing discourses are dissected in Karl-Heinz Bette and Uwe Schimank, *Doping im Hochleistungssport: Anpassung durch Abweichung* (Frankfurt am Main: Suhrkamp, 2006), 357–385; and in a series of wide-ranging essays in Verner Møller, Ivan Waddington, and John M. Hoberman, eds., *Routledge Handbook of Drugs and Sport* (London: Routledge, 2015).

CHAPTER 9

Acknowledgments: I thank the editors for their patience in soliciting this chapter and seeing it through to publication. Chris Young was particularly persuasive in encouraging me to venture into sport history, and I have gained much from the journey. I would also like to thank John Woitkowitz for his stellar help with the research for this chapter.

1. John G. Rodden, "Of Sport, State, and Stasi: Socialism with an Un-beautiful Face," *Midwest Quarterly* 40, no. 2 (1999): 138.

2. Contrary to much that has been written about her (particularly Lothar Mikos, "Prinzessin auf dem Eis—Kati Witt als Sozialistischer Sportstar," in *Sport und Medien: Eine Deutsch-Deutsche Geschichte*, ed. Dietrich Leder and Hans-Ulrich Wagner [Cologne: Halem, 2011], 105–118), all of this happened with the consent of both Witt and her parents. See Katarina Witt, *Meine Jahre zwischen Pflicht und Kür*, 2nd ed. (Munich: C. Bertelsmann, 1994).

3. The first two terms are from "Eiskunstlauf: Geld für die Republik," *Der Spiegel*, January 27, 1986, http://www.spiegel.de/spiegel/print/d-13518121.html; the third is from Tom Callahan, "Skater Debi Thomas: The Word She Uses Is Invincible," *Time*, February 15, 1988, http://content.time.com/time/subscriber/article/0,33009,966709-1,00.html. The original German of the fourth description reads: "jene hollywoodreife Präzision, mit der sie schon früher als systemübergreifendes Lustsymbol betörte." It comes from a 1992 *Der Spiegel* report made after she had already switched from skating to commentating at the Albertville Olympics. See "Eiskunstlauf: Perfektes Produkt," *Der Spiegel*, February 17, 1992, http://www.spiegel.de/spiegel/print/d-13680995.html.

4. Rick Reilly, "Behold the Shining Star of the G.D.R.," *Sports Illustrated*, January 20, 1986, http://www.si.com/vault/1986/01/20/628879/behold-the-shining-star-of-the-gdr.

5. Grit Hartmann, *Goldkinder: Die DDR im Spiegel ihres Spitzensports* (Leipzig: Forum Verlag, 1997), 221.

6. On TV and East German Olympic sports, see Christopher Young, "Sport und Medien: Deutschland und die Möglichkeiten europäischer Perspektiven," in Leder and Wagner, *Sport und Medien*, 13, 18–19.

7. Richard Collins, *From Satellite to Single Market: New Communication Technology and European Public Service Television* (London: Routledge, 1998), 5. Collins notes that the agreements that would eventually create Eurosport were being negotiated in 1987 and late 1988. Ibid., 33–34.

8. Similar transmitter position occurred along the borders with Hungary and Czechoslovakia. See Jean K. Chalaby, *Transnational Television in Europe: Reconfiguring Global Communications Networks* (London: I. B. Tauris, 2009), 8.

9. Claudia Dittmar, *Feindliches Fernsehen: Das DDR-Fernsehen und seine Strategien im Umgang mit dem westdeutschen Fernsehen* (Bielefeld: Transcript Verlag, 2010), 265. The Tokyo Olympics were the first to rely on direct satellite coverage and were transmitted across the world. See Holger Preuss, *The Economics of Staging the Olympics: A Comparison of the Games, 1972–2008* (Cheltenham, UK: Edward Elgar, 2004), 114.

10. Bundeszentrale für politische Bildung, "Deutsche Fernsehgeschichte in Ost und West: Sport im DDR-Fernsehen," August 28, 2017, http://www.bpb.de/gesellschaft/medien-und-sport/deutsche-fernsehgeschichte-in-ost-und-west/245678/sport-im-ddr-fernsehen.

11. Dittmar, *Feindliches Fernsehen*, 343, 429.

12. Mikos, "Prinzessin auf dem Eis," 110–111.

13. "In unserem Land gehört der Sport zum Leben: Diskussionsbeitrag von Weltmeisterin und Olympiasiegerin Katarina Witt auf dem 11. FDGB-Kongreß," *Deutsches Sportecho am Wochende*, April 24–25, 1987, reproduced in Heinz Koch and Angelika Kissling, *Unsere Herzen dem Sport: Dokumentarische Betrachtung zum Zeitraum zwischen dem XI. Parteitag der SED und dem 40. Jahrestag der Gründung der DDR*, Aktuelle Schriftenreihe Gesellschaft zur Förderung des Olympischen Gedankens in der Deutschen Demokratischen Republik 12 (Berlin: Gesellschaft zur Förderung des Olympischen Gedankens in der DDR, 1989), 149.

14. "Zur Information," February 8, 1988, p. 76, DY 30/5096, Bundesarchiv Berlin (BAB).

15. Marc Pitzke, "US-Dokumentation über Katarina Witt: Hollywood on Ice," *Spiegel Online*, August 6, 2013, http://www.spiegel.de/kultur/tv/us-dokumentation-the-diplomat-ueber-katarina-witt-a-914447.html.

16. Katarina Witt, *Only with Passion: Figure Skating's Most Winning Champion on Competition and Life* (New York: PublicAffairs, 2007), 99. For a discussion of fashion rules in figure skating and a picture of Witt's 1988 World Figure Skating Championships costume, see Nancy Yang, "What Not to Wear: The Rules of Fashion on the Ice," *Minnesota Public Radio*, January 21, 2016, https://www.mprnews.org/story/2016/01/21/figure-skating-fashion-rules.

17. The rule was repealed in 2004.

18. The literature on this subject is vast and displays a large degree of consensus. It will not come as a surprise to any sports fan that female athletes are routinely sexualized by sports media outlets or that this sexualization has primarily commercial motivations. For an example of such arguments, see Mary Jo Kane, Nicole M. LaVoi, and Janet S. Fink, "Exploring Elite Female Athletes' Interpretations of Sport Media Images: A Window into the Construction of Social Identity and 'Selling Sex' in Women's Sports," *Communication and Sport* 1, no. 3 (2013): 269–298. Witt is also by no means the first or the last female athlete to believe that selling sex might help promote her sport. Without the space to explore the broader literature on the sexualization of female athletes, I concentrate here on the precise historical circumstances and political strategies that were the context for the creation of Witt's public persona.

19. Witt, *Only with Passion*, 120.

20. Pitzke, "US-Dokumentation."

21. Witt, *Meine Jahre*, 161.

22. Ibid., 163.

23. Allen Guttmann, *The Erotic in Sports* (New York: Columbia University Press, 1996), 168.

24. Mary Jo Kane and Susan L. Greendorfer, "The Media's Role in Accommodating and Resisting Stereotyped Images of Women in Sport," in *Women, Media and Sport: Challenging Gender Values*, ed. Pamela J. Creedon (Thousand Oaks, CA: Sage, 1994), 31.

25. Catriona M. Parratt, "A Testing Time," *Journal of Sport History* 41, no. 3 (2014): 492. Parratt is quoting Guttmann's broader study of women in sport: Allen Guttmann, *Women's Sports: A History* (New York: Columbia University Press, 1991), 1. Parratt acknowledges Guttmann's important role in providing a respectful account of the history of women in sport (she still regularly assigns *Women's Sports* in graduate classes), but she calls him to task for not more clearly laying out the "systematic inequalities that are key to . . . processes" of the "sexualization and sexual objectification of female athletes" (494). As a historian who has explored the long history of the creation of norms of gender and sexuality in Europe, I could not agree more. See Annette F. Timm and Joshua A. Sanborn, *Gender, Sex and the Shaping of Modern Europe: A History from the French Revolution to the Present Day*, 2nd ed. (London: Bloomsbury, 2016). But the argument is much more difficult to apply to Katarina Witt than to female FIFA (Fédération Internationale de Football Association) soccer players, simply because Witt very clearly participated in her own sexualization.

26. Allen Guttmann, "Spartan Girls, French Postcards, and the Male Gaze: Another Go at Eros and Sports," *Journal of Sport History* 29, no. 3 (2002): 382.

27. This term also appears frequently in both the scholarly literature and press accounts about Witt. See, for example, Hartmann, *Goldkinder*, 215; Callahan, "Skater Debi Thomas"; Volker Kluge, *Das Sportbuch DDR* (Berlin: Eulenspiegel Verlag, 2004); and Gertrud Pfister, *Frauen und Sport in der DDR* (Cologne: Sport und Buch Strauß, 2002). Once again, the origins are somewhat unclear, but Gunter Holzweißig attributes the phrase to Walter Ulbricht. Gunter Holzweißig, *Diplomaten im Trainingsanzug: Sport als*

politisches Instrument der DDR in den innerdeutschen und internationalen Beziehungen (Munich: Oldenbourg, 1981), 3.

28. Jasper A. Friedrich, *Politische Instrumentalisierung von Sport in den Massenmedien: Eine strukturationstheoretische Analyse der Sportberichterstattung im DDR-Fernsehen* (Cologne: Halem, 2010), 247.

29. See the various exchanges between Egon Krenz and sports officials in DY30-4968, BAB, and DY30-4963, BAB.

30. Ministerial Council, "Entwurf: Information an den Vorsitzenden des Ministerrates über den Erfüllungsstand des Maßnahmeplans der staatlichen Organe zur weiteren Förderung des Leistungssports der DDR und zur Unterstützung der Vorbereitungen auf die Olympischen Spiele 1988," March 6, 1986, in DR5-3308, BAB, p. 1.

31. "Telephonnotiz Nr. 15" (transcript of a telephone call between Thomas Köhler from the DTSB and the Olympic team leader in Calgary), February 17, 1988, DY30-5096, BAB.

32. Press reports varied about the size of this press conference, citing numbers between 300 and 750. Witt herself put the attendance at 600, which seems a likely estimate. Katarina Witt, "Nicht auf allen vieren," in *Momentaufnahmen: Zeitzeugen zum DDR-Sport befragt von Klaus Ullrich*, ed. Klaus Ullrich (Berlin: Sportverlag Berlin, 1989), 154.

33. Ibid., 157.

34. See various reports and letters in DR510-645, BAB.

35. Friedrich, *Politische Instrumentalisierung*, 254–255.

36. "Information ueber die Berufung Katarina Witts zum UNICEF-Sportsbotschafter," September 20, 1988, DY30-596, BAB.

37. Ibid.

38. Witt, *Meine Jahre*, 50, 60, 76–78, 150.

39. Ibid., 182. See also Kluge, *Das Sportbuch DDR*, 85.

40. On the DTSB's careful plans to pick sports most likely to produce Olympic medals, see Hartmann, *Goldkinder*, 231.

41. Josie McLellan, *Love in the Time of Communism: Intimacy and Sexuality in the GDR* (Cambridge: Cambridge University Press, 2011), 144.

42. Ibid., 145.

43. Witt, *Meine Jahre*, 149–150.

44. Ibid., 50.

45. *Ninotchka*, directed by Ernst Lubitsch (Culver City, CA: Metro-Goldwyn-Mayer, 1939).

46. Empirically supported historical work on the "honey trap" technique is extremely thin. Most of what we know about the phenomenon comes from ex-spies, such as Frederick Hitz, the former inspector general of the American Central Intelligence Agency, and Markus Wolf, the former head of the Main Directorate for Reconnaissance (Hauptverwaltung Aufklärung) of East Germany's Ministry for State Security (Ministerium für Statssicherheit)—the Stasi. Hitz argues that the Soviets and other

East Germans were adept at using "swallows"—female agents—to seduce and black-mail Western agents. See Frederick P. Hitz, *The Great Game: The Myths and Reality of Espionage* (New York: Alfred Knopf, 2004), 99–106. Wolf has famously congratulated himself on establishing a system of using "Romeos" to obtain West German secrets from unsuspecting female government employees. "Since time immemorial," he writes in his autobiography, "security services have used the mating game to gain proximity to inter-esting figures. But if I go down in espionage history, it may well be for perfecting the use of sex in spying." Markus Wolf, *Man Without a Face: The Autobiography of Communism's Greatest Spymaster*, trans. Anne McElvoy (1997; repr., New York: PublicAffairs, 1999), 137. Neither provides specific documentary evidence, and both seem to be capitalizing on the salaciousness of their descriptions to sell their books.

47. Ian Fleming, *From Russia, with Love* (London: Jonathan Cape, 1957), https://www.gutenberg.ca/ebooks/flemingi-fromrussiawithlove/flemingi-fromrussiawithlove-00-t.txt.

48. See, for example, "Ice in the Soul," *Observer Sport Monthly*, November 4, 2001, https://www.theguardian.com/observer/osm/story/0,6903,583607,00.html.

49. William Bridel, personal communication, January 22, 2017.

50. Thomas Brussig, *Heroes like Us*, trans. John Brownjohn (New York: Farrar, Straus and Giroux, 1997), 232.

51. For a useful overview of American and Italian Nazisploitation films, see Daniel H. Magilow, Elizabeth Bridges, and Kristin T. Vander Lugt, eds., *Nazisploitation! The Nazi Image in Low-Brow Cinema and Culture* (New York: Continuum, 2011).

52. *Ilsa, She Wolf of the SS*, directed by Don Edmonds (Aeteas Filmproduktions, 1975); and *Ilsa, the Tigress of Siberia*, directed by Jean LaFleur (Canada: Mount Everest Enterprises, 1977).

53. As I have written elsewhere, American propaganda films like the 1943 film *Hitler's Children* played to Hollywood's fascination with sex under the guise of revealing Nazi crimes. See Annette F. Timm, "Titillation in the Guise of Authenticity: Myths of Nazi Breeding from *Hitler's Children* to *The Kindly Ones*," in *"Holocaust"-Fiktion: Kunst jen-seits der Authentizität*, ed. Iris Roebling-Grau and Dirk Rupnow (Paderborn: Wilhelm Fink Verlag, 2015), 271–294. On the theme of sexual deviance as an explanation for Com-munist evil in James Bond films, see Tricia Jenkins, "James Bond's 'Pussy' and Anglo-American Cold War Sexuality," *Journal of American Culture* 28, no. 3 (2005): 309–317.

54. Howard H. Chiang, "Sexuality and Gender in Cold War America: Social Ex-periences, Cultural Authorities, and the Roots of Political Change," in *Cold War and McCarthy Era: People and Perspectives*, ed. Caroline S. Emmons (Santa Barbara, CA: ABC-CLIO, 2010), 112; Margot Canaday, *The Straight State: Sexuality and Citizenship in Twentieth-Century America* (Princeton, NJ: Princeton University Press, 2009).

55. I am drawing here on Herbert Marcuse's definition of "repressive desublima-tion," which he developed for the Third Reich but also has application here. Marcuse argued that the Nazis used access to sexual pleasure as a means of political pacifica-tion. See Herbert Marcuse, *One-Dimensional Man: Studies in the Ideology of Advanced Industrial Society* (London: Routledge and Kegan Paul, 1964), 72; and Herbert Marcuse,

"Über soziale und politische Aspekte des Nationalsozialismus," in *Feindanalysen: Über die Deutschen* (Lüneburg: Klampen Verlag, 1998), 91–117.

56. McLellan, *Love in the Time of Communism*, 30.

57. This term was a common self-description in the GDR. See Klaus Ziemer, "Real existierender Sozialismus," in *Lexikon der Politikwissenschaft: Theorien, Methoden, Begriffe*, ed. Dieter Nohlen and Rainer-Olaf Schultze (Munich: C. H. Beck, 2005), 823–824.

58. Quoted in Witt, *Meine Jahre*, 49.

59. "Information zur Lage in den Bezirksorganisationen," March 16, 1988, DR5-1428, BAB.

60. Ilko-Sascha Kowalczuk and Bundeszentrale für Politische Bildung (Germany), *Endspiel: Die Revolution von 1989 in der DDR*, 2nd ed. (Munich: C. H. Beck, 2009), 164–165. Witt reflected on this incident in a 2015 interview: "And I stood there, very naïve, on the stage in East Berlin in 1988 and said: I recently met Bryan Adams in Canada. No wonder that the young people thought: Now she's even telling us that she met the guy in Canada—like we'll ever be able to go there." See "Am besten war ich, wenn ich mit dem Rücken zur Wand stand," *Zeit Magazin*, April 2, 2015, http://www.zeit.de /zeit-magazin/2015/12/katarina-witt-eiskunstlauf.

61. For a summary of the press attention, see Joachim Preuß, "Eiskunstlauf: Marktfrau on Ice," *Der Spiegel*, November 29, 1993, http://www.spiegel.de/spiegel/print /d-13682532.html.

62. Witt, *Meine Jahre*, 203.

63. Ibid.

64. See clippings in DX3-730, BAB.

65. Witt, *Meine Jahre*, 253.

66. Mary Evertz, "Katarina Witt Showing Off More Jewels," *St. Petersburg Times*, January 19, 1999.

67. "USA: Skating; Katarina Witt Poses for Playboy Magazine," AP Archive, November 6, 1998, http://www.aparchive.com/metadata/USA-SKATING-KATARINA -WITT-POSES-FOR-PLAYBOY-MAGAZINE/e1edf8a6922983b836201a486c3bc901?.

68. I am respecting Katarina Witt's request, relayed to me through her agent, that I not seek the rights to republish images from her *Playboy* spread here. Although they appear on various websites from time to time, as far as I am aware, they have not been officially re-released.

69. The full title of the magazine was *Die Ehe: Monatsschrift für Ehe, Wissenschaft, Recht, und Kultur*. Without the *Playboy* images for comparison, it makes little sense to reproduce the exact images I am referring to here. But those with access to this rare publication should look at the photos in *Die Ehe* on May 1, 1926 (especially the image captioned " 'Sprung'-Zeitlupenaufnahme," on page 127), and the uncaptioned image taken by Lotte Herrlich on page 146 in the May 1, 1930, issue.

70. Witt, *Only with Passion*, 93.

71. Witt, *Meine Jahre*, 111. See her account of the first time she was recognized, when the young man "did not look into my face once." Ibid., 52. She repeats the story in *Only with Passion*, 93.

72. McLellan, *Love in the Time of Communism*, 101.

73. This theme was taken up with gusto by newsmagazines like *Focus* and *Der Spiegel*. See, for example, "Stasi: Mit Sex und Peitschen," *Focus Magazin*, March 11, 2002, http://www.focus.de/politik/deutschland/stasi-mit-sex-und-peitschen_aid_203726 .html; and "'Liebe öffnet jeden Tresor': Wie die Ost-Berliner Staatssicherheit Frauen für ihr Gewerbe mißbrauchte," *Der Spiegel*, February 25, 1991, http://www.spiegel.de /spiegel/print/d-13489944.html.

74. See the long discussion of these TV shows in Paul Cooke, *Representing East Germany Since Unification: From Colonization to Nostalgia* (Oxford: Bloomsbury Academic, 2005), 141–176, esp. 165–166.

75. Ibid., 170.

76. Harald Martenstein, "Schön war die Zeit," *Der Tagesspiegel*, August 23, 2003, http://www.tagesspiegel.de/kultur/schoen-war-die-zeit/441630.html.

77. Cooke, *Representing East Germany*, 170.

78. Ibid., 251.

79. Mike Dennis and Jonathan Grix, *Sport Under Communism: Behind the East German "Miracle"* (New York: Palgrave Macmillan, 2012).

CHAPTER 10

1. "Sulian tiyu daibiaotuan zai Beijing shouci biaoyan" [The Soviet sports delegation's first performance in Beijing], *Xinwen jianbao* 1953 nian 40 hao [News bulletin number 40, 1953], DVD accompanying Zhongyang xinwen jilu dianying zhipian yingshi ziliaobu, eds., *Xinwen jianbao Zhongguo: Tiyu, 1950–1977* [China news bulletins: Sports and physical culture, 1950–1977] (Shanghai: Shanghai kexue jishu wenxian chubanshe, 2009).

2. Rebecca Karl, *Mao Zedong and China in the Twentieth-Century World: A Concise History* (Durham, NC: Duke University Press, 2010), 77.

3. Thomas P. Bernstein and Hua-Yu Li, eds., *China Learns from the Soviet Union, 1949–Present* (Lanham, MD: Lexington Books, 2011); Lorenz Lüthi, *The Sino-Soviet Split: Cold War in the Communist World* (Princeton, NJ: Princeton University Press, 2008), 31–33; Shen Zhihua and Li Danhui, *After Leaning to One Side: China and Its Allies in the Cold War* (Washington, DC: Woodrow Wilson Center Press, 2011), 118.

4. The Chinese term *tiyu* does not have a sufficient single-word translation in English. As used by Chinese leaders in the 1950s, *tiyu* encompassed physical education, fitness and exercise programs, martial arts, recreational games and activities, and paramilitary "national defense" activities (*guofang tiyu*). The term is perhaps closer to the Soviet term *fitzkultura*, but it is not a direct translation.

5. Dong Jinxia, *Women, Sport and Society in Modern China* (London: Frank Cass, 2003), 36.

6. Xu Guoqi, *Olympic Dreams: China and Sports, 1895–2008* (Cambridge, MA: Harvard University Press, 2008), 7–8.

7. Recent social histories of this period reveal "an astonishing degree of variations and exceptions" to notions of a "swift military takeover" in 1949 and the local impact of land reform or other campaigns on consolidating party control. Jeremy Brown and Paul

Pickowicz, eds., *Dilemmas of Victory: The Early Years of the People's Republic of China* (Cambridge, MA: Harvard University Press, 2007), 7–8.

8. Amanda Shuman, "The Politics of Socialist Athletics in the People's Republic of China, 1949–1966" (PhD diss., University of California, Santa Cruz, 2014), 31–32.

9. Ibid., 3.

10. Karl, *Mao Zedong and China in the Twentieth-Century World*, 85.

11. Xu, *Olympic*, 7–8.

12. Aminda Smith, *Thought Reform and China's Dangerous Classes: Reeducation, Resistance, and the People* (Lanham, MD: Rowman and Littlefield, 2012), 4.

13. Nicolai Volland, "Translating the Socialist State: Cultural Exchange, National Identity, and the Socialist World in the Early PRC," *Twentieth-Century China* 33, no. 2 (2008): 52.

14. Modern *tiyu* had grown alongside Chinese nationalism in the first half of the twentieth century, and by the time of the establishment of the PRC the nation already had a solid base of experienced sports and physical education experts. Andrew Morris, *Marrow of the Nation: A History of Sport and Physical Culture in Republican China* (Berkeley: University of California Press, 2004).

15. Odd Arne Westad, *The Global Cold War: Third World Interventions and the Making of Our Times* (Cambridge: Cambridge University Press, 2011), 69.

16. Ge Wu, "Ye-lin-na.Ge-ji-hao-li ba shi gongchi dilan de jishu" [Elena Gokieli's technique in the 80-meter hurdles], *Xin tiyu* [New sport], August 1953, pp. 24–25.

17. Beijing tiyu xueyuan xiaozhi, ed., *Beijing tiyu xueyuan zhi* [Beijing *tiyu* research institute records] (Beijing: Beijing tiyu xueyuan xiaozhi bianxiezu, 1994), 176–177.

18. Ma-he Ya-luo-mi-er, "Shijie wenming de changpao jianjiang Za-tuo-pei-ke: Yi ge yisheng xinmu zhong de Za-tuo-pei-ke" [World-famous long-distance runner Zátopek: Zátopek in the eyes of a doctor], *Xin tiyu*, January 1953, pp. 18–19.

19. Tim Noakes, *Lore of Running*, 4th ed. (Champaign, IL: Human Kinetics, 2003), 382–385.

20. A. Bu-jia-qie-fu-si-jii, "Za-tuo-pei-ke de changpao lianxifa" [Zátopek's long-distance training methods], *Xin tiyu*, January 1953, pp. 20–21.

21. Ibid., 21.

22. Allison Danzig, "Going the Distance," *New York Times*, July 27, 1952, http://archive.nytimes.com/www.nytimes.com/packages/html/sports/year_in_sports/07.27.html. Danzig wrote, "This little phenomenon of almost super-human endurance and with the most agonizing running style within memory sped 26 miles, 385 yards 6 minutes and 16 seconds faster than an Olympic marathon had ever been traversed before."

23. Ma-he Ya-luo-mi-er, "Shijie wenming de changpao jianjiang Za-tuo-pei-ke."

24. Two athletes from the army who became well known for their international achievements in the mid- to late 1950s were weightlifter Chen Jingkai and female high jumper Zheng Fengrong. However, even in the early 1950s, the army became the source of athletes for many sports. For example, of fourteen top track-and-field athletes profiled in a *New Sport* article in November 1953, eight came from the army, three were students, and three were workers. Diao Yi and Li Youkun, "Chuangzao quanguo zuigao

jilu de yundongyuanmen" [Athletes creating the highest national records], *Xin tiyu*, November 1953, pp. 10–11.

25. That these reports are readily available in Chinese archives also speaks to their continued importance as part of the official narrative on *tiyu* state-building projects in the early PRC.

26. Li Ange, "Zhongguo xuesheng lanpaiqiu daibiaodui zai Jieke" [Chinese student basketball and volleyball delegations in Czechoslovakia], *Xin tiyu*, November 1950, p. 17.

27. Ibid.

28. The transliterated name in Chinese is Su-Ke-Wei. My best efforts to locate this city based on the transliteration have thus far been unsuccessful.

29. Zhongyang renmin zhengfu tiyu yundong weiyuanhui [State Sports Commission], "Tongzhi Sulian ticao daibiaodui jianglai Hua zhi gedi zuo ticao biaoyan shi" [Notice on Soviet gymnastics delegation coming to East China for gymnastics exhibitions], September[?] 1953, B126-1-53, Shanghai Municipal Archives (SMA).

30. Ibid.

31. Khrushchev considered building the Sino-Soviet alliance a crucial part of spreading Soviet influence in the Third World, which he felt Stalin had largely ignored. Westad, *The Other Cold War*, 67.

32. Karl, *Mao Zedong and China in the Twentieth-Century World*, 84–85.

33. "Sulian tiyu daibiaotuan jieshao" [Introducing the Soviet *tiyu* delegation], *Xin tiyu*, October 1953, pp. 20–21. This included Olympic team members Galina Urbanovich, Ekaterina Kalinchuk, Valentin Muratov, and Viktor Chukarin, as well as future stars Sofia Muratova, Albert Azaryan, and Boris Shakhlin.

34. "Shelun: Xuexi Sulian ticao yundong de xianjin lilun he jingyan" [Editorial: Studying the advanced theory and experience of Soviet gymnastics], *Xin tiyu*, October 1953, p. 15.

35. Andrew Handler, *From Goals to Guns: The Golden Age of Soccer in Hungary* (Boulder, CO: Eastern European Monographs, 1994), 44–49.

36. "Zhaodai Xiongyali zuqiudui lai Hu fangwen gongzuo jianbao: Di er hao" [Briefing on the hospitality work for the Hungarian soccer team's visit to Shanghai: #2], February 18[?], 1954, B126-1-86, SMA.

37. Untitled document, February 1954, B126-1-86, SMA. Although this document is untitled, the format and content indicate that it is a State Sports Commission notice sent to the *tiyu* and hospitality committees of the East China and Central China districts about the upcoming visit.

38. "Zhaodai Xiongyali zuqiudui lai Hu fangwen gongzuo jianbao: Di si hao" [Briefing on the hospitality work for the Hungarian soccer team's visit to Shanghai: #4], March 1[?], 1954, B126-1-86, SMA.

39. "Ke Lun," in *Gongheguo tiyu: 110 wei jianzheng zhe fangtan* [PRC Sport: 110 witness interviews], ed. Zhonggong zhongyang wenxian yanjiushi di er bian yanbu (Guiyang: Guizhou renmin chubanshe, 2008), 95. The delegation also included swimmers.

40. Ibid., 95–96.

41. "Zhaodai Xiongyali zuqiudui lai Hu fangwen gongzuo jianbao: Di er hao."

42. "Sulian tiyu daibiaotuan lai Hu biaoyan gongzuo jihua (cao'an)" [Work plan for the Soviet *tiyu* delegation coming to Shanghai for exhibitions (draft)], October 7, 1953, B126-1-53, SMA.

43. Zhongyang renmin zhengfu tiyu yundong weiyuanhui, "Tongzhi Sulian ticao daibiaodui jianglai Hua zhi gedi zuo ticao biaoyan shi." Each of the parallel bars, for example, had to be between 1.6 and 1.7 meters off the ground, 3.5 meters in length, and only 42–48 centimeters apart from each other.

44. Chen, "Shang shiji 50 niandai Sulian ticao dui wo guo xiandai ticao de yingxiang," 126.

45. "Zhaodai Xiongyali zuqiudui lai Hu fangwen gongzuo jianbao: Di si hao."

46. Ibid.

47. Shuman, "The Politics of Socialist Athletics in the PRC," 67, 176.

48. They also complained about entertainment expenses. "Guanyu qing Zhongyang bo zhuankuan xiujian: Xiannongzeng tiyuchang, beihai tiyuchang wenti de baogao" [Report concerning asking the central government for money for building and repairing Xiannongzeng stadium and Beijing stadium], October 14, 1952, 002-004-00126, Beijing Municipal Archives.

49. Zhang Qing, "Huiyi Beijing shi tiyu fenhui de chujian" [Remembering the beginnings of building the Beijing municipal *tiyu* committee], *Tiyu wenshi* [Sports history], no. Z1 (1984): 13–14.

50. Although these numbers seem astronomical by today's standards, even with inflation, these are prior to the currency revaluation that took place in 1955 at a ratio of 1:10,000 yuan.

51. "Guanyu qing Zhongyang bo zhuankuan xiujian." It is unclear whether they received such money or any at all, as the original document has question marks scribbled over these estimates.

52. "Zhaodai Xiongyali zuqiudui lai Hu fangwen gongzuo jianbao: Di yi hao" [Briefing on the hospitality work for the Hungarian soccer team's visit to Shanghai: #1], February 16, 1953, B126-1-86, SMA.

53. "Guanyu huanying Bolan lanqiu daibiaodui de gongzuo xiang shiwei de baogao" [Report concerning work to welcome the Polish basketball delegation], August 1, 1952, B126-1-34, SMA.

54. "Zhaodai Xiongyali zuqiudui lai Hu fangwen gongzuo jianbao: Di er hao"; "Zhaodai Xiongyali zuqiudui lai Hu fangwen gongzuo jianbao: Di san hao" [Briefing on the hospitality work for the Hungarian soccer team's visit to Shanghai: #3], February 25[?], 1954, B126-1-86, SMA.

55. "Zhaodai Xiongyali zuqiudui lai Hu fangwen gongzuo jianbao: Di er hao."

56. Ci Xinwen, "Zhongguo ticao dui shouren duizhang he ta de shoucang guan" [China's first gymnastics team captain and his collection], *Zhongguo qingnianbao* [China youth daily], March 16, 2014, http://zqb.cyol.com/html/2014-03/16/nw.D110000 zgqnb_20140316_3-04.htm.

57. "Jianbao (jue mi)" [Report: Top secret], February 27, 1954, SMA B126-1-86. Although these numbers are prior to the 1955 currency revaluation, they still seem generous given that a monthly issue of *New Sport* cost sixty-six hundred renminbi.

58. "Huadong ji Shanghai huanying bolan lanqiu daibiaodui choubei weiyuanhui tongzhi" [Notice from the East China and Shanghai preparatory committee for welcoming the Polish basketball delegation], July 24, 1952, B126-1-34, SMA.

59. Ibid.

60. "Bolan lanqiu daibiao jieshao" [Introducing the Polish basketball delegation], *Renmin ribao* [People's daily], July 22, 1952, p. 1; "Bolan tiyu yundong de fazhan" [Developments in Polish sport], *Renmin ribao*, July 22, 1952, p. 1.

61. "Bolan tiyu yundong de fazhan," 1.

62. James Riordan, *Sport in Soviet Society: Development of Sport and Physical Education in Russia and the USSR* (Cambridge: Cambridge University Press, 1977), 128–129.

63. Xu Yingchao, "Sulian tiyu de jidian jieshao" [Some introduction to Soviet *tiyu*], *Xin tiyu*, January 1951, p. 14.

64. Ibid., 11–14.

65. "Zhe shi Xiongyali guojia zuqiu lunhedui zai er yue ershiliu ri shangwu baogaohui shang de baogao jilu, weijing zhengli, jingong cankao, buzhun fanyin" [This is the February 26 morning public lecture report records of the Hungarian national soccer mixed team, not yet confirmed, for reference only, do not reprint], February 1954, B126-1-86, SMA.

66. "Bolan tiyu yundong de fazhan." In 1951, two hundred thousand students were awarded badges.

CHAPTER 11

1. Huang Jianren, "Haixia bei qiumi hui guoqi, dahui jingxia" [Fans at Straits Cup Basketball Invitational Tournament wave national flag, startle gathering], *Pingguo ribao* [Apple daily], September 7, 2007, http://www.appledaily.com.tw/appledaily/article /headline/20070907/3797692; "Pi guoqi zao zhizhi, Taiwan qiumi: Nandao yao na wuxingqi?" [Prevented from flying national flag, Taiwan fans: Are we supposed to fly the (PRC) five-starred flag or something?], *Fanshuteng* [Yam], September 7, 2007.

2. Mo Yan-chih, "Ma in Backflip on Right to Fly the Flag," *Taipei Times*, September 9, 2007, p. 3; "The New Ma Lacks Backbone, Too," *Taipei Times*, September 14, 2007, p. 8.

3. Xu Guoqi, *Olympic Dreams: China and Sports, 1895–2008* (Cambridge, MA: Harvard University Press, 2008), 75–113. See also Liu Chin-ping, *Zhonghua minguo Aolinpike weiyuanhui huiji yanbian zhi lishi kaocha, 1949–1981* [A historical survey of the changes of ROC's Olympic Committee membership from 1949 to 1981] (master's thesis, Guoli Taiwan shifan daxue, 1995).

4. Liu Chin-ping, *Zhonghua minguo Aolinpike weiyuanhui*; Liu Chin-ping, *Zhanhou Zhonghua minguo ji guoji Aohui weiyuan gengti zhi lishi kaocha 1949–1981* [Research into the historical succession of postwar ROC IOC members, 1949–1981] (Taizhong: Hongxiang chubanshe, 2010).

5. Susan Brownell, *Beijing's Games: What the Olympics Mean to China* (Lanham, MD: Rowman and Littlefield, 2008), 129–148; Susan Brownell, "'Sport and Politics Don't Mix': China's Relationship with the IOC During the Cold War," in *East Plays West: Sport and the Cold War*, ed. Stephen Wagg and David L. Andrews (New York: Routledge, 2007), 253–271; Xu, *Olympic Dreams*, 75–196.

6. Michael Szonyi, *Cold War Island: Quemoy on the Front Line* (Cambridge: Cambridge University Press, 2008), 7–8, 103, 251–252.

7. "Tixie lishihui" [Chinese National Amateur Athletic Federation Standing Committee meeting], *Dagongbao* [L'Impartial], September 8, 1945, p. 3; Andrew D. Morris, *Marrow of the Nation: A History of Sport and Physical Culture in Republican China* (Berkeley: University of California Press, 2004), 234.

8. Liu Chin-ping, *Zhonghua minguo Aolinpike weiyuanhui*, 30–32; *Dangdai Zhongguo* congshu bianji weiyuanhui, eds., *Dangdai Zhongguo tiyu* [Contemporary Chinese sport] (Beijing: Zhongguo shehui kexue chubanshe, 1984), 402–404; Gu Bingfu, "China's Participation in the Olympics (II)," *China Sports* 336 (September 1996): 7; Jonathan Kolatch, *Sports, Politics and Ideology in China* (New York: Jonathan David, 1972), 171–173; "Xin Zhongguo de 'Feiyu'—Wu Chuanyu de gushi" [The "Flying Fish" of New China—the story of Wu Chuanyu], *XinhuaNet*, February 29, 2008.

9. Liu Chin-ping, *Zhonghua minguo Aolinpike weiyuanhui*, 38–39; Tang Ming-hsin, *Tang Mingxin xiansheng fangwen jilu* [The reminiscences of Mr. Tang Ming-hsin], interview by Chang Chi-hsiung and Pan Kwang-che, recorded by Wang Ching-ling (Taibei: Zhongyanyuan jindaishi yanjiusuo, 2005), 171.

10. Xu, *Olympic Dreams*, 86.

11. Ibid., 92–93.

12. Tang, *Tang Mingxin xiansheng fangwen jilu*, 174–175.

13. See Joseph M. Turrini, "The Purest of Rivalries: Rafer Johnson, C. K. Yang, and the 1960 Olympic Decathlon," in *Rivals: Legendary Matchups That Made Sports History*, ed. David K. Wiggins and R. Pierre Rodgers (Fayetteville: University of Arkansas Press, 2010), 5–28.

14. Gong Shusen, *Tieren Yang Chuanguang* [Iron Man C. K. Yang] (Taibei: Zhongwai tushu chubanshe, 1977), 68.

15. Tex Maule, "Yang of China Is World's Best Athlete," *Sports Illustrated*, May 6, 1963, p. 66; front cover, *Sports Illustrated*, December 23, 1963.

16. Frank Litsky, "C. K. Yang: A Continent Rests on His Shoulders," *New York Times*, May 16, 1963, p. 45; Yang Chuanguang, *Wo de yundong shengya* [My athletic career] (Taibei: Zonghe yuekan she, 1969), 18.

17. Rafer Johnson with Philip Goldberg, *The Best That I Can Be: An Autobiography* (New York: Doubleday, 1998), 172.

18. Gong, *Tieren Yang Chuanguang*, 74.

19. Yang says that he only learned of the plot in 1978 from an ROC intelligence agent. "Sports Legend Alleges Foul Play," *China Post*, April 5, 1997; Johnson, *Best That I Can Be*, 172. A family member of Yang's has contacted me with another explanation for his subpar performance at the 1964 Olympics. However, his Olympic teammate (and fellow

Amis Aborigine) Wu Amin has confirmed publicly that he and Yang were both poisoned in this incident. "Yazhou tieren Malan yongshi" [Asian Iron Man, Malan warrior], *Yuanxiang chang* [Hometown ground], TITV (Taiwan Indigenous TV), August 18, 2014.

20. "All-China Sports Federation Application for Chinese Membership in the Asian Games Federation," August 7, 1973, http://digitalarchive.wilsoncenter.org/document /134616.

21. Xinhua News Agency, "Decision of All-China Sports Federation on Participation in Seventh Asian Games," February 9, 1974, http://digitalarchive.wilsoncenter.org /document/134620; Stefan Huebner, *Pan-Asian Sports and the Emergence of Modern Asia, 1913–1974* (Singapore: National University of Singapore Press, 2016), 239.

22. Hsiao-ting Lin, *Accidental State: Chiang Kai-shek, the United States, and the Making of Taiwan* (Cambridge, MA: Harvard University Press, 2016), 223–225, 238.

23. Jay Taylor, *The Generalissimo: Chiang Kai-shek and the Struggle for Modern China* (Cambridge, MA: Belknap Press of Harvard University Press, 2009), 478, 515.

24. Szonyi, *Cold War Island*, 110.

25. "Taiwan Controversy at the 1976 Montreal Olympics," *As It Happens*, CBC Radio, July 16, 1976, http://www.cbc.ca/archives/entry/taiwan-controversy-at-the-1976 -montreal-olympics.

26. "Taiwan yu Aoyun" [Taiwan and the Olympics], *Taidu yuekan* [Independent Taiwan] September 28, 1976, p. 6.

27. Tang, *Tang Mingxin xiansheng fangwen jilu*, 182; Steve Cady, "Taiwan, Nigeria Quit Olympics; More Withdrawals Threatened," *New York Times*, July 17, 1976, pp. 1, 17.

28. The Provincial Games were held as the Taiwan sheng yundonghui from 1946 to 1973 and then rebranded as the Regional Games (Taiwan qu yundonghui) from 1974 to 1998.

29. "Quansheng yundong dahui, Taiwan jian'er zhan shenshou" [Provincial Games: Taiwan youth show their skills], *Minbao*, October 3, 1946, p. 3.

30. "Shoujie shengyunhui zuo kaimu, Jiang zhuxi qinlin xunci, dui qingnian Taibao xumian youjia" [First Provincial Games begin, Chairman Chiang speaks in person and exhorts the Taiwanese youth], *Minbao*, October 26, 1946, p. 3.

31. "Taiwan sheng di si jie Quansheng yundong dahui teji" [Special report from Taiwan's Fourth Provincial Games], in *Tai ying xinwen shiliao 002 juan* [Taiwan Film Culture Company historical news, volume 2] (Taibei: Taiwan dianying wenhua gongsi, 1949).

32. *China Handbook* Editorial Committee, *Sports and Public Health*, trans. Wen Botang (Beijing: Foreign Languages Press, 1983), 48–49; Morris, *Marrow of the Nation*, 185–229.

33. Kolatch, *Sports, Politics and Ideology in China*, 135–140; Morris, *Marrow of the Nation*, 128–139.

34. Taylor, *The Generalissimo*, 422, 430, 442–443.

35. "Guangfu dalu dajinsai, dengzhe women qu zhengqu, Yu Zhuxi mianli yu hui renyuan" [The great trophy of recovery of the mainland is waiting for us to capture it,

Chairman Yu encourages the games crowd], *Lianhebao* [United daily news], November 1, 1953, p. 3.

36. *Zongtong Jiang Gong tiyu xunci* [President Chiang Kai-shek's instructions on physical culture] ([Taibei]: Zhonghua minguo Tiyu xiejinhui, 1975), 8–9.

37. "Ziyou ri tan zhen ziyou" [On real freedom on Freedom Day], *Ziyou Zhongguo* [Free China] 10, no. 3 (1954): 2–3.

38. Long Yi'e, "Ziyou ri tan yanlun ziyou" [On freedom of speech on Freedom Day], *Ziyou Zhongguo* 12, no. 4 (1955): 14–15.

39. *Zongtong Jiang Gong tiyu xunci*, 12.

40. "Di jiu jie shengyunhui kaimu dianli" [Ninth Provincial Games opening ceremonies], in *Tai ying xinwen shiliao 007 juan* [Taiwan Film Culture Company historical news, volume 7] (Taibei: Taiwan dianying wenhua gongsi, 1954).

41. Morris, *Marrow of the Nation*, chaps. 1–2.

42. What had been the Taiwan Provincial Games were renamed to account for the reassignment of Taipei and Gaoxiong as direct-controlled (and province-level) municipalities, a move that signaled the decreasing likelihood that the ROC would ever encompass any mainland provinces again.

43. Zhang Zhenhai, "Mantan Taiwan qu di yi jie yundong dahui guangan yu li jie shengyun zhi huigu (shang)" [A ramble on perceptions of the first Taiwan area athletic meet and a look back at every Provincial Games, part 1], *Ziyou qingnian* [Free youth] 53, no. 1 (1975): 47.

44. Morris, *Colonial Project, National Game*, 149–166.

45. Morris, *Marrow of the Nation*, 119–120.

46. Chen Chia-Mou, "Guangfu chuqi Taibei shi guomin xuexiao bangqiu fazhan yanqiu" [The research of primary school baseball development in Taipei City in the initial period of restoration], *Tiyu xuebao* [Bulletin of physical education] 30 (March 2001): 92.

47. Liu Junqing and Wang Xinliang, *Shiguang suidao: Taiwan lanyun liushi nian* [The tunnel of time: Sixty years of Taiwan basketball] (Taibei: Minshengbao she, 1999), 135, 161, 166.

48. Ibid., 105; Mao Jiaqi, *Jiang Jingguo de yisheng he ta de sixiang yanbian* [Chiang Ching-kuo's life and philosophical evolution] (Taibei: Taiwan shangwu yinshuguan, 2003), 264.

49. *Han Jung chinseon yagu daehoe jilseochaeg* [Korea-China Goodwill Baseball Series official program] (Seoul: Chayu sinmunsa, 1955), 2–6.

50. "Jianju fu dalu, yixin hui zuguo, Liu Tianlu tan Wang Zhenzhi shi ge aiguo hao qingnian" [Resolutely refusing to travel to the mainland, returning to the motherland wholeheartedly, Liu Tianlu discusses how Oh Sadaharu is a good patriotic youth], *Lianhebao* [United daily news], December 5, 1965, p. 3; Andrew D. Morris, "Oh Sadaharu/Wang Zhenzhi and the Possibility of Chineseness in 1960s Taiwan," in *Japanese Taiwan: Colonial Rule and Its Contested Legacy*, ed. Andrew D. Morris (London: Bloomsbury Academic, 2015), 160–161.

51. Lin Qiwen, "Yundong yu zhengquan weiji: Jiedu zhanhou Taiwan bangqiu fazhan shi" [Sports and the preservation of political power: A reading of the postwar

development of Taiwan baseball] (master's thesis, Guoli Taiwan daxue shehuixue yan-jiusuo, 1995), 47; "Jiang zhuren mian Yazhou qingnian, tuanjie xiaomie gongfei" [Direc-tor Chiang encourages Asian youth to unite to exterminate the Communist bandits], *Lianhebao*, August 25, 1969, p. 8.

52. Szonyi, *Cold War Island*, 41.

53. Sun Jianzheng, "Gelia hao" [Both brothers fine], *Lianhebao*, September 19, 1969, p. 3; "Xiongdi liang yingxiong" [Two brother heroes], *Jingji ribao* [Economic daily news], September 19, 1969, p. 8.

54. This text combines two mostly-overlapping accounts in "Jinmen shizai weida, Mashan qianxiao hanhua" [Jinmen is truly great, forward sentries broadcast from Horse Mountain], *Lianhebao*, September 19, 1969, p. 3; and Wang Fudan, "Cong Jinlong shao-nian bangqiudui chenggong shuoqi: Tan Zhongguo quanmin tiyu de zhiben zhi dao" [On the topic of the Golden Dragons youth baseball team's success: Discussing the is-sues at the heart of Chinese sports for the people], *Guomin tiyu jikan* [Physical edu-cation quarterly] 1, no. 3 (1969): 3. For a more detailed account, see Morris, *Colonial Project, National Game*, 100–101.

CHAPTER 12

1. Susan Brownell, "'Sport and Politics Don't Mix': China's Relationship with the IOC During the Cold War," in *East Plays West: Sport and the Cold War*, ed. Stephen Wagg and David L. Andrews (London: Routledge, 2007), 253–271; Xu Guoqi, *Olym-pic Dreams: China and Sports, 1895–2008* (Cambridge, MA: Harvard University Press, 2008); Ewa Pauker, "Ganefo I: Sports and Politics in Djakarta," *Asian Survey* 5, no. 4 (1965): 171–185; Stefan Huebner, *Pan-Asian Sports and the Emergence of Modern Asia* (Singapore: NUS Press, 2016), chap. 6.

2. Patrick Major and Rana Mitter, "East Is East and West Is West? Towards a Com-parative Socio-cultural History of the Cold War," *Cold War History* 4, no. 1 (2003): 3.

3. Masuda Hajimu, *Cold War Crucible: The Korean Conflict and the Postwar World* (Cambridge, MA: Harvard University Press, 2015), 2.

4. Ibid.

5. Christopher Goscha and Christian Osterman, eds., *Connecting Histories: Decolo-nization and the Cold War in Southeast Asia* (Washington, DC: Woodrow Wilson Cen-ter Press, 2009).

6. Donald K. Emmerson, "'Southeast Asia': What's in a Name?," *Journal of Southeast Asian Studies* 15, no. 1 (1984): 10.

7. Prasenjit Duara, "The Cold War as a Historical Period: An Interpretive Essay," *Journal of Global History* 6, no. 3 (2011): 457–480. For the emphasis on the superpowers' "Third World interventions," see Odd Arne Westad, *The Global Cold War: Third World Interventions and the Making of Our Times* (Cambridge: Cambridge University Press, 2007).

8. Tuong Vu, "Cold War Studies and the Cultural Cold War in Asia," in *Dynamics of the Cold War in Asia: Ideology, Identity, and Culture*, ed. Tuong Vu and Wasana Wong-surawat (New York: Palgrave Macmillan, 2009), 1–16.

9. Chris Baker and Pasuk Phongpaichit, *A History of Thailand*, 2nd ed. (Cambridge: Cambridge University Press, 2009), 146.

10. Ibid.

11. Benedict Anderson, "Introduction," in *In the Mirror: Literature and Politics in Siam in the American Era*, ed. Benedict Anderson and Ruchira Mendiones (Bangkok: Duang Kamol, 1985), 19.

12. Following convention, I refer to Thai persons by their first names.

13. Thak Chaloemtiarana, *Thailand: The Politics of Despotic Paternalism*, rev. ed. (Ithaca, NY: Cornell Southeast Asia Program, 2007), chap. 4.

14. Ibid., viii.

15. Ibid., chap. 6; see also Christine Gray, "Hegemonic Images: Language and Silence in the Royal Thai Polity," *Man*, n.s., 26, no. 1 (1991): 43–65.

16. Thak, *Thailand*, 235.

17. Matthew Phillips, *Thailand in the Cold War* (New York: Routledge, 2016).

18. For example, see Thak, *Thailand*; and Phillips, *Thailand in the Cold War*.

19. Thongchai Winichakul, "Trying to Locate Southeast Asia from Its Navel: Where Is Southeast Asian Studies in Thailand?," in *Locating Southeast Asia: Geographies of Knowledge and Politics of Space*, ed. H. S. Nordholt, P. Kratoska, and R. Ruben (Athens: Ohio University Press, 2005), 122–123. See also Phillips, *Cold War in Thailand*, 1.

20. For discussion and critique of this trope of Thai historiography, see Thongchai Winichakul, "Siam's Colonial Conditions and the Birth of Thai History," in *Southeast Asian Historiography: Unravelling the Myths: Essays in Honour of Barend Jan Terwiel*, ed. Volker Grabowsky (Bangkok: River Books, 2011), 20–41.

21. For an overview, see Charles Little, "South-East Asia," in *Routledge Companion to Sports History*, ed. S. W. Pope and John Nautright (London: Routledge, 2010), 587–598. For more detailed treatment in two countries, see Lou Antolihao, *Playing with the Big Boys: Basketball, American Imperialism, and Subaltern Discourse in the Philippines* (Lincoln: University of Nebraska Press, 2015); and Simon Creak, *Embodied Nation: Sport, Masculinity and the Making of Modern Laos* (Honolulu: University of Hawaii Press, 2015).

22. Sakchye Tapsuwan, "The Role and Function of Physical Education and Sport in the Nation Building of Thailand" (PhD diss., Oregon State University, 1984); Charn Paranut, "Sports in Pre-modern and Early Modern Siam: Aggressive and Civilised Masculinities" (PhD diss., University of Sydney, 2018).

23. Little, "South-East Asia," 588. Besides the Philippines, the colonies and countries of Southeast Asia were minor or nonparticipants in the Far Eastern Championship Games. See Huebner, *Pan-Asian Sports*, esp. 27–28.

24. Organizing Committee for the First South East Asia Peninsular Games, *The Official Report of the Organizing Committee for the First South East Asia Peninsular Games, Bangkok, 1959* (Bangkok: Siva Phorn, 1961), front matter.

25. Wirayasiri, "Ramluek chak khwam songcham thueng phon-ek praphat charusathian" [My memories of General Praphat Charusatian], in *5 rob phon-ek praphat charusathian* [Fifth cycle birthday of General Praphat Charusathian], ed. Chalo Wanaphut (Bangkok: Suan Thong Thin Press, BE 2515 [1972]), 454.

302   NOTES TO PAGES 193–195

26. "Field Marshal Prabhas Charusathiara," in *Moments in Southeast Asian Sport* (Bangkok: Seiko, 1985), 31.

27. Barbara J. Keys, *Globalizing Sport: National Rivalry and International Community in the 1930s* (Cambridge, MA: Harvard University Press, 2006), 1–2.

28. Huebner, *Pan-Asian Sports*, 3.

29. Ibid., 145.

30. Luang is a title bestowed by the king. Following the Thai convention, I refer to Sukhum by his first name.

31. Organizing Committee, *Official Report*, 5. See also "Thai 'Little Asian Games' Idea Told," *Bangkok Post*, May 26, 1959, p. 6. The following description and analysis build on my recent publications (and cite sources used therein). Although those articles note the context of the Cold War, their thematic focus is regional community and friendship and mutual understanding. This chapter is the first to examine the Cold War as a central dimension of the SEAP Games. Cf. Simon Creak, "Eternal Friends and Erstwhile Enemies: The Regional Sporting Community of the Southeast Asian Games," *TRaNS: Trans-Regional and -National Studies of Southeast Asia* 5, no. 1 (2017): 147–172; and Simon Creak, "Friendship and Mutual Understanding: Sport and Regional Relations in Southeast Asia," in *The Ideals of Global Sport: From Peace to Human Rights*, ed. Barbara J. Keys (Philadelphia: University of Pennsylvania Press, 2019), 21–46.

32. Thawi Chunlasap, "Kankhaengkhan kolf thi prathaet Phama" [Golf competition in Burma], December 3, 1956, (3) Office of the Prime Minister (PM) 0201.54/3, National Archives of Thailand (NAT); Raks Panyarachun, "Kansonthana kap phanathan u nu nayok ratthamontri phama" [Conversation with H. E. U Nu, prime minister of Burma], June 3, 1957, (3) PM 220/0201.7/220, NAT. For the bombing incident, see U Nu, *Saturday's Son*, ed. U Kyaw Win, trans. U Law Yone (New Haven, CT: Yale University Press, 1975).

33. American Embassy, Bangkok, "Thai National Athletic Program," Despatch 787, May 13, 1958, 600.3, Box 111, UD3267, Record Group (RG) 84, National Archives and Records Administration (NARA); David Dichter, interview by the author, December 5, 2015, Linwood, NJ.

34. Praphat Charusathian, "Kankhaengkhan kila rawang prathet khangkhiang" [Sports competition among neighboring countries], March 7, 1958, in *Pramuan ruang-rao lae khwam penma khong khaengkhan kila laemthong khrangraek na krungthep phra-mahanakhon wan thi 12–17 thanwakhom phutta sakkarat 2502* [Compiled story and history of the 1st South East Asia Peninsular Games in Bangkok, December 12–17, BE 2502 (1959)], ed. Surachit Charuserani (Bangkok: Government Lottery Printing Office, 1959), 3–4.

35. Secretary of Cabinet, "Kankhaengkhan kila rawang prathet khangkhiang" [Sports competition among neighboring countries], March 21, 1958, in Surachit, *Compiled Story and History*, 5.

36. Praphat Charusathian, "Kankhaengkhan kila rawang prathet khangkhiang" [Sports competitions among neighboring countries], October 9, 1958, in Surachit, *Compiled Story and History*, 12.

37. Letter from Praphat Charusathien to U. Alexis Johnson, December 24, 1959, 600.3, Box 124, UD3267, RG 84, NARA.

38. Organizing Committee, *Official Report*, 2.

39. Simon Creak, "Representing True Laos in Postcolonial Southeast Asia: Regional Dynamics in the Globalization of Sport," in *Sports Across Asia: Politics, Cultures, and Identities*, ed. Katrin Bromber, Birgit Krawietz, and Joseph Maguire (Abingdon, UK: Routledge), 104; see also Creak, *Embodied Nation*, 144–149.

40. Soren Ivarsson, "Making Laos Our Space: Thai Discourses on History and Race, 1900–1941," in *Contesting Visions of the Lao Past: Lao Historiography at the Crossroads*," ed. Christopher Goscha and Soren Ivarsson (Copenhagen: NIAS Press, 2005), 239–264.

41. Thongchai, "Trying to Locate Southeast Asia."

42. "Kanchattang klum prathaet phutthasatsana sueng prakop duai thai kamphucha lae lao phuea totam latthi kommionit" [Forming the group of Buddhist countries consisting of Thailand, Cambodia, and Laos to resist Communism], 1954, (2) Ministry of Foreign Affairs (FA) 16.3/9, NAT; Cabinet, "Kanchattang klum prathaet nai phumiphak esia tawan ok chiang tai" [Forming a group of countries in the region of Southeast Asia], March 21, 1956, FA 93/11, NAT; Ministry of Foreign Affairs, "Kanruam klum prathaet thai—phama—kamphucha—lao (riak wa klum laem thong) pen khwam hen khong thao Kratay Sasorit" [Gathering a group of Thailand–Cambodia–Burma–Laos (to be named the Golden Peninsula Group), being the view of Thao Kratay Sasorit], June 15, 1957, (3) PM 0201.7/221, NAT.

43. Marc Frey, "Tools of Empire: Persuasion and the United States' Modernizing Mission in Southeast Asia," *Diplomatic History* 27, no. 4 (2003): 558.

44. "Thai National Athletic Program."

45. Ibid., 5; David Dichter, interview by the author.

46. "Thai National Athletic Program," 1.

47. Ibid , 5.

48. John Dulles, "Despatch 787," June 10, 1958, 600.3, Box 111, UD 3267, RG 84, NARA.

49. Secretary of Cabinet, "Sports Competitions Among Neighboring Countries," October 20, 1958, in Surachit, *Compiled Story and History*, 16.

50. Letter from U. Alexis Johnson to Walter McConaughy, June 2, 1959, 600.3, Box 123, UD 3267, RG 84, NARA; letter from U. Alexis Johnson to Howard Jones, June 2, 1959, 600.3, Box 123, UD 3267, RG 84, NARA.

51. *Ngan phrarachathan phloengsop Luang Sukhum Naipradith (Pradith Sukhum)* [Royal-sponsored cremation ceremony of Luang Sukhum Naipradith (Pradith Sukhum)] (Bangkok: Government Lottery Printing Office, 1967).

52. Thak, *Thailand*, 121.

53. Huebner, *Pan-Asian Sports*; Phillips, *Thailand in the Cold War*.

54. Roger M. Smith, *Cambodia's Foreign Policy* (Ithaca, NY: Cornell University Press, 1965).

55. Shane Strate, "A Pile of Stones? Preah Vihear as a Thai Symbol of National Humiliation," *South East Asia Research* 21, no. 1 (2013): 41–68.

56. "Les sportifs cambodgiens n'iront pas à Bangkok" [Cambodian athletes will not go to Bangkok], *Réalités cambodgiennes*, November 27, 1959, p. 4.

57. Ibid.

58. "Kila laem thong" [SEAP Games], *Phim Thai*, December 12, 1959, Collected News on Important Events 7/2502/ บ 4, NAT.

59. "Sarit wa khmer ngot song nak kila ma thai atcha mi khon nun lang" [Sarit says Cambodia's canceling of athletes coming to Thailand may have supporter (behind it)], *Siam Rath*, December 4, 1959, Collected News on Important Events 7/2502/ กต 1.7, NAT.

60. Insom Chaichana, *Chiwit lae ngan khong Luang Sukhum Naipradith* [Life and work of Luang Sukhum Naipradit] (Bangkok: Hongphapsuwan, 1964), 174.

61. Ibid.

62. "Sing thi dai chak kila laem-thong" [Things (we) gained from the SEAP Games], *Siam Rath*, December 16, 1959, Collected News on Important Events 7/2502/ บ 4, NAT.

63. Norman Siebel, "Malaya Beaten by Siam at Soccer," *Straits Times*, December 15, 1959, p. 22.

64. "Thai chana kueap mot" [Thailand wins nearly everything], *Siam Nikorn*, December 18, 1959, p. 5.

65. "Sing thi dai chak kila laem-thong."

66. Ibid.

67. "Wiatnam phoei het thai phae futboll khong ton" [Vietnamese reveal reason for their football defeat of Thailand], *Phim Thai*, December 19, 1959, Collected News on Important Events 7/2502, NAT.

68. Samana, "Phap prathapchai ik khrang" [An impressive image again], *Siam Nikorn*, December 20, 1959, p. 3.

69. John MacAloon, "Olympic Games and the Theory of Spectacle in Modern Societies," in *Rite, Drama, Festival, Spectacle: Rehearsals Toward a Theory of Cultural Performance*, ed. John MacAloon (Philadelphia: Institute for Study of Human Issues, 1984), 251–252.

70. Ibid., 252.

71. Organizing Committee, *Official Report*, 60.

72. Unless otherwise noted, details of the opening ceremony are sourced from Organizing Committee, *Official Report*, 41–51.

73. Ibid., 17. The original six member countries included Cambodia but not Singapore.

74. "Colourful Games Opening," *Straits Times*, December 13, 1959, p. 23.

75. Samon Samonkritsana, "Phap prathapchai" [An impressive image], *Siam Nikorn*, December 15, 1959, pp. 5, 7.

76. "Prachachon ruam saen pai chom poet laem thong" [Around one hundred thousand join opening of Golden Peninsula (Games)], *Siam Nikorn*, December 14, 1959, p. 5.

77. Insom, *Life and Work of Luang Sukhum*, 172.

78. Organizing Committee, *Official Report*, 60.

79. Simon Creak, "Rituals of the Masculine State: Sports Festivals, Gender and Power in Laos and Southeast Asia," in *Routledge Handbook of Sport, Gender and Sexuality*, ed. Jennifer Hargreaves and Eric Anderson (London: Routledge, 2014), 112–120.

80. Simon Creak, "Sport and the Theatrics of Power in a Postcolonial State: The National Games of 1960s Laos," *Asian Studies Review* 34, no. 2 (2010): 191–210; Creak, *Embodied Nation*, chap. 4.

81. For a discussion of the revival of royal ceremonies, see Thongchai Winichakul, "The Monarchy and Anti-monarchy: Two Elephants in the Room of Thai Politics and the State of Denial," in *"Good Coup" Gone Bad: Thailand's Political Developments Since Thaksin's Downfall*, ed. Pavin Chachavalpongpun (Singapore: ISEAS, 2014), 79–108.

82. "Malayan Team Leaves for Bangkok," *Straits Times*, December 10, 1959, p. 12.

83. Huebner, *Pan-Asian Sports*, 202–229.

84. See Creak, "Eternal Friends and Erstwhile Enemies"; and Creak, "Friendship and Mutual Understanding."

CHAPTER 13

1. The John F. Kennedy administration, in particular, stressed to Lisbon that it would withdraw its support for Lisbon in the United Nations if the Estado Novo continued to refuse to consider self-determination for the colonies in Africa.

2. See, for example, Pierre Lanfranchi and Matthew Taylor, *Moving with the Ball: The Migration of Professional Footballers* (Oxford: Berg, 2001), 170–176.

3. The relationship between Rhodesia, South Africa, and Mozambique (Portugal), although always cozy because of shared experiences and objectives, was formalized via a secret military alliance consummated in 1960. For further information on this alliance of white minority-ruled states in Southern Africa, see Aniceto Afonso and Carlos de Matos Gomes, *Alcora: O acordo secreto do colonialismo: Portugal, África do Sul e Rodésia na última fase da guerra colonial* (Lisbon: Divina Comédia, 2013); Maria Paula Meneses, Celso Braga Rosa, and Bruno Sena Martins, "Colonial Wars, Colonial Alliances: The Alcora Exercise in the Context of Southern Africa," *Journal of Southern African Studies* 43, no. 2 (2017): 397–410; and Filipe Ribeiro de Meneses and Robert McNamara, *The White Redoubt, the Great Powers and the Struggle for Southern Africa, 1960–1980* (London: Palgrave Macmillan, 2018).

4. Fátima is the site in central Portugal where, in 1917, apparitions allegedly sent from the heavens appeared. Afterward, a sanctuary was constructed to commemorate the events. Fátima remains a popular pilgrimage destination and thus was used by the regime as a symbol for the country's religious devotion.

5. João Malheiro, *Eusébio: A biografia autorizado* (Vila do Conde, Portugal: Quid-Novi, 2012), 112.

6. Ana Santos, "Narrativas da Nação proporcionadas pelas vitórias desportivas e seus heróis," paper presented at IV Congresso Português de Sociologia, Coimbra, Portugal, April 17–19, 2000, p. 6.

7. Malheiro, *Eusébio*, 112.

8. Fernando Correia, *Matateu: O Oitava Maravilha* (Lisbon: Sete Caminhos, 2006), 31.

9. Ana Santos, *Herois desportivos: Estudo de caso sobre Eusébio, de corpo a ícone da nação* (Lisbon: Instituto do Desporto de Portugal, 2004), 92.

10. Ibid.

11. Ibid., 94.

12. Eusébio da Silva Ferreira, *My Name Is Eusébio*, trans. Derrik Low (London: Routledge and Kegan Paul, 1967), 158.

13. Mário Coluna, interview by the author, November 21, 2012, Maputo, Mozambique.

14. Hilário, interview by the author, October 19, 2010, Lisbon, Portugal.

15. "Sport Lisboa e Benfica," N.T. 7366, 4703-CI (2), PIDE/DGS collection, Arquivo Nacional Torre do Tombo, Lisbon, Portugal.

16. A conto is one thousand Portuguese escudos.

17. Gabrielle Marcotti, "Eusebio: The Agony of '66," *The Times* (London), February 16, 2004, https://www.thetimes.co.uk/article/eusebio-the-agony-of-66-ml9jv2khp57.

18. Eusébio, interview by the author, October 28, 2010, Lisbon, Portugal.

19. In the late 1950s, an important and sizable contingent of Francophone African footballers playing in and for France fled the country to support the struggle for independence in Algeria. See Pierre Lanfranchi, "Mekloufi, un footballeur français dans la guerre d'Algérie," *Actes de la recherche en sciences sociales* 103 (1994): 70–74.

20. Gary Armstrong, "The Migration of the Black Panther: An Interview with Eusebio of Mozambique and Portugal," in *Football in Africa: Conflict, Conciliation and Community*, ed. Gary Armstrong and Richard Giulianotti (Basingstoke, UK: Palgrave Macmillan, 2004), 262.

21. Acácio Rosa, *Factos, nomes e números da história do clube de futebol "Os Belenenses"* (Lisbon: Freitas and Freitas, 1961), 565.

22. "Torres: O 'Jogador Médico,'" in *Ídolos do Desporto*, 2nd ser., no. 6 (Lisbon: Bertrand, 1959), n.p.

23. Mário Wilson, "Uma marca na história," in *Académica—história do futebol*, ed. João Santana and João Mesquita (Coimbra: Almedina, 2011), 512.

24. Mário Wilson, interview by the author, October 29, 2010, Lisbon, Portugal.

25. António Brassard, interview by the author, June 19, 2014, Guincho, Portugal.

26. Paola Rolletta, *Finta finta* (Maputo, Mozambique: Texto Editores, 2011), 120.

27. Ibid., 48.

28. João Nuno Coelho and Francisco Pinheiro, *A paixão do povo: História do futebol em Portugal* (Porto: Edições Afrontamento, 2002), 485.

29. Wilson, interview by the author.

30. Malheiro, *Eusébio*, 112.

31. For example, at the end of 1965, the Lisbon CEI had almost 600 members, while the Coimbra house had roughly 115. See Cláudia Castelo, "A Casa dos Estudantes do Império: Lugar de memória anticolonial," paper presented at CIEA7 #6: (Counter-) Memories of Colonialism: Remembrance, Resistance and Transference in Anti-colonial African Narratives conference, 2010, Oxford, UK, p. 8.

32. Ibid., 15.

33. For an account of a particularly courageous and harrowing flight from Portugal back to Africa, see Ruaridh Nicoll, "The Great Escape That Changed Africa's Future," *The Guardian*, March 8, 2015, https://www.theguardian.com/world/2015/mar/08/great-escape-that-changed-africas-future.

34. John Marcum, *The Angola Revolution*, vol. 1, *The Anatomy of an Explosion* (Cambridge, MA: MIT Press, 1969), 37.

35. Tomás Medeiros, interview by the author, June 30, 2014, Lisbon, Portugal.

36. Agosto Matine, interview by the author, November 20, 2012, Maputo, Mozambique.

37. Rolletta, *Finta finta*, 90.

38. Mário Coluna, interview by the author, November 21, 2012, Maputo, Mozambique. FRELIMO was the leftist nationalist party in Mozambique, and MPLA was the Angolan equivalent.

39. Nuno Domingos, "Dos subúrbios da Lourenço Marques colonial aos campos de futebol da metrópole, uma entrevista com Hilário Rosário da Conceição," *Cadernos de estudos africanos* 26 (2013): 236.

40. Armstrong, "The Migration of the Black Panther," 253.

CHAPTER 14

1. Rob Ruck, *Raceball: How the Major Leagues Colonized the Black and Latin Game* (Boston: Beacon Press, 2011), 150.

2. "The Republic of Baseball: Dominican Giants of the American Game," *Voces on PBS*, season 1, episode 3, aired September 16, 2006.

3. Fidel Castro led an attack on the Moncada Barracks on July 26, 1953. The attack was a fiasco and led to Castro's imprisonment, but the insurgency he led after his release adopted the name the 26th of July Movement, and the speech Fidel delivered at his trial in which he said that "history will absolve me" became an iconic defense of the revolution.

4. The Caribbean Series (Serie del Caribe), which began in 1949, pitted the winners of the winter leagues in Cuba, Panama, Venezuela, and Puerto Rico against each other in a week-long tournament. Cuba had won seven of the twelve held before the championship was suspended in 1961.

5. Ruck, *Raceball*, 59.

6. Walt Whitman, quoted in Geoffrey C. Ward, *Baseball: An Illustrated History* (New York: Knopf, 1994), xvii, 3; John Tener and Zane Gray, quoted in Harold Seymour and Dorothy Jane Mills, *Baseball: The Early Years* (New York: Oxford University Press, 1960), 345, 15.

7. Ruck, *Raceball*, 22–25.

8. For the best discussion of Martí, race, and Cuba, see Alejandro de la Fuente, *A Nation for All: Race, Inequality, and Politics in Twentieth-Century Cuba* (Chapel Hill: University of North Carolina Press, 1999).

9. If rapprochement becomes a reality, the struggle over who controls baseball will resurface.

10. Ruck, *Raceball*, 2–8.

11. Louis A. Pérez Jr., "Between Baseball and Bullfighting: The Quest for Nationality in Cuba 1868–1898," *Journal of American History* 81, no. 2 (1994): 509.

12. Ibid., 515.

13. Only exclusive social clubs maintained explicit color lines; their teams played as amateurs. But the professional leagues were open to all men. For more on this era of Cuban baseball, see Roberto Gonzalez Echevarría, *The Pride of Havana: A History of Cuban Baseball* (New York: Oxford University Press, 1999).

14. Barnstorming was a two-way affair, and Cuban teams came to Tampa and other US cities because multiracial, international competitions often drew good crowds.

15. The two central issues were whether Robinson would make the Dodgers' major league squad and open the way for darker-skinned players from the United States and the Caribbean and whether his success would damage the black leagues and players he left behind.

16. Wendell Smith, "Smitty's Sports Spurts: Introducing 'El Diablo' Wells of Mexico," *Pittsburgh Courier*, May 6, 1944, p. 12.

17. These developments strengthened efforts by the American Baseball Guild to organize a players' union and thus made Mexico a more pressing concern.

18. As a boy, Jorge Pasquel had huddled in a basement in Veracruz with future Mexican president Miguel Alemán as US warships bombarded Veracruz and seized the city in 1914. Alemán assumed the Mexican presidency in 1946.

19. Ruck, *Raceball*, 67–70, 120.

20. Cubans had constituted the overwhelming majority of the Latinos who played Major League Baseball before World War II, and their ranks grew afterward. Integration meant that Afro-Cuban players would now become available, too. The Dodgers' Branch Rickey had considered a few Afro-Cuban players as a vehicle to integrate the majors before selecting Robinson. But he realized that adding language and cultural burdens might be too heavy a load for Cubans to carry.

21. "Cuban Criticizes Chandler's Stand," *New York Times*, December 13, 1946, p. 31.

22. *Sporting News*, January 27, 1947.

23. MLB made enough concessions to blunt organizing efforts and kept the upper hand until Marvin Miller became the MLB Player Association's executive director in 1966.

24. For a discussion of Cuba's transition to a post-1959 system of sport, see Paula J. Pettavino and Geralyn Pye, *Sport in Cuba: The Diamond in the Rough* (Pittsburgh: University of Pittsburgh Press, 1994).

25. Rob Ruck, *The Tropic of Baseball: Baseball in the Dominican Republic* (Lincoln: University of Nebraska Press, 1999), 41–46.

26. Manuel Baez Vargas, interview by author, Santo Domingo, Dominican Republic, June 26, 1988; Juan Bosch, interview by the author, Santo Domingo, Dominican Republic, June 19, 1988. I was often told on my first research trip there in January 1984, during the Dominican playoffs, that there was rarely political trouble during the baseball season, only afterward. Shortly after the season ended, street protests against International Monetary Fund demands turned deadly.

27. Santana was a journalist and sports activist for much of the twentieth century. Quoted in Ruck, *The Tropic of Baseball*, 27–28.

28. Quoted in Ruck, *The Tropic of Baseball*, 109.

29. Ibid., 108–109. For more on the 1937 championship, see Rob Ruck, *Sandlot Seasons: Sport in Black Pittsburgh* (Urbana: University of Illinois Press, 1993).

30. Quoted in "The Republic of Baseball."

31. Quoted in Ruck, *The Tropic of Baseball*, 108–109. During Trujillo's rule, most homes had a plaque on the wall that said, "En este casa, Trujillo es el jefe" (In this house, Trujillo is boss). When I was in a bathroom off the dugout in Estadio Quisqueya in Santo Domingo in the 1980s, someone had written, "En este letrina, Trujillo es el jefe" (In this bathroom, Trujillo is boss).

32. Orlando Cepeda, with Herb Fagen, *Baby Bull: From Hardball to Hard Time and Back* (Dallas, TX: Taylor, 1998), 2; Luis Tiant and Joe Fitzgerald, *El Tiante: The Luis Tiant Story* (Garden City, NY: Doubleday, 1976), 221.

33. Ruck, *Raceball*, 149–151.

34. April Yoder, "*Magnifico estimulo*: Baseball and the Dominican Democratic Revolution, 1961–1963," paper presented at the Latin American Studies Association International Congress (LASA), Washington, DC, May 29, 2013–June 1, 2013. Yoder is currently revising her 2014 dissertation in history, "Pitching Democracy: Baseball and Politics in the Dominican Republic, 1955–1978" (PhD diss., Georgetown University, 2014), for publication.

35. Fidel Castro, who had taken part in a failed effort to topple Rafael Trujillo in 1947, was at odds with Trujillo after he took power. Relations between Cuba and the Dominican Republic remained chilly after Trujillo's assassination. But Cuba's isolation from the United States meant that the two nations had little contact in baseball except for the Pan Am Games and after the creation of the World Baseball Classic in 2006.

36. Felipe Alou, with Herm Weiskopf, *Felipe Alou* (Waco, TX: World Book, 1967), 59–60.

37. Felipe Alou, with Arnold Hano, "Latin American Ballplayers Need a Bill of Rights," *Sport*, November 1975, pp. 21, 76–79. For a discussion of the Balaguer government's efforts to promote and manipulate sport, see Yoder, "Pitching Democracy."

CHAPTER 15

Portions of this chapter were previously published in Brenda Elsey, "Cultural Ambassadorship and the Pan-American Games of the 1950s," *International Journal of the History of Sport* 33, no. 1–2 (2016): 105–126, http://dx.doi.org/10.1080/09523367.2015.1117451, and have been reprinted with permission.

1. Tobias Rupprecht, *Soviet Internationalism After Stalin: Interaction and Exchange Between the USSR and Latin America During the Cold War* (Cambridge: University of Cambridge Press, 2015).

2. Carol Hess, *Representing the Good Neighbor: Music, Difference, and the Pan-American Dream* (Oxford: Oxford University Press, 2013).

3. There is a growing historiography on diplomacy and sport, including Claire Brewster and Keith Brewster, *Representing the Nation: Sport and Spectacle in Postrevolutionary Mexico* (London: Routledge, 2010); Heather Dichter and Andrew Johns, eds., *Diplomatic Games: Sport, Statecraft and International Relations Since 1945* (Lexington: University Press of Kentucky, 2014); Barbara Keys, *Globalizing Sport: National*

Rivalry and International Community in the 1930s (Cambridge, MA: Harvard University Press, 2006); and Eric Zolov, "Showcasing the 'Mexico of Tomorrow': Mexico and the 1968 Olympics," *Americas* 61, no. 2 (2004): 159–188.

4. Mark Berger, "'A Greater America?' Pan-Americanism and the Professional Study of Latin America, 1890–1990," in *Beyond the Ideal: Pan-Americanism in Inter-American Affairs*, ed. David Sheinin (Westport, CT: Greenwood Press, 2000), 45–56; Ricardo Salvatore, *Disciplinary Conquest: US Scholars in South America, 1900–1945* (Durham, NC: Duke University Press, 2016).

5. See, for example, Patrick Iber, *Neither Peace nor Freedom: The Cultural Cold War in Latin America* (Cambridge, MA: Harvard University Press, 2015); Stephen Park, *The Pan-American Imagination: Contested Visions of the Hemisphere in Twentieth-Century Literature* (Charlottesville: University of Virginia Press, 2014); and Robert Alexander González and Robert Rydell, *Designing Pan-America: US Architectural Visions for the Western Hemisphere* (Austin: University of Texas Press, 2011).

6. Galvarino Gallardo Nieto, *Panamericanismo* (Santiago: Nascimento, 1941).

7. Katherine Marino, "Transnational Pan-American Feminism: The Friendship of Bertha Lutz and Mary Wilhelmine Williams, 1926–1944," *Journal of Women's History* 26, no. 2 (2014): 63–87.

8. Florence Carpentier and Jean-Pierre Lefèvre, "The Modern Olympic Movement, Women's Sport and the Social Order During the Inter-war Period," *International Journal of the History of Sport* 23, no. 7 (2006): 1112–1127; Steven Olderr, *The Pan-American Games/Los Juegos Panamericanos* (Jefferson, NC: McFarland, 2003), 326; Antonio Sotomayor, *The Sovereign Colony: Olympic Sport, National Identity, and International Politics in Puerto Rico* (Lincoln: University of Nebraska Press, 2016).

9. Cesar R. Torres, "The Latin American 'Olympic Explosion' of the 1920s: Causes and Consequences," *International Journal of the History of Sport* 23, no. 7 (2006): 1088–1111.

10. Ibid.

11. Keys, *Globalizing Sport*, 2.

12. Cesar R. Torres, "The Limits of Pan-Americanism: The Case of the Failed 1942 Pan-American Games," *International Journal of the History of Sport* 28, no. 17 (2011): 2547–2574.

13. "$175,000 Needed to Send Athletes to Pan-Americans," *Boston Globe*, November 19, 1941, p. 20.

14. Eduardo Elena, *Dignifying Argentina: Peronism, Citizenship, and Mass Consumption* (Pittsburgh: University of Pittsburgh Press, 2011), 242.

15. Pablo Alabarces, *Fútbol y patria: El fútbol y las narrativas de la nación* (Buenos Aires: Prometeo Libros, 2007); Raanan Rein, "'El primer deportista': The Political Use and Abuse of Sport in Peronist Argentina," *International Journal of the History of Sport* 15, no. 2 (1998): 54–76.

16. Rein, "'El primer deportista.'"

17. Comité Olímpico Argentino, *Primeros Juegos Deportivos Panamericanos* (Buenos Aires: Comité Olímpico Argentino, 1951).

18. Asa Bushnell, ed., *United States 1952 Olympic Book: Report of the US Olympic Committee* (New York: United States Olympic Association, 1953), 24.

19. *El Universal*, March 5, 1951, p. 8.

20. Harry Grayson, "Los EE.UU. no debían haber mandado sus atletas," *La Afición*, February 21, 1951 (suppl.), p. 1; Buck Canel, "Fué admirable el espíritu civico de los competidores," *La Afición*, March 11, 1951, p. 1.

21. *El Universal*, March 3, 1951, p. 18.

22. "Magnífico epílogo de una gesta inolvidable," *La Cancha*, March 13, 1951, p. 20.

23. Edgar Alvarado Pinetta, "Informe de los Juegos Panamericanos," *Diario de Centro America*, February 26, 1951, p. 5.

24. "The Frankness of Friends," *Time*, February 19, 1951, p. 38.

25. Virginia Lee Warren, "US Aide at Games Chides Argentines," *New York Times*, March 5, 1951, p. 14.

26. Arthur Daily, "Sports of the Times," *New York Times*, February 27, 1951, p. 44.

27. "US Trackmen Upset in Pan-Am Olympics," *Charleston Gazette*, March 1, 1951, p. 22.

28. "US Captures Three . . . ," *New York Times*, March 2, 1951, p. 29.

29. Greg Grandin, "AHR Forum: Your Americanism and Mine; Americanism and Anti-Americanism in the Americas," *American Historical Review* 111, no. 4 (2006): 1042–1047.

30. "Respondió el equipo de pista," *La Cancha*, March 6, 1951, p. 15.

31. "El tiro nos ha brindado buenos triunfos," *El Gráfico*, March 9, 1951, pp. 62–63.

32. Ecar, "Codo con codo," *La Cancha*, February 27, 1951, pp. 12–13.

33. Harold Kaese, "What Price Good Will?," *Boston Globe*, April 9, 1951, p. 11.

34. Jules Dubois, "Argentines Fine Folks as Hosts, US Stars Find," *Chicago Daily Tribune*, March 2, 1951, p. B1.

35. John Cassidy, "What Makes Argentines That Way?," *Saturday Evening Post*, May 26, 1951, p. 152.

36. "Proposal for Patagonia," *New York Times*, March 8, 1941, p. 13.

37. Comité Organizador Buenos Aires, *Primeros Juegos Deportivos Panamericanos: Reglas generales y programa* (Buenos Aires: Guillermo Kraft, 1951), n.p.

38. Jennifer Lansbury, " 'The Tuskegee Flash' and 'the Slender Harlem Stroker': Black Women Athletes on the Margin," *Journal of Sport History* 28, no. 2 (2001): 233–252.

39. Susan Cahn, *Coming On Strong: Gender and Sexuality in Twentieth-Century Women's Sports* (Cambridge, MA: Harvard University Press, 1998), 119–122.

40. Stephanie Elias, "Las mujeres de oro," *Ya: El Mercurio*, July 28, 2015, pp. 16–20.

41. Evelyne Hall, "Report on Women's Track and Field," in Bushnell, *United States 1952 Olympic Book*, 343.

42. "Mexico en Buenos Aires," *El Universal*, March 2, 1951, p. 19.

43. See the official reports on the 1952 Helsinki games provided by the International Olympic Committee, at http://www.olympic.org/helsinki-1952-summer-olympics.

44. "El rostro femenino del deporte," *Revista Amiga*, February 2010, n.p.

45. *Diario de Centro America*, March 6, 1951, p. 5; Fernando Ruíz, "Fallece a los 78 años ex Clavadista Nacional Dolores Castillo," *Prensa Libre*, September 14, 2011.

46. "Es casi seguro," *La Afición*, March 15, 1951, p. 12.

47. See the photographs throughout the February 1, 1951, issue of *Mundo Deportivo*.

48. *Campeón*, February 28, 1951, p. 3.

49. Ibid. Justicialism is a movement based on Perón's political ideology, which rejects capitalism and Communism in favor of corporatism.

50. Napoleon Arraiz, "El hermoso objetivo de los panamericanos," *El Mundo Deportivo*, February 1, 1951, p. 28.

51. Ibid.

52. Bushnell, *United States 1952 Olympic Book*, 326.

53. Ibid., 334.

54. Elias, "Las mujeres de oro," 16–20.

55. *El Universal*, March 7, 1951, p. 15.

56. Gilbert Joseph and Daniela Spenser, eds., *In from the Cold: Latin America's New Encounter with the Cold War* (Durham, NC: Duke University Press, 2008); Roberto García Ferreira, "El caso de Guatemala: Arévalo, Árbenz y la Izquierda Uruguaya, 1950–1971," *MesoAmérica* 49 (2007): 25–28.

57. Arthur Daly, "True Diplomacy," *New York Times*, October 14, 1954, p. 41.

58. United States Olympic Committee, *United States 1956 Olympic Book*.

59. Ibid., 293.

60. *El Universal*, February 18, 1951, p. 14.

61. Alfonso Loya, "Payssé Reyes," *La Afición*, March 27, 1955, p. 13.

62. *El Universal*, March 13, 1955, p. 12.

63. Web Ruble, "Eligio Garcia Back in Bend," *Bulletin*, August 14, 1963, p. 6.

64. Pan-American Sports Organization, *Bulletin* 9 (1956).

65. Pan-American Sports Organization, *Constitution of the Pan American Sports Organization* (Mexico City: Pan-American Sports Organization, 1955), 3.

66. Antonio Andere, "Arenilla de fútbol," *La Afición*, February 13, 1951, p. 2.

67. "Piden de Argentina que vaya nuestro fútbol," *La Afición*, February 13, 1951, p. 3.

68. "Con solo cuatro equipos se Jugará el Torneo Panamericano de Futbol," *El Universal*, March 11, 1955, p. 18.

69. "CONMEBOL Correspondence with FIFA," 1956, FIFA Archive and Documentation Center, Zurich, Switzerland.

70. Lyman Bingham, "Report of the General Manager," in Bushnell, *United States 1952 Olympic Book*, 329–333.

71. *El Universal*, March 8, 1955, p. 10.

72. United States Olympic Committee, *United States 1956 Olympic Book*.

73. Rosario Vazquez Mota, "Ellas en los Panamericanos," *La Afición*, February 23, 1955, p. 8.

74. On the history of sport clubs in Latin America, see Rodrigo Daskal, *Los clubes en la Ciudad de Buenos Aires (1932–1945): Revista la Cancha; Sociabilidad, política y estado*

(Buenos Aires: Teseo, 2013); Brenda Elsey, *Citizens and Sportsmen: Fútbol and Politics in Twentieth-Century Chile* (Austin: University of Texas Press, 2014); and Joshua Nadel, *Fútbol! Why Soccer Matters in Latin America* (Gainesville: University Press of Florida, 2014).

75. Raul Sanchez, "Tornó al volíbol," *La Afición*, February 20, 1955.

76. José Guió Filho, "Campeonato feminino de baquete," *Gazeta Esportiva Ilustrada*, February 1, 1955, pp. 6–8.

77. Alexis Jeldrez, "Marlene Ahrens una ganadora en serie," *Caras*, November 27, 2013.

78. United States Olympic Committee, *United States 1956 Olympic Book*, 297.

79. Omir Arantes, "O atletismo brasileiro no Mexico," *Manchete Esportiva*, November 3, 1956.

80. Pan-American Sports Organization, *Bulletin* 3 (1956).

81. George De Carvalho, "The Triple Jumper from Brazil," *Sports Illustrated*, August 31, 1959, pp. 34–38.

82. Ibid., 35.

83. Ibid., 38.

84. Celeste González Bustamante, *Muy buenas noches: Mexico, Television, and the Cold War* (Lincoln: University of Nebraska Press, 2013), 34.

85. Guillermo Salas, "México cuenta con lo necesario para celebrar una Olimpíada," *La Afición*, March 27, 1955, p. 6.

86. Rein, "El primer deportista," 54–76.

87. "Despite All, a Delightful Show," *Sports Illustrated*, September 14, 1959, p. 20.

88. "En Chicago," *Campeón*, September 2, 1959, p. 1; "El hermoso objetivo de los panamericanos," *Campeón*, September 2, 1959, p. 28.

89. *Folha da Manhã*, August 30, 1959, p. 3. See also Earl Gustkey, "Pan Am Games Legacy: 1959; It's Not Exactly Peace and Harmony," *Los Angeles Times*, August 6, 1987, pp. 1–3, http://articles.latimes.com/1987-08-06/sports/sp-1628_1_pan-american-games.

90. "2,126 atletas," *La Nación* (Costa Rica), August 24, 1959, p. 18.

91. "O publico não está correspondendo," *Folha da Manhã*, August 29, 1959, p. 5.

92. "Em Busca," *Folha da Manhã*, September 1, 1959, p. 8.

93. "Deporte universitario y realidad nacional," *El Gráfico*, August 13, 1959, pp. 44–45.

94. "Mucho calor con bastante frio en Chicago," *El Gráfico*, September 2, 1959, pp. 8–9. The 1959 games provided a forum to criticize the austerity policies of the government of Arturo Frondizi.

95. "El precio de la irreflexión," *El Gráfico*, September 2, 1959, pp. 10–11.

96. "Hoje em Chicago," *Folha da Manhã*, August 27, 1959, p. 10.

97. Odir Cunha, *Heróis da América: História complete dos jogos Pan-americanos* (São Paulo: Planeta do Brasil, 2007).

98. "Os pais de Maria Ester," *Folha da Manha*, July 5, 1959, p. 2.

99. "Pick Girl," *Jet*, January 21, 1960, p. 53.

CONTRIBUTORS

Todd Cleveland is associate professor of history at the University of Arkansas. His books include *Stones of Contention: A History of Africa's Diamonds* (Ohio University Press, 2014), *Diamonds in the Rough: Corporate Paternalism and African Professionalism on the Mines of Colonial Angola, 1917–75* (Ohio University Press, 2015), and *Following the Ball: The Migration of African Soccer Players Across the Portuguese Colonial Empire, 1949–1975* (Ohio University Press, forthcoming).

Simon Creak is assistant professor at Nanyang Technological University. His monograph *Body Work: Sport, Physical Culture, and the Making of Modern Laos* was published by the University of Hawaii Press in 2015.

Mike Dennis is emeritus professor of modern German history at the University of Wolverhampton and has authored three monographs on the German Democratic Republic, including *Sport Under Communism* (Routledge, 2012).

Robert Edelman is professor of Russian history at the University of California San Diego. He is the author of the award-winning *Serious Fun: A History of Spectator Sports in the USSR* (Oxford University Press, 1993) and *Spartak Moscow: A History of the People's Team in the Worker's State* (Cornell University Press, 2009). He is coeditor, with Wayne Wilson, of *The Oxford Handbook of Sports History* (Oxford University Press, 2017).

Brenda Elsey, associate professor of history at Hofstra University, is author of the acclaimed *Citizens and Sportsmen: Fútbol and Politics in Twentieth-Century Chile* (University of Texas Press, 2011). Editor of an issue of the *Radical History*

Review on sports history, she is currently working on a history of sport, gender, and sexuality in Latin America.

Elliott J. Gorn is the Joseph Gagliano Professor of American Urban History at Loyola University, Chicago. His four books examine various aspects of urban life and city cultures in the nineteenth- and twentieth-century United States, including *Dillinger's Wild Ride: The Year That Made America's Public Enemy Number One* (Oxford University Press, 2009) and *The Manly Art: Bare-Knuckle Prize Fighting in America* (Cornell University Press, 1986; 2nd edition, 2010).

James Hershberg is professor of history and international affairs at George Washington University. He was the founding director of the Cold War International History Project at the Woodrow Wilson Center. His major publications include *James B. Conant: Harvard to Hiroshima and the Making of the Nuclear Age* (Stanford University Press, 1995) and *Marigold: The Lost Chance for Peace in Vietnam* (Stanford University Press, 2012).

Alan McDougall is associate professor of history at the University of Guelph. His *Youth Politics in East Germany* was published by Oxford University Press in 2004, and *The People's Game: Football, State and Society in Communist East Germany* was published by Cambridge University Press in 2014.

Andrew D. Morris is professor of modern Chinese history at California Polytechnic State University, San Luis Obispo. He is the author of *Marrow of the Nation: A History of Sport and Physical Culture in Republican China* (University of California Press, 2004), *Colonial Project, National Game: A History of Baseball in Taiwan* (University of California Press, 2010), and *Japanese Taiwan: Colonial Rule and Its Contested Legacy* (Bloomsbury Academic, 2015).

Mikhail Prozumenshikov is deputy director of the Russian State Archive of Contemporary History (RGANI), Moscow. He has edited countless document collections on topics as diverse as the history of development of the virgin lands in the USSR, the Twentieth Congress of the Communist Party of the Soviet Union, the Chernobyl nuclear disaster, and the 1980 Summer Olympics. He has published more than 150 articles on the history of international relations during the second half of the twentieth century and the history of sport, most notably, *Big Sport and Big Politics* (Rosspen, 2004).

Toby C. Rider is associate professor of kinesiology at California State University Fullerton. His book *Cold War Games: Propaganda, the Olympics and U.S. Foreign Policy* was published by the University of Illinois Press in 2016.

Rob Ruck, professor at the University of Pittsburgh, has authored five books, most recently *Tropic of Football: The Long and Perilous Journey of Samoans to the NFL* (New Press, 2018) and *Raceball: How the Major Leagues Colonized the Black and Latin Game* (Beacon Press, 2011).

Erik R. Scott is associate professor of modern Russian and Soviet history at the University of Kansas. His first book, *Familiar Strangers: The Georgian Diaspora in the Soviet Union*, was published by Oxford University Press in 2016.

Amanda Shuman is a postdoctoral researcher at the University of Freiburg. Her 2013 article "Elite Competitive Sport in the People's Republic of China, 1958–1966: The Games of the New Emerging Forces (GANEFO)," was named the *Journal of Sport History*'s Best Article of the Year.

Annette F. Timm is associate professor of history at the University of Calgary. She is the author of *Gender, Sex, and the Shaping of Modern Europe* (Berg, 2007) and *The Politics of Fertility in Twentieth-Century Berlin* (Cambridge University Press, 2010). She is also editor of the *Journal of the History of Sexuality* (University of Texas Press).

Christopher Young is professor of modern and medieval German studies at the University of Cambridge. He is also dean of arts and humanities at the University of Cambridge and coauthor of the award-winning *The 1972 Munich Olympics and the Making of Modern Germany* (University of California Press, 2010).

Manfred Zeller is research associate at the University of Bremen's Eastern European Institute. Currently working on a cultural history of politics at the end of the Soviet Union, he is the author of a monograph on Soviet soccer fan culture (*Sport and Society in the Soviet Union: The Politics of Football After Stalin* [Taurus, 2018]) and coeditor of *Euphoria and Exhaustion: Modern Sport in Soviet Culture and Society* (Campus Verlag, 2010).

INDEX

INTERNATIONAL HISTORY
PROJECT SERIES

Edited by James G. Hershberg

A full list of titles in the Cold War International History Project series is available
online at www.sup.org/cwihp.